CHILDREN UNDER FIVE:

EDUCATIONAL RESEARCH AND EVIDENCE

CHILDREN UNDER FIVE:

EDUCATIONAL RESEARCH AND EVIDENCE

By

Margaret M. Clark

Emeritus Professor of Education,
University of Birmingham, UK

Final Report to the Department of Education and Science,
United Kingdom

GORDON AND BREACH SCIENCE PUBLISHERS
New York London Paris Montreux Tokyo Melbourne

Gordon and Breach Science Publishers

Post Office Box 786
Cooper Station
New York, New York 10276
United States of America

Post Office Box 197
London WC2E 9PX
England

58, rue Lhomond
75005 Paris
France

Post Office Box 161
1820 Montreux 2
Switzerland

3-14-9, Okubo
Shinjuku-ku, Tokyo
Japan

Private Bag 8
Camberwell, Victoria 3124
Australia

The finding's in this Work are those of the consultant and do not necessarily reflect the views of the Department of Education and Science or any other government department.

Library of Congress Cataloging-in-Publication Data

Clark, Margaret Macdonald.
    Children under five.

    Bibliography: p.
    1. Education, Preschool - Great Britain.
I. Great Britain. Dept. of Education and Science.
II. Title.   III. Title: Children under 5.
LB1140.25.G7C55   1988   372'.21'0941   88-7245
ISBN 2-88124-680-X

CONTENTS

PREFACE

This report presents the findings of a personal commission from the Secretary of State, Sir Keith Joseph, "to carry out a critical evaluation of research into the education of under-fives undertaken over recent years". The objects of this evaluation have been "to assist those who wish to refer to existing research, to guide future policy on research in this area, and ultimately to facilitate better deployment of existing resources" (Sir Keith Joseph in a written statement reported in *Hansard* 27.2.85 p.180).

I make no apology that the investigation, which commenced in the summer of 1985, has taken longer than anticipated. Progressively over the past two years it has become a more full-time undertaking, rather than the shorter, part-time study that was expected. The number of researches proved to be much greater than anticipated; identifying, tracking and securing the research evidence was very time-consuming. During the investigation a number of researches have been completed and new publications have appeared whose findings have been included. The magnitude of the task of reading, analysing, synthesising and evaluating the research can be only partly appreciated from either reading the report or studying the reference list. I have consulted and personally evaluated all documents cited.

Those who were seconded to assist me, Peter Heaslip, from Bristol Polytechnic, for two days per week for one year, and Mrs Elizabeth Davenport from Sandwell, for one term, undertook literature searches and made preliminary studies of some of the publications. The grant from DES allowed also for limited time from two consultants, Dr W.M. Cheyne and Dr Brenda Robson, to assist with specific aspects of the study, and part-time secretarial support from Mrs Daphne Fowler. Additional help with typing was given by Mrs Theresa Mason; much of the report I have typed myself. Bill and Rona Cheyne have given support and encouragement, and without their skill and time-consuming assistance in co-ordinating the variety of word processed materials into a unified report it would not yet have been possible to complete this report. A number of friends and colleagues have read and commented on earlier drafts of the report, in particular Miss Wendy Dewhirst, Mrs Margery Browning and Dr M. Erickson. John Whittaker at DES, with whom I have worked most closely during this investigation, has provided stimulation as well as encouragement by his own impressive knowledge of the area. To all those and to others not named whom I have consulted I wish to express my thanks.

The views expressed in the report do not necessarily reflect those of the Department of Education and Science. As stated in the announcement of the commission:

I ALONE AM PERSONALLY RESPONSIBLE FOR THE JUDGEMENTS AND OPINIONS EXPRESSED.

Margaret M. Clark
University of Birmingham,
September 1987

Note

Education of Under Fives: Research Evidence was the title under which I submitted this report to the Department of Education and Science. I acknowledge the funding from DES that enabled me to undertake this study.

My thanks to Gordon and Breach Science Publishers for offering to publish the report, uncut and speedily – a combination rarely offered to an academic researcher. I am particularly grateful to Mark Simon and Fay Miller with whom I have collaborated closely over the brief time needed for publication.

M.M.C.

ABBREVIATIONS

AMMA   Assistant Masters and Mistresses Association
BAESE   British Association for Early Childhood Education
CASE   Campaign for the Advancement of State Education
CHES   Child Health and Education Study
DES   Department of Education and Science
DHSS   Department of Health and Social Security
EME   Early Mathematical Experiences
EPA   Educational Priority Area
ESRC   Economic and Social Research Council
EPVT   English Picture Vocabulary Test
HIPPY   Home Instruction Programme for Preschool Youngsters
ILEA   Inner London Education Authority
LEA   Local Education Authority
MRC   Medical Research Council
NCMA   National Childminding Association
NFER   National Foundation for Educational Research in England and Wales
NNEB   National Nursery Examination Board
PPA   Preschool Playgroups Association
PPVT   Peabody Picture Library
SED   Scottish Education Department
SCRE   Scottish Council for Research in Education
SSRC   Social Science Research Council
WPPSI   Wechsler Primary and Preschool Scale of Intelligence
WISC   Wechsler Intelligence Scale for Children

CHAPTER 1   INTRODUCTION

THE REMIT AND SCOPE OF THE INVESTIGATION

The remit for this report was a personal commission from the Secretary of State, Sir Keith Joseph, who invited me to carry out a critical evaluation of research into the education of the under fives undertaken over recent years. To quote

> "There is now a very substantial amount of research findings available in this field and there is a need, which I believe is shared by academics, practitioners, administrators and elected members of LEAs, to take stock and assess the validity and significance of the results of this research.... the objectives are to assist those who wish to refer to existing research, to guide the future policy on research in this area, and ultimately to facilitate better deployment of existing resources." (Sir Keith Joseph, Hansard 27.2.85 p.180).

It was agreed that the focus would be on funded research which was educational in remit, setting, or implications, and on children aged between two and five years of age. Research would be considered which had been conducted within the last ten to fifteen years in Britain, except where overseas research is frequently cited as having implications for education in Britain. Consideration would be given, within this scope to children from ethnic minorities and children with special needs.

The decision to identify as the area of study 'children under five', rather than pre-school education, was made in the knowledge that the age group in preschool education varies, and to ensure the inclusion of all the major current issues. The inclusion of specific reference to 'children from ethnic minorities' and 'children with special needs' in the interpretation of the remit was to ensure that research evidence on the full range of issues of concern to those involved in the education of children under five was identified. It was never the intention that the investigation would include a survey and evaluation of all the research into young children with severe handicapping conditions. In the last fifteen years there have been many experimental and other studies of children with perceptual difficulties, and of the developmentally young. An analysis of this work would be a major investigation in its own right. Many developments in preschool education have been brought to my attention, often arising from local initiatives. These are not reported here unless they have become part of a research project, whose results are available, and which appears to have a more general applicability.

The investigation began in June 1985, with funding half-time for myself for one year and additional funds for some assistance. The longer time scale, necessitated because of problems in tracking the researches and a number of the research publications and the sheer volume of material uncovered, has at least made it possible to include in the final report important studies whose findings have been published within the last year.

THE REPORT

My style of writing is normally brief and concise. The decision to present such detail was made because of the terms of the remit, reinforced by the many difficulties I had in securing full enough versions for evaluation of some of the work, even studies which are frequently cited. The need for a review such as this became increasingly apparent when studying reference lists and other sources, where we noted frequent citing of some researches, an apparent lack of awareness of others, and assumptions of generalisability concerning some studies not warranted by either sample or the time of collection of the information. For that reason, it seemed important to state for each research discussed the date of empirical work, the geographical area in which the study took place, the sample and any omissions, as well as results and their interpretations by researchers.

There are published reports of some of the studies from which evaluation was possible; others have published versions which because of constraints by publishers or for other reasons are inadequate for such a purpose; still others have not been published and it has been necessary to use a manuscript or final report to the funding body. All sources have been fully documented, with quotations if these seemed necessary to justify points. Where the only available sources are unpublished and thus not easily accessible, and the researches are important, fuller information has been given. Where researches have been frequently cited, and the interpretations appear to have gone beyond the evidence in the original, there also, precise information is given, with full referencing to enable others to check for themselves the conclusions drawn here. If there are large-scale funded studies on a topic, the evidence has been mainly confined to these researches. On important aspects for which there is no such evidence, small-scale studies have also been included, or where these extend the work from the funded study.

The researches are set in their educational and related context. Only then can their current relevance be assessed, the reasons for the precise formulation of topics be appreciated, the expectations of funding bodies and the constraints under which the research teams worked. In Chapter 2 the scene has been set in terms of the assumptions current in the seventies when a number of the researches commenced, even some recently published; the Nursery Research Programme itself; and evidence on variations in preschool provision, (further information is given in the appendices). In Chapter 3 and 4 changes in preschool provision in Britain since 1975 are identified, on the basis of statistical records and research findings. The remaining chapters are devoted to the researches under topic areas. To obtain a comprehensive picture of researches it is essential not to confine attention to a specific chapter, since further relevant information is often cited elsewhere. The issues are interrelated and thus cannot so easily be compartmentalised.

THE APPROACH

The search for research!

The investigation required that all the researches potentially relevant to the education of children under five be tracked. Initial sources included;

a) the report of research ongoing in 1974 on children under five by Barbara Tizard commissioned by SSRC (Tizard, 1975);

b) the report on researches commissioned under the Nursery Research Programme (DES, 1981);

c) a report on preschool observational research between 1970 and 1979 (Flynn and Oates, 1981);

d) NFER registers of research, a list of relevant researches sent by DES, extracts from registers sent by ESRC;

e) replies to letters sent to researchers known to have been involved in research in recent years, or identified through attendance at meetings during the investigation, and replies from other funding bodies.

The aim was to ensure the inclusion of research funded pre-1975 but still ongoing after that date; research between 1975-1979 not supported within the 'Nursery Research Programme', and thus not included in the DES report (DES, 1981); researches since 1980, which though not now funded might be important extensions of previously funded research. This aspect was confined to research in Britain. Yet by March 1986 over 200 possible studies had been identified, from which a selection for detailed study had to be made. Furthermore, in spite of the above research, important studies known to me were not uncovered from these sources. It was decided to make a personal study of all the registers since 1975 of the main funding bodies including DES and SED, SSRC/ESRC, the Schools Council and MRC. This time-consuming task revealed many further researches, and also cleared up some confusions as to whether titles and researchers listed under different names were the same or different! This unexpected and laborious task was important as it made it possible to prepare a comprehensive register of research, and revealed a number of the studies to which detailed reference has been made in the report. Lessons learnt from this aspect, many of which apply to research beyond the current remit, will be reported elsewhere.

Reference to research

A second method of tracking research revealed which researches were cited, and how frequently, and which were ignored. References on reading lists from a number of sources were placed on computer, together with references in recently published books and research reports which appeared relevant (including references to studies in USA). Note was made initially of frequent referencing of specific studies and such publications were at least considered for detailed inclusion. The potential list contained about 1000 references from which researches were identified, and a selection made from those in Britain. The extensive reference list in this report contains only the publications cited, not all those read. Further references may be of value to others.

Other sources of information

During the investigation relevant conferences have been attended, visits have been paid to a number of research institutes and to individual researchers. Peter Heaslip attended a workshop in Israel on HIPPY (Home Instruction Programme for Preschool Youngsters). I was an observer at a meeting in Italy of national representatives from ten countries participating in an international pre-primary project, which provided valuable insights into that project and the issues facing these countries. Separate reports on both of these visits have been submitted.

The full report contains descriptions of the researches and implicit and some explicit evaluation which in the final section is co- ordinated, and summarised. Implications for policy and practice are presented. Important gaps in evidence from research are also noted for the information of funding bodies, and recommendations made for priorities in research funding.

In spite of all the care I have taken in tracking researches and in evaluating and checking, inevitably there will be some omissions or errors in such a detailed report. It is hoped that neither sins of omission nor of commission invalidate any conclusions drawn for policy or practice, or concerning gaps in existing research.

CHAPTER 2   PRESCHOOL EDUCATION: THE SETTING FOR THE RESEARCH

THE LANGUAGE OF YOUNG CHILDREN

Language was a major focus in and justification for the planned expansion in preschool education in the seventies in Britain. To some extent such education was viewed as 'compensatory' to give a 'head start' to children who were 'socially disadvantaged' because of perceived 'deficient language' which would later cause 'failure' in school, and which was claimed to be causally linked to a lack of 'cognitively' demanding language in their homes, with the use of 'restricted' rather than 'elaborated' codes. In short, the aim was for professionals in preschool at an early stage, before 'school' entry, to make good the 'deficiencies of the home'. Hopes were pinned on an early injection of professional input preschool. Little or no attention was directed at possible links between school and its approaches, and the differential attainments of children from so called 'middle' and 'working-classes'.

A deliberate attempt has been made to set the scene by using in quotes as many as possible of the terms which were in frequent use in the late sixties and early seventies. That education, and preschool education in particular, was seen as the solution to educational disadvantage at the time is clear. In a recent publication entitled *Educational Disadvantage Ten Years On*, Nisbet and Watt (1984) consider the developments in Scotland over the period, indicating the inevitability of disenchantment with education as the solution in view of the impossibility of the task it was set, much of the focus being on preschool education.

There were disputes as to how the 'disadvantaged child' should be taught, whether by programmes, and if so, how structured these should be. The deficiencies shown to exist in standardised test situations, and in less formal but 'contrived' situations with an adult, were thought by some to result from a lack of knowledge of language 'structures', others thought these 'deficiencies' were in 'language in use', by children who had already acquired the structures, although they seldom, or perhaps never used them in these settings with a strange adult. If it were the former deficiency then in order to make up for lost time there were those who argued that didactic 'structured language programmes' were essential. If it were the latter then more experience of dialogue with professional adults who would set a more cognitively demanding framework would be required. *Bernstein* was the name most often cited in connection with restricted language use of 'working-class' children, while *Blank* and *Solomon* were cited as advocates of a tutorial dialogue approach. See The Bullock Report *A Language for Life* for a discussion of these issues. (DES, 1975b Ch.5). In seeking to give 'positive discrimination' to 'disadvantaged children' in Britain certain districts or areas were identified for 'priority' in funding, in many instances for preschool services, thus the concept of 'Educational Priority Areas' (EPA), which, were identified for funding of 'action research', also for Urban Aid. The issues briefly noted above and the research projects of EPA predate the current investigation. The view that the best way to give positive discrimination is to identify areas of deprivation and then to place extra preschool resources in these areas has been shown to be simplistic and to lead to provision mainly for less disadvantaged who happen to live in such areas (see Donachy, 1979 for a discussion of this issue). This context influenced those involved in the Plowden Committee (DES, 1967) whose recommendation for expansion of preschool education led directly to the climate for its expansion in the early seventies.

Already by the early seventies voices were being raised in opposition to the expressions utilized so far and their implications of 'incompetence' and 'the deprived child'. Three important papers in a collection entitled *Language and Poverty* reflect some of these points. (See Cazden, Labov, and Bernstein in Williams, 1970). Cazden stresses the importance of the topic, the setting and the listener in influencing the amount and quality of the language which will be produced by a young child, noting possible effects even on performance in a 'standardised test' situation. Labov criticises the assumptions of 'deficiency' in 'nonstandard' (or Black) English and argues persuasively that such language can be used in dynamic and cognitively demanding ways. He also notes the differential effects of adults and the context on the quantity and quality of the language. Bernstein challenges assumptions that an expansion of preschool education on its own would make good those deficiencies resulting from social disadvantage. He also challenges the use of the expression 'compensatory' education for children who in the first place have as yet not been offered an adequate educational environment. Unfortunately, Bernstein seems to be known to a generation of teachers and their trainers mainly as a name connected with a dichotomy of 'middle-class/working-class' with the term 'elaborated code' used for the language of the former and 'restricted code' for the latter. The evidence cited by Bernstein and his co-workers was in experimental, contrived situations, not in the home. Some of the implications for education were developed in what were practical ways which were positive and could have been dynamic in the classroom (see for example Gahagan and Gahagan, 1970).

It is also worth noting that Robinson, one of the researchers who worked with Bernstein in the early seventies, has more recently suggested persuasively that one possible influence on the progress (or lack of progress) of children from so-called 'disadvantaged homes' may be the teachers' judgements and expectations of them which will at an early stage be influenced by the oral language use and response of those children in the formal classroom setting. Such judgements which may be formed early, and which may also influence the children's concept of themselves, are an alternative or at least an additional factor which could be related to attainment (Robinson, 1980). In view of the evidence on language in the home which has become available over the last ten to fifteen years such arguments become even more persuasive and also show the unfortunate effect of a focus on only one aspect of education, such as preschool, in isolation from others. Unfortunately the need for speedy results from research to inform policy urgently for the proposed expansion of preschool education in the early seventies prevented funding of longitudinal, or even extended studies from within the Nursery Research Programme: other researches which later, became longitudinal unfortunately were not designed for this purpose.

Early studies of preschool education and those on language tended to utilize, as one measure at least of the child's ability, a standardized intelligence test. Already by the sixties there were challenges to the appropriateness of such as measures of 'innate' ability. Their amenability to environmental influences and their cultural specificity were also being commented upon. In particular, fluctuations in scores in young children were discussed, and it was suggested that such changes could be real rather than merely the effects of unreliability in the instruments. In this connection it is thus relevant to note that such tests as for example the Stanford Binet Intelligence Scale or the Wechsler Scales for young children (either WISC or WPPSI) came to be used as measures of effects of preschool education. The evidence of differential changes in scores on these tests would themselves challenge any assumption that what is measured is some innate ability (see for example Donachy, 1976). The whole issue of intelligence testing, particularly of young children, its values and limitations, was highlighted as early as the sixties, and before, by Hunt (1961;1969). At the time of the researches discussed here intelligence test scores were still frequently cited, as were scores on language tests such as the Picture Vocabulary Tests, PPVT in America and EPVT in Britain, (see Lomax, 1979c for a discussion of limitations of such measures with young children).

One final reference is pertinent before turning to discuss specific research projects and their implications, *Language and Learning in Early Childhood* (Davies, 1977). The papers and discussions reported there are from two seminars organised by the Social Science Research Council, the first in Leeds in 1974, the second in Bristol in 1975. A study of that publication over ten years later (as someone who was present at the first of these seminars) shows clearly how the concerns of that time in early education were related to the points made briefly in the early part of this chapter and how frequently the expressions cited here in quotes were used in the papers and in discussion. Those who presented papers included Cazden from the United States, to whom reference has already been made, also Tough from Leeds, and Wells from

Bristol whose longitudinal studies of the language of young children will be considered later in this report.

Language development was not necessarily the only or even the main aim for some of the providers of preschool education. For many teachers and assistants social development was regarded as having first priority, followed by more specifically educational aims, preparation for school and linguistic development (see Taylor, Exon and Holley, 1972 and Clift, Cleave and Griffin, 1980). Some types of preschool provision might also differ from others not only in their aims, but also in the reasons for referral of children, all or most of whom might be specially referred, such as for example to day nurseries (see Van der Eyken, 1984). The aims of parents in sending their children to preschool education might give greater priority to social development, learning to mix with others, or preparation for school(see Davie *et al.*, 1984 and Finch, 1981). The aims of preschool education might also be very different as perceived by the schools to which the children proceed from those of the staff involved in preschool education (see Wallace, 1985).

PRESCHOOL UNITS: SIMILARITIES AND DIFFERENCES

Introduction

It is necessary to make some points about different types of preschool units during the seventies, in the early stages of the expansion, when most of the large scale observational studies took place. Furthermore, within a few years, and while the research studies were still underway, the nursery schools and classes in some areas were under threat of closure, in Oxfordshire for example during the SSRC funded research directed by Bruner (Bruner, 1980). It is equally important to note ways in which such provisions may have changed over the last ten or more years. In the following chapters, with evidence from statistical trends and the findings of research, some of these differences and their implications will be discussed. Proportionately more children nationally may now be receiving preschool education, possibly for only one year rather than two, from age three rather than four, and part-time rather than full-time. The staff in nursery schools and classes may now thus have younger children on roll, and also almost a complete turnover of children each year. This has important repercussions both for the amount of administration to be undertaken, and the nature of the context which can be offered, even were the staffing ratios the same. There is now evidence from a number of sources that some children are attending more than one preschool unit, either consecutively, or even a few concurrently. Playgroups may now be attended by younger children, and before entry to nursery school or class, where previously they were often a provision for children under five years of age for whom no alternative was available. There appear also to have been marked differences in recent years in the children attending and referred to day nurseries. Such units could not be distinguished from other units merely as settings providing day long, year long care, and as accepting younger children. That aspect is the subject of a separate chapter.

Only aspects of importance to an appreciation of the current relevance of researches will be noted here. For a short comprehensive overview, including quotations from relevant official and other documents of the seventies (see Bruner, 1980 Chapter 2, and for a brief historical overview see Blackstone, 1973). A summary of the provision of preschool education and care in the seventies is also to be found in Osborn and Milbank (1987 Chapter 2).

Nursery schools

These have a headteacher who will be responsible for administration and for liaison with parents, outside agencies, and the schools to which the children will proceed, of which there might be many, possibly with different entry dates and policies. Staffing might include one or more other teachers, although in some nursery schools the headteacher might be the only teacher (see for example Clark and Cheyne, 1979). The remaining staff to make an adult child ratio of approximately 1:10 would be nursery nurses who might have trained only very recently, and not specifically to work in an educational context. Their career prospects in education would be limited unless they could gain entry qualifications and train as teachers. The headteacher might have responsibility for 100 or so children, and where attendance was part-time, for different young children in the mornings and afternoons. Attendance would be at most for two years, a turnover of at least half the school roll each year with all the accompanying administration. There might also be priority admissions of children with special educational needs. The children would be aged three and four years of age, or perhaps four years of age only. More recently with changes in many local authorities in England and Wales to a single entry date to reception class, the children might have only one year in school, and most are aged three. No fees are charged at nursery schools or classes which are provided by local education authorities.

Nursery classes

These are attached to either an infant, first, or primary school and are the responsibility of the headteacher of that school. They would normally have a teacher in charge in the class, with nursery nurses as the remaining staff, though in some areas there may be no teacher in the class (see for example Hutt *et al.*, 1984). The children attending might proceed to the reception class in that school, or transfer to another school, which might not have an attached nursery class. The teacher in the class will not necessarily have a qualification to teach young children, or children of preschool age (which might also be true of some teachers in nursery schools who had, however, made the choice to work in a setting specifically for preschool children). It is important to note the difference in training and background of nursery nurses. Where a research has indicated which staff were being observed in a research this has been noted here in discussing the findings. With regard to the question of full- or part-time attendance, time in the class, and age-group the nursery class might be similar to nursery schools in that area. In some authorities most of the preschool education-al provision has been in nursery classes either from choice, or because of the restrictions on availability of capital to build new units. Alternatively, the nursery schools might require to be built to serve specific neighbourhoods, with assistance from Urban Aid funds, whereas a nursery class might be started in an available class-room in a local school. It cannot thus be assumed that the populations in the two types of unit are necessarily comparable.

Day nurseries

In contrast these units normally provide all day, all year care, and are run by social services departments. They are normally staffed by nursery nurses, with a matron in charge. The crucial focus is care, and babies as well as older preschool children may attend. Thus staffing must take account of the need for shifts, and the care of babies. Some day nurseries may now have a teacher present all or part of the day, this would have been unusual in the seventies. An important distinguishing feature of most day nurseries is that many of the children attending are specially referred for social reasons. There may be limited, or no possibility of a place for local children whose parent, or parents wish or even need all day care for their child. Thus, the ethos of the unit, the nature of the child population, the possibilities for parental in-volvement, are all very different from the other types of preschool provision discussed above (see Bain and Barnett, 1980). Furthermore there have been chan-ges in recent years in the type of referrals to such units, many of which with long waiting lists cannot now take even single parent families where the mother requires to work (see Van der Eyken, 1984).

Combined Nursery Centres

These were set up to provide a combination of education and all day care. They may have a teacher or matron in charge. The organisation may or may not integrate the children in day long care with the others. Such centres, like day nurseries, may have babies attending. Shortly after their establishment a research project was set up to study their development, which will be discussed later (see Ferri et al., 1981).

Playgroups

These were initially set up informally by groups of parents wishing to provide op-portunities for their young preschool children to mix with other children, often by parents concerned at the lack of other preschool provision in their area. Attendance is normally a few half day sessions per week, and seldom full-time. It is usual for parents to pay a small contribution for their child's attendance to meet, or towards the running costs of the group. Playgroups seldom have exclusive use of premises, which will influence the type of activities which can be undertaken. From their inception there has been in playgroups a commitment to parental involvement, which may involve some or all parents assisting in the group and possibly with management also. Some local authorities have encouraged playgroups, including financially, and even assisted with staffing. Some are authorities unwilling or unable to support sufficient educational provision, others are supportive of the voluntary nature of the playgroup and its philosophy of parental involvement. There are playgroups set up and run by voluntary organisations, which may or may not have parents involved in the management or day to day running (see Ferri and Niblett, 1977). There are also playgroups exclusively for handicapped children.

Some playgroups have on their staff qualified organisers, while some leaders, though working as mothers in the group, may hold professional qualifications, possibly even for work with young children, such as in teaching or nursing. This has been shown in a number of studies (see for example Clark and Cheyne, 1979 and Clark et al., 1982). Playgroups are not spread evenly across the country, are more likely to be concentrated where there are few nursery schools and classes. There is also evidence from a number of sources that more children from middle classes are in attendance at playgroups (Tough, 1977 and Davie et al., 1984) and fewer children from ethnic minorities (Osborn and Milbank, 1987) also more children in rural areas (Haystead et al., 1980).

A national survey of preschool units in 1975 distinguished between 'hall' and 'home' playgroups; over half of the latter did not have parental involvement (Osborn and Milbank, 1987). The topic of parental involvement will be considered later with evidence from several studies. A distinction was made between 'community' playgroups, organised by committees of parents, and 'private' playgroups run by private individuals, in the study in Grampian Region in Scotland by the present author, and a proportionate sample of each type was included in the research (Clark and Cheyne, 1979). Four of the supervisors in the sample of randomly selected nineteen community playgroups were teachers, one a nursery nurse, and most supervisors had attended courses run by the PPA. The nine private playgroups (the relative proportion in that area), were run by private individuals who charged the parents for the children's attendance. Some of these latter were in purpose-built accommodation or parts of homes (in some cases specially converted). Four of these groups had teachers on staff. Thus within the term playgroup may be widely different units for preschool children.

Childminders

These are people who look after children other than their own in their homes, for profit. They are required to register with the social services department. It is not known how many unregistered minders there are, and not clear the extent to which this service has increased dramatically in recent years, or whether the increase is mainly in those who have registered. The research on childminders will be discussed in a separate chapter.

Other provision

This includes private nursery schools, private and workplace day nurseries. Some private nursery schools may be categorised as playgroups (see Kysel, 1982a). Such provision has not been the subject of specific research, although some may have been included in national surveys. It is difficult therefore to know to what extent they differ from other establishments with the same name.

THE BACKGROUND TO RESEARCH IN THE SEVENTIES

The programme of research

The planned expansion of preschool education in the nineteen seventies was intended to make it available in nursery schools or classes, on a full- or part-time basis, for children aged three or four years whose parents wished it for them. This stimulated an interest in research into young children by individual researchers. More importantly it led to the commissioning of research specifically related to preschool education by the Department of Education and Science, and to the identification of this as a priority area for funding by the Social Science Research Council. A Nursery Education Research Management Committee was established under DES chairmanship, one of whose first steps early in 1974 was to set up some short term studies, in six local areas, selected because of the contrasts they offered. The aim of these studies was to identify aspects of nursery education where intensive research might be desirable as part of the programme. Dr. Tessa Blackstone was the Department's Research Consultant for the Programme. The short term studies were undertaken by two members of the inspectorate on secondment together with Dr. Martin Woodhead and others. On the basis of these studies nineteen topics were identified as requiring research or development projects (DES, 1975a). A list of the nineteen topics is to be found in Appendix I, and Appendix II contains a summary of the short term studies.

The Social Science Research Council decided to increase expenditure on the preschool area, and actively commission research into key topics, not all of which would be educational. A decision was made to commission Barbara Tizard to undertake a review of current research on preschool education in the United Kingdom. That study included only work

    a) currently being carried out, or

    b) completed but not yet published.

It did not concern work with handicapped children, except that with severely retarded. The report prepared for SSRC by Tizard listed eleven areas for future investigation, four of which were topics related to the education of 'socially disadvantaged' children (Tizard (1974) for SSRC, then Tizard (1975) for the report with a commentary by researchers. A list of the topics is to be found in Appendix I.

In the light of their own studies and the report to SSRC the DES management committee identified five areas as priority for further research (see Appendix I).

The Direction of the Nursery Education Research Programme as described in a paper of that title by its secretary (Kay, 1975) is summarised in Appendix III.

Researches initiated in or about 1975

Two relevant points are made in the Tizard Report (as published in 1975 by NFER)

a) in April 1975 SSRC awarded most of its money allocated for the initiation of research in the preschool field to Professor Bruner. The research project was to begin in October 1975, to continue for 3 years and the group was to be known as the Oxford Preschool Research Unit (see Tizard, 1975 p.vii for details of remit).

b) after the SSRC review but before the published version DES had already given three new grants for research in this area, namely

i) Prof. J. Hutt and Miss C. Davie (Univ. of Keele) The experiences of young children at home

ii) NFER Developing materials for assessment and evaluation

iii) NFER The aims, role and development of staff in the nursery

It is also important to note that post 1975 SSRC continued to approve grants for research in the preschool field through its normal committee channels (including the Educational Research Board and the Psychology Committee). In SSRC registers those commissioned under the 'Initiative' are listed separately under that heading and 'Preschool Education'. All other grants are listed under the relevant university, and it may or may not be clear from the title whether they are concerned with children under five. (Since 1982 they have been listed under Initiative, or the relevant Committee.)

Similarly DES, SED, DHSS and other funding bodies continued post 1975 to fund research on under fives not within that initiative. Indeed with the then current interest in that aspect of education, and the growing interest of developmental psychologists in the young child, there were many researches, including large funded studies, *not within the programme.*

Research was also commissioned for the Warnock Committee of Enquiry into the Education of Handicapped Children and Young People, which first met in 1974 and reported in 1978. An important aspect of that enquiry was 'Children under Five', to which a chapter in the report is devoted (HMSO, 1978).

Dissemination of the research commissioned in the Programme

The expansion of preschool education in the late seventies was no longer accorded the commitment stated in 1972. As the researches commissioned drew to their completion there appeared thus less interest in any findings of the Under Fives Programme. In relative terms with regard to educational research, a large sum of money had been invested in the programme (about one million pounds over five years). There was a growing emphasis in education on accountability in research (on the contractor/consumer model) and on the need for communication of research findings, to ensure that practitioners and administrators were aware of research and that it was presented in clear policy and practice terms. This led to a decision that a policy for dissemination of the findings should be undertaken as the researches funded under the Programme were due to be completed. Thus in 1980 after discussion between the funding departments involved in the Programme, a group was established "to encourage wide and appropriate dissemination of the results of the current and recently completed research projects funded by DES, SED, DHSS, SSRC and Schools Council in the field of nursery education and day care for the under fives". This Group's function was "to bridge the gap between the research and its potential users". A Handbook entitled *Under Fives: A Programme of Research* (DES, 1981) was the first outcome. Twenty-five projects are listed in the handbook which also includes brief edited accounts by the research workers of these projects of "the aims, methods and results of their projects", and based on information available at that time lists of published references to the project findings.

Two further proposals by the group were also implemented.

(i) The National Children's Bureau was funded to prepare within its 'Highlights' Series, four Highlights specifically on topics related to preschool education and care. These four Highlights are entitled

Why provide for the Under-fives? (No. 52)

Preschool provision in schools, nurseries and playgroups (No. 53)

Home based services for the under fives (No. 54)

Preschool activity and the curriculum (No. 55)

(ii) An appointment was funded specifically to disseminate the research funded within the programme. It was felt by the group that discussions with policy makers and practitioners in a variety of disciplines might disseminate findings in a way that the written word did not, even where written with such a remit. Such an appointment was made, initially for one year part-time. It was then continued for a further year full-time. A report on the dissemination exercise, the meetings held, and those who attended, was prepared entitled *Linking Research and Practice* (Hevey, 1984). An opportunity to discuss research findings on topics of their choosing with someone knowledgeable, interesting, available, and funded to do this, appeared to be welcomed by those who attended meetings.

The impact of such an approach was discussed at a recent meeting of an interdisciplinary group (The Association of Child Psychology and Psychiatry, February 1986) entitled *The Interaction of Research and Practice.* The focus was 'The Case of Research on Children in Care' and 'The Case of Research on Preschool Education' and for each topic a research representative was followed by a consumer (either a practitioner or administrator).

The practitioner who spoke on preschool research, Pat Jefferson, Preschool Advisory Teacher from North Tyneside, reported on the value of such an initiative and the problems for the practitioner and administrator in knowing what research is available, in digesting it, and assessing its relevance to their situation. The anxiety which research generates in the practitioner because of financial constraints, political interests, inadequate reporting of research which by many is therefore seen as a 'weapon' or a 'threat' (particularly in relation to a non-mandatory section of educational provision such as that for the under fives) was noted. The following were all stressed:

- importance of networks of teacher collaboration in raising awareness,

- of the involvement of other staff working in the preschool field,

- of the involvement or knowledge of those taking policy decisions,

- and not least relief from duties to enable the development of a well-informed, teaching profession aware of recent research developments and capable of assessing their relevance for practice.

Limitations of the Programme and its Dissemination

A statement was made earlier that the Tizard Report, now widely cited as a reference point, did not consider other than current (in 1974) or as yet unpublished research, and there were other constraints (Tizard, 1975). Furthermore the Group charged with dissemination was set up to communicate the findings of the *Programme of Research.* The report of that Group, entitled *Under Fives: A Programme of Research*, is now also widely cited, and has been for many their source of knowledge of major preschool research in Britain at that time (DES, 1981). It is thus important to note the implications and effect of the focus adopted. Because of its limited timescale, and funding, the 'Group' charged with dissemination of research decided:

a) to confine consideration to the projects specifically supported under the Programme

b) to confine attention to 'factual' reporting of the projects based on information from the researchers (i.e. no evaluation was included).

Thus no attempt was made to set these 25 studies in a context of

i) work already funded in 1975 but continued beyond that date,

ii) what might well have been equally major studies funded during that same period but not *commissioned*, therefore not in the Programme as defined,

B

iii) work commissioned within some other field, but nonetheless on Under Fives (e.g. the Warnock Committee of Enquiry into the Education of Handicapped Children and Young People, a major focus of which was 'under fives', *Special Educational Needs* (HMSO, 1978).

Finally, there was a timescale with regard to date of funding beyond which studies were not included, even if underway before 1980.

Such limitations are indeed stated in the Preface to *Under Fives: A Programme of Research* (DES, 1981). Their implications for coverage and its limitations are not necessarily clear to the reader, however, and furthermore a subsequent document cites the 'group's' remit as

> "to encourage wide and appropriate dissemination of the results of the current and recently completed research projects funded by the DES, SED, DHSS, SSRC and Schools Council in the field of nursery education and day care for the under fives" (Hevey, 1984, p.5).

A similar statement is in the inside front page. It is noted that evaluation is not a part of the remit but again stressed (also on p.5) that the Group "was primarily concerned to promote a critical interest in all research in the field".

There were limitations set in the Tizard review, (Tizard, 1975) where only unpublished or current studies were included. The basis was mainly interviews with research workers in what was at that time stated to be a field with very limited activity.

There were limitations in the 'Programme' which influenced what research would be commissioned, and which topics could be considered within the available time scale. It is important to appreciate these constraints which is why the article by Kay in which they are discussed is summarised in Appendix III.

There were limitations in the Under Fives Research Dissemination Group's remit with regard to what was included and also lack of evaluation (DES, 1981).

The Current Research: its context

The remit of the current investigation is

a) comprehensive in coverage with regard at least to funded research b) extensive in timescale with regard to funded research at least since 1975

c) extensive in sources of research included, to cover major studies which while they may have been funded prior to 1975 were reported in or since 1975

d) evaluative of individual funded researches

e) contextual in nature in attempting to relate the researches and their findings to each other and to policy.

What then are the limitations and constraints in the current investigation whose remit is clearly so extensive from all points of view?

It is a personal commission, in the announcement of which in a written answer in Parliament, the Secretary of State for Education, Sir Keith Joseph stated that I, the present author, alone would be personally responsible for the judgements and opinions expressed. Clearly this has a number of strengths in a coherence in presentation and conviction in statements not so easily maintained where a group or committee holds responsibility for a report. All references cited have been studied personally; none of the evaluation has depended on assessment by another person. Limitations include the approach adopted, the final coverage, the researches selected for detailed coverage, the personal nature of their evaluation, and any omissions. The timescale and level of funding has also been a limiting factor. To have produced the report sooner would have meant the exclusion of many important studies; to have taken longer would have meant that some of the contents would have become dated. Furthermore, new reports have continued to appear throughout the two years of the study; these have been incorporated where possible.

These statements are made not as any apology for the contents of the report but as a necessary context for the reader to assess its contents.

This report contains many issues which were seen to be important in 1975, or which, though noted, were not regarded as such then, yet now appear to have achieved importance because of the setting in the mid eighties, and ways in which it differs from the educational context of the mid seventies. Some changes in focus may indeed be the direct or indirect result of a range of research findings. Other changes may stem from differences in organisation of services. Still others may be the result of external factors of significance to the provision of early education.

In the mid seventies the term 'Preschool Education' was used as the focus, and indeed, most commissioned or funded studies were concentrated within that framework, rather than a specified age group of children. Some unfortunate effects of that particular focus will be discussed later; it is, however, pertinent to draw attention to that limitation at this stage. It was for precisely these reasons that the remit for this research was defined not as 'preschool education' but 'The Education of Children Under Five'. This was not intended to exclude from consideration topics such as continuity of education, transition, or the curriculum of early education. Throughout the study any relevant studies of children over five years of age have been noted. What was intended by defining the study by age was to avoid ambiguity and also to ensure that it was possible to include studies of four-year-olds in whatever context relevant to education the research took place, whether preschool or not. The importance of that decision will become clear from the following section in which a brief comparison is made between the context in the seventies and eighties based on statistical records and information from research.

CHAPTER 3   EDUCATIONAL PROVISION FOR UNDER FIVES IN BRITAIN SINCE 1975

THE CONTEXT

The expansion of preschool education in Britain proposed in the early seventies was intended to make attendance available, at least part-time, for all children aged three and four years of age whose parents wished it for them. It was to remain *voluntary* and not become *mandatory*; there was thus no suggestion of lowering the compulsory starting age for school in Britain below five years of age. In the early stages of the expansion preference was to be given to areas of 'disadvantage'. Furthermore resources to establish new provision tended to come for example from Urban Aid funds which thereby defined precisely areas in which they could be utilized.

The availability of preschool education in the early seventies already varied widely in extent and nature between administrative areas and even within a single local authority. Some authorities have continued to expand services, others at least to protect them, while still others have cut services. These variations have been influenced by the degree of commitment at a local level, as priority has no longer been accorded to its expansion at a national level, again a victim to economic pressures.

An appreciation of national trends in preschool education over the past ten years is important as a context for assessing the implications of research. Equally important are the wide differences between areas and within areas in the extent, distribution and nature of services available for children under five. A particular authority may have cut its provision over the period, another expanded it. One authority may provide full-time places for fewer children but with the same input of staff, while another provides part-time places for a greater percentage of under fives. One authority may provide mainly nursery schools, another mainly nursery classes, while yet another may admit children under five years of age to reception class in the primary school (i.e. as 'rising fives') a school term earlier than required. Yet another authority may admit children to primary school at the beginning of the school year in which they will reach five years of age (i.e. aged 4 - 4.11). Some authorities may have some or all of these patterns reflected in different areas.

Furthermore the extent of other provision for children under five years in terms of day nurseries, playgroups and childminders may vary from area to area, as well as over time, and may or may not be extensive in the same areas as educational provision for under fives. One authority may utilize early entry to reception class because of lack of preschool educational provision, another may have both preschool education and early entry, and indeed may have many available places also for all-day-care in day nurseries, may have many playgroups and registered childminders.

The flexibility accorded to local education authorities in Britain to plan their own provision for education means that national generalisations are dangerous: equally dangerous, however, are 'national' generalisations based on localised knowledge. Claims which are made that preschool education has suffered cuts *nationally* during the past ten years are not supported by evidence. The expansion may not have been on the scale promised and hoped for, and there may have been cuts in some areas, but the evidence is of a continuing expansion.

RECORDS AND THEIR LIMITATIONS

It seems important to consider the national trends over the period 1975-85, based on statistical records, and where information is available, differential patterns between areas. A study of the various statistical records does reveal, however, just how difficult it is to get a precise picture with regard to the education of children under five years of age, because of the different ways statistical records are collected, and have changed over the period, also because of changes in local authority boundaries. The following points must be borne in mind:

(a) Statistical records for education required to be consulted separately for England, Scotland, Wales and Northern Ireland. Such records may be collected and are presented in different formats: thus some information may be stated in one report, can be calculated from another, and is not available in another.

(b) Date in the school year on which statistical returns are made may differ, as may the point at which age of the children is calculated. As an example the date utilized for age has changed in England in 1980 from January when the statistics are collected to August, the beginning of the school year, and some tables for comparison may use an estimate for January. For this reason trends will be given separately for 1975-79 and 1980-85 for England. In Scottish statistics 'mid year estimate' is used as a basis in estimating percentages.

(c) The terms nursery school and class may or may not be used or shown separately (e.g. DES shows these separately). SED statistics use the term 'nursery school' to cover all provision in preschool education, while DES on occasion uses the term 'nursery class' to include both schools and classes (see p.2 of DES 4/82).

(d) Totals for under fives in preschool education may be shown and also as a percentage of the estimated 3 and 4 year old population. Alternatively it may not be possible to calculate the relative percentages of four-year-olds in preschool education as distinct from those in reception classes in primary school.

(e) The DES statistical bulletins take the school population at a point in January yet children may have entered reception class in January, or the previous September, there is thus a considerable possible variation in how many under fives may have been in reception class at some point during the year (since there is no comparable annual statistical information on point of entry to reception class).

(f) Local government reorganisation has taken place during the period in question. It is possible to show some general trends of importance with regard to preschool education, and some within specific areas. These will be noted below first separately for each part of Britain (that is England, Scotland, Wales and Northern Ireland) then where possible general trends will be deduced.

Statistics will also be presented for day care facilities where available, that is day nurseries, registered childminders and for registered playgroups. Further complications arise in including these in comparisons, since such statistics may be taken at a different time of year, may be based on 'available places' not on children in attendance, may include children in the full age range 0-4 years, percentage availability may be estimated in relation to that wider group.

A table of 'trends in preschool education and day care in England, Wales and Scotland 1975-1985' appears in Osborn and Milbank, 1987 pp.36-37; one page gives the summary figures, the other explanatory notes. The table is provided as a context for their report on a particular research study of the national sample of children born in 1970, the effects of whose early education on later attainment they are considering. Osborn and Milbank in their discussion of the extent of preschool provision in Britain are inclined to give 'explanations' and 'interpretations' or 'causal' interpretations of the trends which are their opinions not based on documented evidence (see Osborn and Milbank, 1987 pp.34-35). The details which are set out here were taken from the original statistical records as indicated and were prepared before the publication by Osborn and Milbank. They are provided as a context for consideration of the current relevance of a wide variety of studies, the empirical work for which was undertaken in the seventies. Furthermore the surrounding text here is confined to further description, or is explanatory in terms of known differences in policy.

NATIONAL TRENDS IN PRESCHOOL EDUCATION

The information below is provided in detailed points for children in England for January 1985. Additional information is then provided briefly for Scotland, N.Ireland and Wales for comparative purposes in order to establish the generalisability of trends.

England:

Education

The trends noted below are based on Statistical Bulletin 10/86 DES *Pupils Under Five Years in Each Local Education Authority in England* (DES, 1986) supplemented for the earlier years by the comparable Statistical Bulletin 4/82 (DES, 1982) from which figures are available for a selection of years from 1950 to 1981.

1. There has been an *increase* in the percentage (and total) of under fives in *education* from 28% to 37% between 1975 and 1979, and from 39% to 43% between 1980 and 1985. (Percentages are of the three- and four-year-old population.)

2. There has been an *increase* in the percentage (and total) of under fives in *pre-school education* from 10% to 18% between 1975 and 1979, and from 20% to 22% between 1980 and 1985.

3. *Nursery class* attendance was *more common than nursery school* attendance, whether full or part-time (about four fifths of children attended nursery classes).

4. With regard t*o nursery classes* for 1985:

(a) there has been an increase in the numbers of children attending

(b) as with nursery school there has recently been a decrease in the number of full-time attenders (since 1982), but a continuing increase in part-time attendance (even in absolute terms both figures are still well above 1975)

(c) in 1985 approximately one sixth of children attending nursery class were full-time (in nursery school it was approximately one third)

(d) the numbers of classes have shown a steady increase in numbers over the ten year period (doubling in number).

5. With regard to *nursery schools* for 1985:

(a) there has been an *increase* in the numbers of *children attending*

(b) there has continued to be a steady *increase* in the number of *part-time pupils* (in spite of the decline in population size)

(c) the number of *full-time pupils* in nursery school increased until 1980 then dropped to below 1975 figures.

(d) there were *more nursery schools* in 1985 than in 1975 (but the numbers have declined gradually since the peak in 1980) (548, 596, 561).

6. Teaching *staff* and *all staff in preschool education* in nursery schools and classes *have continued to increase* over the period 1975-85 from approximately 3, 500 to 6, 500 and from 8.500 to 15, 000.

7. There are *wide variations between LEAs* in the percentage of the three- and four-year-old population attending preschool education. Some authorities have over 50%, others under 5% of under fives attending nursery school or classes.

8. There are *wide differences* in all these statistics for 1985 for *individual LEAs* with some having *no nursery schools* and others *only a few or no nursery classes.*

9. There has been a marked increase in the total number of *children under five in infant classes* in primary schools in spite of the decline in size of the age groups (as a trend over the period).

10. There are wide *individual differences* in patterns *between LEAs* in 1985, from some authorities with over 70% of the estimated population of three- and four-year-olds in edu*cation* to others with under 20%.

Other Provision

This information is taken from *Children's Day Care Facilities at 31st March 1986, England* (DHSS, 1986) which gives trends from 1976-1986. Statistics were taken at 31st March and are given as available places. Rates are given per thousand population under five.

1. With regard to *day nurseries*

The number of local authority and registered day nursery places has increased by 7% (about equal numbers are provided by LAs and registered). The numbers on waiting lists for LA day nurseries have almost doubled between 1976 and 1986 (currently over 19, 000 or 55.2% of those on registers). The rate of provision is 19.4 (9.7 LA) per 1000 under five in 1986. This varies between authorities from about one to over 180.

2. With regard to *registered playgroups*

The number of places has increased recently after remaining relatively constant. (Few places are LA provided and run playgroups, and for these places the number on waiting lists is 38.3% of those registered as attending). The rate of registered places is 138.7 (0.9 LA) and varies between authorities from under 20 per 1000 under five to over 200.

3. With regard to registered *childminders*

The number of places available has increased by about two-thirds between 1976 and 1986 (few places are local authority provided). The rate of places is 46.3 (0.5 LA) and varies between authorities from under 10 to over 120.

Not only does the rate vary widely between authorities for particular services, but also the pattern of services. Some authorities may have relatively low provision, others may have many places available in playgroups and few in other services or vice versa.

Scotland:

The information for Scotland is taken from Statistical Bulletin No. 6/A2/1986 (SED, 1986a) *Provision for Preschool Children*, published jointly with the Social Work Services Group. In addition to *numbers* of children in education it has estimates of *available places* in other provision. From the similar publication No. 8/A2/1984 (SED) information has been extracted for education for earlier years. Only the more recent Statistical Bulletins are jointly issued, earlier publications were on 'Nursery

Education' only. These documents are concerned with provision for *pre-school children*, not as DES '*Under Fives*', so do not contain information on four-year-olds in primary schools in reception classes, a percentage which may be very different from that in England (see later section on Age on Entry to primary school).

These figures provide trends within Scotland; they are not directly comparable with those for England from DES, as the basis for calculation differs. Most of the figures in the 1984 and 1986 statistics are based on the annual September school census, but those provided for the Social Work Services Group (namely on day nurseries, playgroups and childminders) are for March. The precise point in the year at which age is estimated also differs. Furthermore, the term 'nursery school' is used in these statistics to include schools and departments, that is nursery classes (figures for which are not shown separately). The Education statistics are in numbers in attendance, those from Social Services refer to 'places available'.

Education

The following trends are clear for Scotland for *preschool education:*

1. The numbers of children in *preschool education increased greatly* by 40% between 1975-76 and 1979-80 (that is in spite of the drop in estimated population). There was a further increase of nearly one fifth of children in preschool education between 1979-80 and 1984-85.

2. The percentage of the estimated three and four-year-old population in *preschool* education increased between 1975-76 and 1979-80 (rising from 14% to 25%). As there was also an increase in absolute numbers, this is not accounted for by a fall in the population. The percentage continued to rise until by 1984-85 it was 28% of the 3 and 4 year old age group as a percentage of the mid year estimate. The increase over the last five years is in four-year-olds in attendance in preschool education (not three-year-olds).

3. The increase in recent years is in *part-time attendance*, only about 8% of the children attended full-time in 1984-85. There is, however, still an increase in full-time equivalent places thus the trend to part-time does not account for all the increase.

4. There has been an increase over recent years both in the numbers of *teachers* and of other staff (with a pupil/teacher ratio about 26/1 and of staff 7/1).

5. The extent of provision and whether full or part-time attendance *varies widely between Regions* from about 46% to 9% in 1984-85.

Other provision

Some information on *other provision* (in available places) for preschool children provision in day nurseries, playgroups and childminders in Scotland is contained in the recent Statistical Bulletins on *Provision for Preschool Children* which are now published jointly by SED with the Social Work Services Group:

(a) The *available places in day nurseries* in Scotland have remained relatively *constant* over 1980s (at about 4000 places Local authority and registered)

(b) There has been an *increase in available places in playgroups* over the past five years with about 44,000 places now available in 1985 (as compared with 38,000 children in attendance at nursery schools or classes. This is still slightly below the available places in 1974-75 (Osborn and Milbank, 1987).

(c) There has been a *dramatic increase* in the numbers of *registered childminder* places available. The number has more than doubled over the past five years and is now approximately 7,500.

d) Day care provision in Scotland, (local authority and registered), of day nurseries, playgroups and childminders, was available in 1984-85 for about 17% of the 0-4 population (mid-year estimate).

(e) There were *wide variations between Regions* in the amount of *day care provision* available (from about 65% to 13%, 1986 Statistical Bulletin).

Northern Ireland

Education

Information for Northern Ireland is taken from No. 3/1986 Statistical Bulletin for the Department of Education, Northern Ireland, Pupils and Teachers in Grant-Aided Schools - January 1986.

1. Over the period 1981-86 there has been an *increase* in the *numbers* and *percentage* of children in *nursery education*, with *increases* in *full-* and *part-time* attendance and in *nursery schools and classes.*

2. There has been an *increase* in the *numbers of teachers* with the pupil/teacher ratio about 23.5/1 (figures are not given for other staff).

3. Many *more children* attended *nursery schools than classes* (about twice as many children are in nursery schools as nursery classes in 1986)

4. Many *more* children were *full- than part-time*, about twice as many children are full- as part-time in preschool education (in nursery classes about 81% are full-time, and 56% in nursery schools).

5. There has been an *increase* over the last five years in the number of *under fives in schools.* It is stated that about 7,000 of these under fives are receiving nursery education, which is an increase of just over 13% on the level of 5 years ago. A much larger number of under fives (age at December) are in primary school. This represents a slight decrease in the percentage of four-year-olds in school over the past five years (DES N.I., 1986)

Some up-to-date information on provision of preschool education in N.Ireland is available in Wells and Burke (1986a, 1986b) where it is reported that provision of nursery education is for approximately 12.7% of nursery age (based on information from 85% of nursery teachers who took part in the survey). Some evidence on trends in provision and differences between areas is also provided. Details are also provided on the training and experience of the teachers, children's attendance, admission policies, special needs and aims of nursery education. Details on entry patterns to infant school are not given. The figures are not based on Official Statistical Information, but on details collected in the survey.

Wales

Education

This information is taken from *Statistics of Education in Wales* No. 10 1985 (Pub. in April 1986, pages 19-21). It is difficult to make comparisons with the figures cited so far as numbers attending nursery classes and reception classes are not given separately, although the figures are given separately for nursery schools. It is thus not possible to estimate the preschool education provision.

1. At January 1985 about 70% of the population of three- and four-year-olds were in educational provision, age at December (86% of age at August). About 2% of these were full-time and another 4% part-time in nursery schools. A further 42% were full-time and 21% part-time in primary schools (in nursery classes or infant classes).

2. With regard to *nursery schools*

(a) there has been a *reduction* in the numbers of children attending *full-time* over the past five years (about 34% of children attending are full-time)

(b) there has been a *reduction* in the number of *nursery schools*

(c) there has recently been a *slight* reduction in those attending *part-time*

N.B. Full-time equivalent figures are not provided and it was recently reported that an authority was cutting preschool education by reducing part-time attendance to less than half-time.

3. There has been an *increase* in children under five in primary schools over the past five years, both full and part-time (see 1 above) (which in these statistics would include nursery classes).

4. There are *wide differences between authorities* in 1984-85 in the provision for children in nursery schools, in whether the provision is full or part-time, in whether they have many or any qualified nursery assistants, in the proportion of under fives in primary schools and whether these attend full or part-time. Percentages are not cited so it is not possible to assess the relative provision in the various areas, only the contrasts noted above.

5. All authorities have some nursery units attached to junior infant, and infant schools (total 677, schools with such units - percentage of children in these units are not given).

Other provision

Some information is given in No. 10, 1985 from the Welsh Office (p.22) concerning day care facilities 1984. These are at March, are permitted places as in figures for England and Scotland, but are percentages of three and four-year-olds (not as in England and Scotland of 0-4). The places are reported as about 29% but it is not stated whether this is all places in, for example, day nurseries, or places available for three and four-year-olds. Most of the provision is of playgroups in registered premises. There were in addition nine local authority day nurseries (with 220 places) and a further 41 registered nurseries (with 1, 006 places).

A caution

Numbers of places available in preschool education and in other provision for under fives are not necessarily additive. In the national sample of children born in one week in April 1970 whose preschool attendance was studied, it was reported that their most recent provision immediately prior to entry to reception class was the only provision attended for 92% of the sample (Osborn *et al.*, 1984 p.103). The availability of preschool education has increased dramatically since these children were at the preschool stage. In addition several studies have recently drawn attention to multiple use of services, for example childminders taking a child to a playgroup or nursery class (Davie, 1986), or children attending a playgroup at an age before admission to a nursery school or class (Watt and Flett, 1985).

Perhaps such information can more graphically be conveyed by the following dialogue reported by Tizard and Hughes (1984), between a girl aged 3 years 10 months and a member of staff in a nursery class who interrupted a fantasy game with her teacher to announce:

CHILD: Do you know, my baby's one now.

STAFF: Your baby's coming here when she's older.

CHILD: She'll go to playgroup when she's two, though.

STAFF: Will she?

CHILD: Yeah. Because when you're two you go to ... When I was two I went to a playgroup.

OTHER CHILD: So did I.

CHILD: That shows you, that people go to playgroup when they're two.

STAFF: Why do they go to a playgroup?

CHILD: Because they're not old enough to go to school.

STAFF: I see. And how old were you when you came here, then

CHILD: Three or four.

STAFF: Three or four. Then what happens when you're five

CHILD: You go ... When I'm five I'll only ... I'll go to a ... I expect I won't come to here any more.

STAFF: Where will you be, then?

CHILD: Be? In a different school, of course.
STAFF: Do you know which school you're going to?
CHILD: Cross Road [her local primary school].

(Tizard and Hughes, 1984 pp.99-100)

IMPLICATIONS FOR RESEARCH

Perhaps the only points which *are* clear from the statistical patterns and trends cited above are the following:

(a) the dangers of making generalisations for Britain

(b) the problems in making comparisons across the constituent parts of Britain;

(c) the difficulty in estimating exactly how many children are already in education in Britain before their fifth birthday, in what type of education, and for how long

(d) proportions of children under five who are in different types of preschool provision and at what ages.

All this makes it clear that statistical data could be utilized to make many and varied points, most of which could readily be disputed by someone else!

It should be clear that any consideration of the implications of research for policy and practice requires the following minimum information with regard to the setting in which it was conducted:

(a) *the timescale of the empirical work.* The empirical work for the Nursery Research Programme referred to earlier, and for most of the other researches on preschool education studied during this investigation was conducted pre 1980, although in a considerable number of instances the publication is post 1980.

(b) *where the research was undertaken,* whether England, Wales, Scotland, or Northern Ireland, and the Region and area in which the study was undertaken, since this will influence the extent, nature and availability of the provision.

Where less than 5% of the under fives in an authority attend preschool education the characteristics of the actual children attending may be very different from an authority in which over 50% attend.

Furthermore, where a high proportion of four-year-olds are admitted to infant class in primary school the age groups in nursery schools and classes will be affected. Where figures are high both for preschool education, and for under fives in reception classes, many children in nursery schools and classes may be three-year-olds whose chances of preschool education for at least one year are clearly much higher (even where the percentage of under fives in preschool education is similar).

Consideration will now be given to the ages of children in preschool education, the extent to which this may have varied over the past ten years, and implications of any such changes for evaluation of the relevance of research for policy and practice.

CHAPTER 4　CHILDREN IN PRESCHOOL EDUCATION: CHANGES SINCE 1975

THE CONTEXT

The aim in this section is to draw attention to a variety of background features which are important when assessing the relevance to current policy and practice of research over the past ten years.

There are a number of important issues on which details extracted from Statistical Bulletins did not provide evidence (even where figures were given separately for three and four-year-olds):

(a) the age of children's entry to preschool education (whether at three, three and a half or four years of age);

(b) the length of their stay in preschool education (whether one year or two, and whether one year from three or one year from four years of age);

(c) the precise age of entry to reception class in the various authorities.

All of these above points are important in evaluating research on preschool education and assessing its relevance to the education of children under five years of age with regard to the following:

(a) the nature of the roles and duties of the staff in preschool education, and its curriculum;

(b) its relationship to primary education;

(c) whether the curriculum, staffing and roles of those teaching in infant departments of primary schools should change, or are changing, to take account of the increasing proportion of four-year-olds in primary school, and of much younger four-year-olds.

In a report entitled *Infant Behaviour Sparks Study of Reception Classes* it is stated that a research has been commissioned by the Assistant Masters and Mistresses Association to consider how young children react to starting school. It is there stated that the study was prompted after a local survey

> "revealed that many teachers believed standards of behaviour, discipline, social training, language skills and concentration spans had worsened over the previous five years".

This local survey was followed by a questionnaire to a wider group which found teachers expressing concern that

"young children had become more difficult to deal with at school over the years" (Bayliss, 1985)

The report on this research which has recently been submitted (Barrett, 1986) will be discussed in a later section. Clearly attempts to evaluate any such research, and to assess its significance, must take account of national and local statistics, with regard to age on entry to primary education.

Evidence concerning age on entry to reception class will now be considered. 'Entry to school' the expression frequently used is misleading. It gives the reader no indication that a greater or smaller proportion of these children may already have been in attendance at a nursery school, or even the nursery class of the school to whose reception class they transfer.

There is evidence that a number of authorities in England are admitting four-year-olds to primary school at a much earlier age, namely at the beginning of the year in which they will have their fifth birthday. The statutory date for entering school in England and Wales is the term following their fifth birthday.

Where there are *three entry dates* to school in the year (September, January and April approximately) authorities may admit at the statutory age. Many LEAs have admitted children as 'rising fives' (4 years 9 months to 5 years) a term earlier than would be required.

Where there are *two entry dates* (September and January) they may admit 'rising fives' in September and the remaining group in January.

Where an authority, or indeed some of its schools, has only one entry date, then children in England and Wales will enter school aged between four and five years of age (depending on their date of birth) otherwise they would have been denied admission at the appropriate time. This is common practice in a number of Welsh LEAs.

In Scotland, in contrast, where all Regions now have a policy of one admission date per year in August, entry is for children who will attain the age of five years on or before the last day of February of the following year (thus the age range on entry is approximately 4 years 6 months to 5 years 6 months). This is an important difference to consider when making comparisons between England and Scotland with regard to preschool education and to issues such as four-year-olds in reception classes. Such children in Scotland are unlikely to be under 4 years 6 months on entry. This is also an important difference to note when considering appeals for entry to primary school below the statutory age. The number of such requests in Scotland, for example, more than trebled in 1985 compared with the previous year; the massive increase was, however, mainly from one area only 63% of which were successful. (See *Placing Requests in Education Authority Schools* No. 5/B6/1986 SED.) Details are, however, not given of the precise age of children for whom such appeals were made, some of whom might in England have been required to be in primary school, being aged over 5 years 3 months. Still others might already have been in primary school in England had the authority or school only one entry date (thus admitting children aged 4 - 4 years 11 months).

AGE OF ENTRY TO RECEPTION CLASS

Mid-seventies

The study by Osborn *et al.*(1984) of over 13, 000 children who were all born in a single week, 5th-11th April 1970, makes it possible to analyse the wide differences in date of entry to school in England, Wales and Scotland, even of such a narrowly defined national sample.

The following points are relevant on age of entry to reception class for that sample:

(a) more children started school at the beginning of the school year (Autumn 1974) when they were about 4 years 6 months of age (42.1%) than in any other term;

(b) about equal numbers of the remaining children entered school in the statutory Summer Term and the Spring Term (23.6% and 23.9% respectively);

(c) a small proportion (3.4%) had started infant school before 4 years 4 months;

(d) a further 7.1% did not expect to start school until the following school year when they would be over 5 years 4 months.

Thus for this sample, all born within a single week, there was up to a year's variation in age on entry.

Regional contrasts

(a) children in the sample in Wales and the North and North West regions of England were more likely than children elsewhere to start school at the beginning of the school year prior to their fifth birthday or earlier;

(b) about 65% of these children in Scotland did not start infant school until the beginning of the school year following their fifth birthday.

For this sample born in 1970:

- over 80% of the children were attending infant school at age five;

- nearly half the children attended playgroups;

- a further fifth went to local authority nursery schools or classes;

- and a further fifth, who had no preschool designated experience, entered infant school before their fifth birthday

- Only the remaining 7% had no educational or other experience outside the home before statutory school starting date. This, however, varied markedly between regions.

A further important statistic of relevance to a study of research implications which can be shown from this national sample of about 13, 000 children born in 1970 was that:

(a) 33% of children in poor neighbourhoods attended LEA nursery schools or classes - as compared with 14% in 'well-to-do' neighbourhoods;

(b) over 55% of children in rural neighbourhoods attended playgroups and only 8.7% attended nursery schools or classes.

These figures have been quoted in some detail because they are the only national figures for specific children available for all these interrelated factors of relevance to preschool education in England, Wales and Scotland. Furthermore, they indicate that a policy to admit children as early admissions to infant school has been practised in Wales and in parts of England since at least the mid seventies. The pattern even then appears to have been somewhat different in Scotland - at least for children born at the time of year of the children in the Child Health and Education (CHES) Study (See Chapters 6-8 of Osborn *et al.*, 1984 for further details).

A further important point is the extent to which such patterns for age on entry would have been comparable for children born at different times of the year to those in the CHES sample. The effect of local authority policies on numbers of entry dates and age on entry could indeed be very different for children born at different times of the year as will be shown later.

Between 1971 and 1979

In a recent study entitled *Under-fives in School in England and Wales, 1971-9*, Osborn reports that already by 1979 there were many children under five years of age in school in England and Wales who were not in designated nursery provision (Osborn, 1981). Many under fives in primary school were as Osborn states 'rising fives' (i.e. children whose fifth birthday occurred later in the current school term). He reports that even omitting such children in 1977 (the last year for which Welsh Statistics were available for 'rising fives' in nursery classes) the children in infant classes still constitute a sizeable proportion (more than a third of all under fives in LEA schools). He states that over the period 1971-79 the proportion of under fives attending nursery schools and classes increased steadily from 6.1% to 19.0%. Over that period the under fives in infant classes increased from 13.4% to 20%. Thus even in 1979 marginally more under fives were attending infant classes than were attending nursery schools or classes.

Osborn draws attention to a DES circular in 1975 which urged LEAs not to admit children below age five

> "unless they make no additional call on educational resources and do not prevent the redeployment of these resources for more essential purposes".

This same circular, he states, encourages part-time attendance in nursery schools and classes (as was recommended in the Plowden Report and DES White Paper in 1972) as

> "preferable, for most children until they reach compulsory school age" (Osborn, 1981 p.98).

He reports that by 1979 more children in nursery schools and classes in England and Wales were part-time than full-time. In contrast, in 'non-designated infant classes',

> "the number of full-time pupils far outweighed part-time pupils" (p.99).

Thus already in 1981 Osborn was stressing the need for more information about the school experience of under-fives in non-designated classes in primary schools.

1983 and 1986

An article by Cleave *et al.*, 1985 reports a study by the National Foundation for Educational Research of local authorities in England whose policy for admission to infant (or first) school was investigated (the questionnaire was completed by 92 of the 96 authorities). The survey revealed that in 1983 seven in ten authorities reported that they operated a uniform policy for admission (some mixed policies it is suggested are a legacy from reorganisation).

- Only seven of those authorities with a single policy admitted children as late as the statutory age (the school term after their fifth birthday).

- A further eight had a mixed policy which included that alternative.

- A further 21 and 16 respectively admitted all children or some children as 'rising fives'.

- There were, however, 26 authorities which admitted children in the year of their fifth birthday (i.e. from four years of age).

- A further 20 with a mixed policy admitted some such children.

Annual admission was reported to be more prevalent in metropolitan districts; admission termly as 'rising fives' as late as the statutory age was more common in the counties. It would be relevant also to consider the patterns of preschool provision in metropolitan areas as compared to counties, which might also have been different.Thus the age at which children enter school is dependent on where they live. This will influence the possible length of time in preschool, and the age group with which they will mix in a preschool unit.

Further evidence is given that 20 LEAs had modified their policy in the last five years, all but two of these favoured earlier admissions and a slightly larger number were contemplating changes, most in favour of admitting younger children. Further information on length of primary schooling and related issues from NFER is contained in its evidence to the House of Commons Select Committee enquiry into achievement in primary school (reported in Cleave, 1985). In a further study by the National Foundation for Educational Research statistics were collected for 1985-86 for LEAs in England and Wales by means of a similar questionnaire. This study entitled *Starting School at Four* shows that this trend towards earlier admission has continued. This study was of all 108 local education authorities in England and Wales, together with case studies in twelve schools in two LEAs. Returns to the questionnaire were obtained from 90 LEAs (83%).

Slightly over half the LEAs had one admission policy, the remainder had two or three policies. Age on admission could thus vary depending on where a child lived within an authority, as well as between authorities.

    - Annual admission was the majority policy for 37 LEAs, and for some schools in a further 19 authorities (a few children might be as young as three years of age on admission, the rest between 4 and 5 years of age);

    - twice yearly admission was the predominant policy in 13 LEAs;

    - most of the 31 LEAs with three entry dates admitted children as 'rising fives'.

    - All but one of eight LEAs who admitted children at the statutory age were large non-metropolitan counties.

In 32 of 56 authorities with one entry date in some schools and thus 4-5 year olds in school, no ancillary staff were allocated; and where such help was allocated in few instances were NNEB qualifications required. Only half of these authorities stipulated a maximum class size for these infant classes containing four-year-olds and in only ten authorities was it as low as 26 children (Sharp, 1987).

Further details on 1985

A survey of LEAs in England and Wales was undertaken in December 1985 by CASE (Campaign for the Advancement of State Education) concerning policy with regard to admission of children to school below the statutory age, whether this early entry is related to amount of preschool education available, and whether resources are made available where children are admitted early. Replies were received from 76% of LEAs (81 of 104). The results reconfirmed the wide variation between and within authorities. Only nine authorities replying had statutory age entry for the majority of children. Most of the remaining authorities either had one entry date, that is, admitted children from four years of age, or as 'rising fives' (with about equal numbers with each policy for the majority of children). Most authorities admitting at 4+ stated that they gave parents a choice as did about half of those admitting as 'rising fives'.

There was not evidence that those admitting later were likely to have more nursery education. Authorities who replied that they operated a policy of admission as late as the statutory age of 5+ were all authorities with relatively low provision of preschool education.

A number of authorities had changed their policy within the last five years. Because of the complexities and interactions between variables of policy, type of authority etc. it is difficult to make any more complex analysis. There were, however, apparently also wide differences between authorities in whether extra provision was made for children entering school below the statutory age, or only when they reached that age. This did not appear to be more likely where an authority had little preschool education.

Summary

The evidence from Osborn(1981) (and Osborn *et al.*, 1984) shows that:

(a) for many children, in the seventies, early admission to infant classes was the only form of education or care outside the home before five years of age and

(b) already by 1979 in spite of the considerable expansion in preschool education as many under fives were in non-designated infant classes as were in nursery schools and classes in England and Wales

The further evidence from Cleave *et al.*, 1985 shows that such provision in non-designated infant classes is increasing as a result of policies of single entry dates. While there may indeed have been a large increase in younger four-year-olds in infant classes recently, this is thus not a new phenomenon.

The policy of admission of children to reception class below the statutory age for starting school is likely to be one as vulnerable to economic pressure as preschool education. It is also a policy likely to be particularly vulnerable to rise or fall in the birthrate and demand for places in infant school nationally and in particular areas.

The organisation of the nursery school or class (and the infant, reception class) is clearly influenced by both the number of intakes per year to primary school and the age of children on entry. This is made even more complex where, as is frequently the case, the policy differs for different receiving primary schools which are 'fed' by a single nursery school.

MONTH OF BIRTH AND AGE ON ENTRY TO PRIMARY SCHOOL

Much has been written of the disadvantages experienced by 'summer born' children who in a three entry system enter school in the Summer Term. It is frequently stated that they thereby have less time in the infant school, or have only a term in the reception class. Some have given this claimed inequality as a reason for, or advantage of one entry date per year, (with the consequent age range of 4-5 years). In this section only the evidence on differential patterns of admission to school between and within authorities, and over time, is under consideration; other issues will be considered elsewhere. One further important point must be made, namely differential effects of entry policies on children in relation to their precise date of birth.

The effect of numbers of entry dates and age on entry to school on children differs markedly depending on their month of birth. A rough estimate revealed the pattern set out below (assuming birth and date of entry near the beginning of the month):

for a child born in *January* the difference in age on entry to primary school could be 8 months (about 4-7 to 5-3) with one, two or three entry dates with entry date of August/September, January or April;

for a child born in *March* it could be about a year (if Scotland is included) with entry in August/September, January, April or the following August (age about 4-5 to 5-5);

for a child born in *August* it would be similar but with age on entry between 4-1 and 5-1;

for a child born in *September* different policies would make little difference, the only influence really being whether 'rising fives' were admitted in the Autumn or not (age range roughly 4-11 to 5-4);

similarly a child born in *December* would be aged between 4-8 and 5-1 with admission in August/September or January.

ENTRY POLICIES AND RELEVANCE OF RESEARCH

Year of birth could influence the policy under which a child enters school, as local authority policies have changed over the past ten years. Policy may also vary from school to school. The above approximate estimates reveal important differential effects also on children according to their month of birth.

Entry policies have relevance to evaluation of research in early education. Not only must the age group selected be indicated precisely by the researcher, but also the policy under which the authority was operating at the time. See for example Clark *et al.* (1984), where two neighbouring authorities in the research operated different policies at the time of the research (1982 - 1983). The schools in one authority in the study admitted children from 4 to 4-11 in September: the schools in the other authority had three entry dates with entry at 4-9 to 4-11. This latter authority changed the following year to one entry date with entry of 4 to 4-11 in September with permissive entry also in January. The nature of the research was such as to make that an important variable which is discussed in the report.

Where a sample is selected, even a large sample, with births within a particular season of the year, cross national or area differences may appear greater or less than would have been the case if the whole age group had been sampled. For example in the study referred to earlier, *The Social Life of Britain's Five-year Olds* (Osborn *et al.*, 1984) the national sample was a week's births of children born in April 1970. It is clear from the chapter 'Infant School Entry' (pp. 95-99) that there were regional differences between the proportion of children from that week of birth already in infant school by five years of age. It is not possible, however, to ascertain the extent to which the pattern would have been similar for other dates of birth in that same calendar year, or for other years of birth. Certainly the pattern would be very different in England now from 1974-75 when these children entered primary school, even within that narrowly defined week of birth. Depending on school or authority policy, and precise date of birth, a child might now enter school in the Autumn, January, April or the following Autumn - without any change in the mandatory age of entry to school.

CHILDREN FROM ETHNIC MINORITIES; PROPORTIONS AND PATTERNS

One further background trend of relevance in considering research and its implications for early education is the proportion of children from ethnic minorities in the research population in comparison with the population at the time and also with the current position. This is particularly important where consideration is of children whose mother tongue is not English, yet that is the language of instruction in the preschool, and also where different minority languages are spoken by different children.

Some researches have been carried out in areas where there were no children from ethnic minorities, others in areas in which such children may in many schools be in the majority. Some studies, even observational studies, may have omitted from the sample the few children from ethnic minorities, or children whose mother tongue was not English.

A study of integration in ordinary preschool education of children with special needs was carried out in areas with few children from ethnic minorities (Clark and Cheyne, 1979). A similar study was undertaken subsequently in areas with a high incidence of such children and whose mother tongue was not English (Clark et al., 1982). Clearly the issues in the two areas were very different and had such children been omitted from the latter study would have grossly distorted the picture, oversimplifying the issues faced by administrators and by practitioners in the integration of children with special needs (see Clark, 1987).

Evidence of changes

ational evidence of trends over the period is not readily available for proportions of children from ethnic minorities in preschool education, or of under fives. Nor is there evidence on the exact number of children for whom English is not their mother tongue. Evidence which is available from a single area, namely Birmingham, may serve to highlight the problems, the speed with which changes can take place and the implications of this for schools. These figures are taken from the research report by Clark et al. (1984 pp.8-11) and were based on birth statistics for Birmingham available for the period to 1981 and thus covering children in the City likely to enter school up to 1985-6. Although there are no similar birth statistics for Birmingham beyond 1981 there is no reason to believe that the trend has reversed.

Patterns of ethnic origin of parents of children born in Birmingham are shown below as percentages :-

	1962	1967	1972	1977	1981
Afro-Caribbean	12.2	10.0	6.8	7.1	9.1
Asian	2.6	8.8	15.5	20.0	25.0

Two important points not necessarily peculiar to Birmingham can be seen from the above:

  - the increase over the period in the proportion of young children from ethnic minorities in the population of under fives

  - the change in pattern of ethnic background, with currently most of these young children of Asian ethnic origin.

Furthermore, most of those of Asian ethnic origin have both parents of that ethnic origin, whereas for those of Afro-Caribbean ethnic origin a number have one parent only of that origin.

Finally two out of every three births of wholly Asian parentage in 1981 were to women who had lived in the United Kingdom for less than a decade.

See Clark *et al.* (1984 pp. 8-11) for further details of these patterns and their possible implications not only for the City as a whole but also for particular schools.

Implications

Thus, in cities like Birmingham, where many children entering school are of Asian ethnic origin, or indeed have a mother tongue other than English, any evaluation of research evidence and its implications for current policy and practice must take into account whether:

  (a) any study conducted in such an area was undertaken at the time when there were no, few or many children from ethnic minorities,
and

  (b) sample selection explicitly excluded children whose mother tongue was not English, even where such children did live in the area or attend the preschool unit (in more detailed studies, of children's language for example).

Some might argue that since these children are second generation immigrants the young children will now enter school with a reasonable facility in the English language. The study referred to above would, however, not endorse that view. An assessment of the children's competence in English after entry to the reception class, and in their mother tongue if it were Punjabi, was part of the above study. Furthermore, parental interviews in the home were conducted in Punjabi for a number of the children in two schools in Sandwell (see Clark *et al.*, 1984 and for further details Whittaker, 1985). The language in the home was Punjabi and indeed a number of the mothers had little English even where they had been many years in U.K.

Further related studies, both in the Birmingham area, have been conducted by students of the author. One of the studies by Ahmad (1986) involved interviews of mothers of preschool children of Asian ethnic origin in the homes shortly before the children's entry to reception class, some were attending nursery school or class (Ahmad, 1986). The mothers were interviewed in their mother tongue and the children have been assessed both in their mother tongue and in English shortly after entry to school. The language of the home was Punjabi, and not English, also the parental attitudes to young children and to their early education were very different from those reported in studies of language interaction in the home by Wells and by Tizard and Hughes for example. In both of these studies children whose mother tongue was not English were excluded (see Wells, 1986 p.223 and Tizard and Hughes 1984 p.25), as was also true in the earlier longitudinal study by Tough (1977a see p.3). These frequently cited language studies will be discussed in a later chapter.

A second study has just been completed in a Birmingham nursery school by the head teacher of the school, where almost all the children are of Asian ethnic origin and most speak little English on entry to nursery school. Pearson's study has involved observation in the nursery of children soon to move into infant school (at age 4-5 years of age). The language in play of a selection of these children has also been recorded using a radio microphone, their language has been assessed in their mother tongue and in English prior to entry to infant school. Where the children have used their mother tongue during the play, which was true of most, this has been translated into English by native speakers. It should be noted that the head teacher and the staff of the school, as of most schools, do not understand the children when they speak in their mother tongue (Pearson, 1987).

There are important implications for practice, staffing and teacher training from studies such as these. Such studies, all of which were conducted by experienced teachers, are cited here in illustration, although they are small scale, because they have been completed recently, in 1985-6; furthermore, there has been little evidence of large scale or funded studies of relevance involving children under five years of age. Further reference will be made to the DES funded study to which they are related on *Early Education and Children from Ethnic Minorities* in the relevant section(s) of this report (Clark *et al*, .1984).

Ethnic minorities and preschool education

A further point of relevance in any attempt to assess effects of attendance at different types of preschool provision is evidence that differential proportions of children of indigenous white, West Indian (Afro-Caribbean) and Asian ethnic origin may attend different types of provision.

There is evidence from the national sample for England, Wales and Scotland of children born in week 5th-11th April 1970, referred to earlier, that there were ethnic differences in attendance at different types of preschool provision. The percentages of the different groups who had attended were as follows:

	LEA Nursery Schools or Classes	Playgroups
Ethnic origin European (UK)	18.5%	44.3%
West Indian	41.5%	14.6%
Asian	30.9%	18.9%

Where one parent only was from an ethnic minority background it is reported that the patterns were similar to those where both parents were 'of' European (UK) background. Details are not given for day nurseries as figures were too small for patterns to be reliably assessed. The terms used in that study have been used here (See Osborn et al., 1984 pp.118-9).

There is further evidence from a survey of preschool provision in 1975 (Van der Eyken et al., 1984). One third of those attending preschool provision who were identified as of West Indian origin were in social services day nurseries, a proportion ten times higher than for the two other ethnic groups (accounting for 11% of the children in these nurseries. A relatively greater proportion of those identified as of Asian ethnic origin in preschool provision attended nursery schools or classes than of the two other ethnic groups. Such differences could not be accounted for by factors such as the greater concentration of playgroups in rural areas of LEA nursery schools and classes in 'poor' or 'average' urban areas as there still appeared to be differential use between the two groups of ethnic minorities where there were known concentrations of both groups (See Van der Eyken et al., 1984, pp.101-103).

This information is based on a national survey of preschool units in England, Wales and Scotland in 1975 by means of questionnaires through local authorities and thus the information on ethnic origin may not be fully reliable. Furthermore there were differential patterns of return from different types of unit, from 93.2% for LEA nursery schools to 64.2% for playgroups and 88.8% for day nurseries (see p.81). The differences are, however, large enough to be worthy of note.

In a more recent study in 1979-80 (Clark et al., 1982) an assessment was made of the incidence of children in ordinary preschool units with special needs in Birmingham and Coventry. Information was not gathered on ethnic origin but such data as was available suggested that even within a single city there were differential patterns of attendance at different types of preschool provision of children for whom English was a second language. Children with second language problems were

c

found predominantly in *educational* preschool provision: few were in day nurseries or playgroups. Even within specific types of preschool educational provision there were wide differences. Some nursery classes for example had no such children, others up to a third of their children and in some, most of their children were so identified. (See Clark *et al.*, 1982 Ch.5 for a discussion of these issues).

CHAPTER 5   LANGUAGE AND THE HOMES OF PRESCHOOL CHILDREN: RESEARCH EVIDENCE

In this chapter evidence from four British researches on the language of preschool children will be considered. The studies by Tough, Wells, and Tizard and Hughes are possibly still the most frequently cited in relation to preschool education: they will be discussed in some detail because of this. The contradictory nature of some of the findings and concern that in some secondary sources the findings are over-stated, or generalised beyond what is felt to be legitimate from the samples on which they are based is a further reason for treating them in such detail. Evidence from a follow-up study at ten years of age of some of the children in the study by Wells will be included. The fourth study, that by Davie and others, though published more recently, was undertaken in the seventies, as were the three referred to above. The context was set by a brief summary in an earlier chapter of the sort of assumptions about the language of young children prevalent in the seventies when these studies were undertaken.

THE DEVELOPMENT OF MEANING: TOUGH

Joan Tough's study of the language of preschool children was completed by the early seventies (Tough, 1973). She was then funded by Schools Council until 1983 for a curriculum project entitled 'Communication skills in early childhood', to develop curriculum materials for language work with young children and also by DES within the Programme of Research from 1976 for a study entitled 'Fostering the Development and Use of Language by Young Children'. Video tapes and resource materials were prepared for use in training nursery assistants. She has subsequently published a series of books with guidelines for teachers and others working with young children with associated audio visual materials for use in training courses and these latter materials have recently been updated. Her work is referred to in DES 1975a and 1975b and is reported in Tizard (1975, see p.5-6). Tizard notes in her SSRC review of ongoing research that Tough's was one of the very few curriculum or compensatory projects to be derived from a prior study of development (Tizard, 1975 p..5).In *A Language for Life* (DES, 1975b) her categorization of purposes for which language is used was cited, and the differences she found between her 'advantaged' (middle class) and 'disadvantaged' (working class) samples. To quote:

> "But there is a range of uses which children from 'educating' homes seem to have developed more extensively than children without these home advantages" (DES, 1975b p.53).

While there are many publications by Tough herself, or which cite the longitudinal study undertaken by Tough, there appears to be only one publication which gives details of the research study (Tough, 1977a). It should be noted however that *The Development of Meaning* is not a research report in any strict sense and that the full information for a summary and evaluation of findings is not always available even in that source. Briefly, the study was as follows: a longitudinal investigation of a group of 64 children, samples of whose language in 'contrived' situations arranged by the researcher were tape recorded and analysed at the ages of 3 years, 5+ and 7+ years.

The sample

This is referred to as the 'advantaged' and 'disadvantaged' group within each of which was a group who attended nursery school or class, and a group not attending (each of the four groups had equal numbers of boys and girls). It was possible with the insertion where required of 16 additional children to ensure that 12 children in each of the four groups could be compared at each stage (Tough, 1977a, p.5).

The advantaged group had one or both parents from "professions which are generally reached through a course in higher education" (teachers, doctors, lawyers and other similar status). The disadvantaged group had parents who "completed their education at the minimum age, and worked in unskilled, or semiskilled occupations" (p.2).

Excluded from the sample were children:

   a) whose IQ was below 105;

   b) from a family of more than six children;

   c) if there was known or suspected evidence of rejection and emotional stress;

   d) if the mother did not speak English as her first language,

   e) who were West Indian, because of problems with use of nonstandard English;

   f) if they were shy, withdrawn or hostile to the observer;

   g) in the nursery if they were not happily settled in school;

   h) unless they spoke clearly enough for transcriptions to be made of what they said. (p.3.).

Two relevant points are noted:

   a) that it was difficult to find children for the advantaged group who were not in some form of preschool experience.

b) the composition of the group had excluded the most disadvantaged section of the population (p.4).

Teachers in nursery schools and classes were asked to select children who fitted the criteria. The non-nursery children were selected initially by the head teacher of infants' schools who were asked to identify families who might have children who would fit the criteria.

These schools were in areas where there were no nursery schools or classes available, schools which "served the large housing estates on the edge of the city, or the 'down town' areas of the city" (p.4).

Thus this study is of children in an urban area, the city is not named and details are not given of the pattern and proportion of children who attended preschool education at that time (about 1970). Reference is made on page 130 to the children living in "Yorkshire towns and cities". No reference is made to the selection of the advantaged group other than a) above. Clearly a final process of exclusion of children referred was still open to the investigator. All the above points about the sample are important and are thus cited in some detail as they are not normally noted in secondary sources, and must clearly limit the generalisability of at least some of the findings. They are also important when attempting to compare and contrast findings of this study with others since as may be seen from the above, both groups were highly selected.

Samples of language

At three years of age each child was recorded in conversation with a 'chosen companion' with a collection of play materials. An observer was present during the approximately one hour of recording. The observer's role is referred to, but there is only passing reference to its possible importance (which could have been differential). There is reference to the extent to which the group addressed the adult; it is clear that the perception of the adult was different in the groups. For example the advantaged non-nursery group addressed the adult almost twice as often as the nursery advantaged group and in contrast, the disadvantaged non-nursery group addressed the adult more frequently than the disadvantaged nursery group, but the absolute number of such questions or comments is not given (see p.81). With current knowledge, and even from the above and a study of extracts of dialogue it would appear that the adult, by her very presence, would have influenced the dialogue. At a later stage in the study the adult did leave children to talk in her absence, but not at three years of age.

Little attention is given to possible effects of the 'chosen companion' which might have been differential. Dialogue is a two-way process, not only one child initiates, similarly language surrounding imaginative play depends on reciprocity between the two participants. Were the chosen companions of the advantaged more likely themselves to be advantaged and those of the disadvantaged similar to the target child? Two extracts are given as a context for discussion, a brief extract from Billy and Michele (on p. 72-3), and a longer extract with Tom, Sally and the observer (on p.74-77) which make such a suggestion at least plausible. What might have happened if all the advantaged children had played with a less advantaged playmate and all the disadvantaged had the benefit of a more advantaged companion? The samples of language from the children at 5+ and 7+ were taken in the context of a variety of tasks (described in Tough, 1977a Chapter 8). Since what was regarded as the appropriate context in which to record was different at each age, and within these later age groups the task set was shown to influence strongly the amount and complexity of the language it is not possible to make generalisations across these age groups.

The findings and their implications

This study was a pioneering attempt to record and analyse the language of a relatively large sample of young children in as near natural settings as seemed possible at the time, and not by tests. It is important not to generalise the findings beyond their legitimate boundaries and to bear in mind their limitations. The highly selective nature of both samples of children means that the data cannot be generalised to all three year olds, since only those who already spoke clearly were included. Thus there could be many children entering preschool education at three years of age, or even infant school at four or five years of age, whose language structure and use is even more limited than the most limited cited in that report, at least in such contexts. Furthermore there is no way of knowing from the description of this sample just how selective from the point of view of articulation it is. Thus teachers may well be faced with many children who on entry to school have articulation so poor that their communicative attempts are difficult to follow for the adults, and their peers. One may assume that the 'chosen companions' also spoke clearly which would also influence the quality of language elicited from the three-year-olds. Finally, differences in competence between the chosen companions could also affect the extent to which dialogue was sustained and imaginative play developed in pairs of children.

One of the most important findings, which remains in spite of limitations in the sample, is mentioned less and yet is of crucial importance to education. That is the effect of the context on the children's apparent competence. The data from the children at three years of age does not allow such information to be extracted as only one setting was used: nor can effect over time be assessed as that same setting was not used at 5+ and 7+. Some information on the effect of context is, however, available at 5+ and 7+, showing within age differences and in particular that the gap even between means of the advantaged and disadvantaged groups is much narrower in some settings than in others. This has important implications for education since teachers who utilize only certain limited contexts from which to judge young children's language competence may assume a wider gulf between the less advantaged (for whom some such situations may be unusual, unknown or alien), and the more advantaged (for whom they may be common everyday experiences in which they comfortably express their views at length to an adult or other child).

At five years and at seven years of age there were striking differences in the groups in the complexity with which they expressed interpretations of a picture, the more advantaged it is claimed "injected, meaning into the situation" (p.101). The disadvantaged children tended to give short responses which treated the picture as a series of objects and thus it is argued "the children were orientated to examine the situations differently" and thus used "different strategies of language" (p.103). Such evidence is important since it shows that even in such a highly selected group of 'disadvantaged' children response to such commonly used materials as pictures, unless supported and encouraged, may lead only to labelling of unrelated objects. This may be reinforced by use of pictures of discrete objects where a labelling response may be all that is required by the teacher! In a section entitled 'Some contradictions in a chapter called *Language and Disadvantage at School*, crucial points for understanding the language knowledge and use of young children are made (based on the evidence from the children at 7+ years of age).

1. "For all the activities except free conversations the disadvantaged children's utterances tend to be considerably shorter than those of the advantaged children" (p. 157);

2. The advantaged children talked more than the disadvantaged in these settings and the difference "was greater when imaginative projection was asked for" (p.158);

3. When retelling a story the disadvantaged had a mean length of utterance which was almost twice as high as in other situations. They showed they were able to remember sequences and reproduce the story line with much of the detail, (Note, the story was repeated to a companion in a meaningful context);

4. Tough expresses caution at the ways in which linguistic data should be interpreted as follows:

a) although the disadvantaged children showed lower mean scores for all measures, *the range of scores is not necessarily less*

b) *all the children produced long complex utterances at times.*

She also notes that when retested at seven years of age the IQ's of the disadvantaged group were lower than when initially tested at three years of age, that they were inclined for some types of items to respond with 'I don't know', or otherwise avoid answering the question. Thus the tests may be an underestimate of their knowledge and understanding. It may not be "a lack of resources of language that governs what they do. The child's disadvantage in school seems to stem more from a lack of motivation to think in those ways ....." (p. 165-166).

One major difference between the children in these groups in these situations appears to be according to Tough "in their disposition to use language for particular purposes". Frequently when pressed further the disadvantaged children "moved towards the answer given spontaneously by the children in the advantaged groups" (p. 170).

To quote:

> "All that can be inferred from this is that in this context, and others that were used, the children in the disadvantaged groups did not refer to past experience as explicitly and readily as did the advantaged groups" (p.111).

This relates to the paper by Cazden mentioned earlier, Cazden (1970). Clearly in many situations in school the child is likely to be judged by the more limited responses and this may in turn lead to lowered expectations - perhaps in the way suggested by Robinson in the article referred to earlier (Robinson, 1980).

As was noted earlier the initial sampling for this study was such as to ensure half of the children in each group attended nursery school or class. The children in the nursery groups were selected from eleven different nursery schools and classes, supervised by experienced teachers. No detail is given as to whether the advantaged and disadvantaged groups were in the same, or similar preschool units (as was the case in the study by Tizard and Hughes to be discussed later). The first recordings at three years of age were made shortly after the children had started in preschool education. At that stage there were already some statistically significant differences between the nursery and non-nursery disadvantaged groups. Tough suggests this may be explained by the fact that these children in the nursery schools and classes were already gaining experience of talking with a friend in the presence of an adult. Even were that the only explanation it could have important implications in that a 'disadvantaged' child who had experience of preschool education might on entry to infant school reveal to the teacher, even without probing, greater apparent competence in language situations in the classroom which might in turn result in increased expectations of the child. Furthermore, it is stated that at three years of age, contrary to what might have been expected, the disadvantaged groups asked more questions than the advantaged groups, and the nursery disadvantaged group asked twice as many questions as the three other groups (p. 83).

It is difficult to evaluate the results in this study on nursery attendance and its effects on language as only a few pages are devoted to this discussion (p. 170-172). Little detail is provided on the comparability of the groups in relation to the nursery education they received, on date of entry to infant school or similarity of language experiences in school between the ages of five and seven years of age.

Implications for early education

It is stressed that the situation, and also whether there were probes, influenced the children's language differentially and that there was considerable overlap between the groups. The discussion tends, however, to be in terms of means and extracts which are cited and selected to show contrasts between groups. It would have been valuable had some examples been cited of less successful advantaged children and of individual children in the disadvantaged group who were successful. Parental interviews could have been used to put 'flesh' on to such studies. One unfortunate effect of this approach in presentation, and of the classification of uses of language which Tough developed is that in most secondary sources it is to this classification that reference is made. There is often reference to absolute differences between advantaged and disadvantaged children in their uses of language and the need to teach the latter what the former have grasped already. There are successful children from 'disadvantaged' homes and less successful children from advantaged homes. Even with such highly selected groups as in this study one feels there may have been some hidden within the mean scores. This was certainly true in the larger and more representative sample from Bristol of Wells, discussed in the following section. A study of young children who were already able to read with understanding on entry to school, at five years of age, also included some who were from so called 'disadvantaged homes' (see Clark, 1976).

Joan Tough as an educationist was influenced by the work of Bernstein and by the views of Piaget to whom she refers frequently. Her views on the 'egocentric' thinking of young children and on their stages of cognitive development are the contexts within which she discusses, for example, the development of logical thinking and moral concepts. The experimental work of Donaldson and of Bryant was only beginning to appear when *The Development of Meaning* was published in 1977. Both have shown that, even in experiments such as those on which Piagetian evidence was based, the precise context will influence the child's apparent competence (Donaldson, 1978). Gordon Wells whose language study of young children will now be discussed, also wished to follow the development of normal children and at a stage where their uses of language was more complex than had previously been studied. To that end he wished to study their language in natural settings, in the home. Consideration of the similarities and differences in the work of Wells in relation to that of Tough is important. Wells (1977) undertook a critique of the study by Tough in direct response to *The Development of Meaning* the reference used for the discussion in this chapter.

A critique of the research findings

Wells raises the issue as to whether such marked differences as Tough found between her groups could have been "an artefact of the way in which the groups were selected" (p.3), and thus whether the conclusions would be supported were the full spectrum of family backgrounds from which the school population was drawn to be studied. Wells selected from his own sample a group to give equal representation to four classes of family background across the full spectrum, using the same criteria of occupation and education of both parents. Four boys and four girls in each group were studied (with no cutoff for IQ or exclusion of children). The recordings were of *spontaneous speech* in the home which was then analysed as described by Tough. According to Wells, the Bristol data revealed large *within-group differences* particularly for the more complex categories and much smaller differences between classes, "with very few cases of a clear trend over all four classes of family background (p. 4-5). Wells raises issues similar to those noted earlier including:

a) the danger of making generalisations about habitual use of language from speech samples in one limited situation;

b) the danger of claiming from later evidence in different but also limited situations that the differences between the groups in habitual use of language had increased;

c) that all the situations were 'non-spontaneous' and one cannot assume that each child's perception of the task was the same;

d) that because a child did not use, or seldom used, certain forms of language in these situations it cannot be inferred that they would not do so in a different setting with different communication partners.

The above points concerning young children's language would be confirmed also in studies by the present author. Language samples collected in a variety of contexts using radiomicrophones revealed wide differences in the child's apparent competence; indeed some of the most complex language was found in discussion around relevant tasks in a 'contrived' situation but with peers, with no adult involved, even the arrival of the adult affected the dialogue as the children began to defer to her (Clark *et al.*, 1984 and Coates, 1985). One further point which Wells makes is the danger of assuming that educational success can be predicted for individual children by means of the type of categorisation in the Tough study. He discusses what variables were found to be predictive in his sample. Finally, Wells stresses, from his language samples from young children at home in their spontaneous conversations, that the type of dialogue which Tough refers to as 'enabling' occurs rarely even in the more advantaged homes (see also Davie later in this chapter). What he feels is important in sustaining dialogue is "the presence or absence of genuine reciprocity and collaboration" (p.10). Should this prove to be the case, and there is now further evidence to support this view, then it will also have important implications for language stimulation in young children. Dialogue with adults in a 'contrived' situation (that is arranged for the purpose of talk) may indeed merely serve to reinforce teachers' ideas about children's limitations, which a wider knowledge of these children might have dispelled (see Clark *et al.*, 1984 and Tizard and Hughes, 1984). It should be noted that retelling a story in a meaningful context elicited some of the most complex language from the disadvantaged in the Tough study. Further evidence on the complexity of language elicited in such situations in the home, is to be found in other studies including those of Wells and Davie.

STUDIES OF LANGUAGE AT HOME AND AT SCHOOL: WELLS

These studies by Wells and related studies by co-workers have been extensively funded since 1972 until 1984 among other sources by SSRC (and later ESRC) by the Nuffield Foundation and latterly by DES also. Over the period of the grants there have been numerous articles on the studies by Wells, and by his co-workers and more recently a series of books. The sources from which most of the following information has been taken are the following books, Wells 1981, 1985a and 1986, also the unpublished report to DES in 1984 on *Linguistic Influences on Educational Attainment*. A collection of papers has also been published in 1985, based on papers which were in circulation at an earlier stage to which where appropriate reference will also be made (as 1985b). The Bristol study began as an investigation of language development with two main aims:

a) to describe the sequence of language development in a sample of children learning to speak English as their first language,

b) to investigate the environmental factors that might have an influence on that development. It was also hoped to describe these children's conversational experience and to investigate the relationship between preschool experience and success in school.

The study of language preschool involved a sampling by means of a radiomicrophone of *naturally occurring conversation* which was sampled in 90 second spells for a complete day from 9 a.m. till 6 p.m. once every three months over a period of two-and-a-quarter years. There was no observer present during these recordings and contexts were identified by replaying the tapes to the parents at the end of each day. Wells found that although the 'route' of the children's language development was similar there were wide differences in the rate of development which appeared to be related to the quality of the 'child's conversational experience'. The quality and quantity of the conversational experience was the best predictor of the child's oral language at entry to primary school. Furthermore attainment at seven years of age could be strongly predicted by differences between children on entry. Wells attempted to identify aspects of conversation which appeared to be related to later attainment in school at seven years of age, and in particular, 'literacy related' activities. Those he found to be the most powerful in their effects were the contexts related to story and he has developed this theme and its implications for education in a number of publications. One example is the recently published book *The Meaning Makers* (Wells, 1986). Through data from the longitudinal study Wells states that one of the most important features found in the homes of children whose success could have been predicted early was 'the sharing of stories' whose role he suggests in relation to literacy development is more important than any early introduction to features of print. He also suggests that "stories have a role in education that goes far beyond their contribution to the acquisition of literacy" (p. 194). The book referred to above is not only the most recent overview of the Bristol Studies by Wells, but it is also the publication in which he develops in the greatest detail the implications of the research for education. If, however, one wishes to have the full details of the sample selection, the language sampling and analysis, and the linguistic analysis of the language, then it is to the publication *Language Development in the Preschool Years* (Wells, 1985a) that one must turn. The earlier publication *Learning through Interaction* (Wells, 1981) has contributions from Wells and a number of co-workers.

In view of the points which were made earlier concerning the sample in Tough's study it is pertinent to make a more detailed statement on that studied by Wells.

The Sample

A pilot study was undertaken in 1971-2 to test the feasibility of the design and the main study commenced in 1973. Full details of the sample are set out in Wells 1985a, Chapter 1. The sample as drawn from birth records in the City of Bristol of children born in 1969-70 and 1971-2. Those excluded initially were children:

   a) of multiple births,

   b) with known handicaps,

   c) whose parents were not native speakers of English,

   d) who were in institutions or full-time day care,

   e) likely to move soon,

   f) had siblings already in the study.

The sample consisted of 128 children from a larger randomly drawn sample in Bristol of children representative in sex, month of birth and family background (based on occupation and education of both parents). Half of the sample was aged 15 months and half 39 months at the start of the research. A sample of 32 children from the younger group was followed into school and over their first two years in primary school, and a further assessment was made when the children were aged 10 years 3 months. A first visit to seek agreement was made by a health visitor and after the above exclusions and those who refused to be interviewed by the researchers 63.4% of the initial pool was left (see Wells 1985a, p.26-7). The commitment which would be required was then explained to these families by interviewers. Of those interviewed 87.4% agreed to take part, (more of those who refused were in lower social classes). Age of the children was spread through the year with selection from eight months of birth. Random selection was then used to enable appropriate patterns with regard to the grouping by occupation and education of parents, month of birth and sex. Additional children were included as replacements. Details are given of any withdrawals after an initial observation which were selective in ways that gave concern to the research team (e.g. more boys than girls). However, the final sample of 125 (of the 128) children for whom few observations were missing did cover:

a) a younger and older age group;

b) a spread across the year in date of birth;

c) a range of family backgrounds;

d) roughly equal numbers of boys and girls, both in the total, and within each category.

Other features of the children and their background were allowed to vary randomly but details are given on some aspects in Chapter 7, 'The children and their families', in which the parental interviews are also reported.

Implications for early education

Of some importance to this present report is the fact that in the mid-seventies in this sample from Bristol a number of children were already attending either nursery school or class, or playgroup, (or both) by the age of 3 years 6 months. At the time of interview this was already as high as 81%, although it is stated that:

"few of the children in the younger age-range were attending nursery school at the time of interview. However, the proportion increased as the children grew older" (Wells, 1985a p.290).

In the various publications little further reference is made to how many children in the full sample had attended nursery school or class or playgroup before entering school, or how many of those in the longitudinal study to ten years of age had pre-school education experience. Careful reading of the many publications has revealed only passing reference (for example in Wells, 1985b p. 81, 83-84). It is briefly referred to as not being associated with attainment at age seven, but suggested that those already judged to be educationally at risk at three years of age might have been given priority admission to nursery school or class. The absence of detail on this aspect of the study is all the more surprising in view of the detail in all other aspects. Reference is made to checking whether the child attends nursery school or playgroup, and if so, on what days, to determine appropriate days for recording (Wells, 1985a, p. 26). Since most of these children did appear to attend preschool units it is legitimate to wonder to what extent these preschool educational experiences supported the home developments or whether they reinforced the differences already apparent; also how many of the children described in detail in case studies did attend preschool units.

It is thus a matter of concern that in the book entitled *Language Development in the Preschool Years* (Wells, 1985a) there should be as a subtitle 'Language at home and at school', yet the 'school', to which reference is made there and repeatedly in the more recent reports of the longitudinal research is the infant school entered about five years of age, studied in detail with classroom observation over the children's

first two years in school. It was logical to seek funding and to gain extensive funds
to utilize such detailed language samples and to obtain information for these children
after entry to primary school, which could then be compared and contrasted with
their day at home (see Wells, 1985b Chapter 6, and 1986 Chapter 5). What is dis-
turbing is the tenor of a number of the comments which may appear to suggest to
readers that for all or most of these children entry to infant school was their first experience of education outside the home. Clearly even from this limited information
this was not the case. The dialogue of Gary in the home (Wells, 1986 p.71-78) for
example clearly owed something to stimulus in the nursery school (or class?) yet
only passing reference to his attendance is made to explain topics under discussion.
Reference is made only in passing to Rosie's prior attendance at nursery class (on
p. 96). Indeed all but three of the group of 32 children followed into school had previously attended some form of preschool unit (personal communication). The
following and other quotations *which all refer to infant school,* could give the impression that was the child's first school, or even in the third quotation that it was
preschool which was studied in this research.

    i) "From Home to First School. By the time children come to school at five, therefore,
they have learnt a very great deal and have done so as active meaning-makers" (Wells,
1985b p.156).

    ii) "Children's experience at school in this respect is almost the exact reverse of their
experience at home. Compared with parents, teachers it appears, are typically far more
concerned to pursue their own topics - to follow their own agenda - than to accept and
extend the topics offered by the child" (Wells, 1985b p.160).

    iii) "As with other researchers who had compared the language experiences of younger
children at home and in the nursery or preschool playgroup, what we found is that,
compared with homes, schools are not providing an environment that fosters language
development" (Wells, 1986, p.87).

Wells goes on to state that even the most linguistically deprived children in his study
did not have in the classrooms language experience which was richer than that of
the home (these were classrooms in infant schools). He compares his findings in this
connection to those of Tizard in her study of young preschool girls at home and at
school (a study which will now be discussed) and to similar findings by Wood in
preschool playgroups and classes (to be discussed later).

Based on the classroom observations in the infant school Wells gives examples of
'enabling' contexts and dialogue between children and some teachers and shows
how this effects the children's responses. The in-service materials and courses which
Tough developed have raised the awareness of many teachers about young children's
ability to communicate given a variety of contexts, appropriate materials and skilled
probing by a genuinely interested enquirer. Wells, particularly in the most recent
publication (Wells, 1986) gives further important pointers about effective communication both between child and adult, and adult and child.

LANGUAGE AT HOME AND AT PRESCHOOL: TIZARD AND HUGHES

This study was funded by SSRC in the late seventies. The most widely cited report of this research is *Young Children Learning* (Tizard and Hughes, 1984) in which the research findings and their implications for education are presented in a style of communication to a wide readership, with many and extensive extracts from conversations at home and school. A number of papers based on the study were already in print much earlier in academic journals (Tizard *et al.*, 1980, 1982, 1983a, 1983b). In Tizard *et al.* (1980) the focus is on contrasts between the language of the young children when talking with mothers and teachers; in 1982 the focus is on adults' cognitive demands in the two settings; in 1983a the children's questions and adults answers are reported. The issues raised earlier on 'verbal deprivation' are discussed in the context of the research findings in 1983(b) under the title *Language and Social Class : Is verbal deprivation a myth?* These topics are also covered in a more narrative style in Tizard and Hughes(1984). A study of that publication shows the extent to which Tizard and Hughes challenge the formulations about disadvantage in the home and the need to teach working-class parents how to talk with their children, as some interpreted the earlier findings of Tough. Their findings with regard to the home as a language context are linked to and shown to support those of Wells discussed earlier, and those of Davie (to follow).

The research by Tizard and Hughes is based on recordings with a radiomicrophone of naturally occurring dialogue of girls with staff at preschool in the morning, and at home with their mother in the afternoon. These recordings over several sessions of about two and a half hours were then transcribed and analysed.

The Sample

This study was of 30 girls of about four years of age. Half the girls were working-class (with fathers who were working-class and mothers who left school at the minimum age with no educational qualifications), half were middle-class (with fathers in professional or managerial positions and mothers who have or had qualified for tertiary education). The other criteria in selection were that the children should attend nursery school or class in the morning and spend the afternoon at home with their mothers: the children from the two social classes were drawn from the same nine nursery schools in two LEAs, where more than two children fulfilled the criteria, selection was random. All schools and parents agreed to take part in the study which involved recording, and the presence of an observer, at home in the afternoons, as well as recording in the nursery school. The recording at home which was analysed covered the early part of afternoon (1pm - 3.30pm), those at school covered two mornings (9am - 11.30am) (excluding any formal story or music sessions for the whole group). Recorded but not analysed from the school samples was the children's talk with other children. Only two girls selected refused to co-operate and were thus replaced by two others. It should be noted that the following were excluded:

a) boys,

b) children not attending part-time preschool education,

c) children not at home with their mothers in afternoons (thus any whose mothers worked full-time),

d) children whose father was at home in the afternoon,

e) who came from families with more than three children,

f) children in homes where the main language spoken was not English.

In short to quote:

> "The working-class children in our study could not in any reasonable sense be considered 'deprived'; they lived in small, two-parent families, the majority in Council housing, and appeared to be well cared for, much loved, and plentifully supplied with toys. Since nursery schooling in Britain, although free, is not compulsory, it is possible that they came from particularly caring, or educationally orientated families. At any rate, they were probably typical of the majority of working-class children who attend half-day nursery school, and who are nevertheless seen by their teachers as in need of language enrichment" (Tizard *et al.*, 1980 p.52).

Thus this study was similar to that of Tough in having two groups, one middle-class and one working-class, and contrasted with Tough but similar to Wells in analysing naturally occurring language (Tizard with an observer present, Wells without, but both by means of a radiomicrophone). Like Wells, Tizard recorded at home and at school: Tizard undertook those recordings concurrently: Wells had no information on the language of his group in the preschool unit, but recorded in infant school at a later stage. Tizard's sample was aged about four years, while Tough's sample was initially aged three years of age, but highly selective, presumably more able to be understood without any preselection except that noted earlier. Unfortunately Tizard and Hughes seldom make reference to the fact that their sample was all girls, using the word children in the title *Young Children Learning* and on almost every occasion in the book (although of course girls' names are used throughout). They do, however, indicate how similar to the findings of Wells theirs are, in showing extended and complex conversations in the homes. In the Tizard and Hughes study the sampling of language is for a shorter period, but the recording is continuous, while for Wells it covered the day from 9am - 6pm but in 90 second 'bursts', and was also longitudinal. Thus neither study is able to give evidence on dialogue at bedtime (and particularly perhaps story reading then). Because of their criteria both may undervalue the contribution of fathers to their children's language development (see Davie, 1984). Taken together, however, they give new insights into the contributions of the home to the language development of young children.

The findings

The following is a summary of points made by Tizard and Hughes concerning the conversations, with comparisons between social classes and between home and school:

1) Number of adult - child conversations : no social class differences in numbers were found, but fewer at school than at home.

2) Length of conversations : no social class differences but conversations at home tended to have more 'turns' than at school.

3) Who initiated: in all settings the children initiated about half the conversations - no differences between social classes or between home and school.

4) Past and future events : the majority of school conversations concerned play activity whereas at home a number were on a range of topics including past and future events. There was also a social class difference with conversations with middle-class children more often concerned with the past and future.

5) Length of conversation : both at home and at school much the longest conversations concerned books which the adult was reading aloud, or had just read aloud and/or when engaged in a joint activity. There were more stories recorded in the working-class homes than the middle-class homes, it is suggested this was because the 'peak' story time in the latter would be evenings.

6) Numbers and type of questions : children asked many questions at home, few at school with no social class difference. The number was highest in relation to books and past and future events. At home and school middle-class children however asked a higher proportion of 'nonspecific' why and how questions, and the proportion for both classes was higher at home.

7) Adult responses : proportion of 'elaborate' answers was higher at school and both at home and at school 'middle-class' children received more elaborate answers.

8) Relationship between child's conversation at home and school: correlations were low and not significant thus a child who talked a lot or asked a lot of questions at home or who tended to initiate conversation is not necessarily likely to do so at school.

All the above points are taken from Tizard et al.(1980 p.55-68).

Finally, it should be noted that the children's intelligence was assessed after the study by someone not involved in the study. The results showed a difference on a standardised test between the two social classes, matched to be comparable on other variables as indicated earlier (working-class girls IQ 106.4 (S.D. 13.2), middle- class girls 122.3 (S.D. 11.3). This is an important point which may reflect differences in the two groups in intellectual development, or may instead reflect the differential effect of a formalised setting with a strange adult on the young girls in the two groups. This relates to points made by Tough (1977a) concerning her two groups of children whose IQ changed differentially and by Davie (1984). The possibility that the level of language competence of 'working-class' children may well be underestimated in such situations and in other formal situations is raised by such findings . This may then result in adults providing less challenging dialogue with the child than the child has potential for, and may indeed show in other naturalistic settings. Tizard and Hughes do discuss the relationship between IQ and other factors of language, showing that there was a tendency for the working-class children with higher IQs to talk more at school and ask more questions than those with lower IQ, a finding which could be related to the point made above. (The above points are based on Tizard *et al.*, 1980 p.55-68. These expanded and illustrated by extracts are in Tizard and Hughes, 1984).

For the sake of clarity and completeness the comparisons between language at home and at school by Tizard and Hughes are placed in this chapter. Further studies in pre-school units will be considered in the following chapters. It is important to note that the study by Tizard and Hughes in school considered only the language that the girls had in the free play-setting with the adults (teachers and others). Dialogue which they might have had there with other children was not analysed. Some of this might have been made possible by other settings planned by the adults as a stimulus to language, as well as to social interaction. (This aspect will be considered later in connection with evidence from Clark *et al.*(1984) on peer interaction in educational settings). Tizard and Hughes make little reference to the possibility that the attendance at a preschool each morning by each girl in their sample may have influenced either the content of the language in the afternoons, or the readiness of the mother to indulge in such extended dialogue over a period of time. The question that remains unanswered is how different the evidence would have been had these girls not attended preschool in the mornings. Had the sample included boys at home in the afternoons, would the social class patterns indeed have been the same and the home/school differences been the same, less - or greater? Would a comparable sample of young girls not attending nursery school have given similar results at home? Indeed, would there have been some mothers in such a sample who would not have agreed to participate?

In Tizard and Hughes (1984) there is discussion on parental attitudes and ways in which these may differ across the classes. There is also in Chapter 6 some discussion of subtle social class differences in line with some of the points made earlier by Tough - to quote one example:

"We found that the middle-class mothers used language for complex purposes significantly more often than the working-class mothers - on average, adding the different usages together, fifty-one times an hour compared with thirty-eight times an hour for working-class mothers. The proportion, as well as the rate, of these uses of language was higher in the talk of the middle-class mothers. The averages conceal wide variations and there was a good deal of overlap between the social classes. However, five of the working-class mothers had lower scores than any middle-class mother" (Tizard and Hughes, 1984 p.141).

It seems important to consider the relationship between mothers' views of their own contribution to their child's development and the dialogue in which they engage. The assumption current in the early seventies of deprivation of language and deficiencies in homes could well have reinforced attitudes of incompetence in parents such as these. A discussion of such attitudes in parents from a much more 'deprived' section of the community than were involved in these studies, and of ways in which not only their attitudes but that of their children's teachers to the parents contribution might be modified is reported in Donachy (1979).

EXPERIENCES AT HOME: DAVIE, J, HUTT AND OTHERS

The parallel studies of 'the young child's experiences at home' and 'play, exploration and learning in the preschool', directed by John and Corinne Hutt at the University of Keele, were among the first researches to be funded by DES within the Programme (both are reported in Tizard (1975) and Kay (1975)). The empirical work for both was undertaken in the seventies. The report of the research on experiences in the home which was published in 1984 as *The Young Child at Home* (Davie, Hutt, Vincent and Mason), is the source for the evidence discussed here. The parallel study in preschool units which became the responsibility of John Hutt after Corinne Hutt's death in 1979 is not available in published form and the report to DES in 1984 was therefore the source consulted. Supporting evidence from that research in the preschool units is cited by Davie and Hutt. At present, however, attention will be confined to the study in the home as the parallel study did not involve the same sample of children. Davie and Hutt (like Wells and Tizard) studied the young children in natural settings in the home, but unlike them extended their study in time to the child's waking hours and in space beyond the house.

They had an observer like Tizard (and not Wells), and also attempted to assess and minimize observer effects. Unlike Tizard and Wells they did not record language by use of a radiomicrophone; they did, however, categorise language interactions and devote a chapter to language.

This study gives a picture of the experiences at play and interactions with parents, siblings and relatives over the equivalent of a day, sampled in two-hour blocks over several days, for a group of normal preschool boys and girls. Thus the relative pattern of experiences over the day of boys and girls is studied, their interactions with both mother and father are considered. Lacking are full transcripts of the content of the dialogue which could be reanalysed by others (as is now possible with the language from Wells' study). Details of the observational schedule are provided in their Appendix. As in the other researches discussed here, social class was a major concern because it was felt that:

> "so much attention has been paid to it in earlier research, using different techniques and the findings from this research have affected the attitudes of people concerned with the education of the young child" (Davie *et al.*, 1984 p.177).

From their evidence they claim that social class does not operate as strongly as has been suggested. They found that the vast majority of the children in their sample had plenty of toys and that working-class parents spent as much time talking and interacting with their children as did middle class parents. They note on p.177 that:

"The differences we did find were subtle and qualitative".

Middle-class parents were more inclined to provide toys of so-called educational value, their children had more plentiful supplies of books and were encouraged to spend time on activities more related to developing the beginning of academic skills. On the completion of the observation period the children were assessed by the observer on the Stanford Binet Intelligence Scale and social class differences were found which it was suggested could have been related to the experience in activities such as are in these tests. A sex difference was also found with the girls scoring higher on the test. Greater competence in language was shown by some children in the natural setting (see p.151-2).

Like Wells they noted that 'abstract' explanations were rare even by middle-class parents. They do suggest, however, that there were differences which were subtle and qualitative in language usage of parents to their children, with, for example, more use by some of the working-class parents of 'instructions' which were redundant as the child already knew the labels. In contrast the novelty of the 'instructions' from some of the middle-class parents, "appeared to stimulate their children to demand more 'instructions'" (p.178). Both groups used what they categorised as 'options' as effective ways of controlling their children, that is suggestions or invitations to take part in a new activity, or to deflect from a less acceptable : this and praise it is claimed were more frequently used by middle-class parents. Middle-class children were also receiving more 'options' from peers - suggesting "that older siblings were developing similar tactics to their parents towards their siblings" (p.149). Their categorisations of speech were based on the work of Bernstein (p.148). Speech was 'categorised' rather than recorded and they themselves note that very subtle differences in language production could not be revealed in their study (p.136).

The Sample

This study was of 165 children living in Stoke-on-Trent and the immediately surrounding area. The sample was balanced for, sex (boys and girls), age (3-3.5, 3.5-4, 4-4.5 years) and family position (eldest, only, youngest). Documentation available locally was used for initial approaches to large numbers of families with assistance from local personnel to obtain a representative sample, (as in Wells' study). Details are given (in Davie *et al.*, 1984 Chapter 2) of sample selection and of possible bias as a result of families unwilling or unable to co-operate.

Children were excluded who:

a) had any serious health defect

b) were not of UK or Eire origin,

c) were from single parent families,

d) were attending nursery school or class, a day nursery, or a playgroup more than two sessions per week.

Because of the balanced sample it was possible to study a more complex pattern of variables, not only social class but sex differences if any, and the effect of position in the family on interaction with adults and young children. It was found for example that there were differences between boys and girls not only in their toys but in preferred activities and in types of fantasy play (found also in free play in nursery schools by Lomax, 1979b). Position in family strongly influenced interaction with adults and children, 'oldest' were more like 'only' children, youngest children interacted less with adults and more with children. There was not evidence of differential interactions of mother and fathers with young sons and daughters, even in rough and tumble play, although fathers were more inclined to play football with sons. Fathers were less inclined to interact with 'youngest' children. Girls neither spoke more nor received more general or particular forms of speech, although they did score higher on the intelligence test.

Implications for early education

The published report does contain sufficient detail on a number of points for replication to be possible (including details of the observation schedule). It would have been helpful to have known how much overlap there was between groups where differences were found, particularly where comments were made on social class differences. Details are given concerning the social and physical environment of the area and of the children in the two social classes, an important consideration in assessing the generalisability of the findings, yet one which is not provided in sufficient detail by some research workers. A summary will be given of the features of the environment detailed by Davie and Hutt to assess the generalisability of their study. It also illustrates how differences between home environments might plausibly explain some patterns of interaction, rather than differences in preferred styles of child rearing between classes, to which they may be attributed by some researchers.

The following points are noted with regard to the area in which the study took place:

a) the children all lived in or near Stoke-on-Trent (thus urban);

b) the employment in the area is in the potteries and mining, also a large tyre factory (influencing patterns of employment including of females);

c) the area has many parks;

d) the city has a history of early provision of preschool education with already by the seventies nursery schools and classes, also day nurseries;

e) provision of preschool education was increased because of women's employment in the potteries;

f) nursery school attendance was normally full-time (See Davie *et al.*, Chapter 3 and p.160).

Points d), e) and f) could all be important in any attempt to replicate the study.

A chapter on preschool provision and parents' attitudes to this (Chapter 9) is based in part on the wider sample of over a thousand families contacted initially. Parents were shown to be confused about the nature of different types of provision for young children. The reason for sending children to a playgroup or nursery school most frequently cited was to mix with other children. It is reported that more middle-class than working-class parents in the sample were in favour of keeping their child at home, for child-centred reasons, especially where nursery school was concerned, (noted there as normally full-time). The sample excluded children attending nursery school or class or day nursery, or playgroup more than two sessions per week. Middle-class parents in the sample were more likely than working-class parents to give 'developmental' reasons for wanting their children to attend playgroup. About half of the sample attended playgroup at the time of initial contact and there was a highly significant class difference, with many more middle-class than working-class children attending.

The following points are noted with regard to the sample of children and their families:

a) about half the sample (of both classes) lived in 'semidetached' houses;

b) most of the middle-class parents and a high proportion of the working-class parents were owner-occupiers (there were cheap terraced houses for sale) almost a third of the working-class were in council accommodation;

c) few lived in flats and where they did it was on the first floor (it was the city's declared policy not to house families with small children in high rise apartments),

d) all families had sole use of toilet facilities, (although in a few old properties the toilet might be outside);

e) overcrowding was not a problem;

f) only one family had no outside area which was their own;

g) few were living adjacent to very busy roads;

h) the majority were car owners (with a social class difference);

i) all families had television sets;

j) all but four fathers were working;

k) few mothers worked full-time but 39% were working, (more middle-class than working-class);

l) fathers or relations tended to be caretaker when the mother worked, although a few went to a childminder;

m) most of the families had close relatives in the area (both maternal and paternal).(See Davie *et al.*, 1984 Chapter 3).

As may be appreciated these conditions are very different from the multiple deprivation from which some families suffer who may live in overcrowded conditions in high rise flats, near to busy roads, with no outside play area, a low income or unemployment and with no relatives in the area. Some children in addition to all the above may be from single parent families, and with very young mothers. It is important to consider the environment in which these children live and all the constraints they place on parental interaction with their children, and between siblings. There is growing evidence of the depression of many young mothers in these circumstances, its effect on the children in the home and yet the parent's inability to take advantage of preschool facilities which may be available (Shinman, 1981). It is essential, however, that 'multiple deprivation' is not confused with social class influences. Davie and Hutt comment that the conditions of their sample are very like those described by Bryant, Harris and Newton (1980) for under fives in Oxfordshire which was the area in which the major SSRC study funded within the Nursery Research Programme was conducted about the same date.

This study by Davie and Hutt is rich in insights into the lives of these 165 preschool children within their extended families. Its plan and the range of day covered makes it one of the few studies in which the relative interactions of mothers and fathers is studied in relation also to the sex of the children and their position in the family. The activities and interactions available to these young preschool children are shown to be wide and varied. Any differences related to social class are at most 'subtle and qualitative'. Social class differences may be widened in 'contrived' and experimental settings which may have differential effects on parents and children from different social classes. In relation to the contexts in preschool units they suggest that:

> "the preschool setting may have a similar effect, constraining and inhibiting the young working-class child, so that, for example, his speech and fantasy play are curtailed, enhancing differences that are not apparent at home" (Davie *et al.*, p.178).

This observation would be supported by the evidence from Tizard and Hughes' study on the differential effects of school on the social classes, with the middle-class children displaying a competence in school more similar to that at home. This is certainly not a situation peculiar to the preschool unit. Indeed the gulf found by Tizard and Hughes might have been greater had the children been in the more formal setting of the infant classroom, as may be seen from the findings of Wells in the latter setting. Transition from preschool unit to infant school was studied by Cleave, Jowett and Bate (1982) and by Barrett (1986). These researches and others on continuity and discontinuity between preschool and reception class are considered in detail in a later section of this report.

In view of these findings on the differential effects of contexts on language between social classes, the proposal by Robinson noted earlier becomes all the more significant. He suggests that teachers predict children's attainment partly on the basis of what he refers to as "the language management of children", that they overestimate the size of the correlation between social class, speech and academic potential and that the "differentials are communicated to and perceived by the children" (Robinson, 1980 p.38-9).

CHAPTER 6   EXPERIMENTAL AND INTERVENTION STUDIES IN PRESCHOOL UNITS

THE CONTEXT OF THE SEVENTIES

Assumptions about 'deficiencies' in the language development of many 'disadvantaged' children related, it was claimed, to 'inadequacies' in their homes, set the priorities for establishment of preschool units in areas of disadvantage, and for the emphases on language development and the role of the professional. Most of the research studies in preschool units in Britain have had a focus on language development, in most instances the interactions between adults and children in 'ordinary' preschool units (as in the study of young girls at home and in school by Tizard and Hughes, 1984), rather than in experimental units such as were the base for a number of the studies in USA. It is thus important to bear the following points in mind:

1) The promotion of language development was only one aim in preschool education, indeed not necessarily that with the highest priority in the view of the staff, or any priority in some preschool units (see Taylor, Exon and Holley, 1972).

2) Social and emotional development may have equal or higher priority for some staff, and for many parents, for whom preparation for school may also have high priority (see Davie *et al.*, 1984 for examples of the views of parents in that study). In the study by Clift, Cleave and Griffin (1980) in nursery schools and classes the teachers and assistants emphasised social aims (before educational preparation for school and linguistic aims).

3) Some types of preschool provision may have different aims from those of others, for example day nurseries (see Van der Eyken *et al.*, 1984 pp.106-109 for the views of a national sample in 1975).

4) There could be differences in the priorities accorded by staff and those assumed by others to be their aims, including their colleagues in the infant departments to which the children may proceed (see Clark *et al.*, 1984, and Wallace, 1985).

5) The children attending certain units or types of unit may differ in characteristics, particularly for example in day nurseries where there may be criteria set for admission of all or most children (see Van der Eyken, 1984).

D

It is thus important in considering evidence from observations of language interaction in preschool units to bear in mind the extent to which that was a priority for the staff. Furthermore in any comparison between units it is also important to assess the extent to which the characteristics of the children are similar, or whether the problems faced by particular units in promoting language development might be much greater than those in others.

Some professionals felt that to make good children's language deficiencies language programmes more or less structured were required; others felt that some form of dialogue tutorial approach between an adult and child was required for poorly functioning children. Others, particularly those in preschool education in Britain, felt that the context should be a relaxed setting which would stimulate play, with a good adult-child ratio, a variety of educational toys and equipment and natural materials for creative play. A wide choice was to be available to the child who should be free to move around and select activities and companions within this safe and stimulating environment. All or most of the day (or half day) would be available for free play chosen within limits by the children themselves. The role of the adults would be partly to respond to children's initiations, to talk with the children, and not least to organise the setting in ways that would lead to creative use of materials. In Britain there were few examples in preschool education of the use of highly structured didactic programmes, which at that time were in type and philosophy against the above trend, and were as a result rejected by most preschool educators.

In some of the preschool experimental projects in USA a highly didactic approach or structured programme was used, in others a more tutorial dialogue approach, still others were referred to as 'Piagetian' preschools, while others more closely resembled the natural play settings described above. The experimental projects in USA rigorous enough in experimental design to be included in the evaluation of the long-term effects of preschool education covered a variety of approaches, and included more or less parental involvement (Consortium for Longditudinal Studies, 1983).

The projects funded in Britain within or around the time of the Nursery Research Programme in the seventies took place mainly in 'ordinary' preschool units, in most cases without intervention in the sense of additional staff or an experimental programme. Furthermore they were planned in the early stages of the expansion, indeed in some instances the units had only recently opened, or the staff begun to work together. Yet while the projects were still underway the climate changed dramatically and contraction and threats of closure were already underway.

Few ordinary preschool education units at that time would have been characterised by active parental involvement. Research studies involving parents tended to involve home visiting or tutoring programmes where, for example professionals demonstrated to parents how to interact with their young children in ways that were thought to stimulate language development. One study which did incorporate in an experimental design the variables of nursery attendance in an ordinary preschool unit and a programme for parents at home, with or without nursery attendance, in an area of deprivation was that of Donachy (1976 and 1979). Pre- and post-testing on psychometric tests of experimental and control groups was part of the design. Improvements in language development as assessed by tests were found as a result of nursery school attendance, increased where parental involvement was added.

It is seldom possible in educational research of relevance to practice to adopt a 'pure' experimental design, with random allocation of either children or staff to different types of unit or programmes. There is a danger that this limitation may lead in some studies, as a consequence of possibly hidden selective factors, to findings being erroneously attributed to type of unit, to staff ratio or training, or social class or some other feature (see Cheyne, 1979).

Most studies in the preschool environment have been either small-scale laboratory studies over a short period, or large-scale studies in established preschool units. The former can have the advantage of tighter experimental control but are limited in time-scale and numbers. The latter, which have the advantage of natural settings, may differ in variables other than those being investigated, thus making it dangerous to infer causal relationships. Large-scale funded studies in Britain, such as those which will be discussed in the following chapter, have mainly involved observation of the behaviour and interaction of staff and children in ordinary preschool units, rather than intervention or experimental studies, or the evaluation of language programmes. In the present chapter brief reference will be made to a number of studies which have been either 'quasi-experimental' or have involved the implementation of a language programme or specific language activities. From these it is possible to highlight some of the issues in the interpretation of results, and the complementary nature of naturalistic and experimental studies.

In a 'quasi-experimental study (that is one in which an attempt was made to match preschool units and children on a number of important variables), Tizard and others studied the relationship between the cognitive level of staff behaviour and children's performance (Tizard, Philps and Plewis, 1976). In a small-scale study in a day nursery in Newcastle, Moxon assessed the effects of a language programme devised and implemented by the staff (Moxon, 1979). Turner and Whyte (1979) monitored the implementation of a language programme by the teacher and assessed its effects on the development of four-year-olds in a pre-reception class in a primary school in Belfast.

Detailed observations over time in a single preschool unit are as important as large scale studies in providing evidence on the relationship between staff behaviour and that of the children. Between school and between staff differences in approach and success in interaction are seldom fully considered in large-scale studies, and important differences both in approach and success may therefore be overlooked. Murphy undertook a series of observational studies over a period of months in a purpose-built nursery school in a deprived area in the West of Scotland in the mid seventies, a school staffed by experienced staff with qualifications to work with young children

(Murphy, 1980). Lomax (1977a, 1977b), undertook several detailed observational studies funded by the Scottish Education Department and the local authority involved, over a period of years in the mid seventies in comparable schools in similar areas in the West of Scotland.

A study of features of spatial design in preschool units was funded by the Scottish Education Department, also in the West of Scotland, in the mid seventies when it was anticipated that a large building programme would be required for the intended expansion in preschool education (Neill, Denham, Markus and Schaffer, 1977). In an SSRC funded study Smith and Connolly (1980) established an experimental playgroup which enabled them to 'manipulate' variables such as group size, amount of equipment, staff ratio, or nature of staff interaction, and to assess the effects.

More recently Sylva, Smith and Moore (1986), with support from the Nuffield Foundation, undertook a one-year evaluation of the implementation of the High/Scope curriculum in a number of preschool centres, following the involvement of staff in a training programme.

STAFF BEHAVIOUR IN PRESCHOOL UNITS

In this research by Tizard and others (Tizard, Philps and Plewis, 1976), a study was made of the cognitive level of staff behaviour in preschool units, and of the children's test scores in relation to different features of the units. An attempt was made to match units on a number of important variables, such as size of unit, equipment and resources. When units had been matched on the important variables, and in addition the presence or absence of a language session as part of the unit's programme, units selected could no longer be representative or typical of that type of preschool unit. This is an important point to note in relation not only to this study but to others where little detail may be given on a number of these variables.

This study involved 12 preschool units, 51 staff and 120 children. Some of the units had predominantly middle-class children, others predominantly working-class, some in each category had a language session during the day. The care adopted in design made it possible to exclude certain explanations for the findings and to appreciate the complexity of the interactions. The design included observations within the units over the day, during free play and snack times, and not only during the language sessions. This part of the design further clarified the issues and excluded yet other interpretations which otherwise might have been given for the results.

"Significantly more 'cognitive' staff behaviour was observed in middle-class than working-class centres, and the amount of 'cognitive' staff behaviour was also significantly influenced by the educational orientation of the centre. The working-class children in schools with a language programme had significantly higher language scores than other working- class children" (Tizard et al., 1976 p.33).

The observations made it possible to study staff behaviour outside the language sessions, which were indeed short in all units, and did not involve all the children. It appeared that in centres where there were language sessions there was also a sensitivity in staff to the cognitive aspects of their work, a variety of situations being used as opportunities to stimulate children's language development. The design of the study made it possible to establish that there was not a straightforward relationship between involvement in the programme and the effects, or the training of the staff or staff ratio. It would thus not be legitimate to assume that the cognitive level of interaction would automatically be raised by the introduction of a language programme, or raised further by devoting more time to the language sessions, as these might merely have served as a stimulus to staff to focus on language during other parts of the day. Though associated with the language sessions, the effect was not necessarily caused by these, since the working-class children in these centres who had not themselves participated in the sessions still had higher scores.

An important element, even where a research does measure 'product' outcomes in terms of scores on psychometric tests for example, is 'process' studies which include observation of staff and child behaviour time-sampled over a period outside the particular intervention, as in this and the following study.

LANGUAGE STIMULATION IN A DAY NURSERY

This small-scale study in 1976-77 involved assessment of the effects of the introduction of a language programme in a day nursery in Newcastle for twenty minutes per day. The matron had sought help for her staff in improving the children's language skills, Thus the initiative came from the nursery, the staff of which were also responsible for developing the programme to meet their needs, and for its implementation (Moxon, 1979). This action-research involved two parallel groups, each of about fourteen children, mean age about three years, and length of stay in the nursery about nine months. The nature of the unit meant that even with a programme as short in duration as four months there were changes in the children attending. Also there was a wide age range in each group, from under three to five years of age.

Pretesting of the experimental and control groups on a number of psychometric tests was carried out, and re-testing after the completion of the programme (only 11 were assessed in each group before and after the study). There were improvements in test scores on both groups of children, with significantly greater improvements in the experimental group on some tests. Observation of staff behaviour, using a similar schedule to that used in the study by Tizard et al., 1976, showed that in this study also the amount of cognitive staff behaviour and talk to children in the experimental group outside the specific language sessions had increased. Such changes in staff behaviour could have been as important as the programme itself in achieving the changes in the children's scores. In preliminary discussions with the staff it was found that their aim was to provide an environment which would satisfy the children's emotional and social needs. The staff were at that time 'wary' of anything which might be seen as teaching. Participation in the programme might have alerted the nursery nurses to possibilities for language development. One feature of the experiment was that each child in the experimental group received twenty minutes of individual attention in the form of a story. This may have sensitized the staff to unrealised potential in some of the children and/or helped the staff to develop knowledge of the children which could have facilitated dialogue with them at other times.

In this study as in the previous one it would thus be erroneous to attribute any changes in the children's assessed cognitive development to the language programme, and certainly to these specific language activities. The desire of the matron to focus on language development, the involvement of the staff in the planning and implementation, the opportunity that was created for the children to have sustained individual attention, and the increased level of cognitive interaction between the staff who participated and the children for whom they were responsible might all have played a part. Assessment of other children for whom these staff were responsible, but who did not take part in the language programme, could have helped tease out some of these issues (as in the study by Tizard *et al.*, 1976). Unfortunately studies in the 'real' situation of a preschool unit may not always provide a residue of children on which to test such hypotheses further.

A LANGUAGE STUDY IN A RECEPTION CLASS

The importance of a teacher's belief in the value of an innovation in relation to the progress of the children has been little investigated, and might indeed have been a further variable in the study described above. The present study by Turner and Whyte (1979) was initiated in the reception class of a primary school in Belfast with what are described as some of the characteristics of an EPA area. Few of the children entering this primary school had the opportunity to attend either a playgroup or nursery school. It had therefore been decided to admit in January children who were four years of age between August and December, thus giving then an additional two terms in school. At the commencement of the study in 1974, there had already been three groups of early entrants for whom a semi-traditional nursery school curriculum had been developed. The teacher involved in the study was an experienced infant teacher in a school which encouraged a variety of approaches. She felt that language development was the key to helping these children, but was not sure how to tackle the problem in the setting with which she was faced.

The aims of the study were to assess whether an intervention programme would benefit these children in the short- and long-term and whether it could be carried through by the class teacher. The teacher was to retain control of the content, sequence and methodology of the programme, which was to be covered in ten weeks, with a different theme for each week. The programme was used twice with classes of early entrants, with one class for two terms, and with another for one term. This made it possible to compare the effects of two and one term experience of the programme. The children were aged about 4 to 4.5 years.

A battery of psychometric tests was administered before and after the intervention, and the tests were repeated later to study long-term effects. Control groups formed from children who had entered earlier without the intervention were also assessed. The performance of a random sample of children was also assessed each week during the programme. The results were discussed with the teacher and could lead to adjustments in the programme.

Developments in the programme and problems in its implementation are discussed in the report. These insights were possible because of the presence in the classroom of an observer throughout the study. From initial unfamiliarity with the programme, the problems changed at later stages to those of staleness, which caused difficulty in attempts to implement the programme comparably with each group.

Pre- and post-test scores for the experimental groups showed significant gains on some of the tests as compared with the control groups, indicating that the programme appeared to be successful in improving the children's language functioning, at least on such measures. Later data suggested that two terms of intervention were necessary for lasting effects.

As with the two other studies reported so far, the researchers express caution in any interpretation of the results. They still feel, however, that there was some evidence of lasting effects after two terms of intervention. What cannot be established is the precise features which led to any effects. The programme was devised in such a way that, taking account of the available literature at the time, it would utilise readily available materials, and it went through modifications in methods and materials though not in its basic objectives. The changes in practice were implemented by an experienced teacher, who wished to improve her practice, and who was observed and supported throughout by a researcher with whom she could discuss progress and problems. The continual presence of the researcher was felt to have facilitated the development of the programme as well as its assessment. Indeed, it is not possible to know whether without her presence the intervention would have continued, as she also looked after the other children while each small group of five or six children was taken by the teacher for 15 minutes each day of the language activities. It is stated in the report that it was found essential that there should be a second adult in the room for such activities to be implemented with children of this age. It is unlikely that in the eighties the same type of assessments would be used as were used here and in the two previous studies and in most other studies at that time, mainly standardised psychometric tests. There are also now further ideas available in the literature which might be incorporated in any such language activities. The brief report of this study does have many useful insights for anyone even now considering either the introduction of a language programme, or its evaluation.

STAFF AND CHILD BEHAVIOUR IN A NURSERY SCHOOL

Detailed observations over time in a single preschool unit can provide evidence on the relationship between staff behaviour and that of the children. Murphy undertook such studies in a purpose-built nursery school in an area of multiple deprivation in Renfrewshire in the West of Scotland in the mid-seventies. These studies have been reported in a number of articles, on staff behaviour, the children's cognitive development and children who appear to drift from one activity to another (Murphy, 1980; Murphy and Wilkinson, 1982 and Wilkinson and Murphy, 1983).

The nursery school, which was staffed by experienced teachers qualified for work with preschool children and by nursery nurses, had about 140 children on roll, attending mornings or afternoons. Little compulsion was placed on children to take part in particular activities and there was no formal language programme. The attitude was not 'laissez faire', but rather a belief in planned placement of staff and activities and intense staff involvement. The placement of some activities was fixed, that of others varied. Observations of eight members of staff and of 29 children were carried out regularly over a four month period. The staff spent a large part of their time at activities likely to facilitate language development. It is commented that while both teachers observed were well-organised and appeared successful in stimulating dialogue they adopted very different styles, one showed a preference for direct teaching, the other, interaction and shared play with the children. An important point is made that each has a place provided there is prior organisation and verbal interaction is ensured. It may also be that different styles also appeal to different children.

The cognitive level of staff interaction with children was high in this school, both for teachers and nursery nurses, and greater than that reported by Tizard in the study reported earlier (Tizard *et al.*, 1976), with which it is compared (in Murphy, 1980). The materials found were comparable to those found in most nursery schools: what was felt to be important in achieving the high level of interaction was the careful preparation of equipment, and the staff organisation. This made it probable that the children were involved in a range of activities of their choice. Off-task child behaviour, often found to be high in free play settings, was very low. Group size for the majority of staff observations was between two and six children, thus allowing more extended dialogue, while large groups were formed for certain activities. An important point made from the observations is the tendency for the boys to prefer certain types of more physical and construction activities, activities at which staff involvement was likely to be lower. The importance of monitoring the boys' play and ensuring sufficient staff involvement in dialogue with these children is noted. Lomax (1977a and 1979a), in a longitudinal study in a similar nursery school found differences in the free choice activities of boys and girls, and differences by age, thus reinforcing the importance of careful monitoring of children's choices of activities over time.

A further analysis of the results on the 29 children in the study is reported (in Murphy and Wilkinson (1982). These children were about four years of age when assessed initially on a variety of psychometric tests and were retested after the four month observation period. The analysis of the results is considered by socioeconomic grouping, by level of IQ and for boys and girls. As there were no control groups it is not possible to assess the extent to which the improvements in test scores found were 'real', or were the effects of practice for example. What is interesting, however, is the comparison between choice of activities and these measures. This showed that the children in the higher socioeconomic group spent more time at the cognitive activities, less time alone and more time talking, both in play and in communication with others, particularly other children. The children with higher IQ spent more time listening to stories, and more time communicating with others, adults in particular. When the gainers and losers in terms of scores, from initial to later testing were compared it was found that the losers spent less time on cognitive activities and more time on open-ended pursuits. As noted earlier there was very little 'flitting' or off-task behaviour. When high and low flitters were compared (Wilkinson and Murphy, 1983), it was found that the former were more inclined to spend time on the climbing apparatus for example where staff contact was likely to be supervisory rather than interactionist although there was not evidence that there was avoidance by these children of communication with adults. Some aspects of this part of the study were limited as the sample on which it was based was that used for the remainder of the study which was merely divided into two for this aspect and thus did not focus on children at the extremes of high and low concentration. What cannot be established from this admittedly exploratory study is causal relationships. It does, however, confirm findings in other studies, and reinforce even further the need to monitor both staff interactions and the activities in which the children engage over time.

INTEREST IN BOOKS AND STORIES

Nursery schools and classes typically provide a number of activities at the same time and allow the children considerable freedom in choosing what they do. This may make it difficult, particularly in a large-open plan unit, to keep track of who does what, and for how long. The play activities of younger and older children, and of boys and girls, were recorded by staff in a study by Lomax (1977b and 1979b) in a large open-plan nursery school in Dunbartonshire. There were changes in activities in which the children were interested between the ages of about three and five years of age, and sex differences in choice. Boys were significantly more interested than girls in tower and brick building with large apparatus at both ages. Girls were more interested than boys at age three in books and music, and in puzzles and Wendy house activity at age five. Both boys and girls had become more interested in books by five, and by five most girls had lost interest in sand and water. What it is not possible to know from such studies is the extent to which in the nursery school the children are continuing to engage in activities which they experience at home, or even in which interest was actually stimulated by the home. In another study by Lomax in a similar nursery school, observation of the children in school was planned to select children who showed high or low interest in books and stories. The two groups of children were then compared for involvement in other activities. Parental interviews, and questionnaires to staff on the children's activities made comparisons between home and school possible and an assessment of the extent to which the children differed in other aspects of their behaviour. The headteacher of the nursery school in which the study took place was particularly concerned to foster an interest in books and stories, a lack of which has often been associated with educational disadvantage in young children. The nursery school in Dunbartonshire, financed by Urban Aid, had only recently opened in the mid-seventies when this study took place (Lomax 1977a and 1979a). The first phase of the study involved several days of observation of the grouping at the various activities of adults and children. Simultaneously a second researcher observed in the book corner, noting which children entered, how long they stayed, and what they did. From the observations two groups of 14 children were selected, matched in pairs for age, sex and session attended, one of each pair having high interest in books and stories, the other low. The mean longest time in the book corner was 22.5 minutes for the former, and 4 minutes for the latter.

It is interesting to note that in this school story telling and looking at books, taken together, were among the most commonly observed activities. Children were observed seeking out adults to tell or read, or particularly to reread, favourite stories. There is little evidence from other studies of the extent to which such activities are as common in other preschool units. A further aspect that it was possible to observe in the first phase of the study was the effect of the presence of an adult at an activity on its popularity. Some of the activities concerned with books and stories would require the presence of an adult. It was found, however, that other activities which were observed with and without an adult were more popular when an adult was present, even if the adult was not actively involved.

The children in the two groups were assessed on a number of tests, and further observations of their activities were made. No differences were found on the test measures. They were also relatively similar in their choice of other activities, except that the children with low interest in books and stories were found to engage in more activities, but for shorter periods, and to spend more time doing nothing in particular. The interviews with parents revealed that the two groups were relatively comparable in their activities at home and in their preference for playing alone or with others. The only significant difference was that the high interest group had a story from an adult at home more often, in most cases once a day. Some differences between the groups in school were perceived by the staff. The high interest children were seen to enjoy playing alone, the others to dislike this; no difference was observed in their preference for contact with adults.

Precise details have been given of a number of aspects of the design of this study, indicating the care in matching the two groups of children and the extended observation in the nursery on which the general findings were based. The parent ratings of the children at home and staff ratings at school were also important. From a study of the full report of this research, and the related one on record-keeping, it can be seen just how much care was taken to ensure that causal relationships were not erroneously attributed. The time-consuming nature of carefully controlled, but small-scale studies such as these is also apparent. Researches such as these are important in ensuring that hypotheses are fully tested in as near experimental conditions as possible. The research by Smith and Connolly (1980) was also experimental in design, but added a further dimension, in that the studies were undertaken in two parallel experimental playgroups established for the purpose.

DESIGN FEATURES IN NURSERIES

A study of 'Psychological Influences of Spatial Design Factors in Nurseries', funded by the Scottish Education Department, was carried out in the mid-seventies in the West of Scotland, at a time when it was anticipated that an extensive building programme would be required for the then planned expansion of preschool education. That study involved five preschool units, nursery schools and day nurseries, differing in design. Much of the study reported in the research report (Neill, Denham, Markus and Schaffer, 1977) is concerned with architectural aspects of the buildings. In a more recent publication (Neill, 1982) some relationships between design and child behaviour are discussed. Interpretation must take into account staff aims, and in these units the staff were in general agreement that their role was one of supervision and assistance, with the children allowed to learn from direct experience. Much of the time was found to be in child-directed activities. It is suggested that in these units where staff felt intervention was appropriate they tended to choose the more school-orientated activities. Several of the 'classic' preschool activities, (such as sand, water, Wendy house play and pretend) appeared to receive little staff attention, although their presence there might have encouraged manipulative play and talk (a finding in other studies also). Child behaviour was analysed in relation to building design and it was found that playroom openness was the most important building factor. Children in the more open-plan units spent less time on school-orientated activities, had less staff contact, spent more time moving around, doing nothing, in aggression and active play. The conclusions, while tentative because of the small number of units and the correlational nature of the study, could be of practical significance were they to be confirmed elsewhere, as large open-plan designs were those being used in a number of the new nursery schools being built at that time.

STUDIES IN AN EXPERIMENTAL PLAYGROUP

About the same time as the study reported briefly above a series of studies was underway to investigate experimentally, but in as natural as possible a setting, the effects of different features of the preschool unit on children's behaviour. With a grant from SSRC, Smith and Connolly established a playgroup in Sheffield, for which children were recruited from the surrounding area. A single site was used, but two parallel groups were established, each with its own characteristics. Staffing included a supervisor with infant school or nursery school experience. In these two groups the effects of environmental variations were studied. The project made it possible over three years to study the effects of variables such as class size, space, amount of equipment, not confounded by other variables, and in each instance to check whether findings were applicable in both groups (Smith and Connolly, 1980 and 1986).

Variations in space were found not to affect levels of social play or aggression significantly. More space led to more running, chasing and rough and tumble play. The amount of available equipment clearly affected social behaviour. When there was more equipment children split into smaller subgroups or played alone and were less likely to play in large parallel play clusters. Less equipment also led to more physical aggression. There was an effect of variations in class size on choice of play activities and on the number and sex of partners, Subgroups of four or more were commoner in the smaller classes, possibly because the children knew each other better making social groupings easier for these young children to maintain. In the larger classes where there was more choice of companions, there were more strong friendships observed, and more same sex companions. More fantasy play was observed in the smaller classes, and in the larger, more frequent records of no activity.

An experiment over eight months was carried out to compare experimentally a structured activities programme with a free play programme. Both programmes had the effect of increasing the amount of adult-child contact during the experimental period. Those in the more structured programme engaged in fewer activities, but stayed at them longer. There was evidence of increase in persistence by children with adult involvement. There were no differential effects on the children's cognitive abilities as measured by tests. These findings illustrate the need for caution in attributing any changes either in the behaviour of staff or children to a specific language programme where no alternative innovation has been compared with it. Elsewhere it is reported that fantasy and sociodramatic play tutoring, at least for children whose play is limited, may assist staff to be more sensitive in their planning of activities to talk in stimulating ways to the children. This may also encourage such children to maintain social interaction with their peers (Smith, Dalgleish and Herzmark, 1981). The increased adult-child contact in the present study was at the expense of reduced peer interaction, and the children appeared to be less able to manage conflicts successfully. It is suggested that the free play situation may have helped the children to learn to manage conflicts. There was evidence that the quality of adult-child interaction worsened with more children per adult. Conversations became fewer and shorter, and more often about routine matters or concerned with prohibition. Also more communications from the children remained unanswered. A balance of free play and more structured situations seemed important, bearing in mind the advantages and disadvantages of each, and also possibly more adult involvement in the former, especially for children who appear less competent in sustaining social interactions with their peers.

A CURRICULUM INNOVATION

The High/Scope curriculum developed in the States for preschool units aims to encourage the development of problem-solving skills in the children. It explicitly addresses the role of intervention by adults and of careful monitoring of progress in the preschool unit in helping children to develop such skills, to assume responsibility and to take initiative (Hohmann, Banet and Weikart, 1979). In 1984-85 a training programme in High/Scope was carried out in Britain, with twelve representatives from eight agencies (including voluntary and statutory, national and more local, some with a care orientation and others in education, two representing ethnic minorities). Those who attended the workshops were nominated by their agency and were expected to return to their centres and train the staff to implement the programme, adapting it to suit their own needs. A one-year evaluation, supported by the Nuffield Foundation, was carried out in 1984-85 by Sylva, Smith and Moore (1986). The aim of the evaluation was to consider the expectations of the agencies and their representatives in taking part, and subsequently the extent to which these had been met. An observation study was also carried out in five preschool centres involved in the training programme to assess any differences in the interaction of staff and children before and after the programme.

This study was not experimental and neither selection of participants nor centres was under the control of the evaluators. Most of the agencies taking part had some prior knowledge of the innovation, some having already visited the States to see it in action. The agencies had a variety of reasons for selecting their representatives who took part, and the centres with which they were associated. Not all representatives were in charge of a centre, or even worked in a centre, which would have made attempts to implement what they had learnt very different for the various participants. Details of the centres and the background of those who took part are given, most of whom were either trained teachers (and nursery nurses) or trained in social work. It is difficult to assess precisely what were the effects on the various units, and whether any changes were the result of the training. Even more difficult to assess is the effect of the specific programme, as distinct from factors such as the commitment of the agencies to the venture, the nature of the staff selected, effects of intensive training, the opportunity to share experiences with other similarly committed practitioners, some with very different perspectives, even the need to make presentations. It is stated that the training provided was of a high standard (and it was by a team from the States), it was in a small group, was intensive and with a selected group of participants.

It is clear from the report that the programme did not meet the needs of all the agencies, or of all the participants. One wish in some of those who took part was to increase parental involvement, yet there was no such effect during the year in which it was evaluated. The views of those who took part are difficult to estimate, as responses are not quoted for all (even in tables there may be 8 or 10 only). Furthermore it would appear that only eleven of the initial twelve completed the course. As the plan was for a two-tier training, with the participants then training the workers in their centres, questionnaires were given to the staffs in the centres to assess their views before and after the implementation of the programme. These workers saw no change in their assessment skills of monitoring children's development or in observation. They also reported that at staff meetings topics of routine and rearrangement of equipment were frequent with lower priority than previously to parental involvement and other aspects. Such a balance might have been redressed later, but it is important to note that second tier perceptions of an innovation may already be very different from those intended by the initial trainers. It is interesting that the agencies, both educational- orientated and care-orientated, saw a lot of change in room arrangement and in organisation of the day, the five education-orientated agencies saw minimal change in children's activities.

The observation part of the study was carried out in five centres selected to give a sample of the various types of provision. Details are not given of the precise position in the centre of the participant. In each of these centres ten children aged between 3-5 years of age, randomly selected, were observed before the programme was implemented, each for twenty minutes on two occasions. Ten comparable children in each centre were observed after two terms of the programme, to determine any changes in interaction in the units. It was found that there was greater involvement of the adults in dialogue with the children, but less peer interaction. There was also a greater emphasis on the more 'cognitive' activities and a reduction in the more creative. When not with an adult the children were more likely to play alone or in pairs. Information is given only for the total sample, which could mask very different practices in the different centres. The evaluators stress that "a curriculum as broad and complex as High/Scope cannot be implemented in just one year" (Sylva *et al.*, 1986 p.86). The emphasis on the cognitive aspects, and organisational features, possibly at the expense of the social- emotional, may have been temporary only, but may not. It is stated that:

> "At the very least, then, the pilot year left participants disappointed at High/Scope's approach to parental involvement" (Sylva *et al.*, 1986 p.81).

One problem in assessing the impact of this training, and the curriculum is that it is not clear how similar or different were the various centres in their interactions, organisation and layout prior to the training. Thus it is not possible to determine the extent to which in some centres the changes towards greater planning of the environment were desirable and led to positive effects, while in others the effects might have been less, or have provided a straitjacket. It is also not possible to determine whether even as intensive a training as this, with as high level trainers with first hand experience of the innovation, and committed participants, will have had any long term desirable effects on the centres. When training is no longer conducted by those who are so intimately involved in and committed to the innovation, as were the team from the States, one must question precisely how effective the more widespread dissemination would be - also at what cost. These points are not specific to this innovation, but to any. The problem here is that the positive and negative effects of this particular innovation cannot be adequately assessed where there is no alternative innovation to balance some of these novelty effects. This curriculum appears to have had some effects similar to those noted in others studies after the introduction of other language programmes.

CHAPTER 7   LANGUAGE AND INTERACTION IN PRESCHOOL UNITS : THREE FUNDED STUDIES

INTRODUCTION

Three major funded researches in preschool units with a focus on language development will now be considered, reference will also be made to other studies. Two of the studies were funded within the Nursery Research Programme.

One research within the Programme was the major study funded by SSRC directed by Jerome Bruner under the title 'Oxford Preschool Research Project' from 1975-1978. Within that research there were a number of projects - Observational and interactional studies in preschool units, (nursery schools and classes and playgroups), studies in day nurseries, concerning childminders and parents and preschool. The findings of the research were reported in six books, the first by Bruner entitled *Under Five in Britain* (1980) was an overview and summary of the project, that and two of the other publications will be referred to in this chapter, namely *Childwatching at Playgroup and Nursery School* (Sylva, Roy and Painter, 1980) and *Working with Under Fives* (Wood, McMahon and Cranstoun, 1980). These studies are perhaps the most frequently cited references to observation within preschool units. In addition, a number of later studies by Sylva and by others have utilized the observation schedules developed within this project. These have also been used within playgroups and elsewhere for training of staffs in observational techniques. In a critical evaluation of the project by the present author concern was expressed at a number of aspects of the study including some of the statements made by Bruner in his overview which on close study of the relevant report of that aspect were felt to go beyond or not to be borne out by the data. (For further details the reader is referred to Clark, 1982). The other research within the Programme, directed by Corinne and John Hutt at Keele University, funded by DES from 1975-79 was entitled 'Play, Exploration and Learning in the Preschool'. It was planned to be a parallel study to that in the homes reported in a previous chapter (Davie *et al.*, 1984). Unfortunately this research and the related studies are not yet available in published form, therefore the material presented here will be based on the research report submitted to DES in 1984 under the title *A Natural History of the Preschool* (Hutt, Tyler,

Hutt and Foy, 1984). The third study which was also funded by SSRC from 1975-78 was based at the Open University and directed by Asher Cashdan. The source on which the material in this chapter is based is the final report to ESRC entitled *Teaching Styles in Nursery Education* (Cashdan and Meadows, 1983) as the research has not yet been published in book form.

While all three studies were underway threats of cuts to preschool education were already a possibility rather than the major expansion programme towards which they had been directed and planned.

CHILDWATCHING AT PLAYGROUP AND NURSERY SCHOOL

This study, and the following one, both part of the Oxford Preschool Research Project, were undertaken in Oxfordshire. While clearly it would have been unfortunate if all the studies in preschool education had been undertaken in areas of multiple deprivation it is important to bear in mind the area in assessing the generalisability of findings. Bruner cites reasons for the choice of Oxfordshire for the study, and for inclusion of the range of services, which he states, within the limited budget and time scale, would be considered in terms of whether and to what extent each was fulfilling its function (rather than comparisons across types of provision) (Bruner, 1980 p.53). It is, however, difficult within the framework as presented not to become involved in comparisons across types of provision. Thus it is important to note possible limitations in the selection of nursery schools and classes and of playgroups.

Aim

The aim of this aspect of the research was to assess the extent to which the various contexts in preschool units stimulated complex activity, concentration and conversation between the children and between them and the staff. This was studied by means of an observational schedule with target children observed for twenty minutes on two occasions with the activities recorded each half minute on an observation schedule. Speech was not recorded thus only an approximate rendering could be included in the notes and only where this was audible to the observer. None of the centres studied had special language tutorial schemes. A comparison was made, however, of the units with more or less 'structure' in their day's routine. A further comparison in this connection was made between the sample of units in Oxfordshire and preschool units in Miami U.S.A. where structure was a feature of the routine of the day.

The Sample

The study took place in 6 of 14 nursery schools, 6 of 14 nursery classes and 7 of 120 playgroups. One major concern is the statement that, to quote:

> "we did not choose our centres randomly, as some were eager to collaborate in the study while others remained cool to outside research" (Sylva *et al.*, 1980 p.46).

The sample is referred to as 'fairly representative' but no indication is given as to how this was assessed or what it means. In Bruner 1980 p.41 and again on p.42, in the description of Oxfordshire reference is made to 250 playgroups rather than 120: it is not clear whether this was a dramatic increase over a very short period or 120 was already selective in some way.

The playgroups appear to be differentially selective as it is stated that:

> "our playgroups are probably drawn from amongst the better ones; that is, most had well-established histories and highly trained staff" (Sylva *et al.*, 1980 p.46).

The reference to 'highly trained' staff and 'well-established' would hardly have been typical of playgroups at that time. Furthermore in later reference to the organisers in the playgroups it is stated that:

> "seven of the nine playgroup supervisors in our sample had formal credentials in work with young children, such as a teaching certificate, an NNEB qualification, or an advanced PPA training" (Sylva *et al.*, 1980 p.119).

In the composite pictures of the three types of unit, nursery school, class and playgroup the supervisor of the latter is portrayed as:

> "a formally trained primary school teacher who gave up practice when she started a family" (Sylva et al., 1980 p.107).

The 'composite nursery school' described has several teachers on staff as well as nursery nurses and the nursery class has one teacher plus other staff in the unit.

Points such as these on staffing and selection of units are important in considering the implications of patterns found within units, and in comparisons between different types of units. Size of unit is one variable considered, but it must be borne in mind that most of the largest units in this study were nursery schools and many of the playgroups were small.

Staff ratio is considered also in relation to interactions; here again it is important to note that 'staff' as a term is used for any adult regularly in the unit (including 'rota' mothers in playgroups and students, but excluding visitors) when comparisons are made on the effects on interaction of what are referred to as 'good' and 'very good' staff ratios. One might question whether it would have been more appropriate to have made such analyses within types of unit or in such a way as to have allowed for factors which are not randomly distributed across types of provision (see discussion earlier on the study by Tizard *et al.*, 1976).

The sample of children selected as targets for the observations were as follows:

- 120 children, with equal numbers in each of the three types of preschool unit (nursery school and class and playgroup) - half of each group aged 3-6 to 4-6 and half 4-6 to 5-6 years of age, which enabled a comparison to be made between younger and older children.

To quote:

> "Although the centres studied were far from a random sample in the county, the individual children were selected on a random basis" (from registers) (Sylva *et al.*, 1980 p.46).

Excluded were children with obvious physical handicaps or children who had started school within the last month. No reference is made to ethnic minority children in the sample but in the composite picture of the nursery school it is noted that a few are attending (p.98).

Implications for early education

It is important in studying the summary of findings in Bruner (1980) and the more detailed report (in Sylva *et al.*, 1980) to bear in mind the definition of staff used, the selective nature of the sample of units, as well as the area in which the study took place, namely Oxfordshire. There are important findings in this study, even allowing for these reservations. It should be noted, however, that anyone seeking to study the role of teachers in the educational units as compared with the other staff (nursery nurses) will not find such information in this study. There are references to teachers and nursery nurses in the text, in the 'composite' units referred to above. These are also identified in the detailed description of a large nursery school selected as a case study to illustrate a setting which gives stimulus to the children within a carefully planned framework.

Size of unit

Size of unit is considered in relation to complexity of play and some important points are made on adverse effects of some large open plan units. Some of these analyses are confounded by other differences in units which distinguish large from small units. Furthermore the nursery school singled out as a detailed case study because of its positive dynamic pattern is indeed a large unit.

The danger that an open-plan free play setting in a large unit, far from resulting in complex play and dynamic interchanges, may lead to flitting and distraction and low level activities is stressed. Likewise the dangers that 'routine' and 'structure' may become a 'straitjacket' are demonstrated from the parallel study in Miami where, in preschool units, many of the children spent much of the day in compulsory activities (See Sylva *et al.*, 1980 Chapter 9).

Shared activities

One finding of this study relates to that of the research referred to earlier by Tizard *et al.*, (1976). Units in which there was higher 'task' structure were found to encourage greater complexity during the free play settings. Even in these settings most of the day was in freely chosen activity. Furthermore, the 'structure' referred to is shared activities and not a formal tutorial language programme which was not used in these units. Children were found on occasion to choose to continue some of these shared activities when such a session was over. It was also suggested that these may have provided a common focus for children and staff for conversation. Bruner suggests also that:

> "the findings surely suggest an interest and readiness in the children for more intellectually demanding tasks" (Bruner, 1980 p.71).

Conversation and complex activities

Study of staffing is confounded by the definition of staff used (adults regularly in the unit) which makes it difficult to draw practical implications from the findings. There is evidence of limited conversation between adults and children, one effect of the presence of a limited number of adults and many children. Furthermore many of the interactions between adults and children were of a one-off variety. Certain types of contexts were found to stimulate more complex play, greater concentration and more extended dialogue.

Much of children's time was spent in interaction with their peers and in this connection it was found that children in pairs were much more likely to engage in higher level play: it is therefore suggested that opportunities for such play should be actively encouraged.

The activities which were found to be associated with the most complex activity by the children were those which had a clear goal and a means by which it was possible a goal might be achieved. It was also important that there was what Bruner refers to as a 'real-world feedback'. This meant that the child appeared to know at what he or she was aiming, whether it was building or drawing or doing puzzles. The pair setting was the best social setting for this, particularly with the younger children. For the older children play with an adult was even more stimulating. There was, however, disappointingly little utilization of this as a context for the stimulation of complex activity and extended dialogue.

It was possible to study turn-taking in conversation and the length of time an adult was engaged in conversation with a particular child or group of children. Any evidence on the cognitive content of the dialogue is based only on notes taken by the observers also involved in recording on the observation schedule. Observation backed by recording of the language of adults and children in preschool units by Tizard and Hughes (1984) and by Clark and others (1982 and 1984) would support and extend the evidence from this study.

Further evidence on language interaction between staff and children was obtained within the Oxford research by a study of recordings made and selected by staff in preschool units. The implications of that study will now be considered.

CONVERSATIONS IN PRESCHOOL UNITS

In the introduction to *Working with Under Fives* (Wood, McMahon and Cranstoun, 1980) in which this aspect of the Oxford Preschool Research Project is reported, Wood and his colleagues consider the priorities in aims of preschool practitioners as reported in other studies. They stress that in any attempt to assess the extent that such aims are operationalised in practice it must be borne in mind that a particular activity may serve a variety of purposes. Time allocated to a particular aspect is not sufficient as an assessment of its priority. There is evidence of the importance of

> "sustained interactions between adult and child, in which the adult acts in the service of the child's ideas and actions" which it is reported "exert a positive effect on a variety of measures of the child's developing competence" (Wood *et al.*, 1980 p.11).

Wood and his colleagues consider the dangers of uncritical acceptance of this and particularly of the assumption that such can be translated into practice in preschool centres with limited adult resources. As they stress, it would not be practical to suggest that each child should be given sustained attention by an adult for long periods. They even question whether or not it would be advisable. They cite evidence from the study of their colleagues that an adult faced with a fairly large group of children and motivated to increase her personal involvement with them may "push herself into more directed group activities". To quote:

> "Sylva's research suggests that such organised activities may well produce uninterested, passive children. Our own research, as we shall see, points in a similar direction ..... The practical question we must ask, given that practitioners accept the importance of their interactions with the child, is whether they are able to translate their desires for interaction into effective practice" (Wood et al., 1980 p.11).

Aims and Methods

Differences in style of language interaction between adults and children are explored by case studies based on recordings by practitioners (two nursery teachers and a playgroup supervisor). The question is raised as to whether differences in style matter and whether this might be affected by the particular child's nature as well as the adult's. The incentive for this aspect of the study came from concern expressed at a meeting by a nursery teacher in whose setting observation of interactions had taken place. She felt these did not capture the purpose behind the observable: as noted earlier the precise language of any interactions was not recorded. For this present aspect the language of selected interactions was recorded (by means of a small powerful microphone) then transcribed and analysed. The selection of what was recorded was the choice of the practitioner. The team felt that this approach with the additional facility for the practitioner to add comments about the context and purpose behind the dialogue was valuable. It was also possible for the practitioner to undertake a further recording. In the early part of the report three case studies are presented from the above and some analysis is made of the conversations.

In the following year of the research a further 21 practitioners were recruited to take part (19 playgroup workers and two teachers). It is stated that this shift of emphasis to the playgroups was partly that two of the researchers' "principal contacts were in the playgroup movement"; also that "nursery schools are not very numerous around Oxford", and particularly

> "a growing concern about the cuts that were looming in the State sector, cuts that eventually culminated in the contraction of nursery provision in the County. The threat introduced by the economic and political climate was hardly conducive to a forward looking, research attitude" (Wood et al., 1980 p.32-3).

The above statement has been quoted in detail both because it shows a clear shift in emphasis but also explicitly stated is the nature of the change in climate in which these major studies funded for a climate of expansion were operating before their completion.

Findings and their implications

This research lends support to points cited earlier and extends these. A statistical analysis of all the tapes of conversations indicated that the framework the adult offered for dialogue influenced the nature and extent of children's responses.

Frequent adult questions received answers but little more, and were associated with fewer questions or contributions by the child.

> "The more an adult questions a child, the less likely he is to elaborate on his answers, to take double turns or to ask questions of his own. Too much control leads to children giving short often monosyllabic answers ..." (Wood et al., 1980 p.80).

Topics of conversation and 'time domains' are analysed and show how frequently the utterances by the adult were 'here-and-now' and how few were related to past or future, how frequently they referred to the child addressed or objects and possessions and rarely to other people, present or absent.

A number of the practitioners recorded noted with regret on hearing the tapes

> "quite frequent attempts from children to engage in conversations about events elsewhere that failed because they had not understood fully or listened attentively" (p.101).

The frequency with which adults asked children questions to which they, the adults, already knew the answers and the effect is commented upon.

Evidence from a separate small experimental study with mothers of young children is presented (on pages 121-2) which could usefully be replicated with practitioners in training.

- One of the three groups of mothers of four-year-old children played with their children,

- a second group drank coffee while their children played but did not see them and

- the third group observed the children by closed circuit television as they played with another adult with the toys.

The mothers were then asked to encourage the children to talk about the play, with very different results from the three groups. The mothers who had observed their children were able to coax their children into more elaborate and sustained conversation. They had the knowledge to do so, and the children had purpose in responding. Where the mothers had played with the children, in contrast, the children were least likely to talk freely:

> "It was quite clear that the children appreciated that mum could answer the questions herself and they often made their reluctance to play what was effectively a silly game quite plain" (Wood *et al.*, 1980 p.122).

This has important implications for practitioners for their style of management in dialogue, also for the provision of activities which stimulate 'real' conversation between small groups of children to solve the task, extend the play, or inform the uninformed. Participation may not always be the most effective use of the adult's time, unless it is to help a child solve with assistance a task he could not solve alone (or with another child) but may complete, on this occasion, with adult assistance.

The analyses of conversations, mainly in playgroups, confirmed the interaction studies reported in Sylva *et al.*(1980) that contrary perhaps to expectations there was little evidence of the involvement of adults in children's play themes, possibly a conscious decision for some adults. It is suggested that on tape there were different styles of adult play represented such as 'parallel' player, playmate or co-player, play tutor or spokesman for reality. The dangers and benefits of adult involvement are discussed in Chapter 7 of Wood *et al.*, 1980.

A study of subsequent tapes by the three practitioners involved in the initial study showed that they had been able, as they had planned to achieve a dramatic drop in 'management' talk and to increase the length and, even more important, the continuity of their conversations. These three practitioners, all highly committed and involved it would appear, are reported to have shown great flexibility. The 24 practitioners in the later study were not particularly interested in the issues of topic or time domain, but were interested in who starts initiations and how to continue these.

Some of the dangers of a focus on conversation as such to change adult style of interaction are to be seen in Chapter 8 of Wood 1980. All changes were not for the better, some adults increased their level of questioning or in attempts to be involved in play became directive and controlling (see p.182-3). By utilization and further development of these techniques, materials about management styles, and conversational styles and sample transcripts were prepared which were employed in group work with practitioners. This work, which is reported in Appendix A of Wood *et al.* (1980), is valuable for training of staff in analysis of the conversations, as are the interaction schedules of Sylva *et al.* (1980) mentioned earlier.

Some reservations

In any consideration of implications of that research for the education of children under five it is important to note the views of the research workers made explicit in the final pages of the book, certainly not those likely to have been in the minds of the funding bodies, or of educators in the early seventies. It seems important to quote these as they do colour the tenor of the report:

> "Playgroups seem to be here to stay. Given the present political climate it is not clear that many nursery schools are. Where government seems to have given up any intention or even aspiration to provide proper care and education for the children of women at work, the future which seems most likely and desirable is some form of full day care on the lines of our current playgroups" (Wood *et al.*, 1980 p.206).

This quotation at the start of a section entitled 'Is training the way forward?' indicates clearly the exclusion by these researchers of educational provision from any significant continuing contribution to the education or care of children under five, which may have been true in Oxfordshire at that time, but is scarcely borne out nationally.

Playgroups have continued to increase, as has educational provision for under fives, both in preschool education and in reception classes. Furthermore there is evidence from some research studies that attendance at playgroups rather than being an alternative to attendance at nursery class or school may, on the contrary, precede it (See for example Hutt *et al.*, 1984 and Watt and Flett, 1985). With the increase also in four-year-olds in reception class the age group for which playgroups are catering is likely to be younger than was perhaps the case in the children in this study in Oxfordshire in the late seventies. Such changes may have important implications for the role and nature of, and difficulties in, sustained conversation with the young children who attend.

Further evidence from related studies

Wood, with colleagues in the University of Nottingham, with a grant from the Medical Research Council, has continued to develop the line of enquiry initiated in analysis of conversations in preschool settings in Oxfordshire. A number of the hypotheses tentatively formulated from the evidence on the self-selected tapes have been tested in experimental settings: in particular the relationship between teacher demand (especially in the form of questions) and the cognitive level of children's responses. In one publication Wood suggests that a weakness of the Oxford study was that they did not have evidence of the children which would enable them to assess the extent to which some factors to do with particular children were responsible for any such effects. In an experimental study an experienced teacher was encouraged to change her style of conversation in ways that enabled the effects on the children to be assessed systematically. As it was accepted that dramatic effects would be achieved with linguistically able children care was taken to include some who were not so, and also whose mother tongue was not English in the six children. A detailed analysis of the relationship between teacher style and length and complexity of child responses did support a number of the points raised earlier.

That children's stage of language development and powers of understanding place constraints on what teachers can achieve in language interaction with them is not disputed: what is clear from the evidence is that:

> "The way in which a teacher talks to young children helps to determine how active, forthcoming and competent they may appear. Whether the children involved are preschoolers or older pupils; deaf, hearing or perhaps coming to English as a second language, the same basic 'rules' of conversation hold. If a teacher seeks to get children talking and thinking through question after question, then she is unlikely to hear children spontaneously elaborate on the theme of conversation, or go beyond her questions to add more information" (Wood and Wood, 1983 p.160).

Furthermore, excessive use of questions, particularly questions to which teachers already know the answers, has an adverse effect on the quantity and quality of the children's responses and thus may reinforce in the minds of the teachers a picture of a lower level of competence in the child than is legitimate from other evidence. Wood and his colleagues have included in their research extensive work with young deaf children in which they found similar evidence and evidence which challenges some of the assumptions about the appropriate ways of focusing language 'lessons' with young hearing impaired children. This is discussed in Wood, Wood, Griffiths and Howarth, 1986 (see particularly Chapter 3 'The Nursery Years'). Based on their research in preschool units with hearing children and in special schools with hearing-impaired children they provide a valuable structure for analysis of conversation showing how different teacher strategies and levels of control affect the quantity and quality of the children's contributions (See Wood *et al.*, 1986 pp.53-64).

The focus in the Oxfordshire studies, and the subsequent ones referred to above, is on the role of the adult in the initiation and development of conversation and not on any possibilities in appropriate settings of peer-peer interaction even for young preschool children. Peer-peer dialogue is not necessarily more limited, shorter and less cognitively demanding. It also is dependent on the context, and under appropriate conditions in preschool units can provide a fruitful context for stimulating and cognitively demanding dialogue, on occasion more complex than any recorded for these children in adult-child sessions. It can even provide valuable insights for the adults to improve their own practice and raise their expectations (See Robson, 1983). If adult-child interchanges are to assist children's cognitive development and are to be more than 'brief encounters' of adult controlled language with minimum child response, whether in ordinary preschool units, reception class, or in special schools, it is important that the insights from researches such as these are incorporated into pre-service and in-service training. The planning of the setting, the adults' perception of their role and their views of the children's competence are all important. Their teaching style may facilitate or inhibit dialogue with and between the children. Further supportive evidence is to be found in the research in preschool units of Corinne and John Hutt and their team which will now be considered.

PLAY EXPLORATION AND LEARNING IN THE PRESCHOOL

The main studies in this section were funded by DES from 1975 directed by Corinne and John Hutt at the University of Keele. The final report to DES entitled *A Natural History of the Preschool* (Hutt, Tyler, Hutt and Foy, 1984), prepared after Corinne Hutt's death in 1979, also incorporated a number of related studies. In the parallel study discussed earlier, *The Young Child at Home* (Davie *et al.*, 1984) a chapter is devoted to comparison between the findings of the two studies. Since different children were involved in the two researches and the study in preschool units is not, yet available in published form, it was felt to be essential to summarise the studies in preschool units here. As the source is an unpublished manuscript which may have changes of wording before it is available to a wider readership it did not seem appropriate to give precise quotes with page references as has been the practice elsewhere. The report presents the findings of a series of studies addressing different aspects of preschool education, and with different samples. For clarity each in turn is reported briefly, with a note in brackets of the chapter in the report concerned with that topic.

The Context (from Hutt *et al.*, 1984 Chapter 3)

The main project in preschool units was undertaken in two contrasting areas: one area, the northern part of Staffordshire in the West Midlands, had a comparatively long tradition of support for nursery education and includes the area in which the parallel study in homes was conducted. The provision of preschool education there was influenced by the demand for female labour and a local authority with interest in education of the young child. There were also day nurseries and many playgroups. The nursery tradition in the second area, parts of Cheshire, was very different, was more recent and tended to be in nursery units or classes attached to schools: in the former attendance was more likely to be full-time, and in the latter part-time.

Background information about the units to be used in the study was obtained by means of a structured interview. In Area A all 21 nursery schools and 6 day nurseries were visited and a random selection of about one-quarter of the nursery classes and playgroups (11 of each). In one area studied nursery classes were staffed by nursery nurses only, the head teacher of the school being in charge. All children in the day nurseries had extended day care, two thirds of the children in nursery schools and classes attended full-time and none in the playgroups. The day nurseries had, as expected, most children who suffered from difficulties and most mothers worked. About half of the mothers of the children in the nursery schools and classes worked, in the playgroups about 18% : some worked only part-time or evening shifts. In Area B the sample included seven nursery classes and one nursery school and few children there attended full-time. While about half of the units reported that many mothers worked, this was mostly in part-time employment.

Activities and Materials (Hutt *et al.*, 1984 Chapter 3)

To investigate the availability and use of materials and activities, observations were made in eight nursery schools, classes and playgroups and six day nurseries. Each unit was observed on two separate mornings at intervals of 20 minutes using a scan method of sampling. Immediately preceding the scan the observer recorded the various activities available: during the scan the numbers of children at the various activities were recorded. 'Free-play' periods were contrasted with periods of adult-led organised activity where children were constrained to attend. Comparatively little of the latter type of activity was observed in any of the four types of nursery, free-play was the emphasis; it was however greatest in nursery schools and classes and least in playgroups. Story or singing sessions occurred in all types of provision; use of audiovisual aids was observed in nursery classes but seldom elsewhere. The range of activities and materials available included in most nurseries a 'Home' or 'Wendy' corner, a book corner and some miniature adult objects. Most had a range of table-top activities and construction toys. Little gross physical activity was involved in the children's play indoors. There were differences in the extent to which different types of activity were simultaneously available during free-play (as distinct from potentially available) being greatest in playgroups as compared with other preschool units where their availability was usually selective. From their observations the researchers reported that there appeared to be general agreement concerning the range of activities which were appropriate for children aged three to five years of age and also in a belief in the value of play in the child's development.

Aims of Staff (from Hutt *et al.*, 1984 Chapter 4)

The aims of the staff in the preschool units were explored by use of a brief questionnaire based on that used earlier by Taylor *et al.* (1972) which has been used also in a number of other studies. The biographical details about the respondents revealed important differences between staff even with similar training. As found in other studies, many of the nursery nurses in day nurseries were aged less than 21 years unlike those in other units, and many staff in all other types of provision had children of their own (see Bain and Barnett, 1980 for a case study of a day nursery where there were similar findings and the implications of such young staff in such difficult and complex situations is explored). A difference in perceived role was seen between nursery nurses working in day nurseries and those in educational preschool units. As in the Oxfordshire study a number of the playgroup staff had formal qualifications (of 44, four were qualified teachers and ten were trained nursery nurses).

The benefits that staff considered most important from preschool provision were ability to mix with others, enhanced language development and the opportunity to discover and use potential. Staff in nursery schools and classes emphasised language development most, day nurseries emphasised emotional security more than others, and the playgroups social-emotional development. Somewhat similar results were obtained in Area B except that staff in the latter area tended to be younger and less experienced.

Greater emphasis was given by the staffs in nursery schools and classes to the role of the adult in giving guidance and instruction in contrast to day nurseries and playgroups where it was more generally perceived that the adults should allow the child to play. Staff tended to give a low ranking to the involvement of parents in the process of tuition and the lowest priority for this was given by nursery nurses in both types of establishment.

Parents interviewed saw preschool as a means of preparing the child for the routine and discipline of schooling rather than as an intellectual training (a possible conflict in aims). Many of the children in this study had attended playgroups before entering nursery school.

Adult's activities (Hutt *et al.*, 1984 Chapter 5)

An observational study was undertaken in a sample of each type of preschool unit with eleven staff from each type of unit; staff were observed during free play for 30 minutes on each of two separate days; by means of a time-sampling procedure. A check was made on inter-observer reliability and only when this was high were items retained. Most of the observation was in the playroom. Staff appeared to spend comparatively short periods of time engaged in a particular behaviour before switching to another and differences which emerged appeared to be related to practical aspects of running the unit. Involvement of adults in children's activities was found not only to be limited but also to be brief when it did occur, partly it was suggested because of the fluidity of the free-play situation. (Hutt et al., 1984 Chapter 5). It is suggested that a degree of restructuring of the environment might have been necessary to change this.

Children's activities (Hutt et al, 1984 Chapter 6)

So far the study was concerned with the attitudes and roles of staff and the availability of materials in the preschool units. The next step in this sequence of studies was to consider the pattern of children's activities. The researchers who, as in other studies of observation, attempted to assess the effects of the presence of an observer, report that there appeared to be no evidence of a systematic effect of their presence.

A check had been made on which activities were regarded by staff as most important and a notable feature was the high value placed on books and materials, particularly by the teachers. Playgroups supervisors were more inclined to emphasize water play and large climbing apparatus while parents tended to emphasize academic activities. In the 'scans' of the room representational toys and home corners were often seen to be used in children's play - despite the low value placed on these by the staff (Hutt *et al.* Chapter 6). The use of sand and water was relatively infrequent in view of the time they were available.

To study the involvement of children in the various activities in more depth 96 children were selected and observed for two separate periods of 30 minutes (12 boys and 12 girls) from each of the four types of provision. A comparison was made in the times devoted by the children to play with materials, fantasy play, physical play and looking and watching. Wide individual differences were found in children's pattern of play, but not sex differences on these dimensions. Only in regard to the amount of physical play was there a significant difference, with more of this in playgroups, where more such activities were available indoors, and there was in that setting also a sex difference with boys more involved than girls. It is noted that in spite of the importance accorded by the staff to books children spent comparatively little time looking at books. It is suggested that a major influence here could be the need for the presence of an adult. (See Lomax, 1977a and 1979a for different findings from observational studies in a nursery school with high priority given to books and stories).

Most of the observations had been indoors. As it was thought that there might be differences between that and play outside a small study was undertaken specifically to investigate that, involving 18 children aged between 3.5 and 4.5 years, the sample from several nursery schools. Any differences in the results were as might have been anticipated, with a greater effect of area on boys. In connection with emphasis on activities in different types of preschool unit it is noted that, in the area in which that study was conducted, playgroups tended to cater for younger children than those in nursery school or class. In addition supervisors may have been concerned about anticipating work in the reception class - or nursery school or class. The study which had now established the extent of popularity of various kinds of material and activity in the preschool units next directed attention to what children appeared to do with the various materials.

Use of Materials (Hutt *et al.*, 1984 Chapter 7)

This aspect of the study involved 71 children in six nursery schools and 59 from five day nurseries who were observed at play.

An interesting difference was found in the nature of play with dry and wet sand; the former was commonly associated with stereotyped repetition of two actions though with younger children there were more exploratory patterns; the latter produced much more varied sequences of behaviour. Water was associated with an even greater range of patterns, though there tended to be a need as the session continued to remove unwanted objects, which often also occupied adults. Activities which were 'product-orientated' (like brush-painting and clay and dough) produced different patterns of activities. The younger children tended to concentrate on brush-strokes whereas older children engaged in more exploratory activities. Most play with clay and dough was by older children for whom it was still relatively novel. Finger-painting, which was rarely available, elicited much exploration by older and younger children - possibly related to its comparative novelty. Collage yielded patterns which were more like that with sand and water with one action tending to predominate; there was, however, more variety in the materials.

The 'social content' of the various materials was different with little adult participation with sand and water play. Collage in contrast was one in which an adult was almost always present. The child there had a 'captive' partner and it was observed that some of the most sustained and lively discussion took place there; though the collage itself was possibly only incidental. There was most conversation with other children during play with wet sand and water. The pattern was similar in day nurseries to that in nursery schools but it is suggested in 'a more exaggerated form'. The researchers suggest that in so far as staff regard sand and water play as associated with cognitive development greater adult presence might be appropriate.

Fantasy play (Hutt *et al.*, 1984 Chapter 8)

There is a belief among many educationists concerned with young children that fantasy or imaginative play has an important role in children's cognitive development. This was explored with a sample of 40 nursery and reception class teachers of young children. Although all teachers were able to give examples of their own definition of imaginative play there was not consensus of its essential attributes. Comments, were that it was a replay of either an experience observed first hand or fictional, a re-enactment of roles or imitation. The majority of teachers mentioned the importance of props in its creation. The benefits suggested by the teachers covered all aspects of the development of young children, cognitive, emotional and social.

Observations in nursery school

In the observational aspect of the study of fantasy play nine nursery schools were involved. The observations here were of groups of children, in contrast to earlier aspects of the research which focused on individual children's activities. The aim was to make a study of the type of themes and their frequency and of where in the classroom they were to be found. Most observations were indoors during free-play and covered ten sessions of free-play. The observer scanned the whole classroom and made detailed notes of observed incidents of fantasy play. These records were divided into 'episodes' and events within these.

Domestic themes were found to predominate (but with a sex difference). Representational play with objects was present in more than half the events with two or three children involved, or a child alone. The availability of representational objects in a particular area (such as the home corner) was associated with a great deal of parallel play: adults tended not to be involved. It is suggested that representational object play tended to be a relatively low level activity with children in parallel and without adults. Fantasy person play involved groups of children, again rarely adults: each sex tended to adopt 'sex appropriate roles'. Fantasy play with food was commonly associated with the 'home corner', usually solitary or parallel with adult involvement rare. More boys than girls tended to be involved in fantasy object play which tended to be with construction toys, children were rarely seen alone, rather in groups of about three and rarely with an adult. Themes were varied but tended to be local.

Immaterial fantasy play was only apparent in about one-fifth of the events observed, usually involved groups of children and this might take place in a variety of parts of the nursery: here also adults were not closely involved. A media theme was often involved in events in this category. Clearly to identify fantasy or imaginative play does tend to involve the verbal component. Indeed fantasy person and immaterial fantasy play can only be identified from the child's verbal behaviour. Thus this aspect of the study has so far only been considered from a surface aspect. A further analysis was therefore conducted between children as regarded by their teachers and their linguistic competence as assessed on the Reynell Developmental Language Scales. This study involved observation of 12 children aged about 4 years of age in a nursery school, (six reported to show high levels of imaginative play and six low levels) observed for 100 minutes during twenty observation periods. It was found that the amount and complexity of fantasy play was closely related to the verbal competence shown on the test.

Observations in day nurseries

The limited language of children in day nurseries had been observed in everyday utterances and it seemed worthwhile to make a comparison of their language in fantasy play, also to assess whether or not it was equally limited. In this study a detailed analysis was made of twelve children from five day nurseries. It was found that the children displayed greater competence in their language during fantasy play than in their 'ordinary' speech. Extensive extracts are given from the children's language during fantasy play and in the ordinary setting - each of which was recorded with a radio microphone. Their everyday performance did not give insight into their competence. What is more significant, but not explored, is the fact that what is categorised as 'ordinary' setting is in all five instances with an adult who is adopting a manner which does not extend or expect any extended language from the children. The effects of this style have been stressed on a number of occasions during this report. The expectations of children's language of the young staff in the day centres was very low: furthermore developing language had not been listed as high in their priorities. The availability of evidence of the language of these children in these different settings is thus important. It is likely that were these adults with their present expectations, and what would have been referred to by Wood and his colleagues as 'managerial' style, to have joined the fantasy play the language and play might well have 'dried up'.

Implications

From the evidence of these various studies the authors stress that much of what they observed as fantasy play was repetitive, low level, not necessarily social and seldom involved adults. The fact that more complex play and extended fantasy play was differentially seen among children who were linguistically able does not require a causal relationship to be deduced with fantasy play *per se* improving children's cognitive development. Repetitive, unchallenging and solitary play may have an important role, a 'recuperative' function but there may be important further dimensions before play can fulfil other functions. One dimension which was not explored in these studies was the extent to which the children who showed the most complex and extended play, and were linguistically able, were children who already had these skills in the home setting rather than acquired them in the preschool unit in which they were observed. Clearly the presence of such children might raise the level of play of the children who joined them in play but their own complex extended play might have been developed elsewhere, and could for example have had adult involvement.

In an attempt to assess the extent to which adult tutoring can raise the level of fantasy, and creative play, particularly in children from 'economically disadvantaged backgrounds', a number of experimental studies have been undertaken. Encouraging effects on social, linguistic and cognitive development have been reported. Smith and colleagues from Sheffield University have undertaken experimental studies funded by SSRC to assess whether tutoring in fantasy play is essential to achieve such effects or whether the effects can be attributed to the increased adult involvement. Their study, and a review of other experimental studies, is reported in Smith, Dalgleish and Herzmark (1981). Smith and his colleagues suggest that fantasy and sociodramatic play tutoring, at least for those children whose play appears to be limited, may assist the staff to be more sensitive in their planning of activity, to talk in stimulating ways to the children, and may encourage the children to maintain social interaction with their peers.

Attention and choice (Hutt *et al.*, 1984 Chapter 9)

A further aspect considered in the Hutt researches in preschool units was activity span and in particular the role of the adult in extending children's attention. This analysis was based partly on the data collected in each type of unit. It was found that activity spans of the children without an adult were highest in the nursery school and class, but with an adult this was increased in all types of unit, suggesting the important role of the adult in stimulating and sustaining children's attention on an activity. From the data from a variety of studies it is reported that the average length of activity span tended to be about a quarter of an hour, but often with frequent interruptions. Attention spans of anything from one minute to over an hour in a few cases were found.

Observations were made in an attempt to assess whether or not certain features led children to be attracted to specific activities. It was found that girls more frequently chose activities where an adult was present than boys. Most approaches were decisively child initiated, but girls had more adult initiated activities especially product-orientated and structured activities. Children's departure from activity rarely appeared to be aimless. It is however important to note that while in 'product orientated' activities children did leave when they had completed the activity, in many instances the product was not completed and this was more common with boys. Adult intervention was commonly a cause of departure from free play or representational play.

The picture which emerges is of children purposefully engaged, often in activities of their own choice, but with frequent interruptions. The importance of planning the placing of adults and changes in the position of specific adults becomes clear from these studies, though clearly this could not be explored fully because there were some activities at which few adults were present.

Use of Language (Hutt *et al.*, 1984 Chapter 10)

Reference was made earlier to the studies of language at home and at school by Tizard and Hughes (1984) and that in schools by Sylva *et al.*(1980). This aspect of development was also studied in the Hutt research project with a large scale observation study with a check list (but not recorded speech). This involved 80 children aged four years of age in six nurseries of each of the four types noted earlier (20 children of each sex in each type of nursery). A study of interactions suggested that some adults are sought out by children rather than others, but that the adult's nominal role may not be the explanation. Children tended more readily to approach an adult already involved in an activity with children.

The findings in this study were in accord with those of others, there was little evidence of complex conversation or discussion of past or future events. As this was true in all types of unit, all of which had an extended free play context, the research raises the possibility that this could be one feature of relevance. Features of the environment could be one aspect militating against such interactions between adults and children. Attempts to respond to overtures of all children may thus result in short and relatively superficial interchanges, and, as a result of the sheer quantity and range of demands with which the adults are bombarded, in some children rarely being involved.

Types of Play

The authors of the report use the word 'play' throughout for the children's activities in the preschool unit, because it is the term which is in common use by staff. They make an important distinction however between what they call ludic behaviour which is self-amusement, less focused and mood dependent and epistemic behaviour which is concerned with acquisition of knowledge and information and is more 'focused'. Some kinds of activity have the objective inherent in the task itself, or are productive of change, or of competence in a new skill. The authors suggest that currently the environments of preschool units are structured to encourage ludic rather than epistemic behaviour, with day nurseries most so. It is claimed that the type of activity they term epistemic is very important towards learning and cognitive development and clearly requires a sufficiently good adult child ratio for work with individual children or small groups. They stress, as have others cited here, that the ratio is not sufficient. Adults may merely dominate the interaction rather than extend it particularly if they adopt a questioning managerial role (as shown by Tizard and Hughes, 1984 by Wood *et al.*, 1980 and the present author (Clark *et al.*, 1984)).

Implications for early education

During the course of the Hutt researches the behaviour of around a thousand children in about fifty preschool units in a range of types of preschool unit, nursery schools and classes, playgroups and day nurseries, located in urban areas around Stoke-on-Trent and South Cheshire was studied. Ethnic minorities were under-represented in the area, and children whose mother tongue is not English are not discussed in the report. The children in the studies were relatively comparable to those in other urban areas and the preschool units relatively comparable. It is noted that in nursery classes, staffed by nursery nurses and not teachers, in outlook and aims the nursery nurses were more closely in accord with teacher colleagues than with nursery nurses in day nurseries.

In all types of provision a wide variety of activities was potentially available and at the time of this research all were organised for free-play to which the staffs were committed, and during which the various studies were undertaken. In all provision during free-play children were most frequently seen using representational objects. Sand and water appeared to be used for very limited stereotyped and repetitive activities and adults were seldom available at such activities: they were more likely to be at the clay, collage and painting. More children were present at a task when an adult was present. The frequent and multiple demands which adults faced in these environments meant that adult attention spans were very short. This feature militated against any extended dialogue with children, which was found to be rare and normally concerned with the present.

Children's decisions about choice of activities were firm both with regard to start and completion; they attended for longer periods to the activities they chose though not necessarily at a high level. The evidence on play with sand and water and on fantasy play was disappointing in the findings of its limited and often repetitive nature; although quite complex themes developed with some more flexible props. It was suggested that fantasy play rather than being regarded as an aid to cognitive development was better regarded as an aid to diagnosis of children's mood, complex language facilities and other hidden talents.

Adult and child interaction patterns were similar to those found in other studies, with most adult responses in the form of questions, explanations were infrequent (though slightly more common by teachers). Day nursery staff were found to talk less to the children than staff in other settings and talk tended to occur in response to children's actions. It is suggested that some of problems in achieving coherent extended conversations were the result of the setting:

> "the efforts of adults to give equal attention to the fragmentary verbal gambits provided by children (the significance of which is often not understood by the adults) may result in verbal exchanges which are anything but conversation" (Hutt et al., 1984, p. 16.14).

It is clearly important to explore further which adult styles, organisational patterns and activities are associated with more extended and elaborated activities, greater concentration and more extended and meaningful dialogue between adults and children, and between children themselves. Some points have already been given in the studies discussed so far, either explicitly or implicitly. This study has shown, as have the others so far, the dangers of a large free-play setting as the entire context within which preschool children in large groups can learn. These issues will be explored further in the third large scale study funded in this period in preschool units.

TEACHING STYLES IN NURSERY EDUCATION

This study based on the Open University was funded by SSRC from 1975-78. The final report to ESRC by Asher Cashdan and Sara Meadows is the basis for the discussion (Cashdan and Meadows, 1983). It is unfortunate that so far little of this large scale study has been available in detail in published form. The two authors left the Open University, Cashdan before the analysis was complete, Meadows at the end of the grant and the other director became ill and withdrew. At the time that this research was planned in the mid-seventies and those discussed earlier, there was little evidence from observational studies of what were the patterns of teacher and child behaviour and activities within ordinary preschool units.

Aims

One aim in this research, as with the Oxford and Keele based studies, was to provide descriptive material based on observation of the day-to-day activities of staff and children. In this study the focus was on teachers and the children in their classes in a sample of mainstream nursery schools not involved in any other research or intervention project. It was also planned to institute an experimental tutorial language programme with these teachers and to assess its effects on teacher behaviour and children's progress.

The Sample

This study took place only in nursery schools, in order to have units with at least two teachers for the experimental study in addition to the head teacher. Ten typical nursery schools in Outer London Boroughs from forty were selected, with a reasonably wide social class mix in each. Details are given in the report (Section 2) of the method of selection of schools and exclusions. The two teachers were selected by the head teacher. Thereafter, within each teacher's class or group eight children were selected for observation and testing, four children whom the teacher regarded among the most able and four least able and functioning poorly.

Children were excluded who:

1) had a recognised physical or mental disability;

2) were known to be leaving by summer 1976 (as the experiment went beyond that);

3) whose parents were known or thought to speak a language other than English at home (from the detailed tables about the catchment areas in Appendix A1.2 to the report there may have been a considerable number of such children in the area of some of the schools, even if not in attendance);

4) were absent during teacher observation.

Details are given of any replacements required among children initially selected.

The Study

In addition to observations of the teachers' behaviour on eight days and child-focused behaviour on five days, each teacher completed a repertory grid, and was interviewed concerning all the children she taught. Tape recordings were also made each term of each teacher working with eight children for about ten minutes on a one-to-one basis. Eight children (balanced for sex) were observed in each class in each term during free-play. The children participated in the one-to-one sessions and were assessed on EPVT at least on two occasions. Half of the teachers were involved in a 14 week teaching intervention programme, using a dialogue approach which was developed by Marion Blank. Related to that these teachers discussed their work with the research team, including selected conversations with children in their classes.

In a paper delivered by Meadows and Cashdan in 1982 on 'Children's Play in Nursery Schools', the authors report on the findings and implications of the observational study. This involved a trained observer making a written narrative record of the target child's activities and conversation for a period of three minutes then coding immediately. Observations were made in mainstream nursery schools during free play and children were observed in random order on at least four occasions over two days in each term. It was found that the children's play was interesting and purposeful: the children were contented and busy. The researchers felt, however, that the play was often brief and repetitive, and lacking in complexity and much social participation. The play of the older children was, however, more complex and less repetitive. There were sex differences in choice of activities and also girls were more often near the teacher and showed greater duration in their play. There was little evidence of sustained or uninterrupted conversations between children and adults. While stressing the pressures under which the adults were operating with large numbers of young children, the authors question whether the ideology of free-play with the adults adopting a noninterventionist role is an environment providing sufficient intellectual challenge. It may leave many children contented but spending much of the time in brief spells of repetitive play with little language interchange rather than providing contexts which stimulate and develop curiosity and extended dialogue. They thus raise similar issues to those raised earlier.

Implications for early education

The results of this study support the other evidence cited so far in this chapter in that teachers' verbalisations to children concentrated on simple questions and statements. They also found that negative comments were rare: so also were complex statements or instructional talk. There were substantial differences between teachers in their behaviour.

After the experimental teaching intervention (and support and discussion) there were small changes towards higher demands being made by teachers who took part. It is noted in the report (Cashdan and Meadows, 1983 p.52) that the one-to-one sessions were "interesting at an intuitive level", but that no formal analysis has been carried out. Meadows and Cashdan (1982) report that after the intervention they obtained changes in the behaviour of the children observed in these classes, especially encouraging since the target children observed had not all had personal experience of the tutorials and the training period had been short. The shift was towards higher-quality play, and more interaction with adults. Unfortunately the children's utterances during observations were not coded because of problems in audibility (Cashdan and Meadows, 1983 p.5). This study did not use radiomicrophones during free-play settings without which a detailed analysis of the content of the children's language is difficult to assess.

The other studies cited so far have covered much of the ground covered in the observational work. The more complex analysis of different teachers' interactions with children in relation to their other characteristics is not available in the report.

Evidence on observation in natural settings in preschool units and comparison between language at home and at school, has already been considered in some detail based on a number of studies. It is perhaps sufficient to indicate that Cashdan and Meadows, with different observational schedules for teachers and children and in a different area, obtained comparable data, with in their case a focus on schools and teachers as the adults observed. By the time this research report and that of the Hutt study were written the published findings of the Oxford Preschool Research and the Tizard studies had already received wide publicity. Thus the authors of these two last researches, at Keele and the Open University, who were working at about the same time in different preschool settings, though independent in their collection of data, were familiar with and frequently refer to the work of these others in their reports.

In the Oxford study reference was made to attempts to sensitize practitioners to their own ways of talking with children and the influence of that on the children; furthermore they were encouraged to attempt to change their practice. In this current study that possibility was also present but for the same practitioners who were involved in such interchanges there was also a dialogue language intervention programme introduced. It is thus not possible to separate out the extent to which the small change in language behaviour reported in the teachers was the effect of either or both of these aspects. The experimental design required pairs of teachers, one of whom would become involved in the programme. In the climate of the mid-seventies it is not surprising that there was among the teachers hostility to the researchers' philosophy (Section 6, p.54). It is reported that although that was the situation initially they were:

"enthusiastic about it by the end",

and,

"only one remained doubtful to the end. Among the others some confessed that only now were they learning about pupils who had previously been strangers to them"; (Cashdan and Meadows, 1983 Section 6, p.54).

The teachers involved, it is reported, prepared pamphlets on the experimental work for other teachers. From the evidence in this present study it cannot be deduced whether or not the experimental programme was an essential element in any change or new insights that took place.

All but two of the teachers involved in this study had been two or less years in their present school and for a number this was their first teaching appointment, furthermore few appear to have had experience in any other preschool unit, though most were trained on a nursery/infant course (Cashdan and Meadows, 1983 Appendix V). These relevant details provided in this study would probably be fairly typical for teachers in non-promoted posts in nursery schools at that time.

There is not evidence in this study, or in the others discussed in this chapter, on the extent to which the training of the teachers who were observed in the preschool units had prepared them for such work, or had even included any observation in preschool units. Limited or no attention may have been paid in their training to the planning of free-play contexts and choice of activities for these younger less mature children, many likely to have limited competence in relating to 'strange' adults; to organisation of other staff and the need to relate to other adults including parents in preschool units.

The studies reported here have shown differential staff attention to certain activities, and thus the possibility that children who spend time at these may have more staff attention. Two further studies will be mentioned briefly. Cooper (1979) describes a study of 112 children aged 36-50 months in seven nursery schools, in which she compared the quantity and distribution of speech in two different settings, when the presence of the adult was incidental, and when the adult was more involved. In the settings analysed staff were found to be talking more with the older children, particularly older girls. Interpretation is limited as differences between nurseries, staff and children are not analysed, or the extent to which the results were influenced by specific activities selected by the boys and girls. Ingham (1982) compared the behaviour, language and social groupings of twenty children aged three and four of West Indian ethnic origin with similar indigenous white children in day nurseries, using a modified version of the observational schedule used by Sylva et al.(1980). She found sex differences in the amount and type of children's contact with adults. The girls of both ethnic groups were more often engaged with adults both in supervisory and more positive interactions. She stresses that the boys of West Indian origin were those who did not appear to be receiving the same opportunities; even supervisory talk was less. An analysis of play activities showed that the girls of both ethnic groups tended to engage more in activities such as art, puzzles and small-scale construction. These activities which produced a higher degree of concentration and potential for dialogue were settings in which boys, particularly those of West Indian origin were rarely seen.

The evidence from the studies in preschool units clearly highlights a number of important issues about the context provided by a completely open-plan free-play preschool setting as a setting for large numbers of young children. It could be, as some of the researchers have suggested, that the environment and its 'implicit' structure can be utilized successfully by the more mature confident outgoing children, who concentrate on more complex activities and stimulate those who join them to participate also. Dialogue with adults, which is in short supply because of so many competing demands, may also be selectively available to the more linguistically able children. What is also clear from such studies is the pressures under which the staff in such settings are placed, throughout the day. The organisational abilities, enthusiasm, range of skills, ability to share experiences with young children, stimulate them but not constrain them, may require skills to which their training does not sensitize them. The demands placed on staff working in educational settings with young children may not only be excessive, and ones for which they are not adequately prepared, they may also be in conflict with each other.

CHAPTER 8   RESEARCH ON DAY NURSERIES AND COMBINED CENTRES

RESEARCH CONTEXT

The diversity of preschool provision in Britain has already been indicated: the numbers and the types of preschool units available in a given area vary widely. For families whose circumstances require day-long care for their preschool child the alternative tends to have been limited to either a day nursery or childminder. Day nurseries provide all day, all year care for children, in many instances from a very early age. Childminders provide care for limited numbers of young children in the minder's home. Research into day nurseries will be considered in this chapter, studies of childminders in the following chapter.

A survey was undertaken on behalf of DHSS by the Office of Population Censuses and Surveys, Social Survey Division, into *Preschool children and the need for day-care*. The survey involved interviews of the mothers of children under five years of age. The population sampled was defined as children aged under five in private households in England and Wales and it was calculated that a sample of 2500 children would give adequate representation in each year group and single need category. The interviews were undertaken in 1974, much of the data in the report is related to a variety of needs and not specifically to education, much is concerned with 'needs' in children under three years of age. The population characteristics would be very different now, thirteen years later. For that and the above reasons the findings of the survey will not be discussed in this present report. Readers interested in the details of the survey are referred to the published report (Bone, 1977).

Funded studies of day nurseries and combined nursery centres and of childminders will be reported and the relevance of the findings to the education of children under five considered.

Two researches funded within the Nursery Research Programme commenced in 1975 as did a study of some of the then recently opened combined nursery centres. The two studies of day nurseries, by Bain and Barnett (1980) and by Garland and White (1980) both took place in London. These and the study of combined nursery centres by Ferri and others (1981) will be discussed in some detail in this chapter. Reference will be made to a more recent study by Van der Eyken (1984) which provides comparative information from a survey of day nurseries in England in 1975 and a sample of these in 1983. Evidence will also be presented from two studies directed by the present author, one of these studies was undertaken in the Grampian Region in Scotland in 1976-77, the other in the West Midlands in 1979-81 (Clark and Cheyne, 1979 and Clark, Robson and Browning, 1982). The major concern in these latter two studies was the integration of children with special needs in ordinary preschool units, a topic considered elsewhere in the report. Both studies involve interviewing the person in charge of each of the day nurseries in the research. These interviews provide evidence of relevance to the issues under consideration here. The findings of the studies funded specifically to study day nurseries are important in their own right, and as a context for analysing the evidence on long term effects of preschool education reported recently for the national CHES sample (Osborn *et al.*, 1984; Osborn and Milbank, 1987). These children were born in 1970, and were thus in preschool units, some in day nurseries, about the time of the above studies. It is equally important to note research evidence on similarities and differences in the population and aims of day nurseries in the seventies and eighties in order to appreciate the current relevance of their findings. Available evidence suggests that there may indeed have been considerable changes in the children attending and in the roles of the staff.

CHILDREN AND DAY NURSERIES

The aims of the study

This research directed by Bruner (as part of the Oxford Preschool Research) was concerned with the organisational patterns of care in different types of day nurseries and with the nature of care provided for the children.

There were two main aspects to the research, one concerned with organisational features, the service provided, history of the unit, links with other agencies etc. This information was gathered by interviews which it is reported were informal, "note-taking during the interview was kept to a minimum" (Garland and White, 1980 p.8). The second aspect of the study concerned the day care provided in the various units, based on relatively informal observation. Recordings lasted for 20 minutes at a time and were in total between five and nine hours. The observer recorded in a notebook what was seen and heard in as much detail as possible. Focus was on individuals - more often than not a member of staff, but occasionally also a child:

"if what it was doing seemed interesting, or relevant to that day's activities in that nursery":

"more time was spent observing in nurseries felt to be successful in providing a good standard of care ..." (Garland and White, 1980 p.9).

The sample

Nine day nurseries in London were studied, three of which were State nurseries, selected as representative of 'the best practice'. The other six units were chosen to give samples of other types and were not necessarily

"considered to be the best practice in any particular field" (Garland and White, 1980 p.7).

They were

an all-day playgroup, a factory nursery,

a university nursery,

a nursery run by and located in a hospital,

a 'community' nursery and

a private nursery run by a charitable organisation.

The research is reported in narrative style without quantitative data to back the statements or the stance of the two researchers on what they would regard as 'good practice' made explicit. In a review of the publication the present author expressed concern at the methodology (Clark, 1982). It is difficult from the publication, because of its style and format, and the fact that the data on which the case histories and interpretations are based is not quantified, to extract the information for this current report. For a summary which highlights the main points the reader is referred to Bruner, 1980 Chapter 7.

It is important not to assume homogeneity in any aspect of organisation or care in units catering for children who need all-day care. This study covered only nine units, three State and six private nurseries, all in one area, London. A few units took children under two years of age, the hours they were open and number of weeks they were available differed, and whether they took any children part-time. In one unit those working with the children were mainly parents, in another they were all in nurses' uniforms and physical care was the feature emphasised. In one of the State nurseries groups of the older children went to the nearby nursery school in the afternoons; in another, children were accepted only if the parents were not working and therefore free to co-operate. In three of the nurseries most children were from ethnic minorities:-

- the State nursery referred to above, (where many of the children were of West Indian origin, as were many of the staff);

- the factory-based nursery where many of the children could not speak English on entry;

- one of the other private nurseries which had a specific emphasis on language training for children of minority groups.

The findings

Within the nine nurseries studied there were widely different practices, patterns of organisation, staff attitudes to children and to parents. In some day nurseries there was an authoritarian approach with a considerable emphasis on compulsory education-related tasks, in its narrowest interpretation, undertaken in a way which caused concern to the observers. All children were expected to take part in these activities: furthermore in some units there was a marked contrast between these 'work related' activities and any free play which was more regarded as a time-filler to keep the children occupied - a very different focus from that reported in the preschool units in the previous chapters. What was referred to as a child-centred approach with an emphasis on social-emotional development (contrasted with adult-centred) was reported in the three State nurseries (initially selected as examples of good practice) and two of the other units, the university nursery (whose children were mainly those of students), and the all-day playgroup (which involved parents in the unit). In those nurseries which were less child-centred it is also suggested that there was a more hierarchic system of management and junior staff were regarded as less competent.

In the publication by Garland and White the term 'cognitive goals' is used in a very different way from that found in most other studies consulted. It tends to be used in association with large groups, very didactic teaching of school-based topics at this early age - and indeed reports situations which appear to have achieved little positive interaction and many negative controlling moves. To quote:

> "Nurseries with an adult-dominated approach, and cognitive goals as their predominating aim, are those in which negative alliances tend to occur" (Garland and White, 1980 p.113).

It is difficult to assess how typical these nine day nurseries were of units providing all-day-care when the study was underway in 1975-8 and how comparable the pattern would be now. On the basis of the evidence in Van der Eyken (1984) it would appear that the situation has not eased for staffing or the nature of the child population served. That survey concerned only local authority day nurseries, which accounted for only three of nine in the above research and those were selected as representative of 'good practice'.

In summarising the findings of the Garland and White research, Bruner (1980 p. 160-163) draws attention to the numbers of staff in the day nurseries who were only in their late teens or early twenties with NNEB training. Others had no training and amongst these were a number of young girls who had only recently left school. Furthermore the staffing ratio was better in the State than private nurseries. To quote:

> "Training and qualifications in the private nurseries are distinctly lacking. Job tenure is short, hours long, and pay low. There are virtually no opportunities for nor routes to advancement and little sense of professional pride" (Bruner, 1980 p. 163).

and further

"It must be said finally that there is no reason of merit that compels the recommendation that day nurseries *as they now operate* should be greatly increased in number" (Bruner, 1980 p.168) (Italics in the original)

A STUDY OF A DAY NURSERY

The information in this section is based on the report to DHSS of a study entitled *The Design of a Day Care System in a Nursery Setting for Children Under Five* (Bain and Barnett, 1980). Bain and Barnett report that even in 1978 over 30, 000 children were in public local authority day nurseries and there were long waiting lists. They claim that few of the public have any conception of what a day nursery is, they confuse it with other types of provision such as nursery schools and classes and playgroups. There was a climate of opinion that day nurseries are good places to put a child.

In 1970 the DHSS commissioned the Tavistock Institute of Human Relations to undertake a fact-finding study into day care provision for under fives. That study in the Greater London area, completed in 1971, justified feelings of unease which had prompted DHSS to fund the study. Its findings led to the action research by Bain and Barnett

"to build a model of day care in a nursery setting, giving the optimum care possible (within the limitations of the system, and resources available) for the under fives and their families during day time separations" (Bain and Barnett, 1980 p.4).

The project was initially funded from 1975-8 (with a six month extension).

The aims of the study and setting

The day nursery selected for this study was chosen to be typical of local authority nurseries in Great Britain in terms of their problems and resources. The aim of the project once the nursery had been selected was

"to try with the staff to make it as adequate as possible with these constraints for the children, parents and staff" (Bain and Barnett, 1980 p.17).

It was felt that the project should be based in a nursery where the level of care was already high and one where the team felt they could work with the staff. Final choice was also influenced by accessibility to the team who were to visit the nursery twice a week during the study. The focus was on facilitating desirable changes in the role of staff, the organisational structure of the nursery, its boundary relationships and working culture.

Twelve children attending the day nursery in early 1976 were selected (representative of the nursery in terms of age, sex, cultural background, reason for admission and length of stay). These children were followed through their career in the nursery and eleven were reassessed clinically and educationally in 1978-79.

The aim of the research team in this action research was not to tell the staff how to change (which is what some staff expected initially)but to work collaboratively with the staff. Unfortunately the matron of the day nursery left during the project, an inevitable hazard in an indepth study. This report has interesting insights into the processes of change, the strains and frustrations these produced. Even where changes were seen by the staff to be desirable it was not always possible because of external constraints to implement the changes. Examples were the evidence of a recruitment gap in filling vacant staff appointments and the extensive administrative duties required of the matron, and problems in the institution of a parent/staff room.

The day nursery in this study was a 54 place nursery (47 in attendance) admitting children from 3 months to 5 years of age; a wide range of cultural backgrounds was represented although for most children English was their first language. Stated reasons for admission for most of the children were 'unmarried mothers' (21), parents separated (10), or mental health of the mother (7). There were ten nursery staff including the matron, and all staff were NNEB trained. Most of the staff were young and all but the deputy had been in their posts for less than a year. Turnover of staff was high and the nursery had previously depended greatly on agency staff. The nursery was open from 7.30 a.m. to 6 p.m. each week day throughout the year with two 'shifts' for the staff. There was only a half-hour lunch break for staff and yet the unit was fully staffed for less than half the day.

The findings: the children

One reason for referral to day nurseries often given is to ameliorate bad effects of home background, according to the research workers. The study of twelve children over their period in what was a relatively good day nursery which became better during the project, gave an opportunity for an indepth study of this. The results were not found to be encouraging:

> "On the contrary there are indications that the day nursery experience for most of the children caused added difficulties for their development which became very apparent at school" (Bain and Barnett, 1980 p.25).

All except one of the twelve children studied were in the nursery from under the age of three years; all except one, who was only briefly in the nursery, had numerous caretakers within the nursery. Details are given for seven of the children with regard to major caretakers (defined as a nurse who stayed more than one month). These range from 12 to 20 'caretakers' in between two to three years in the nursery and for one with a shorter time in the nursery it was six preceded by a childminder. Not only were a number of the twelve children reported to have been unwanted but also the mothers of seven were being psychiatrically treated or had recently been treated. Two others had alcoholic problems. Half the children were from large families with 5+ children. Furthermore only four of the twelve mothers themselves were from intact families. Although some of the mothers were working the jobs were generally temporary, unskilled and numerous. At the beginning of the project these mothers did not know the names of any other mothers in the nursery. During the project, however, parents began to spend some time in the nursery, revealing some of their problems to the staff. The staff in turn became less critical of the mothers. The background of these families, psychologically as much as physically, must have placed the child under considerable pressures.

Many examples of "painful separations and consequent difficulties" are given (Bain and Barnett, 1980 p.34). The physical health of the twelve children was also clearly well below average with chronic problems in a number. Of the nine children assessed all but one is reported to have scored at least average intelligence: although it is noted that the majority of the children had language difficulties. The range of tests given to such young children is surprising. Of those three children not tested two were babies both of whom, from observation, were thought to be emotionally and mentally retarded, the other, a two-year-old, was unable to be tested.

It seemed important to provide considerable detail on these children not only for a full understanding of this particular study, but also to give the reader some appreciation of the complexity and range of difficulties suffered by children in a day nursery. To suggest that a day nursery differs from other provision only in providing all-day all-year care is so strikingly a misrepresentation. Bain and Barnett give the important warning (on p.43) that the impression was being given that day nurseries catered for normal children needing extended day care. From their interviews with staff, this was also implicit in their training. It is now pertinent to consider the detailed findings on the staff in this day nursery.

The findings: the staff

It is not surprising that the research team found that there was a very high staff turnover, high absence and sickness rate, although these were reduced during the project. This high turnover and absence rate increases the stresses not only for the children but also for other staff. During the project 1976-78, 26 permanent nursery staff worked at the day nursery, 15 permanent staff left and 32 agency staff.

The important feature that stands out is the extreme youth of the nursery nurses on permanent staff. Seventeen of 22 qualified nursery nurses were under 25, most were single. The staff were thus mostly young, unmarried and few had children of their own.

Furthermore many of the staff had as children experienced abnormal experiences themselves, which the researchers associate with the pattern of high staff turnover and the nature of the relationships of the staff with the children. For most of the nursery nurses the job was seen as something in between leaving school and getting married, one where it was not possible to see a career development. The researchers felt that those aspects of the staff background were important in their effects on the environment it was possible to provide in the day nursery.

It will be possible from other sources to consider the pattern of background of nursery nurses who are working in the education service in nursery schools and classes, many of whom seem to have very different characteristics. Of about 100 nursery nurses working in Avon nursery schools and classes interviewed in a study by Heaslip between 1979 and 1981, only one had been under a year in the present post, nearly half had been in their current post for over ten years and a number had extensive other experience: thus a very different pattern (Summarised in Heaslip, 1985)

Two organisational changes which were introduced into the nursery as part of the action research are of relevance to the present report. The first of these involved the introduction of a group for two and three-year-olds. Separation of these children was decided upon because of the differing needs of the wider age range of 2-5 years and the stresses this had caused for younger and older children. Accompanying this change were discussions with parents and two members of staff each taking responsibility for half the children in the room. It is difficult therefore to separate out these various elements and their relationship to the success of the venture which led to these members of staff forming more attachment with the children for whom they were responsible.

The other initiative which was monitored during the project was the introduction of a nursery school teacher on a half-time basis. There were some initial resentments about the appointment, partly from the expectations of the nursery school teacher, and also her higher pay and status, shorter hours and longer holidays. Initially also the organisation of the day nursery was a problem. One development after her arrival was the separating of the three-and-a-half to five-year- olds then integrated with the work of the nursery school teacher. The introduction by the borough of a nursery teacher was to help prepare the older children for school. Bain and Barnett note that although the placement of the nursery teacher was not a part of the project, their presence enabled the staff to work through their feelings and helped facilitate the necessary organisational changes. While they felt that the children in that setting did benefit they question whether such attachments of teachers were desirable in the longer term. They suggest that such an appointment might prevent nursery nurses developing a more educational role which might lead to their having a more satisfying role. It is debatable whether such could or would develop without changes in the training of staff, in-service training and guidance and support. Clearly in view of the sensitivities of the staff and the complexities of the situation very great care would be required in planning any 'educational' input. In one of the State nurseries described in the study by Garland and White (1980 p.12) there is reference to a group of older children attending a local nursery school in the afternoons, an alternative model.

The setting in the day nursery

Bain and Barnett had noted high levels of aggression in the day nurseries in which they had observed, and became concerned as to whether this could at least be partly the result of the child's exposure to the day nursery. Their aim in this part of the study was to look at nursery-specific factors within a single day nursery. They felt the following factors were important: the size of group, the ratio of caretakers, the structure of care, the constancy of the caretaker. Ten pairs of children were observed simultaneously, one with greater exposure to the nursery (a combination of duration and average hours). These observations, they claim, gave some support to their hypothesis, as did a comparison of children between two and five years of age as rated for aggression by their nursery nurses. There is the alternative possibility that children who were placed in the day nursery at a younger age and/or for longer, also had greater adverse circumstances outside the day nursery which could have been related to their aggression. This was not studied in detail although it is commented that

"We do not however know of any overall difference in the family backgrounds of the children in the paired sample who were more aggressive which would distinguish them from the children who were less aggressive" (Bain and Barnett, 1980 p.106).

These researchers suggest a possible relationship between aggression and 'discontinuity of care' which was evident in the organisation of the day nursery and would be most extensively experienced by children with greatest exposure to the regime. They recommend a change in focus in the nursery nurse's role to a primary concern with the 'child's psychological well-being' and 'a case assignment system' and a regrouping of the children (Bain and Barnett, 1980 p.146). They managed during the study to encourage greater mutual understanding between staff and parents (including joint meetings, and home visits).

"The changes in the nurse's role, relationships with parents, and structure of care enabled some children in the nursery to form deeper and more stable attachment relationships with their particular nurse" (Bain and Barnett, 1980 p.147).

A number of the statements made in this study are not supported by empirical evidence. They are, however, based on several years of in-depth study of and involvement with the institution by the two researchers. A number of the findings are in line with other work on children in institutions in stressing the importance of an approach and organisation which enables and encourages young children to develop close relationships with a few members of staff rather than have indiscriminate, even if good, physical care from a number of caretakers.

COMBINED NURSERY CENTRES

In the early seventies a number of local authorities began to develop a new kind of nursery namely a 'combined nursery centre', to provide preschool education and day care in a single unit, in several cases established as a result of joint applications by education and social services for Urban Aid funds. Clearly such units were likely to meet a considerable challenge and many problems in bringing together in a joint venture two services with separate administrative and professional settings. It was felt necessary to study such developments and thus DHSS and DES provided funds to the NationalChildren's Bureau to evaluate some of these centres. This research, between 1975-78, which was within the 'Programme', involved a study of four of the seven combined nursery centres which had by then been established in different areas under Urban Aid. The information in this section is taken from the published report of the research entitled *Combined Nursery Centres: a new approach to Education and Day Care* (Ferri, Birchall, Gingell and Gipps, 1981).

The study

This evaluative research focused on four main areas: children and parents, staff and the framework within the centre (See Ferri *et al.*, 1981 p.11-12). An experimental design was not possible, but for comparative purposes in parts of the study three nursery schools and six day nurseries were chosen in similar areas. The study involved regular visits by a member of the research team over the period of the research about every two months to a combined centre and its 'control' nurseries. Each visit had a focus - on assessment of children, interviews of parents or observations. In considering the generalisability of any findings of this study it should be remembered that it involved only four centres all of which had only recently been established in a pioneering venture.

The Sample

All four Centres studied were purpose-built and jointly administered but differed in size. Details of centres not included in the research, and the reasons are given by Ferri *et al.* (1981 p.14) and Chapter 2 is devoted to detailed descriptions of the Centres in the research. A study of that chapter shows just how varied were these four centres in staffing, organisation, size and certainly therefore in the experience that a child would have who attended one or another, this in spite of the fact that all were purpose-built and had opened between 1971 and 1973. All children might attend full-time, or some might be part-time. There might or might not be babies. The amount of autonomy permitted to the head of the Centre in allocating any or all of the places varied, for which children fees were paid, when and on whose decision. Staffing also varied: all four centres had a teacher in charge, and in two the deputy was also a teacher.

Staff: their training and aims

Information on training and experience was collected for the staff in the four combined centres and three day nurseries and nursery schools. This information was collected for 30 teachers and 124 nursery nurses. Only half of the teachers had specialised in nursery/infant training. One in three of the teachers who had come to the combined centres had no previous experience in a preschool setting. Most of the nursery nurses had NNEB training and most had had an educational placement during training. For about a third, however, this post was their first in preschool and many were very young, almost one third were under twenty years of age and this proportion was higher in combined centres. Few of the staff had been motivated to apply to work in the combined centres either by knowledge of or interest in such a venture. There were wide differences in pay and conditions for different members of staff in the various centres. There was little evidence of difference in staff turn-over between the combined centres and comparative day nurseries: there was some evidence of turnover of teaching staff in the centres.

The teachers and nursery nurses in the combined centres and in the nursery schools and day nurseries in the study were asked to describe their own role and that of the other professionals. In Chapter 6 (Ferri *et al.*, 1981) the findings are presented, mainly in narrative form, with quotations. Teachers in combined centres and in nursery schools also, saw themselves as responsible for the planning and implementation of the educational programme. It is noted that the teachers in all four combined centres interacted mainly with the children aged three and over. The nursery nurses saw themselves as more concerned with the all-round development of the child, and with care and physical well-being particularly where they worked with the younger children.

There had been difficulties in forming working relationships in all four centres, more or less successfully resolved in different centres. Some of the stresses are reflected in the perceptions by the different professionals of the roles of others. It is clear that neither the misperceptions, nor the negative attitudes to the contributions of others had developed only because of working in this close proximity and new type of setting. In some of the centres it appeared they might have been exacerbated, particularly where some of the staff lacked experience and/or appropriate qualifications, and this was combined with differences in status, pay and conditions. What was observed was how different the patterns were in the four centres. In the centre where the head gave clear and direct guidance, where the teaching staff had remained in post, harmonious relationships had been established with clear perceptions of and respect for the roles of each other. In other centres defensive attitudes on the part of teachers and nursery nurses were reported.

The researchers suggest that the present system of separate training for the two groups may have been at the root of some of the problems. The fact that a number of the teachers were neither trained for, nor had previous experience in the preschool field is a matter for concern, and would hardly be-conducive to a respect for their professionalism and may also have led them to be more sensitive in preserving their status.

Observations of staff

Details of the observation aspect of the study are given in Chapter 7 of Ferri *et al.*, (1981). This involved in addition to the combined centres, the nursery schools and day nurseries. To keep the observations comparable in setting the younger children were excluded from this aspect (although a separate study was undertaken of under-threes which is reported in Ferri *et al.*, Chapter 10). Observations were made for each member of staff, predominant activity or behaviour and the nature and context of verbal interactions were recorded on a schedule. Just over half of the staff activity recorded involved interaction with children with wide differences between the schools and the day nurseries and combined centres (76%, 57% and 55% respectively). Clearly there was likely to be more necessary domestic and related work in the two latter types of provision.

Measures of staff involvement in what the researchers referred to as cognitively-orientated activities was recorded as 16% in nursery schools, 9% in combined centres and 5% in day nurseries. Day nursery staff were, however, more frequently observed in 'child care' or 'affective' behaviour.

The researchers suggest thus that in relation to balance of educational/caring role the staffs in combined centres lay between the nursery school and day nursery.

Differences were noted in the proportions of observations during which staff were talking to each other with only 5% of such instances in the schools and 16% in the other two types of provision. Staff in schools were also less likely to be observed giving minimal supervision to children.

There were only 13 teachers in total in this aspect of the study and thus comparisons of the teacher's role in the nursery schools as compared with the combined centres must be treated with caution. More involvement of the teachers in activities other than with children was reported in the centres than in the schools. It is not clear the extent to which this was partly at least the effect of differential administrative duties in a physically larger unit.

There were major differences reported in the child-involved activity by nursery nurses in the different types of nursery (from 71% in nursery school, to 57% in day nursery and 52% in combined centres) and in their 'cognitively orientated' activity (17% in nursery school, 7% in combined centres and 5% in day nursery).

Much more time was observed during which nursery nurses were talking with other members of staff in day nurseries and combined centres than in nursery schools. An examination was made of these patterns within age groups for nursery nurses (the number of teachers was too small for such a comparison) and this showed a higher level of involvement with the children for the oldest group of staff (over 35 years of age) a greater amount of cognitively-orientated activity and social and verbal interaction. These older members of staff also spent less time speaking with other members of staff.

Differences were found between combined centres in relation to involvement with children, one centre in particular was reported to be high in quantity and quality of verbal interaction of staff with children - 'cognitive', social talk and in giving praise, comfort and encouragement to the children. This centre had established the most successful relationship between teachers and nursery nurses.

In this published report details are not given for the observational study. It is difficult therefore to assess the limitations on its generalisability as a result of the nature of the schedule, the selected times of day for observation, whether or not staff in promoted posts were included or not and if so how allowance was made for their differential duties. In Appendix 2 the reader is referred to the British Lending Library for an extensive list of tables: only two summary tables are included in the book (in Chapter 7). It does seem a matter for regret that in a published report of research it has not been possible to include some of the relevant information at least in an Appendix.

Observations of children

The behaviour of the three and four-year-old children in different combined centres and other types of provision was studied, 40 children from the combined centres and 30 each from the schools and day nurseries (with part-time and full-time children, except in the day nurseries where all children were full-time). Two schedules with predefined categories of behaviour were used for the observation study which is reported in Chapter 9 (Ferri *et al.*, 1981). The first schedule recorded predominant activity and social grouping and the second contained categories of verbal interaction. The actual content of speech was not recorded. A ten-second time sample was used and each child was observed at regular intervals for a total period of two hours. These observations took place during 'free play' which was in effect the greater part of the child's day.

It is reported that:

"in the combined centres and nursery schools there appeared to be a much more conscious planning and structuring of activities, built around particular themes or concepts, than was discernible in the day nursery setting, where activities seemed at times to be 'provided' as part of the daily programme in much the same way as meals and toilet routines" (Ferri *et al.*, 1981 p.130).

One strikingly consistent finding cited is the relatively unfavourable position of the children in one of the combined centres where there was more 'drifting' and less contact or verbal interaction with staff which it is suggested may be partly a result of the size and design of that centre; although one of the other centres which was only slightly smaller, had avoided such effects because of differences in organisation and approach of staff. This relates to the findings of Sylva *et al.*(1980) referred to earlier where the size of units is commented upon adversely if open-plan and large, and yet the nursery school there selected as an example of good practice was also large.

Many comparative percentages are cited by the researchers in Chapter 9. It is difficult to assess the generalisability of these, or their statistical significance, as the subgroups are very small and there were different patterns on occasion in different types of provision, or within a type of provision for different groups of children. Another matter of concern is the fact that the observations took place only during 'free play' which it is reported was "the greater part of the child's day in each nursery". There is no detail given as to how the rest of the day was occupied and whether this was differential in the various units or types of unit. It is possible for example that in some units the remainder of the day was devoted to activities of a higher level of cognitive play and greater or lesser contact with adults. The children might or might not have been in groups with adults; children might or might not have been directed to these. In the absence of this information it seems inappropriate to cite these findings in any further detail.

Assessment of children

Information was collected on children's development, based on two successive groups of children. In Chapter 11 (Ferri *et al.*, 1981) the study of children's development is reported which involved 281 and 271 children in the two groups. This aspect involved three combined centres with matched nursery schools and day nurseries. The two groups were initially tested in 1975 or 1976 when the children were about three years six months and they were retested about the end of that school year and the children in the second group were assessed on a further occasion. It was possible to retest 80% of the children. Details of the tests used are given on pp.147-9 of Ferri *et al.*, (1981). It is reported that scores varied with age and social background. There were no differences in either sample of children in their progress after the level of their initial scores was taken into account. On post-test of the group followed into the infant class no differences were reported after pretest scores were taken into account.

Using the same samples a study was made of the children's classroom behaviour as reported by staff. The researchers were less concerned with initial differences than with relative changes. There was little evidence that any differences were maintained into the infant school in the sample followed there, and there were no differences in children who had attended full-time.

These sections of the study are very confusing in presentation as differences are given for one sample, then it is often reported that these did not apply to the second sample. This does show the value of two separate samples from successive year groups. In view of the conflicting information from these on occasion, it could have been made easier for the reader to determine which were generalisable differences being found in both samples. More data could also have been supplied to enable the reader to assess the legitimacy of the conclusions.

DAY NURSERIES 1975-1983

In a recently completed research funded by DHSS, Van der Eyken has reported a comparison of a national study of local authority day nurseries in England between 1975 and 1983. The source of the following information is the report to DHSS entitled *Day Nurseries in Action* (Van der Eyken, 1984).

In 1975 the Department of Child Health Research Unit at Bristol University carried out a study of all preschool provision in England, Scotland and Wales which included 469 local authority day nurseries. In 1983 a random 25 per cent sample of the day nurseries in England was asked to complete the same questionnaire with some additional questions.

In the 1975 CHES survey it was found with regard to day nurseries that:

1) their children were considerably more disadvantaged than those in other provision;

2) they were the only type of provision to take children under two years of age;

3) they contained the largest proportion of handicapped children;

4) they were the only institution capable of offering regular meals, and a large proportion of the children qualified for free meals;

5) 'crisis cases' tended constantly to take preference for admission;

6) day nurseries were found to pay less attention to cognitive development and 40 per cent reported that they made no conscious attempt to facilitate language development.

In short, the picture of day nurseries which emerged in the mid-1970s:

"was one of a hard-pressed service, overwhelmed by demand (often from severely deprived or one-parent families), with a rather traditional 'welfare' approach to the care of children and somewhat isolated from developments in other sectors of preschool provision. Staff tended to be young, qualified in terms of basic NNEB training but with virtually no educational input, and somewhat remote from both other agencies and from the families they tried so hard to serve" (Van der Eyken, 1984 p.12).

In the 1983 survey it was found that the number of Social Services day nurseries in England had increased between 1975 and 1983, the increase in places for children was only about 10 per cent.

1) Many local authorities had changed their criteria for entry to nurseries to give priority to, or include, children considered 'At Risk' or in danger of non-accidental injury. (It was not possible from a study such as this to ascertain whether there had been an increase in such cases:)

2) It is further reported that there was by 1983:

"far less chance of working parents, or even the single working parent, obtaining a place for a child in a day nursery on the simple grounds of their need for day care" (Van der Eyken, 1984 p.viii).

In the 90 day nurseries in the 1983 survey three-quarters of the children had been referred to day nurseries by social services personnel (compared with 44 per cent in 1975). Arrangements were more flexible with some part-time places available if required.

3) There was also evidence of a reduction in the age of children attending.

4) There is some evidence of an increase in ethnic minority children in attendance at the day nurseries in the survey. It is not clear from the evidence how much this can be attributed to demographic changes. There were few staff identified as from ethnic minorities.

5) Some authorities it is reported, had introduced contractual arrangements with families for placement in a day nursery.

6) Between 1975-83 the giving of parental support to parents by staff in day nurseries had increased. Working with parents, a task undertaken by most nurseries, was reported to be causing considerable stresses to staff. There was a dramatic increase in parents' rooms and mother-and-toddler group sessions. Most officers-in-charge expressed concern at the level of training of their staffs which they felt were inadequate for the demands being made on them. The training for most of their staffs was NNEB.

So far the evidence has shown that the staffs in day nurseries were faced with more complex problems, younger children and more priority cases in 1983 than in 1975. A number of officers-in-charge had additional qualifications. A basic training only was common in their staffs who had to work with the children, and now even younger children, a number of handicapped children and children from ethnic minorities (although few of the staff were from ethnic minorities) and with parents.

The necessity for shift systems meant that even with apparently 'adequate' staffing ratios there were still problems for continuity for individual children and major organisational problems for the officers-in-charge. They had to relate to any outside agencies, undertake the necessary administrative work and organise their staff's interactions with the children. In their aims as stated, the staff in the day nurseries in 1983 were more likely to make special efforts in the area of language development and some reported they developed special programmes for children about to enter primary school. There can be no evidence of the extent to which this was carried out in practice, as no observations were made in the units.

One aspect which is particularly relevant to this report is the availability of teachers in day nurseries, made possible according to Van der Eyken by the 1980 Education Act which meant that teachers working in nurseries would continue to be subject to the general directions of their head teacher (Van der Eyken, 1984 p.120). The aim was to make possible interchange of expertise and resources. By 1983, however, only 15 of the day nurseries in the study had the services of a teacher at least once a week and only seven full-time. Some of these were members of staff who had a teaching qualification rather than the type of arrangement referred to above. Indeed one such day nursery with three teachers on staff changed its function in 1982 to that of a family centre (p.122). Day nurseries with teachers attached reported greater involvement with individual children or groups to facilitate language development. The teachers working in day nurseries are reported as working in a variety of ways either alone or alongside day care staff and helping with parents and family groups. Although there was some increase in contact with schools in day nurseries where there were teachers this was still reported to be limited (p.128).

The evidence presented so far is taken from the questionnaire returns. Also available on this aspect, however, is some evidence, cited by Van der Eyken, from the first year of one authority's project introducing teachers into day nurseries, that of the Inner London Education Authority (See Van der Eyken, 1984 pp.129-134). Reference is made to the defensive attitude of the day nursery staffs who saw the teachers as a threat. Problems of high staff turnover in the day nurseries are also mentioned (noted also in Bain and Barnett, 1980). Some of the possible areas of impact from the introduction of an experienced qualified teacher are noted, including acting as a model for inexperienced NNEB staff, helping set up assessment procedures, setting up a toy library, making contact with other preschool provision and with statutory agencies.

Van der Eyken claims that there is evidence from the survey that day nursery staffs are struggling with considerable changes

> "whose cumulative effect not only challenges their ability to cope with rising demands, but whose ramifications affect the wider field of under-fives provision within the community, and therefore have important implications for policy makers" (Van der Eyken, 1984 p.220).

A number of recommendations for policy and further research are made which include the following needs:

- to attempt to recruit more mature students to work in day nurseries, and those from ethnic minorities;

- for a further examination of interdepartmental liaison;

- to study factors related to staff turnover and absence;

- to examine both initial and in-service training for staffs;

- a study of the subsequent development in primary school of children who have attended day nurseries;

- support for childminders from DHSS and their integration with other services to enable a 'flexible day care service' to be provided. (See Van der Eyken, 1984 pages 221-223).

DAY NURSERIES: SOME EVIDENCE FROM INTERVIEWS OF STAFF

The present author undertook two studies which involved day nurseries as well as other types of preschool unit. These studies had as their focus integration of children with special needs in ordinary preschool provision. The studies included interviews with the person in charge of each unit to explore their training, views of and knowledge concerning handicapped children and also other aspects of the life of their unit. Some of the interview information is pertinent to the current discussion, the remaining aspects will be reported when discussing issues of integration of children with special needs. Both of these studies were funded by DES, the first in Scotland in 1976-77, the second in the West Midlands in 1979-81.

The study in Scotland in 1976-77 directed by Clark, included all nine local authority day nurseries in the Grampian Region, referred to in that Region as pre-school day centres, (with 321 children attending, most full-time). At that time all day nurseries were the responsibility of a nursery nurse with additional staffing of nursery nurses; none had any teachers on staff. The day nurseries reported a higher incidence of children with handicapping conditions attending than other types of unit and it was clear from the descriptions that some of these children were very disturbed or hand-icapped. Other agencies were involved with a number of these children and some had parents who were psychiatrically disturbed or handicapped. (See Clark and Cheyne, 1979 pp.178-180). This is clearly an additional problem faced by the staffs in such units. The study in the West Midlands in 1979-81 (see Clark, Robson and Browning, 1982) involved a similar design and all twelve local authority day nur-series in the research area of the City of Birmingham (with 724 children, most attending full-time), almost half the children in such day nurseries in Birmingham. All nine day nurseries in Coventry were also included in the study (with 536 children, most attending full-time). The person in charge of each of these 21 units was inter-viewed. Many preschool units in Birmingham and Coventry had many children of Asian ethnic origin for whom English was a second language: there were, however, many more such children in nursery schools and classes than in day nurseries.

The day nurseries were similarly staffed to those in Scotland with an 'officer-in-charge' or matron and nursery nurses (sometimes supported by unqualified child assistants). Details were not collected in these studies on the age of the staffs. Four of these nurseries had the services of a teacher on a full-time basis and two on a part-time basis. The person in charge (officer-in-charge or matron) of most of the day nurseries felt the accommodation was inadequate even for present purposes, before considering any changes required for handicapped children. Lack of space was the main problem reported, and it is significant that most matrons mentioned in this con-nection the need for a parents' room since parent counselling was now an important function. Outside play areas were considered inadequate, important in view of the fact that most of their children attended for long hours each day, all year.

Most of the matrons of the day nurseries held NNEB or equivalent qualifications. Most felt their training had not been adequate for their present responsibilities, or even for the post of nursery nurse (although they felt that current training was becoming more sensitive to these needs). They cited in this connection that they felt the function of the day nursery and hence of the matron had changed dramatically during the past ten years. They felt that previously the day nurseries had catered for children whose parents were in full-time employment. Now many of the children came from one-parent families or were 'at risk' in the home. Almost all the children were priority admissions suffering from some degree of social/emotional deprivation. In addition to dealing with parent counselling they reported they often had to cope with psychiatric illnesses of which they have little experience.

In addition to interviews of staff in charge in all the preschool units, an observational study of children with special needs and control children in 15 ordinary preschool units was part of the research design, included were three day nurseries (See Clark *et al.*, 1982 Chapter 8).

These two studies by Clark reported briefly above, which involved all the local authority day nurseries in selected areas, indicate yet another dimension of the stresses under which the staffs in day nurseries operate. They also support the comments in the survey by Van der Eyken, 1984) indicating that the nature of the population of children in day nurseries appears to be changing. The problems may now be even more complex than those in the day nurseries in the studies undertaken in the seventies.

A RECENT PROJECT

A more recent project on 'Parents in partnership: services for families with young children, ' based at the National Children's Bureau from 1983-86. was funded by DHSS and had an additional grant from the Scottish Office. A recently published report contains case study descriptions of selected centres including family centres and a day nursery. The schemes included in the project were selected from those working towards improving relationships between parents and professionals (Pugh *et al.*, 1987)

CHAPTER 9   CHILDMINDERS

'Childminder' is the term used in Britain for a person who cares for children other than their own in their home, for reward. Such persons are required by law to register with their local authority. It is clear from the DHSS statistics that there has been a dramatic increase in the numbers of registered childminders. The extent to which that represents as large an increase in available places for children is not clear: there may have been an increase in the proportion of childminders who register.

It is clear that currently State provision in day nurseries is unlikely to be available for the young children of mothers who wish to work or require to work, or even for those of single parent families. Where there are no relatives to care for such young children, or the parents cannot dovetail their working hours, many such children must spend much or all of their day with childminders, registered or unregistered, (or in private day nurseries possibly such as those described in the study by Garland and White, 1980).

THE CONTEXT IN THE SEVENTIES

A small-scale study was conducted in London Boroughs in 1975-76 for DHSS by the Thomas Coram Research Unit, London University, to investigate the quality of care given by registered childminders. It involved interviews of minders and mothers, observations of 27 children with minder and with mother and assessment of the children's language. The 39 registered minders studied were together looking after 155 young children and a further 21 older children before and after school.

In the report of that study published as *Minder, Mother and Child* (Mayall and Petrie, 1977) concern was expressed at a number of aspects of the care. This included the large numbers of children cared for by some of the minders single-handed and in conditions, which though materially adequate, were not thought appropriate for the stimulation of young children. These were minders who were registered and a number had some relevant experience and training. Indeed the manner of selection of the sample means that they were probably a favoured sample of such a group at that time in the London area (see Mayall and Petrie, 1977 pp. 20-21).

Any suggestion that such provision at that time was providing a day care which was 'domestic' with warm 'maternal-like care rather than institutional' was not accepted by the researchers. The hours for the minders were long, the pay was low and many of the young children had frequent change of minder. In the Foreword to the report Jack Tizard states:

"The picture we get from this study is of sad, passive children, of anxious, harassed mothers, and hard-pressed minders insensitive to children's needs and distrustful of the mothers - who in turn are resentful of the minders" (Mayall and Petrie, 1977 p.11)

Mayall and Petrie in Chapter 9 discuss the implications of their findings and in Chapter 10 make a series of proposals to improve the service.

In the mid-seventies great concern had been expressed by a number of people, including the research workers noted above, concerning the conditions in which some children in such provision were spending their days (see Bryant, Harris and Newton, 1980 Chapter 1, 'What do we know about minding?'). As a result studies were funded within the Nursery Research Programme into such provision.

A further study by Mayall and Petrie was funded by DHSS with as its focus day care in day nurseries and at minders for children aged under two years of age. The focus in their earlier study having been on children over two years of age.

In view of the focus of this current report it is not appropriate to give a comprehensive assessment of the research on childminders, particularly that with a focus on children under two years of age. Two studies of childminders with a focus on children over two years of age which were funded within the 'Programme' were felt to be relevant to the current report. The first, which was part of the Oxford Preschool Research directed by Bruner, was carried out in Oxfordshire using a similar methodology to the study in London in 1975-76 referred to above (Mayall and Petrie, 1977). The other study funded by DHSS and undertaken in Staffordshire by Davie has recently been completed (Davie, 1986).

CHILDREN AND MINDERS

This study of registered childminders was undertaken in Oxfordshire starting in 1976 at a time when in that county there was low provision of day nursery places. A local working party set up to review provision of preschool facilities for children aged 0-5 years had made a number of recommendations with regard to supervision of childminders (see Bryant *et al.*, 1980 pp. 29-30). The research workers expected to find minding in Oxfordshire rather different from the picture which had been painted of minding in large cities, (as in the study by Mayall and Petrie, 1977). They expected to find better housing, fewer children per minder, fewer language problems, more part-time minding and better local facilities such as parks and open spaces.

Aims

There were two aims of the survey, first to determine who were the main users and second the quality of care provided. It was the intention also to look at unregistered minders; this was not in the end undertaken.

The Sample

The sample of minders was 'randomly selected' from the registers kept by the Social Services Department; a two in five sample was drawn of which 68 were currently minding, 75 further were available but not currently minding and a further 26 were no longer interested in minding. This immediately reveals limitations in any such register (noted also by Davie to be discussed later). The sample traced and willing to co-operate was 165 minders, 91 per cent of those in the original two-in-five sample (66 active, 73 inactive and 26 ex-minders). The mothers and children were selected from those attending (98 children including some siblings). One child from each minder was selected. Just under half the children were the only minded child currently with the minder. Details are given of differences between the selected children and the total number of children with these minders (Bryant *et al.*, 1980 pp.35-36). The 66 'mothers' selected (of which 63 agreed to be interviewed) included, it is noted, four fathers who are throughout the text included within 'mothers' (as distinct from childminders)!

The Study

The information was obtained by means of a structured interview. Detailed information was gained on a previous day's events. In addition to utilizing the interview to gain information from minder and mother the interview was used as an opportunity to observe the behaviour of the child in relation to mother and minder during the first twenty minutes of the interview (to provide similar observations to those undertaken in London (by Mayall and Petrie, 1977) for comparative purposes. Additionally an assessment was made of all toys available at home and at the minders.

Mothers and minders

Data on minders is available on a total sample of 165 (including active, inactive and ex-minders) and 63 mothers, one for each minder (p.37). The minders were older on average than the mothers, more likely to have had lasting marriages, all but one had a family but only half had preschool children, they had larger families (half had three or more children). Most minders had lived in the current area for a number of years (in marked contrast to the mothers) and were more likely also to have parents or relatives in the area.

In this study mothers were found to come from higher social class than minders (using husband's occupation) and there were differences in mothers' and minders' educational background. Reasons for working given by the mothers who were using minders included need for money, being bored and lonely. In a third of cases the mother already knew the minder, in others the recommendation was from the mother of another minded child. The Social Services list and to a less extent health visitors were sources for children to mind.

Reasons for minding given included 'starting as a favour', but common was 'company for their own child' and the fact that they did not want to leave their own child. 'Helping a friend' and 'love of young children' tended to be given as a reason by different minders and it is suggested that in some of the former the 'minding' might be a 'onceoff' situation. A number of minders registered only after initial experience of minding. They had learnt of the need to register from a variety of sources. After registration some had been asked to make alterations, which some had undertaken. Minders appeared to regard registration as useful in that it meant they were within the law and also that the register was a source for children. The minders in this study did not appear to be actively seeking children even where they had vacancies. In most instances no 'rules' concerning the minding had been put on paper by the minder.

The children selected for study and the others attending the same minder ranged in age from under six months to over four years of age, but there were few babies at minders.

There were wide differences in the time at the minder from as little as four hours on one day a week to 70 hours over seven days a week with about 30 hours as the average. For over half the children the greater part of their waking hours was with the minder and the amount of time was not related to age.

Children and Minders

The majority of the three and four-year-olds at minders went to playgroups or nursery school or class as well as the minder. Those arrangements had sometimes been suggested by the minder (for example if their own child was already going) and it was sometimes the minder and not the mother who had taken the child on the first day.

With regard to stability of childminding arrangements, it was found for a number the arrangements were more stable than had been reported by others and there were only a few instances of frequent changes. It should be noted that the way of sampling would have tended to include in the survey the more stable arrangements (noted by Bryant et al., 1980 p.148).

The children's life at the minders was generally at a physically high standard, most had gardens, and most were allowed the free run of the house. About a similar proportion of mothers and minders had a good or poor selection of toys. Two-thirds of the sample children had other preschool children to play with at the minders and some appeared to have formed close friendships and some of the others also attended playgroup. The minder's husband is reported in a number of instances to have played an active part.

This picture is contrasted with the study by Mayall and Petrie, in 1977 in London where it is reported that the minded child was rarely the only preschool child and that in some instances there were five or more other under-fives.

Observations at minders

The final aspect of this study is the evidence from the observation of the children made during the early part of the interview of mother and minder. This was based on eight measures, praising, caressing, ability to give a detailed picture of child's development, of the child's interests, expression of sympathetic awareness of child's need, having spent time actually involved with child the previous day and not speaking slightingly of the child, finally the number of approaches initiated by the child to mother or minder. The interviewer also rated the child's behaviour and on a five-point scale the warmth shown by minder or mother to child (see Bryant *et al.*, 1980, Chapter 8).

The authors compare the children's approaches to mother and minder and of the 'minded' child and minder's child. They found most children did make approaches to the minder and did not find similar evidence to that reported by Mayall and Petrie. Numbers of approaches were not related to numbers of adults present or age of child or numbers of hours at minder. A study was made in detail of the 19 children who took virtually no notice of the minder; who appeared to be having difficulties in making relationships (p.171). This measure of 'approach' is a difficult measure to assess as it could be the result of an active child with a warm relationship with an adult or a demanding or insecure child. Furthermore lack of approach during the interview could be a mark of a self-possessed young child not wishing to interrupt an adult conversation, or lack of warm relationships, or indifference to other people.

It is difficult to assess the significance of this and some of the related evidence as there are so many other variables including, among others, the age of the children, the presence of the interviewer actively involved with the adult. Likewise the mother, more than the minder, might have attempted to show a concern for her child in the presence of the interviewer concerned with the care of young children of working mothers. That there are difficulties in interpretation is noted by the researchers (on pp.178-9). They do, however, discuss differences between their groups described as 'quiet' (15), 'mixed' (26), and 'lively' (17). In several instances in the quiet or mixed group there had been a reported break-up in the family. There were others where the researchers felt the relationship with the parents was poor. They note several instances in the mixed group, however, of a parent with particularly good relationships with their children including the divorced or separated parents (including a 'single' father). There were also a few mothers who were either neglecting or abusing their children, several involved in legal action, there were several instances of mental illness in the parents, there were children who had persistent illness.

In short it is suggested that the children's home lives had some influence on how they behaved at the minders though what the actual causal relationship is they admit is not clear (p.189). There were some of the children who were 'quiet' at the minders without any such traumatic circumstances; the background of these minders was then studied.

There was some evidence of differences in the minders' attitude and approach to the children in the 'quiet' group but what cannot be established by this study is whether there is a causal relationship and if so to what extent the quiet, withdrawn unresponsive child is a cause or result of the minder's behaviour.

From their evidence in this study the researchers do not feel it is possible to conclude that for most children the relationships with the minder are "close and satisfying ones": To quote:

"Three in five children seemed to be quiet and detached, or at least not very involved with their minders, and more than one in four were disturbed or distressed there or had impoverished speech" (Bryant *et al.*, 1980 p.201).

They suggest that this is not because they are "cold and unloving women, nor that they are indifferent to the children they mind" (p.201). They point out that there is, however, not evidence that these particular children would necessarily be better at home with their parent(s), many of whom were coping with very stressful circumstances, were single parents or were suffering from mental illness.

"Furthermore, it is quite possible that the very good relationships we found between some mothers and children in this group were made possible just because the mothers did go out to work and got away from their children for a while" (Bryant *et al.*, 1980 p.204).

In the book from which this material has been taken (that by Bryant *et al.*, 1980) considerable detail is provided and the interpretations of the behaviour and interactions observed between minders, mother and children are in the main cautious and tentative. The reader who only consults *Under Five in Britain* (Bruner, 1980, Chapter 6) to obtain a picture of this study could, however, be forgiven for assuming a rather different kind of study had taken place since he claims:

"There seems every reason for concluding on the basis of this study that the present practice of childminding will increase maladjustment in the generation exposed to it" (Bruner, 1980 p.127).

This may be a legitimate concern, but is not a justified conclusion from a study of a small group of preschool children from a wide age range and variety of backgrounds in which the children were studied in the two settings of the home of the minders and mothers, while mother and minder in turn were interviewed.

Minding in Oxfordshire probably compares favourably with minding elsewhere, at least in inner city areas. There were certainly good physical conditions, fewer children with each minder, and indeed many minders who were not currently minding children. There were in Oxfordshire good housing conditions and fewer single parents. It is thus important not to over generalise either from a study such as this or from studies in urban areas of multiple deprivation with fewer long stay inhabitants to provide stability in home day caring.

The more recently completed study by Davie will now be considered to establish how comparable were its findings to those noted above.

CHILDMINDING : PRACTICE AND POTENTIAL

The study funded by DHSS within the Nursery Research Programme directed by John Hutt and Charmian Davie at the University of Keele entitled 'An Investigation into Childminding Practice' was funded from 1979 for four years. The report on the study of childminding in Staffordshire recently submitted to DHSS (Davie, 1986) is the basis for the following information. In her introduction Davie gives some detail on the current position with regard to childminding. She notes for example, that DHSS circulars now recommend that individual childminders should only be registered for care for up to three children under the age of five years. Furthermore local authorities may use childminders in a similar way to day nurseries for placing priority children; in which case the local authority may pay the necessary fees. There are reported to be considerable savings in cost in utilizing such provision as an alternative to day nurseryattendance. In the majority of cases, however, the arrangements between minders and parents are private. Thus as Davie reports, DHSS was interested in what arrangements parents make and how knowledgeable they are on preschool provision. The extent to which the care by unregistered and registered minders differs was also a matter for concern.

Evidence on childminding

For Stage 1 of the study four separate primary school catchment areas in Staffordshire were identified with different characteristics. Leaflets were distributed to households, followed by visits in order to contact everybody with a child aged under five years of age or who looked after a child under five years old in order to find out their views on preschool facilities. About 1600 households were contacted and 160 interviews conducted. In 'Asian ethnic origin' households where there was no English speaker to act as interpreter the team returned with an interpreter for Urdu and Punjabi, or for Bengali. Additional interviews of childminders were included outside these areas to make up the numbers. All childminders in these areas were also contacted. Few were found to be currently minding children under five years of age: this sample thus provided insufficient numbers for the planned observational aspect. Further minders were therefore identified from the register.

The researchers contacted 375 minders, 72 of these registered were minding a child under five years of age at the time. Of 150 minders who had minded children in the past, 27% had only minded one child and about half from two to five children. There were a few who estimated that in the course of their minding career they had cared for over a hundred children. A number of those who were now no longer minding reported that those for whom they had minded had been made redundant; some felt they had now little chance of getting children to mind; some had advertised with no success. All but three of the 72 current childminders were interviewed covering a total of 121 minded children and 64 parent interviews were completed.

A study was made of the knowledge of preschool facilities of those parents and minders interviewed. Playgroups were the most frequently cited facility and the adults seemed better informed on them than local authority facilities. They were for example, found to be particularly unsure about payment. The childminders interviewed were on the whole better informed than parents. It was found that a greater proportion of two and three-year-olds attending minders were attending an additional preschool facility than those not attending minders and they were more likely to use playgroups than were mothers. In the four to five year-old age range very few of either group were not attending any preschool unit.

Nearly half of the mothers interviewed who did not use childminders had worked in some capacity since the birth of one or all of their children under five at the time of the interview (32% were working at the time of the interview). Many were not working full-time and fathers played an important role. No child was reported to have more than three different caretakers. Of the children of Asian origin whose parents were interviewed and who were not attending childminders, 15 of 16 parents were not born in Britain.

All the children aged over three and a half years were attending nursery school or class and all those interviewed realised there was such a facility and intended sending their children. Lack of information and misunderstanding about available preschool facilities was identified in a number of those interviewed, including the headteachers of two of the primary schools interviewed during the project.

In this study the minder and minded children's households were mainly working-class. Where mothers used childminders they were more likely to have continued in the type of job they had had before the children's birth. Most minders were willing to accept children under two years of age and the majority would accept babies. A number of children had had a change of minder because of the parent's dissatisfaction with the arrangement. The potential in such situations for spread of rumour and the difficulty in refuting or even checking the evidence is stressed. Thus it was difficult to ascertain how valid were any of the criticisms where the situation was not one under observation.

A wide range of practical issues is discussed in Chapter 5 of Davie (1986), covering child rearing, discipline, safety, illnesses, contacts between minder and parent.

Parents were in general satisfied with food provided by the minders although there were in some instances differences of opinion concerned with the amounts of snacks or sweets allowed. Most parents reported having opportunities to chat at least briefly with minders about the children. There neither appeared to be a greater number of accidents or greater ill-health in children attending minders.

Misunderstandings on occasion appeared concerning fees to be paid where there had not been sufficient clarification with regard to extras, increases or payment during absence. It is suggested guidelines could help minders with this aspect and also avoid friction.

Observational Studies

In the two settings, at home and at the minders, fourteen children aged between 28 and 39 months, each attending a different minder, were observed. To keep a relatively homogeneous group, the children selected were those who were both walking and talking. It had been hoped to observe these children as compared with the minder's own young children; few minders were found to have their own young children at home at the same time as the minded child. For 14 children observations were made in behaviour and speech categories of the minder's behaviour and speech and of the mother and the target child on a two minute observation cycle. Behavioural conflicts or 'incidents' were particularly concentrated upon. Each child was observed on a 'dummy' observation in each situation to habituate the target child, adults and siblings.

The findings are reported and compared with those of the two other researches (discussed earlier, by Mayall and Petrie, 1977 and Bryant *et al.*, 1980) whose methodology they attempted to replicate in addition to their own observational study.

There were a number of practical difficulties in this aspect and in the evaluation of any evidence collected (see Davie, 1986 pp.100-104). Davie draws attention to the fact that even in their independent observations other preschool children were present at the minders and not at home. Thus the minder's attention was spread over several children. They found the range of toys available to be similar, and comparable to their study of children in their homes (Davie *et al.*, 1984).

They found higher levels of speech to children from minders than mothers to children. On 'demands' and 'questions' to adults children showed higher levels at home, that is on items which required child initiation.

The child appeared less assertive at minders, which is reflected in 'incident' measures where children appeared to provoke more behavioural conflicts at home.

These observations are in agreement with the interview data from minders and mothers. It is pointed out by Davie that the sorts of analyses undertaken in the two other studies to which she refers were made retrospectively and about this she expresses concern (that is in the studies of Mayall and Petrie (1977) and that of Bryant *et al.* (1980) cited earlier).

Implications of the findings

Davie considers relevant information from the studies by Garland and White in day nurseries, and by Bain and Barnett(1980) in a single nursery discussed earlier in this report) and from other studies in preschool units (also reported here) and evidence from a study by Cleave *et al.*, 1982 concerning children's transition from various types of preschool settings to primary school.

Davie claims, when consideration is given to the amount of time the child receives attention in different types of preschool setting, the childminders and home settings gave by far the greatest percentages. There were high figures also for initiations at home and the minders, with the children initiating far more themselves in both these settings. Davie then observes from a range of this evidence that, to quote:

"All these studies would suggest that the child at home behaves differently to when he is in any other environment. The child is less confident and assertive and more likely to be watchful and make less frequent demands on adults. To suggest that this is a characteristic specific to the childminding situation alone appears contrary to the evidence" (Davie, 1986 p.112).

Davie considers areas in which there appeared to be conflict between parent and minder. The minders were found more often to be critical of parents than were parents of minders. It was also found that parents did not appear aware of the minder's criticisms. Davie recommends the use of contracts to cover a number of basic points to do with practical aspects such as fees, holidays, food, incidental expenses, parental permission for outings. Other aspects which could be discussed to avoid later conflict, though not contained in any contract, are childrearing and the child's interests and fears.

From the evidence of this study the register of childminders was out of date and therefore was not a useful source for parents seeking minders. Chapter 9 of the report by Davie is devoted to issues concerned with registration and relationship between the minders and Social Services and a number of recommendations are made (on pages 156-157).

In the final chapter of her report Davie notes that:

"Two recent reports on childminding undertaken in London and Oxfordshire, respectively (Mayall and Petrie, 1983 and Bryant *et al.*, 1980) have suggested that there is something uniquely unsatisfactory in the childminding situation. They consider that children at minders' may behave in a withdrawn and passive manner. Our data suggest that children may be more inhibited at the childminders' than they are at home but not in a manner which should cause concern" (Davie, 1986 p.162).

Evidence is then provided of differences in children's behaviour in a variety of settings from that in their own home.

"This inhibition in the children's behaviour is therefore not exclusively confined to the childminding situation. The assertion that this inhibition is damaging is questionable" (Davie, 1986 p.162).

Davie notes, that the childminders in Staffordshire did not have to contend with overcrowding and lack of outdoor play space and steep flights of stairs; there was also a relatively low level of immigrant families in contrast to an area such as London. The role of childminders is changing and she suggests mothers using childminders may well be women pursuing professional careers.

She also stresses that to see a childminder as a mother substitute would be a mistake, their job on which they were concentrating was the care of young children. Indeed those in her study were careful not to usurp the mother's role. The childminders are reported for example to have encouraged the children to talk about experiences they had with their parents.

Children in Staffordshire who were attending the childminders in this study were found to be experiencing homelike care by one person with whom they could form a warm attachment and were also able to benefit from attendance at playgroup or nursery school with a continuity of care at the minder which might continue when they entered the infant school.

Davie, on the basis of her study, gives priority to improving channels by which parents may be helped to find childminders and to the encouragement of local authorities to extend their supervision of registered childminders to ensure those listed do provide at least minimum standards of child care.

FURTHER RESEARCH ON CHILDMINDING AND DAY CARE

Brief reference will be made to two further studies funded by DHSS.

The first of these researches which was on childminding was undertaken by Elsa Ferri and Dorothy Birchall at the National Children's Bureau. It was concerned with support services for childminders in the form of supervision, meetings and material assistance. The study commenced in 1983, the report has recently been submitted to DHSS and a publication is expected shortly. The research was undertaken in 20 local authority areas, selected because of the extensive and varied nature of the support they provided. Following investigation of the nature of these services semi-structured interviews of 200 childminders in four of the areas were undertaken to assess their perceptions of the support they receive and would wish.

The second research which is at the Thomas Coram Research Unit, University of London is a 'longitudinal study of the effects of different forms of day care on infants and young children with full-time working mothers'. Some preliminary results of this study, directed by Peter Moss and Edward Melhuish, were reported at a meeting of the Association of Child Psychology and Psychiatry in London in June 1986. The study is concerned with the experiences and development of children who receive different forms of day care because their parents are in full-time employment. This is a study of dual earner households where the mother has resumed full-time employment within nine months of the birth of the first child. The study includes care by relatives, minders and in day nurseries. None of the children were, however, in State nurseries (they were either work-place, voluntary or private).

Economically disadvantaged families are underrepresented particularly in certain types of placement. This could be because of the relative youth of the sample of children, but also the criterion of dual earner households. The sample is from around the London area and women in professional and managerial jobs are over-represented. Most of this sample is of mothers who returned to work before the 'statutory maternity leave' ended. By the time the children were 18 months one quarter of the mothers were no longer in full-time employment. This is an ongoing project with detailed observations over time of the continuing sample of young children in the different settings. Its findings, while they may be of concern to social policy makers in relation to the ways in which these very young children spend their days, the numbers of caretakers to whom they must relate, and their development over time, are not of specific relevance to the current report.

CHAPTER 10 PARENTS AND PRESCHOOL EDUCATION

INTRODUCTION

Research on two issues will be considered in this chapter, namely, parental involvement in preschool education, and home visiting by professionals concerned with the education of preschool children. There has been encouragement and perhaps even pressure to involve parents, but what is not always clear is the aims in such involvement, and the extent to which it is for the benefit of the child, the parent or the professional. The parents of children attending a preschool unit may be encouraged or expected to become involved, or discouraged from involvement unless the circumstances are exceptional. Parental involvement might mean any or all of the following:

a pre-entry visit by child and mother to the preschool unit,

a brief settling in of the child,

attendance at parents' meetings,

regular parental help in working directly with children in the unit,

fund raising or other such help,

direct concern with management.

In the introduction to a recently published report on 'Partnership in Action', a useful framework for discussion of parental involvement in preschool centres is set out under five headings, as follows:

1. Non-participation

    active, by choice (because the parent is working, or wishes time away)

    passive, where the parent might wish to participate, but for a variety of reasons does not (lack of confidence, or of English, depressed, or has younger children)

2. Support(external)

    moral support, fund raising, materials etc.

3. Participation

    as helper, or as learner

4. Partnership

between individual parent and professional, parents and professionals in general, with parents as workers in the unit or home visiting, or parents and policy-makers

5. Control

selecting children, or staff, managing resources.

(Pugh, Aplin, De'Ath and Moxon, 1987, 1 and 2).

A development project based at the National Children's Bureau from 1983-86, funded by DHSS and a small grant from the Scottish Office, is reported in the above publication. Following a postal enquiry to the main providers of services for the under fives, social services, health, education and the voluntary sector, 130 schemes were visited.

The team then studied 16 schemes in detail, including some jointly funded schemes. Those chosen were all attempting to improve a partnership with parents. Case histories describing twelve of these schemes are presented in the recent publication.

RESEARCH CONTEXT

'Parental involvement in nursery education' was one of the five priority areas identified by the DES Management Committee for research (DES, 1975a). Two funded researches on parental involvement listed in the DES report on Under Fives (DES, 1981) were those by Barbara Tizard, and by Teresa Smith within the Oxford Preschool Research. In the reports of these studies a section is devoted to the research background and issues then current which led to such a focus (See Tizard, Mortimore and Burchell, 1981 Chapters 1 and 2 and Smith, 1980 Chapter 2). This topic was considered earlier in this report, including the assumptions then current of inadequacies in the homes of many preschool children, and the way these led also to the establishment of home visiting programmes aimed at encouraging parents to play with their children in what were regarded as more dynamic and cognitively demanding ways. One such initiative was that in the Lothian Region in Scotland, where a research project was funded to extend it and evaluate its effects (Raven, 1980 and McCail, 1981). Another study, also in Scotland, was that by Donachy whose programme encouraged parents to interact with their preschool child. It was a school-based project which involved parents attending either a primary school or nursery school for weekly group discussions which were chaired by a teacher (Donachy 1976;1979). Although the above studies took place in the seventies, and thus some of the findings may now be dated, many of the issues they raise are still pertinent. It therefore seems important to note their main findings. Some of the studies reported in other sections of this report, while not funded specifically to study parental involvement, do consider this, for example in the context of observation in preschool units, where some of the adults observed might indeed be parents of the

G

children attending. Others have included questions on parental involvement in interviews or questionnaires to staff or to parents.

One such study, on 'demand and uptake', took place in Lothian Region of Scotland, an area which already in the seventies had a high enough level of preschool provision for most children to attend a nursery school or class or playgroup before entry to primary school (where the educational home visiting scheme referred to above took place). Parental involvement was one of the topics discussed in the interviews of about 600 parents. Over 20% of parents whose children attended playgroups were involved in its organisation, and a comparable number stayed on rota days, however, over 20% did not have the contact of taking and collecting the child, or even where they did about 20% did not go into the facility; others went in for only a few minutes. In contrast, while few parents were involved on a rota in attendance at nursery schools or were involved in its organisation, almost all parents had the contact of delivering their child, and over half went in at least for a few minutes. In day nurseries, most mothers took their child, some might stay until their child was settled, but were not involved in other ways (see Haystead, Howarth and Strachan, 1980 pp.81-85). Some parents although involved with their child at home did not wish to be involved in the preschool unit, or to have other parents involved; some felt they would not have been welcome. While one reason for some parents not taking the child was shared transport, it is important to note that parental involvement in all forms of provision varies greatly in relation to circumstances, as well as the views of staff and parents.

Two other studies are *Combined Nursery Centres* (Ferri, Birchall, Gingell and Gipps, 1981), and *The First Transition* (Blatchford, Battle and Mays, 1982). The latter research in addition to detailed study of a small group of children at transition from home to preschool included a survey of preschool units whose attitudes to parental involvement at the point of children's entry were explored. Even with regard to this specific aspect there were widely different views held by staff as to whether parents should be expected to stay, should remain only if the child was felt to be upset, or be actively discouraged from staying. As these studies also were undertaken in the seventies, it will perhaps suffice to draw attention to them, and to cite evidence only from the large scale CHES national sample of children and the related national study of preschool units based on the University of Bristol.

A four-year evaluation of Home-Start over the period 1974-78 by Van der Eyken, sponsored by SSRC and DHSS, gives a description of a rather different type of parental involvement (Van der Eyken, 1982). Home- Start is aimed at under-fives but is equally concerned with parents in their own right also, and involves volunteers rather than professionals. Further details on this and other initiatives are to be found in *The Needs of Parents* (Pugh and De'Ath, 1984).

Several recent studies contain evidence relevant to the roles of parents in their children's education, and on differences between the attitudes of staffs in many preschool units and expectations of the teachers of reception classes. In reception classes there will now be a greater proportion of under fives, and younger four-year-olds, children who, had they been of preschool age at the time of the researches noted above, might have been either still at home, or in a preschool unit. Two relevant studies are *Starting School: an evaluation of the experience* (Barrett, 1986) and *Continuity in Early Education: the role of the parents* (Watt and Flett, 1985). These researches are reported in detail in the section on Continuity. Although 'parent' is the term most frequently used in the reports of research, there is seldom any reference as to whether or not any fathers were involved, and if so how many. In most instances the researches appear to have been on maternal involvement. One interesting exception is the experimental parental involvement study of Donachy. In that study comparisons were made between the young children's cognitive development when the mothers were involved in a home programme, when the child attended nursery school, and when in addition to attendance the mother was involved. Donachy noted whether or not father as well as mother was involved, and found this to be the case in a number of the high gain children (Donachy, 1979). It is possible that the attitudes of staff to the involvement of mothers and fathers in the preschool, or in working with their child at home, might be very different.

PARENTAL INVOLVEMENT: A NATIONAL SURVEY

A book has been published recently entitled *The Effects of Early Education* (Osborn and Milbank, 1987), the main focus of which is a consideration of long term effects of preschool education based on a follow-up at ten years of age of the national sample of children born in a single week in 1970 in England, Scotland and Wales. Much of the evidence from the national sample collected when the children were five years of age has already been published, as has the information on the national survey of preschool institutions in 1975, the former among other places in Osborn *et al.*, 1984, the latter in Van der Eyken *et al.*, 1984. For the purposes of this discussion on parental involvement probably the best reference is Osborn and Milbank, 1987 Chapter 9, which brings together in a single source the data from the two studies referred to above.

In view of the relatively recent dates of publication of much of this research it is important to note that the information from the national survey of preschool units was collected in 1975 and was based on questionnaire returns, not observation or interviews. Furthermore the children in the national sample were born in 1970, and their preschool education was completed by the time their parents were interviewed in 1975. Since the information is retrospective, the parents may possibly have overestimated their involvement. Furthermore, as was noted earlier, at that time fewer children would have attended preschool units pre 1975 when these children were under five than currently, and the pattern of units attended would also have been different.

The nature and size of the sample made it possible to consider differences in the extent of involvement in different types of preschool provision, and according to social background and region of the country. It seems worth summarising the findings to set a context for the other researches which were also undertaken in the seventies. The limitations of the evidence and its generalisability must be borne in mind.

Survey of preschool units

The national survey of preschool units involved a questionnaire to staffs, which among other aspects sought information on the extent of involvement of parents in various aspects of the unit, including working with the children. It is admitted that there may be some ambiguity in the question on staffing from which the data on direct parental help was elicited. Many playgroups were established and staffed by parents, or only with the help of parents; it is thus no surprise that a much higher percentage of 'hall' playgroups reported regular or rota parental help than did nursery schools or classes. It should be noted, however, that 22.8% of these playgroups reported no parental helpers. A distinction is made between hall and home playgroups, and in the latter type 63.4% had no parent helpers, more comparable with about 70% in the various maintained provisions. Unfortunately the analysis of involvement in other ways including practical help, attending social events, and involvement in planning and management is tabulated for each type of provision as the percentage of units in which at least one parent is involved. This is very misleading as a comparison since in some units this could be based on an isolated instance of a particular parent. In that aspect also there is the expected evidence that more hall playgroups than nursery schools had at least one parent involved in planning and management (though the difference is only 52.2% and 37.5% measured in this way). Home playgroups are different here also in recording only 7.8% with at least one parent involved in planning and management and an even smaller percentage for consultative committee as compared with these other types of unit. A survey such as this may give an impression of a fair degree of parental involvement in a number of aspects. What cannot be assessed is precisely how many of the parents are involved, and in what ways. Some assessment of this is possible from the related study.

Survey of children

For the total sample of 5, 056 children who attended a preschool unit only 26% of the parents reported that they had given even occasional help with the children (only 12% of the most disadvantaged), while 68.3% of mothers are listed as not giving help to the unit. There are clearly difficulties in teasing out causal factors for differences in relation to social class, region, etc. as these are also related to the type of preschool provision attended. Even in hall playgroups where the incidence of mothers helping was highest, only 38.1% of mothers reported that they had helped with the children (including the category 'less than once a week'); in the home playgroups this was only 14%.

It is easy to assume that lack of parental involvement was due to lack of interest or time. It could also have been a result of staff attitude to parental help, or how the staff and parents view their roles. From a survey study such as the above it is not possible to assess the reasons for involvement or lack of it. The two studies which are reported below make it possible to look at these aspects and to consider the extent to which the level of parental involvement can be raised in units with a wish to do this, also obstacles in the way, for both parents and staff.

PARENTAL INVOLVEMENT IN SCHOOLS: AN INTERVENTION STUDY

In 1975 Barbara Tizard was asked by DES to put forward a proposal concerning parental involvement in nursery education. This three year study from 1976 funded by DES is reported in a book entitled *Involving Parents in Nursery and Infant Schools*, subtitled 'A Source Book for Teachers' (Tizard, Mortimore and Burchell, 1981). The book contains a valuable overview of the context which led to such an emphasis in the seventies, from

> "a variety of relatively distinct but mutually reinforcing influences",

which included

> "evidence of underachievement among working-class children, despite post-war educational reforms"

Among explanations which had been put forward for this had been -

> "working-class ignorance about education, a lack of interest, or a restricted style of parent-child communication" (Tizard *et al.*, 1981 p. 21).

All of these were felt to point to the need for parental involvement, with particular emphasis on the importance of the first five years of children's life. Tizard points also to the growing evidence at that time from parental involvement in the expanding playgroup movement. It was clear that there was official approval in principle for parental involvement, but what this did, or should, mean in practice was less clear.

Aims of the study

One aim of Tizard and her colleagues in their intervention project in 1976 was to study which parents do take up opportunities for involvement when such are made available and what kind of involvement they prefer. Another aim was to study the attitudes of nursery teachers to parental involvement, since there were clearly very different views on which if any roles parents could, or should fulfil in schools. Even where teachers wished to co-operate with parents their training had not prepared them for such roles; the team thus also considered ways to make such ventures more successful. The project is referred to as a descriptive study of parental involvement in action in which the above issues are addressed, rather than an experimental project. The team did not consider it part of their remit to convince teachers that they should involve parents; thus they selected schools where the head teacher and class teacher wished to increase their parental involvement and to be involved in the research. In these schools an intervention study was undertaken to support and extend parental involvement.

The sample

Seven units were selected for the intervention project, all within reach of London, some were nursery classes others nursery schools. They differed in social class composition, educational level of the families, whether or not many of the mothers worked, and if so full- or part-time, and the extent of cultural and/or language barriers to parental involvement. All the units in the study had both three- and four-year-olds, all were staffed by teachers and assistants, and all were run mainly on 'free-play' lines. In all the units the mother stayed for a certain amount of time initially to 'settle' the child. Three of the units, the more middle-class, are reported to have had active parental involvement programmes. The remaining four relied on informal contacts having tried and failed to develop more active involvement. In the units with a high proportion of nonindigenous children there were cultural and language differences, and also many of the mothers worked full-time, with the children cared for by relatives out of school hours.

The findings

The book on the study (Tizard, Mortimore and Burchell, 1981), contains only a brief, very general report of the research, no tables, or precise details of the number or proportions of parents who were interviewed at each stage, and only percentages of parents involved in particular initiatives. The reader is referred to the British Lending Library for nine tables which report the findings in greater detail. General points and specific examples of teacher and parent answers to questions are given, but not details of the interviews. A section is devoted to a brief report of implications of a study involving parents in the teaching of reading which was not part of this research project and to interviews of parents who were involved in toy libraries attached to other units. Much of the book is concerned with practical advice to teachers involved in parental involvement based on the research. Policy recommendations are made, and some of the difficulties encountered are discussed, particularly in the units where a high proportion of the children were from homes differing in language and ethnic background from the staff and where many of the mothers worked full-time. The book contains a number of helpful ideas for those instituting policies of greater parental involvement in schools, or as an aspect in teacher training. Evaluation of the research is, however, not possible from this published source.

Initial observations revealed that the extent of informal contacts with parents tended to be affected by differences in the routine and that conversations were very general. There was little evidence of teachers sharing knowledge with the parents on the child's learning either at school or at home or of suggestions for further work at home. The researchers therefore interviewed the teachers, and parents in their homes (with the aid of an interpreter where necessary) concerning the aims of nursery education to assess the extent of comparability of their perceptions. The most frequent answer by staff, teachers and head teachers, (by 11 of 14) was to enrich the children's language mainly through the medium of play. For some, this was seen as needed to make up for the deficiencies they believed were in the homes. In addition some staff saw as important giving these children 'security'. It is reported that none of the staff mentioned teaching English as a second language as a priority, although all had at least one child for whom English was a second language, and in three units there were many such children. As in a number of other studies in which mothers' views were sought, the mothers are reported not to have been aware of the priority that the staff placed on language and intellectual development, seeing the nursery unit as a place where the children learnt to mix with others. Indeed a number were found to wish that their children were starting on reading and writing, and not to appreciate the educational intent in the available play materials, although they had not expressed this concern to the staff, not wishing to be seen to interfere. Not only did the parents see the role of nursery education differently from the staffs, but also they saw their own roles differently. As was found in most studies at that time, the teachers tended not to believe that the parents were indeed capable of assisting, or willing to help their children at home. As in other studies where the parents were interviewed at home it was found that the parents were both willing and anxious to help their children. They tended, however, to regard as teaching only more didactic instruction in reading and writing. It was felt that even in units such as those in this study staff saw only a one-way model of parental involvement, a wish to change some aspects of the parents' behaviour.

The team discussed with each teacher the evidence from the observations and interviews, and on this basis ways of extending and improving parental involvement were planned. In the first year of the project two days per week were spent in each unit by a member of the research team and in the second year occasional visits were made to four of the units. Twice termly meetings attended by the teachers, head teachers and by advisers were held in London to discuss developments. At the end of the first year staff and parents were interviewed and a second year's projects planned. A questionnaire to parents after the second year's intervention received a very low response rate in some units even after reminders. The researchers give a warning against the use of such a strategy to gauge parental views or interest, as they were aware from other sources of the continuing interest of parents.

A year after completion of the project, by which time the children were in infant school, 42 parents were interviewed, six from each unit, three of those who had been most involved, and three least involved. These interviews were undertaken by a community worker who had not been involved in the project.

The types of intervention which were extended or introduced had the following aims:

Communicating the teachers' aims and methods - which included videos, notices, copies of rhymes and songs used in schools, mother and toddlers' groups;

Widening parents' educational horizons - groups of parents taken to libraries, toy shops etc.;

Involving parents in helping their children at home;

Increasing parental contributions at school;

Organising an exchange of views with parents - which involved in some instances a different pattern in parents' evenings, or home visiting.

During the first year of the project between 30 and 68% of the parents in each unit had been involved in more than half of the activities arranged, and by the second year this had increased to between 50 and 94%. Most mothers were involved, including helping at least once in the nursery unit. In one unit many of the mothers helped on a rota basis, in other units this was true of only a few mothers in each class. Few fathers were involved, and even then mainly in attendance at evening meetings. It is not clear, however, to what extent the staffs were encouraging of the active involvement of fathers within the units.

The most popular activities were the libraries and the parents' meetings which during the project had high attendance. This was attributed to both the care taken to arrange repeat meetings during the day and in the evening to suit parents, possible creches, and particularly the organisation of the meetings around topics of particular concern to the parents. It took longer to gain involvement by more than a very small number of parents in the three multi-ethnic units, and particularly that unit where most children were of Asian ethnic origin. This did, however, increase during the second year of the project. Parents' evenings were well-attended in these units, particularly when videos of the activities were shown. Toy libraries set up in two units were closed because of loss and damage, as was one library. Some families appeared to see toys, and books also, rather as something to keep children amused, possibly on their own. Because of the lack of response to the activities offered in one of the multiracial units a research officer visited the homes to gain a better understanding of the views of the parents concerning education. Lack of support for the activities in the schools was not associated with lack of interest in their children's education. Half the mothers were working and many had grown up in a different culture and educational system. This reinforces the need to ensure that means are found to help parents to understand the aims of the education which their children are receiving, particularly parents from different cultural backgrounds. Otherwise they may not even appreciate that the experiences their children are receiving are indeed education.

> "Our project demonstrated that given extra resources almost all mothers and about 50 per cent of fathers can be drawn into one aspect or another of a nursery parent involvement programme, provided that staff are prepared to visit some parents at home, and provided that when necessary a bilingual relative or friend is available to act as interpreter" (Tizard *et al.*, 1981 p.58).

A year after the end of the project a number of the activities had ceased, some had not had the effect intended by the teachers, while others had survived. Most teachers wished for more time to talk with parents either in school or on home visits. Resources were clearly an important limiting factor. Some staff were positive about involvement in the project, others stressed the difficulties. What became clear was that increasing parental understanding was not easy, even with additional resources. The danger of associating parents' lack of involvement with the school either with lack of involvement with the children, or lack of interest in their education is stressed. The interviews after the end of the project showed that even parents who had been less involved were not necessarily uninterested in their children. Other factors, including working full- or part-time, caring for younger children, or ill-health were among possible reasons. There are many lessons to be learnt from such a project, not least the need to ensure that parents are aware of the aims behind the activities their children are experiencing in school.

PARENTS AND PRESCHOOL

A study of parental involvement in preschool units formed part of the Oxford Preschool Research directed by Bruner, other aspects of which have already been discussed. Since this study took place in only one area, Oxfordshire, which had at the time a very low proportion of mothers working full-time, and since the research was in 1977-8, the findings may no longer be representative of the extent of, nature of, or attitudes of staff to parental involvement. The issues raised in the report are still of current concern, therefore a brief outline of the study will be given (for further details see *Parents and Preschool* (Smith, 1980).

The aims

The nature of parental involvement in a sample of preschool units, also the views of selected staff and parents on different types of involvement was studied. At the time of the research Oxfordshire had 29 nursery schools and classes, and 290 private groups (250 of which were members of the PPA).

The study

An observational study was undertaken in 15 preschool units (3 nursery schools, 4 nursery classes, and 8 playgroups), selected to be representative of different characteristics, which included high and low parental involvement. The observations covered two sessions during which at five minute intervals a note was made of what parents were doing and whether working with children. Discussions were then held with staff and parents in 13 of these groups which did involve parents. In eleven groups parents were actually involved during observations: the numbers involved varied widely, as did the attitude to such help, the way it was organised and its nature.

Staff in all 15 units were interviewed to elicit their views on parental involvement. For some the focus for the unit was the child, and any parental involvement in such contexts might be concerned with settling the child for example. Others saw their unit as for parents and child, with more of a sense of partnership and mutual learning between home and school. These latter were more likely to have parents working alongside children with guidance, and to be more open and accessible to parents at the beginning and ends of sessions.

Interviews of about 60 parents were conducted to explore their views, ten names were taken at random from the register of each of six groups, chosen to give a playgroup, nursery school and class with high and low involvement. 'Servicing', which included maintenance and fund-raising, was the commonest type of help, and management the least common. In the three units where parents helped at the sessions there was considerable variation in numbers who did, and in the nature of what they did. Among parents who were not helping were some who had in the past, but who for a variety of reasons were not able to at present. Some parents who had not been involved or who were not currently involved would have liked to help, others had not been asked or felt their offers had not been taken up. Some parents who had been discouraged from contact with the unit, or had felt so, were thought to be hindered by this in their attempts to help their child at home. An important point made on the basis of the parental interviews, and one made in other studies also, is that parents do not seem to be aware that in their shared relationship with the child there may indeed be a teaching/learning relationship. Some parents who were involved had such an awareness. For some parents the view expressed by staff that at this age one does not 'teach' children, but rather respond to their initiations, caused some confusion. If parents are to see preschool attendance as an aspect of education, and not merely as a preparation for it, clarification of the learning potential in and purposes behind the activities in the preschool need to be spelt out, and illustrated.

The findings

There was no single philosophy with regard either to the advisability or nature of parental involvement. Furthermore there was not a pattern which clearly differentiated the playgroups from the other types of provision, or those with different types of catchment areas. Even where there was active parental involvement within the sessions it was also possible to find some parents who were in the 'network', who were active, and others who were not. This was found even in an open democratic group where involvement was encouraged, but where social class, education or ethnic group might have a subtle effect on who was indeed involved. The extent to which mothers rather than fathers, or indeed only mothers, were interviewed or involved is not clear as the expression used is 'parents'.

What is clear from this study is the complexity of this issue, also that an important determinant of the nature and extent of parental involvement is the philosophy of the staff in the unit, which may, however, not always be explicit. There also appeared to be an untapped reserve of parental interest, of which the staff were not always aware. This book, and that by Tizard referred to earlier (Tizard *et al.*, 1981), could provide evidence as a basis for discussion of this topic in pre- and in-service training of teachers involved in early education to heighten their awareness of assumptions which lie behind educational practices, not least concerning the extent and nature of parental involvement - whether it is expected, encouraged, or tacitly discouraged for at least some parents.

AN EDUCATIONAL HOME VISITING PROJECT

The Lothian Home Visiting Scheme was evaluated in a two-year action research project funded by the Scottish Education Department, and carried out by the Scottish Council for Research in Education. A pilot scheme had been started in 1975 in the Lothian Region of Scotland, with one home visitor attached to a nursery school, to stimulate parental involvement with their children at home. This was extended in 1976 to the appointment of six educational home visitors, teachers selected for their sensitivity and capacity to work with parents in their homes. Five of the home visitors were attached to nursery schools or primary schools with a nursery class, in areas judged to be socially disadvantaged, the other visited families with a handicapped child. Each visited about ten families per week, and about 180 families with a child aged between two and three years of age were involved in the project. The criterion for selecting families was that they were thought likely to benefit; excluded were those where multiple problems were thought likely to prevent them focusing on the educational activities of the project. The brief for the home visitors was to visit the homes for about one hour per week and work with the children in the presence of the mother. While the general approach was influenced by the then current views, the styles adopted by the visitors varied. A number of fathers were involved, some actively during the visits.

The Divisional Educational Officer in Lothian Region, on whose initiative the home visiting scheme was established, has outlined the context and thinking behind the scheme (MacFadyen, 1980), which was strongly influenced by the work of Levenstein in the U.S.A. who employed toy demonstrators, initially trained as social workers, to visit mothers in their homes. MacFadyen was impressed, not only by the measured effects quoted on the children's intelligence, but also by the fact that the programme was within the natural setting of the family. He was clearly not as convinced as others at the time that the parents were incapable of helping their young children, or were disinterested in their education, rather, many were isolated and lonely, overcome by their problems. While expressing interest in their children's education, such parents avoided contact with the traditional educational establishments. It seemed valuable to set up a scheme such as that described above with the express purpose of visiting the home "to encourage and enhance the mother's unique and irreplaceable role in the educational development of her children" (MacFadyen, 1980 p.13).

The teachers, who had been influenced by the work of Tough, stressed language and cognitive development, with use of stories, rhymes and jigsaws, plus 'messy' play; outings were also suggested. Story reading was encouraged, but in that context, it is noted by McCail (1981) that there was the danger that the mothers' questioning could become a testing of memory. The purpose in the activities was to encourage the mother to work with her child, and to close the gap between home and school, also to provide the mothers with some opportunity to take part in activities outside their home (MacFadyen, 1980). While the visitors in the initial stages, and during the evaluation, were specially selected teachers, there was the intention to develop at a later stage the use also of volunteers, as had Levenstein. McCail notes that this development did begin, with support for the volunteers from the educational home visitors. An important point is made by McCail that:

> "unless, at the end of the day, the mothers are encouraged to develop self-supportive networks, they may easily be in a more dependent situation than if there were no home visiting project, and the problem of loneliness which afflicts so high a proportion of them, and which could well have important implications for their children, will not have been overcome (McCail, 1981 p24).

This project was not seen as an alternative to early education in preschools, but as a preparation for it so that these families were more likely to take up the places on offer, either full- or part-time when their child was about three years of age. It was also not intended to replace links between home and school at later stages, but rather to lay a foundation for better communication between home and school at the nursery and primary level.

The research, which adopted a mainly 'illuminative' approach, is reported in detail in *Parents. Teachers and Children* (Raven, 1980). This involved close observation of the project as it developed, interviews with those involved, and a small scale study of the attitudes of the parents involved and others in the same and other areas. *Mother Start*, a related publication, contains a brief description of the development, mainly in the form of case studies based on notes kept by the home visitors; also discussed are other schemes, and the issues raised by such interventions (McCail, 1981).

This was a pioneering local initiative, clearly influenced by the knowledge of research and sensitivity of an administrator. Because of the way it developed, and many problems that affected the research project, described in detail in Raven (1980), it is difficult to evaluate it. The resources available to the project do not appear to have been adequate for the plan as established, and as a result neither the samples interviewed, nor those who undertook the interviews, appear to have been adequate for legitimate conclusions to be drawn from that aspect of the study. This was an ongoing innovation, whose planning and development were not under the control of the research team, thus presenting almost insurmountable difficulties for a rigorous evaluation, as distinct from a description of the progress of the initiative. In addition there was a change in researcher, there were also changes in home visitors, and in some of the families involved. There is little precise information on the backgrounds of the families interviewed, how many refused, how long they had been visited (some were visited for only a few weeks, others for two years), or on the interviews. Thus, what was intended to be a major part of the research, is not fully reported.

Because of the innovative nature of the home visiting scheme it seemed important to give the above details and to indicate the limitations of the research, particularly as some of the problems are not unique to this project. They can so easily befall an evaluation of what is already an ongoing educational intervention; although here they were compounded by change of research personnel in the early stages. It is important that educational innovations are evaluated; yet such researches are even more difficult to make rigorous as well as relevant than those where the researchers are involved in the planning as well as later evaluation.

A SCHOOL-BASED HOME PROGRAMME FOR PARENTS

In the early seventies, while working as an educational psychologist in Renfrewshire in Scotland, Donachy undertook a number of small-scale home-visiting programmes in which health visitors and others attempted to foster verbal interaction between mothers and their preschool children. In the early studies, toys and books were used, subsequently books only. Later a school-based system was used to extent this work, and include more families, involving the primary school which the preschool children would attend. With support from Renfrewshire, and the Scottish Education Department an experimental project was established (Donachy, 1976 and 1979).

The experimental design included 96 children in areas which had many characteristics of deprivation. There were six equal groups; two school-based groups took part in the programme (one of children aged three and one aged four years), two nursery school groups of four-year olds (one involved in the programme), and two control groups, one aged three and one aged four. The school-based groups were selected from children due to attend the primary school, then the other groups were matched as closely as possible. The mothers were invited to come to the primary school (or nursery school) once a week, borrow a book for the child and take part in group discussion chaired by one of the teachers, during which time the children were looked after. The mothers were asked to spend about 30 minutes per day talking with their child, reading from the books they borrowed, and involved in the tasks which were described on sheets which were issued. The discussions were about the experiences during the previous week, although they ranged over other topics also.

The children were assessed on a number of tests before and after the programme which lasted for four months. The mothers kept notes, and were also interviewed. Significant differences in scores were found on a number of the tests for the children attending nursery school, and greater differences when in addition the mothers were involved in the programme. There were also significant effects of the school-based programme. From records kept by the mothers it emerged that involvement of fathers in the carrying out of the programme was associated with high gains in the children. What cannot be established from this study is whether this was the result of additional time being devoted to the activities, or whether it was related to the combined effects of maternal and paternal interest.

An important feature, which resulted from the involvement of the infant teachers in the primary school, was that these teachers were able to meet the mothers in advance of the children's entry to school, and that they learnt that these mothers were indeed interested and willing to help their children. It was also possible to show that such a venture was viable in the present educational system. The project stimulated a number of additional schools to set up similar projects. Subsequently Donachy has moved to Northern Ireland where he has developed this work further, and also for younger children. His current project is being supported by the Northern Ireland Council for Educational Research (Donachy, 1987).

An attitude scale which was administered to the mothers before the study revealed that the mothers of the children attending nursery school had initially a more positive attitude, an important point related to demand and uptake of preschool provision. This is a point which has been commented upon by others also, and one on which further evidence will be considered in the following chapter.

CHAPTER 11 DEMAND AND UPTAKE: EVIDENCE AND ISSUES

THE SETTING

'What parents want and why', one of the five priority areas for research in preschool education identified in 1975 (DES, 1975a), was set at a time when a massive increase in such provision was planned, to make it available for those parents who wished it for their three- or four-year-old children on a full-time or part-time basis. Estimates of likely demand had not been based on empirical evidence, thus one of the purposes in commissioning research was to gain such information. One project funded by DES and SED to investigate this issue took place in the Lothian Region of Scotland, an area which by the mid-seventies already had a high proportion of places available in preschool education (Haystead, Howarth and Strachan, 1980). Included in the research was a study of non-users. In an intervention study an attempt was made to assess the effect of increasing knowledge of the existing facilities. A second research, in a contrasting area, is the frequently quoted study by Shinman, *A Chance for Every Child?* (Shinman, 1981). In that study in the London area, also in the seventies, it proved possible to compare the characteristic not only of users and non-users, but also of non-users who expressed an intention to use the facilities when available, and who then failed to do so. It is ironic that by the time the information from studies such as the above was available the political climate had changed. Already by 1976 the issue had become 'Low Cost Provision for the Under-Fives', the title for a joint conference of DHSS and DES (DHSS, DES, 1976). In addition a number of other issues had become more explicit, such as for example, whether the provision would or could suit working mothers. Under debate also was the role of the playgroups, whose numbers and importance had increased, with the cost-cutting climate leading some local authorities to provide them with funding as an alternative to nursery schools and classes. Lady Plowden's presidential address to the Preschool Playgroups Association in which she transferred her support to playgroups received considerable publicity, (especially in view of her former chairmanship of the committee which had advocated the expansion of preschool education, already under threat for economic reasons), particularly when she followed it with an article to the Times Educational Supplement (Plowden, 1982).

The term 'playgroup' so often used in research, statistical tables, policy documents and elsewhere as if it referred to a specific type of provision, may indeed cover a wide variety of provision for preschool children. Some playgroups are self help groups set up by mothers for their children within which they themselves participate, and which they organise and fund. Others, such as those investigated by Turner in her study of playgroups for deprived children in Belfast, may be receiving public funding, or be organised and staffed by voluntary agencies, as were 52 such groups at the time of her study (Turner, 1977). In an appendix to that report, Turner reports on the characteristics of the leaders of 27 such groups. The majority of the leaders were married and had children of their own, in many cases older and not part of the group. Most of the leaders had previous experience with another group of at least three years. Although few had attended full-time courses, most were currently attending, or had completed part-time or day release courses. Most of the 30 playgroups in areas of special need in twelve local authorities in England and Wales studied in the research by the National Children's Bureau, which will be discussed later in this chapter, were run by or received financial support from the local authority, or were run by voluntary organisations (Ferri and Niblett, 1977). In contrast, those 'working- class' playgroups studied by Finch (1983;1984) were initiated by a community worker or councillor, but run by local mothers, with or without continuing help. Finally, the term playgroup can be that used to categorise a private nursery school (according to Kysel(1982a) in an ILEA survey of use of preschool provision).

The precise details of the researches on this topic carried out in the seventies may be less relevant in the eighties and beyond, in view of changes in circumstances and in patterns of provision as outlined earlier in this report, including the increase in the numbers of younger four-year-olds already in reception class in England at least. Some of the evidence may also be area specific, indeed even the characteristics of that area may have changed dramatically. Haystead et al., 1980 set their results against a background of relevant features of preschool provision in the rest of Scotland at the time of their study, and relate them to the main issues which each aspect was planned to address. Thus the report is a valuable base for anyone wishing to investigate the current situation in other areas. Shinman (1981), likewise presents her empirical data in such a way that the issues discussed may still have contemporary relevance.

A third research to which reference will be made is more recent, and was undertaken in 1980 by the Inner London Education Authority's Research and Statistics Branch. The aim of the survey was to investigate, by means of a questionnaire, the types of facilities which were used, and whether there were differences in use by social and ethnic groups. The issues were then studied in more depth by interviews in one particular borough ((Kysel, 1982a;1982b).

Brief reference will be made to several studies which were concerned with the use of playgroups by 'disadvantaged' parents, since this topic seemed to fit most appropriately into this section. The studies which will be cited are those by Ferri and Niblett (1977) and Finch (1983;1984).

Differences over time and between areas, such as those cited earlier in this report, will clearly influence availability of provision for particular families. Range of available provision will also vary, and that available in the neighbourhood may or may not suit the needs of particular groups. Attendance at some units may involve expenditure, while other provision such as nursery schools and classes is free. Some units might be accessible but only with expenditure on transport, or for those with their own transport. Even statistical information for a local authority does not provide sufficiently detailed information to assess whether or not any or a choice of provision is available in a particular neighbourhood. Even within a type of provision the hours available for a particular child may not be suitable, and could vary from full-time to a few sessions a week. With regard to some types of provision, such as for example day nurseries, there may be lengthy waiting lists, and in addition certain requirements such that even families living in the immediate neighbourhood may not be eligible for admission. In few areas will there be a real choice for particular families, such that they are likely to consider the advantages and disadvantages of different forms of provision, in aims as well as in costs, accessibility and hours. Parents' choice may have been limited to whether or when to send their child to the single available provision. Among non-users may be some who are lacking in support for, or interest in, attendance for their child at such an early age. Where only one possible unit is available, specific features about that particular unit, its approach, a member of staff, or the children currently attending might be the reason for non-use. A research project in an area such as the Lothian Region, with a high level of provision, made it possible to explore the views of parents and possible gaps in provision even in such areas (Haystead *et al.*, 1980).

DEMAND AND UPTAKE IN AN AREA OF HIGH PROVISION

Using primary school catchment area as the unit, three geographically distinct areas in Lothian Region were included in the study by Haystead *et al.*, 1980, namely city centre, the outskirts of the city and a rural area. Also considered in choice of areas was type and amount of preschool provision and availability of work for women; all areas selected were socially mixed; there were at that time few children from ethnic minorities. Most 3-5 year-olds not yet in primary school were attending a nursery school or class, or a playgroup, or would do so before they started in primary school. In the city centre area studied over 90% of the children in the 3-5 age-group attended either a nursery school or class or a playgroup, with twice as many in the former as the latter. In the area in the outskirts a similar proportion attended nursery school or class (61%), but fewer attended playgroup (12%). In contrast, in the villages studied there were only 27% attending nursery school or class, and 53% at playgroup. A few children in each of the city areas attended a day nursery. A number of children under three years of age were already attending playgroups (in the city centre over 20% of children aged 2-3, including a number of younger two-year-olds).

During the study about 600 mothers whose children attended preschool provision were interviewed. Most current users expressed satisfaction with the unit which their child currently attended. Of the children in the sample 31% had changed the facility they attended (or a few had stopped attending) some for a variety of domestic reasons. Some had chosen to move the child from one type of provision to another, some had seen a move from playgroup to nursery school or class as a natural progression. Even in an area as well-provided as this there were certain groups who were unlikely to have choice. Those in outlying villages were likely only to have the possibility of a playgroup; those in disadvantaged areas with large numbers of young children had less choice. Even where there is extensive provision it is difficult to ensure that it keeps pace with the movement of population. The third group with little choice were those for whom all-day provision was essential, and who tended to have to come to a private arrangement with a childminder.

Most children in this study attended preschool five days per week, part-time. This included 38% of those attending playgroups, most of which were open in mornings only. Attendance at nursery school or class was half-time for most children, more in the mornings than afternoons. A number of those whose children attended in the afternoons would have preferred mornings as they felt the children became bored in the mornings waiting to go, or were too tired in the afternoons. Few of the mothers worked full-time currently, but over 20% in each of the three areas worked part-time. A number hoped to work, or to work longer hours when their children were older, either for financial reasons or their own preference. In a number of families grandmothers, friends or neighbours gave additional help on a voluntary basis.

Preschool facilities were sufficiently close that the majority of those attending nursery school or class or playgroup could go on foot, others went by car, very few went by bus. In contrast half of those attending a day nursery went by bus: furthermore the number of hours per day attended and weeks in the year would have been greater. An attempt was made to assess the extent to which the parents were knowledgeable about the different facilities. It was found that they were more likely to name the types that were available in their immediate locality, and were also better informed about them. The commonest source of information was friends and neighbours.

Most mothers currently taking their children to any kind of preschool provision thought that it was advantageous for them to go; those who thought it was a disadvantage were referring either to inconvenience of taking them, or to missing the child's company. When the parents were asked why they sent their children to preschool provision the commonest response for those attending nursery units and playgroups was for social reasons; child development and preparation for school were the next most frequent reasons given. Domestic reasons for a few might have determined the precise time the child started. Some parents were reported to see education in terms of a 'race', and therefore one advantage of preschool education was that subsequently the child would settle down more quickly to the business of learning. Most parents expressed satisfaction with the activities in which their children engaged. Some thought their children could be more profitably engaged, with more direct teaching, or structuring of activities; a view more often expressed by parents of older children.

It was possible in this study to look at the extent of parental involvement in the different types of unit. The extent of parental involvement reported by the mothers of children attending playgroups was perhaps less than might have been expected; namely only about 20% stayed all the time on rota days, and about 27% helped with organisation. 22% of the children attending playgroups had mothers who did not even have the contact with the facility of taking the child; a further 21% did not go into the facility; even of those who did enter a number were likely to stay for only a few minutes. Some of the differences were in that certain playgroups required or encouraged parental participation. Some of the mothers of children at playgroups were working, or studying. Few mothers of children attending nursery schools or classes reported taking part on a rota, or being involved in the organisation of the unit. Most mothers, however, took their child to and from the unit, and about half the mothers went in at least briefly. There was little parental involvement in any day nursery provision. Some mothers did not become involved in the preschool unit because they had felt discouraged, or were embarrassed, others because their child did not want them to. Many mothers reported that they did not wish to be involved in the organisation. Reasons for not wishing to be present at sessions often referred to lack of confidence in their own ability, or that of other parents, and with this went a belief in the expertise of trained staff. In an intervention study in a different area, various ways of providing information were explored, and their relative effectiveness. The commonest reason given for selection of a facility was that it was nearest. The additional information provided did not appear to change preference, but some of the approaches did increase knowledge of the activities in the various preschool units.

The reasons why people are not using existing facilities is an important element in planning. It is dangerous to assume that the reason is only lack of sufficient facilities. In the three mixed social class areas in the first part of the study less than 4% of the mothers had not taken, or did not intend to take their children to preschool. Some said they did not want preschool facilities, saying they thought it was better for the children to stay at home with them. To investigate this aspect further a special study was undertaken in two primary school catchment areas, in a part of the city which had the severest shortage of places, areas with considerable fluctuation of population, high unemployment and poorer housing. There, a group of non-users was studied, some in the sense used above, others were dropouts. A group of irregular users was also studied. The reasons given by the mothers for wanting places were similar to those who did attend. Several mothers are reported to have believed their child did not need to go unless the mother had failed. Others reported that they would have been lonely without the child. Although they might feel that attendance could have benefited the child they had not sought a place, even where the child had no children to play with and no outside play area.

Most of the 'dropouts' had attended the facility for a very short time. In several instances the reason given for stopping was that the child did not like it, or did not settle. Several who had dropped out had initially been persuaded by a professional to take the child (health visitor or social worker), but perhaps had not believed in it themselves. One of the features which distinguished the non-users and dropouts from the others was that the mothers said they enjoyed having their children at home, and would be lost without them. In contrast children on waiting lists in this area were described as difficult by a number of the mothers.

When nursery education is not compulsory, even where units are placed in disadvantaged areas, middle class children from nearby areas may be among those attending. Some of those in most need may not make the effort to attend, for a variety of reasons. In the disadvantaged areas the units reported pressure for any full-day places, for which there were waiting lists. Some mothers did not feel it was worth taking their child for a shorter period, because of financial problems and younger children. Some showed already, even with children as young as these, a powerlessness to control their children's actions and quickly accepted the young child's wishes. Facilities would need to be extremely flexible if they are to have any chance of meeting the variety of needs of some of these families. To make extensive provision is not in itself sufficient.

CHARACTERISTICS OF USERS AND NON-USERS OF NEW FACILITIES

Two small-scale studies are worthy of brief mention, although they took place in the early seventies, because they specifically address the characteristics of non-users of preschool provision (Shinman 1981). The first study was of parents who did and did not make use of newly opened playgroups; the second concerned the use by registered childminders of newly opened centres which they could attend, and to which they could take the children. Many of the studies of uptake of preschool provision have been in areas of extremely bad housing, or with lack of social amenities. Shinman felt that it was important to study a community without such obvious disadvantages and where the community had been active in seeking the establishment of the provision. In 1972 the London Borough of Hillington decided to allocate resources to provide custom-built premises to be used as playgroups in seven council estates. The catchment area for each unit was clearly defined and socially homogenous. The project took place in the second area, the catchment area for the proposed playgroup and the local primary school. The Tenants' Association had been active in demanding a playgroup, much of the cost of which was to be financed by the local authority.

Lists of families with children under five supplied by the authorities were not found to be adequate, so were supplemented by door-to-door visits. Semi-structured interviews were then conducted of 77 mothers identified as having children aged three or four years of age. Those who initially refused to be interviewed later agreed, an important point, as among those were a number of the mothers subsequently identified as 'alienated'. Three groups were identified;

Group 1 those who made no use of the new provision, and who did not already go elsewhere (22);

Group 2 those who made use of the new facilities (37);

Group 3 those who continued to make use of preschool facilities outside the area (18).

Distance was not regarded as a factor influencing use of the new playgroup, which was custom-built, conveniently close to all the families. Few of the mothers went out to work; these who did tended to be in Group 3, already using provision outside the area. Mothers already using facilities tended to have smaller families, some were one child families. Much of the cost of the playgroup was met, and although a small payment was required those who did not participate did not suggest that money was a factor.

Attitudes to education of some of those in Group 1 were less positive than those in the other groups. A disproportionate number of mothers in Group 1 were relatively isolated within the community. Not only were they less likely to see friends and neighbours, but also their own mothers and relatives. There were, however, others whose continued non-use of facilities was for very positive reasons. Likewise, in Group 3 there were some who had sought out provision elsewhere because of lack in the immediate community, and for child-centred reasons, and who continued to use that even after the establishment of the local playgroup. Others had been guided to use of provision by outside agencies, or the need to work. Even among those who registered their children for the new playgroup there were interesting differences.

Shinman accepted that the group was less homogenous than had appeared, and that there might even be very different subgroups within users and non-users. She identified seven characteristics for what she termed an Index of Maternal Alienation, as follows: dislike of messy play, the youth of the mother when she married, dislike of neighbours, comparative isolation from family and friends, lack of child-centredness, little time available for relaxed play with her children, a 'less mature' mother.

Those classified on the above as High Alienation included all but one of the one-parent families, mothers, who were coping with considerable pressures. Most of those classified as LA, if they used preschool provision had taken steps to seek it out for themselves. Checks were made among Group 2 during the first term of the new playgroup, and 7 of 8 who were either nonstarters or spasmodic users had been classified as HA. In Group 1, LA mothers were non-users for child- centred reasons. They enjoyed having their children with them, but also called on friends for baby-sitting. They had some social life themselves, and the children were integrated into it. They appear similar in many ways to mothers who did not send their children to preschool provision in the study by the present author of children who could already read with understanding on entry to school at five years of age (Clark, 1976). Those among the non-users classified as HA were identified by withdrawal from the community and a distrust of anything educational. The LA mothers in Group 2 had welcomed the idea of the playgroup, and involvement in it. They regarded it as valuable for the children, and would therefore support it. Among Group 3 mothers were some who had sought out a preschool facility before the establishment of the local playgroup, only two of these ten subsequently changed to the local provision. Within this Group 3 were HA one-parent families and others whose children's attendance was following the intervention of an agency.

It appears from this small study that the issues of use and non-use of a voluntary provision are much more complex than would appear from some of the literature, and that the scale adopted by Shinman may help to throw some light on the issue. Depending on the amount and range of preschool provision in the community, and the expectations of the primary school to which the children may proceed, some of the LA mothers currently non-users might decide to become users, for their children's sake, either in terms of companionship, or future educational achievement. Rather than regarding part-time attendance as a disadvantage, such mothers might prefer that to full-time. In an area where attendance at nursery school or class was full-time, there were some mothers who for child-centred reasons did not wish their children to attend (Davie *et al.*, 1984 p.160). Some of the characteristics referred to here as associated with HA may be found among those who do not use part-time provision, who are spasmodic users, who register their child then do not take up the place, or whose children attend very briefly then leave. Among these may be some mothers who may feel inadequate to cope even though their families are smaller than average. Others with family problems may not wish to admit to these, as a result they may appear to withdraw from family and friends, and to show alienation from those in authority. Following the analysis of users and non-users among mothers using the concept of high and low alienation, Shinman then used a similar analysis of users and non-users among childminders.

The study of childminders was conducted in two deprived areas of inner London, with rather different characteristics. The sample was registered childminders; (in both areas about half those on the register were no longer minding, a finding in other studies also). Free informal centres were to open in both areas, for two sessions each week, and all childminders were told about them individually and consulted on days and times which would be convenient. The aim was to offer the minder an opportunity to get out of the house, meet others and relax. The project workers spent some time talking with the minders and some playing with the children. After 18 months a check was made on the extent to which minders used the centre, and an assessment was made as to the extent that a modified Index of Maternal Alienation would be predictive of users and non-users who were a cause for concern. Characteristics of the childminders are given in Shinman (1981). On initial interviews the minders tended to report that they were minding for the money, but about three months later after regular visiting while money was given as a reason for starting, more gave a liking for children as a reason for continuing. Some differences were found in the two areas, including the relative ages of the minders. In one area they were younger, more likely to have young children of their own at home; in the other their families were likely to be older, and larger.

Both centres attracted as many minders as could be coped with, including as regular users, some who had initially indicated possible problems. For child-centred reasons some decided to attend, and became regular users, some at considerable inconvenience. Minders with young families of their own were more likely to use the centre, but also to play with the children, and enjoy friendly relationships with other adults there. The distribution of users and non-users found among mothers was also reflected among the minders. There were some who did not use the centre, but for what are termed 'child-centred' reasons; they were non-joiners who were likely to have organised their homes around the children, and to enjoy the children. Also found were 'High Alienation' minders, who were nonstarters or irregular users. In both areas, as in the previous study, among those were the isolated, and those suspicious of authority. Some had negative attitudes to child care, were not using other services like health clinics, were more likely to be living in cramped conditions and without outside play space. In short, some were those most in need of help. Some improvements in childminding were facilitated by the centres, which were both a forum for raising problems, and a support to those who attended. The challenge remains of how to support and improve the conditions of those termed 'HA' non-users, whose isolation was likely to continue, and to reflect on the quality of care they provided.

PATTERNS OF USE OF PRESCHOOL PROVISION IN ILEA

In 1980 a survey was conducted by the Research and Statistics Branch of the Inner London Education Authority into the use of preschool provision in young children in the year prior to entry to reception class (Kysel, 1982a). A random 20% sample of the authority's primary schools was drawn (126 schools), and the headteacher of each was asked either to complete or ask the parents to complete a questionnaire concerning such use, and other features of the child's background for those who entered in Spring Summer and Autumn of that year. Four schools did not take part, and responses were available for 88.4% of the reception class entrants to the remaining schools, though not necessarily to all questions. It was found that 87% of the children in the sample had attended a preschool facility in the year before entry to school, 62% had attended a nursery school or class, or both, 22% attended a playgroup, 7.8% day nursery and 3.1% a childminder. Since nearly 40% of all pre-school places available to three and four-year-olds was in playgroups, it would appear that this must be more used by younger children. More than one facility had been used by 10% of the children, the commonest combination was nursery class or school and playgroup; it is not clear whether these were used concurrently or not. Over 70% of the children attending a childminder went to another facility also.

Much of the information in the report is of specific interest to ILEA in planning its own policy and will not be listed here. What is of interest is for example use according to background features, including ethnic background. In the survey in ILEA, 57% of the children were indigenous, 12.3% of West Indian background, 9.4% of Asian background and 3.7 % African. The remainder were mixed or of other ethnic background. Most of the children had been born in the United Kingdom. It is important in considering pattern of use to note that one-fifth of the children came from one parent families, but 42.6% for children of West Indian origin, a feature which might influence need, for example, for full-day provision. The Asian and African origin groups made much less use of preschool provision than those of indigenous or West Indian origin. There was little difference in use of nursery schools and classes, but less use of playgroups. Those of West Indian or African origin made greater use of day nurseries and childminders.

There were social class differences in use of facilities, and in the type of facilities used. For example, there was lower use of facilities generally among children whose fathers were unemployed, and lower use of playgroups but higher use of day nurseries. Some divisions of ILEA had full-time nursery places, some had relatively more provision in nursery schools and classes. The relationships were very complex, and could be explored only to a limited extent in a survey. It was particularly difficult to attribute causal relationships within the findings.

It is important to note that the term playgroup as used in this survey, and in a number of other studies, could have meant a very wide range of facilities. Some might have been 'self help' playgroups; others playgroups organised and run by a voluntary organisation, or the local social services department; while yet others might have been private 'nursery schools', which it is stated in the report on p.19 were categorised as playgroups. These are not distinguished from each other in the survey.

From this survey it was found that although a high proportion of children in ILEA had attended a preschool provision in the year before entry to primary school, in spite of ILEA policy to give preference in the provision of nursery places to areas of social need, there was no evidence that children from socially disadvantaged backgrounds did make more use of nursery provision. Groups who made particularly low use of preschool facilities were children born outside the United Kingdom, or whose fathers were unemployed, those from large families of four or more children, and those of Asian background.

In a more detailed study in one area of ILEA, the mothers of 98 children who had entered the reception class in schools in the area were interviewed at home (Kysel, 1982b). The aim of the study was to investigate use of preschool provision from birth, reasons for choice of facilities, and knowledge which the parents had of different types of provision. A comparison is provided between this area and the findings for ILEA as a whole. A higher proportion of single parents were working before the child was two years of age, and related to work pattern their children were more likely to have had care outside the home before the age of two, but by age four a difference in proportion of working mothers was not evident. Already by two years of age 34% of the children were attending some provision, 70% between three and four, rising to 94% between four and five. With increasing age the proportion attending nursery school or class increased. Because of the way the information is presented it is not possible to look at the proportion of children attending either two types of provision in a year, or two simultaneously. About equal numbers of the children had attended full or part-time in the year before entry to reception class, most in a nursery school or class. In addition, there were seven children whose mothers worked either full-or part-time who were multiple users, of a nursery class plus childminder or playgroup. Nearness to home was a common reason for selection of a particular facility, or having another child already there. Knowledge of facilities was often from friends or neighbours. A few facilities had been rejected because they did not offer full-time places, and a few after visits. Some nursery classes were attended mainly by local children, others attracted children from further away. The mothers were reported to have limited, and on occasion erroneous information on different types of facility. About one-third of the mothers did not know what a day nursery was, for example. Some mothers were confused at the difference between a nursery school and class, as they stated wrongly which their child attended. This should not be a matter for surprise in view of the very widely different characteristics to be found even within a particular type of provision. In general mothers were satisfied with the preschool provision their child had attended, but in most instances with little knowledge of possible alternatives.

DISADVANTAGED FAMILIES AND PLAYGROUPS

Financial support was provided by DHSS for a study by the National Children's Bureau of playgroups which appeared to be successful in attracting children and families of 'high need' (Ferri and Niblett, 1977). In order to obtain a national picture of provision in England and Wales a letter was sent to all social services department and to a number of voluntary organisations known to be involved in such provision to ascertain whether they operated any such playgroups, or provided financial support. Replies were received from 86 of 116 local authorities indicating

H

current involvement. Visits were then made to those who supplied most information. Some playgroups were excluded from further study either because although sited in an area of 'deprivation', a sizeable proportion of the children came from more advantaged areas, or because of their 'precarious position' at the time of the visit; two points which are themselves noteworthy.

The sample investigated was 30 playgroups, within which an attempt was made to include some run by social services, others by voluntary bodies and a variety of independent groups, and to have a variety of policies and practices represented. Twelve local authority areas were involved. Information was obtained from the playgroup leader about the organisation of the group, and concerning the children who were attending, and who joined during the project. Regular visits were paid to each playgroup, every four or five weeks, during five months in 1975.

Six of the playgroups were run by social services departments, and a further 15 received financial support either for general costs or for specific children. Six groups were in addition closely involved with the Preschool Playgroups Association. Accurate information concerning the origins of the groups was difficult to find as only about half the leaders had been with the group since its inception. More than half of the groups had been in existence for more than two years. At the beginning of the study most of these groups were full, and several had long waiting lists. Most of the groups contained some children who had been special referrals from social workers or health visitors. Only two of the groups were charging anything near an economic fee, and most had arrangements for free places. Most groups received grants from social services, some of which was Urban Aid funds. In most instances the children could walk to the playgroup; three provided free transport as a policy.

Details are given of a number of characteristics of the total sample of children in the study, but these will not be listed here since it is not clear how this varied in different playgroups, nor how representative these were for children in that age group and their families in these areas. For example a percentage is given for children from ethnic minority backgrounds. However, one of the playgroups took most of its children from a community where most families were of Asian ethnic origin, and it was drawn to the attention of mothers.

The question is raised as to whether these were playgroups in high need areas, or for high need children. 'Need scores' were allocated to the children, and it was found that about half of those who had been specially referred had high need scores. It was felt that the siting of the playgroup in an area of need was the feature, apart from acceptance of special referrals. There was no evidence that seeking out of such children was part of their aim, furthermore the few groups that did do so had considerable resources at their disposal and the seeking out was not done by the leader. It is stressed, that any such policy would require considerable outside resources.

All but one of these groups had a leader who had undergone some form of training relevant to work with young children (some through the Preschool Playgroups Association). Eight leaders were NNEB trained, one was a teacher, and one a nurse. Furthermore most had some experience of working with preschool children before joining the group. These groups were clearly dependent on the skills and expertise of these committed leaders who were undertaking a taxing and stressful job. It is therefore important to note that the 'salary' they received was in some cases a token, and in all low. One was not paid, one paid on a matron's scale, and the amount per session of the others varied from 68p per session to £3.25, for half it was £2 or less. They were also operating in a number of instances with little or no regular contact with outside agencies. While all the playgroups in the study had some contact with outside agencies for support, in practice this varied from frequent to none. Some groups had contacts with local schools. Finance was one of the major problems faced by leaders, particularly if they were responsible for raising sufficient income to run the group, this could operate against the acceptance of certain children, and lead to cessation of attendance of those unable to pay.

An important aspect in relation to benefits to particular children is the length of their stay, and the regularity of their attendance, both of which were considered. Those who left during the study were more likely to have been referred by an outside agency, which was the case also among short stay children, who remained less than three months. Attendance rates over the five month period were not found to differ significantly between those who had been allocated high need scores and those who had not. Here also there was evidence of lower attendance rates for those who had been specially referred. A significant point is made that in one in three of the special referrals there had been no follow-up contact with the group by the referring agency. These findings highlight the necessity for support and encouragement to continue to attend, and to attend regularly, particularly for families with special needs sufficient for their children to be specially referred.

Less than half of these playgroups had a management committee, and in only five cases were mothers represented on it. Furthermore, in only half of the groups were mothers involved in the day to day running of the group; in some this was only a small group of regulars, in only one playgroup were all mothers involved. In most groups some mothers took part in activities such as fund raising, or outings. A specific group is referred to where by sensitive and energetic work the leader had been able to involve about half the mothers. It is commented that for many of the mothers one function of the playgroup was to meet their needs, and to provided them with a few hours respite. It is suggested that in such playgroups the type of involvement which can be expected, initially at least, may be very different. Furthermore, the time, skills and effort may be beyond even the most gifted leaders, who already have the responsibility for planning for the needs of the children while they attend. Cautions are sounded by the authors of the research report against regarding the mother's involvement as an essential requirement. The needs of these children for opportunities for stimulating play, and of the mothers for some respite, and or a sympathetic listener, may be sufficient justification for the establishment of such playgroups without requiring parental involvement either in participation or organisation.

PRESCHOOL PLAYGROUPS AND WORKING-CLASS MOTHERS

A three year longitudinal study of five playgroups in Lancashire was carried out by Finch between 1978-81, the final year of which was supported by a small grant from SSRC (Finch, 1981). The criteria for selection of four of the groups was that they were recently registered, located within inner city areas or less popular council estates, and as far as possible were self-help working-class groups run by local women whose educational background and qualifications were minimal. With the assistance of the social services department only four such groups were found in the whole of Lancashire, showing as Finch states, that it was a rare phenomenon. A fifth 'middle class' group was added for comparative purposes, in a new town development, including private and corporation housing. After the three year period only two of the groups had survived, one working-class group and the comparison group. One group did not get under way, another failed because of lack of children, and a third closed after about two years and a series of difficulties, disagreements and lack of children. This group was observed in detail over that period. The 'working-class' groups were found to have difficulties in attracting children, which in turn meant limited income. They also had problems in actual handling of funds. Finch reports conflicts also in relation to those who were involved and those whose children attended, including concern about the competence of those actually running the group, and even fear expressed by some mothers for the safety of their children..

Finch paid a series of observational visits to the groups over the three year period, and also conducted 47 semi-structured interviews with those who ran the groups and some of the mothers who used them. The working-class mothers interviewed almost all expressed the hope that attendance would be a preparation for school; a view rejected by many in the comparison group. None of the working-class groups had successfully sustained a mothers' rota; all were run by a group of leaders. None of the working-class groups was a self-help group, but rather a group being run by somewhat older mothers for the younger mothers in the area. For some of these women the money they earned was important; they also made friends. In contrast virtually none of the non-involved mothers had formed friendships. Finch suggests that there were boundaries established between the two groups in the community. Some of the leaders appreciated that the playgroup could provide a meeting place for the mothers, but felt they had neither the skills nor the resources; most mothers welcomed the break. Three of the playgroups had been initiated by community workers, all of these had closed by the end of the research. That which remained open longest initially had a leader who had trained as an NNEB, and it was after her departure that disputes developed. The playgroup which remained open had been initiated by a local councillor of many years standing in the estate, who remained active as an authority figure, and firm chairman of the committee throughout. That structure was felt to have been important in establishing outside contacts when necessary, possible in the comparison group through individuals, in arbitrating in disputes, indeed in maintaining that group's existence.

In two articles Finch discusses the issues involved (Finch, 1983 and 1984). Tensions between self-help and charitable provision, is one issue she raises, since she feels that these groups were tending to the latter, with low paid helpers in charge. The competence of these leaders is also questioned, and was by the mothers themselves, who were paying for their child's attendance. In more mixed, or 'middle-class' groups, while those acting as leaders may be there as 'ordinary mums', their competence and status as perceived by the mothers whose children attend may stem partly from qualifications they possess and/or their organisational skills. There is indeed evidence from other researches that many playgroup leaders of mixed, or middle-class groups do have professional qualifications, although they are not being paid for such. The need in times of crisis to be able to link with outside agencies was a further problem to groups such as these. Finch questions whether in some ways such groups were even providing these mothers with what they wanted for their children. In considering the role of playgroups it is essential to consider evidence from groups such as these, and those initiated, funded and run by voluntary organisations or from public funds, and not only those which approximate to a self-help model.

CHAPTER 12   CO-ORDINATION AND CO-OPERATION IN PRESCHOOL EDUCATION

It must be made clear that any attempt to separate the two 'Cs' of co-ordination and co-operation is really artificial and that they are indeed perhaps two aspects of the same issue. Likewise the third 'C' of continuity is difficult to treat in isolation from the other features. Perhaps for present purposes it is helpful to consider co-ordination as the feature which relates more to the administrative structures, co-operation to the personnel involved whether professional, volunteer or parent, and continuity as focusing on the children and their early experiences of education. With this distinction in mind, but accepting the inter-relatedness of the three aspects, co-ordination and co-operation will be discussed in this chapter, continuity will be discussed in the following chapter.

'Co-ordination of Services' and 'Continuity and Progression' were among the nineteen items considered as requiring research based on the short-term studies on behalf of the Management Committee of the DES Nursery Research Programme. Furthermore co-ordination and continuity were two of the five priority areas for research identified by the DES Committee on the basis of their own studies and the report by Tizard to SSRC (DES, 1975a).

RESEARCH CONTEXT

Two studies were funded on co-ordination, one supported by DES and DHSS, the other funded by DES/SSRC; although neither study is listed in *Under Fives : A Programme of Research* (DES, 1981). The first of these researches on, 'Co-ordination of Services for Children under Five' was a two-year project funded by DES from 1979-81. The final report on that project by Martin Bradley was submitted in 1981 together with a comprehensive summary for wider distribution to the local authorities and others interested in the survey. It was subsequently published under the same title and it is from the published version that the information for this report is extracted (Bradley, 1982). The other research referred to above on 'Co-operation' directed by Joyce Watt and funded by SSRC, was published as a monograph by SSRC under the title *Co-operation in Preschool Education* (Watt, 1977) and it is to that source that reference will be made.

Studies of co-ordination of services which have as their focus organisational patterns within a country, as in the case of Bradley's survey, or within an area as in the research by Watt, are unfortunately likely to become dated at least as regards their detailed information. In the ten or so years since these studies, that of Bradley in England, and by Watt in Scotland, there have been major organisational changes in both countries. Furthermore, there have been very considerable differences in the numbers of children under five in attendance at preschool units and in the nature of the units they attend. There are also many children aged four years of age who, depending on their exact month of birth, may already be in attendance at reception class in a primary school. While the more detailed findings of the two studies may now be less relevant, recommendations and also the concerns expressed are pertinent. Readers interested in the details of these two clearly presented studies are referred to the publications by Bradley (1982) and Watt (1977). The nature of the two studies and the topics covered will be summarised below.

CO-ORDINATION OF PRESCHOOL SERVICES

The research by Bradley of St. Katharine's College, Liverpool, on 'Co-ordination of Services for Children Under Five' was a two year project funded by DES between 1979-81 with three purposes:

a) to examine co-ordination of services for children under five;

b) to study ways in which such policies are planned and carried out;

c) to provide information which would give a base for planning future policies.

The research was in two phases: the first concerning co-ordination procedures involved a postal survey of 95 English local areas with education and social service departments and 87 area health authorities (with the exception of the Inner London Education Authority Area). Over 700 voluntary organisations were also involved. The second phase involved follow-up visits to 25 selected areas to cover different types of area and forms of co-ordination identified in the first phase.

The first phase of the survey identified a number of types of co-ordination of services including formally constituted subcommittees, semiformal structures and informal procedures. The high response rate to the survey indicated a greater interest in under fives than some would have expected. The patterns of co-ordination identified were widely varied and councillors appeared to be less involved in discussions than might have been expected. Social services departments were reported to be central to the co-ordination procedures, especially with regard to informal contacts with voluntary organisations. Already by the time of the survey, playgroups and childminding advisers had been appointed in some areas. It was noted that where there were co-ordinating groups these seldom reported to voluntary agencies as they did to council committees and departments. Furthermore few voluntary organisations were found to be involved in co-ordination procedures (those which were involved included Preschool Playgroups Association PPA, The British Association for Early Childhood Education BAECE, and The National Childminding Association NCMA).

Bradley (1982 Chapter 8) does not recommend a prescription for co-ordination at local level but stresses that in successful arrangements the following were of importance:

a) clarity and simplicity with the place of the arrangements in local administration explicitly stated;

b) representation of interests since in some areas it was found that certain aspects were isolated from any co-ordination (e.g. childminders);

c) communication, consultation, negotiation and collaboration as elements to ensure discussion and presentation of ideas from a variety of participants;

d) access to enable those at the level of policy decisions to be in direct touch with 'grass roots' practices;

e) mutual awareness, respect and support with links between officers and voluntary services stressed.

There was evidence that a number of developments had been strongly influenced by particular personalities in key posts. A number of issues in relation to this aspect which were found to affect co-ordination are equally pertinent now and these include:

a) adverse effects of non-replacement of specific personnel reducing effectiveness;

b) the importance of interest and involvement of councillors;

c) the necessity that new officer appointments involve contact with other sectors;

There were clearly important issues related to administrative structures and procedures which could vary in the different sectors of the local authority.

The third major issue considered, apart from personalities and administrative structures, was the financial arrangements relating to the various services. Concerns were reported on closure of playgroups as school entry age was changed without consultation; unevenness in provision between areas leading to some families moving; an increase in part-time childminding for the hours not covered by nursery classes. The considerable disparity in age on entry to reception class in many neighbouring authorities is also noted.

The research project team received a great deal of information on a variety of aspects of co-ordination much of which is still relevant (see Bradley, 1982 p.122-140). The recommendations and issues concerning co-ordination with regard to personnel, administration structures and finance which are summarized by Bradley on p.97-108 are important evidence for any area now considering ways of improving policy and practice for children under five by co-ordination of available services. From documents consulted during this current research and from interviews, co-ordination of services is clearly an aspect of at least as great concern as it was at the time of Bradley's research. Many of his warnings, as well as the examples and suggestions, are highly pertinent to local and national policy-makers even in the changed circumstances. Studies such as this reveal just how fragile are some developments, susceptible to the vagaries of changes in personnel and/or lack of replacement of personnel, boundary changes, reduction in funds or even reorganisation of local services.Cuts in funding may lead to this non-mandatory area of services for under fives having low priority. The development of co-ordinating structures, formal and informal, may lose momentum in face of other aspects competing for time, and finance. A final point of relevance from Bradley's report is the following:

> "The practices of some departments in allowing 'market force' factors to determine access to services has not been generally beneficial to sectors. Variations within an authority in admission to schools require careful monitoring if a balanced approach is to be maintained and care is also needed to avoid annual fluctuations caused where a school might admit four-year-olds one year, rising fives the next and so on" (Bradley, 1982 pp.101-102).

And further,

> "The main value of administrative structures and procedures is that as a framework they can add coherence and relevance to service planning and delivery".

> "We suggest that developments in services in local areas be related to the current range and distribution of services, and that an examination of this range and distribution should be the foundation upon which developments are made" (Bradley, 1982 p.103).

CO-OPERATION IN PRESCHOOL EDUCATION

In contrast to the survey of local authority policies on co-ordination undertaken by Bradley in England, the study on co-operation by Joyce Watt (funded by SSRC) was a detailed study in Scotland of a single community, shortly before regionalization (Watt, 1977). Fife, the selected area (which retained its boundaries after regionalization) was chosen as an area in which one of the highest proportions of three and four-year-olds in Scotland attended preschool provision. It was also a relatively compact area, yet had wide variation in size and type of community. One disadvantage in its choice was the absence of any day nurseries or nursery centres at the commencement of the research in 1974.

The aim of the research, based on questionnaires and interviews (but not observational studies), was to analyse factors which appeared to promote or inhibit co-operation. About 44% of the estimated population of three and four-year-olds (of about 11, 000) were in attendance at some form of registered preschool unit in 1974, most on a part-time basis. There were nursery schools and classes, playgroups and private groups. Children of working mothers were found to be in attendance, with family support for the remainder of the day in a number of instances. Information was collected on over 150 units, on the characteristics of over 4, 000 children attending these and on a 'random sample' of over 1, 500 children in the three to four year age group. Information was collected on staff attitudes to 'professionalism', to 'parental involvement' and 'co-operation' in preschool education from over 400 staff and a number of interviews of staff. Over 500 parents were also interviewed to assess the demand for preschool education and attitude to involvement in it. The researchers note an important imbalance in the sample of parents of non-attenders and those from community playgroups. In the former there is a suggestion that some families from lower social classes may have been omitted by health visitors who were responsible for identification. In the latter instance two difficulties are noted, in identifying parents in some community and private groups, also prior consultation of parents before releasing their names.

Watt reports that lower social classes were under-represented in preschool education at that time, and particularly in community playgroups. Children from 'problem families' were also seriously under-represented. Staffs in the preschool units tended to see the under-representation of children from deprived families in terms of inabilities in the families. Staff in the community were more inclined to be critical of what was offered to such groups.

There was a demand by parents for preschool education both full and part-time (but if part-time, mornings rather than afternoons). Some mothers were also found to favour playgroups for the younger children and nursery school or class for the four-year-olds. Watt found, as have others, that parents tended to perceive preschool education in terms of social benefits. Parents not interested in preschool provision tended to be those with large families and from lower social classes.

Attitudes to professionalism amongst staff varied widely from those who rated high professionalism as important, to those who feared that professionalism created barriers to voluntary effort. It is noted that co-operation between professionals and voluntary groups was generally accepted in principle as was the need for co-operation between staff of preschool groups and professionals working in the community. In practice, however, it was felt that the former did not have priority and the latter tended to be affected by misunderstandings and 'popular stereotypes' rather than a clear appreciation of the roles of other professionals.

It is important to note that even in an area such as Fife with a relatively high proportion of preschool children attending some form of provision there were wide differences in the amount and the type available in different communities (even within the two major towns). In one rural district there were no children in nursery schools or classes, but about 20% in playgroups: in contrast in a mining district almost half the children attended a nursery school or class, and none were in either playgroups or private groups. In different parts of the area it was also possible for all, or none, of the children to be catered for.

Clearly some of the findings of this study may be less relevant in the eighties: the main thrust is, however, still as pertinent today and indeed, is made even more forceful by the very nature of the community in which the study was undertaken. This was an area with a concern for preschool education and with a relatively high level of provision, yet even there the amount and type varied dramatically from place to place. Furthermore, even in an area with a tradition for preschool provision there were clearly problems in co-operation. In the final chapter of her report Watt proposes a possible framework and in so doing also analyses a number of the problems in establishing co-ordination and co-operation between services. She stresses the need for a regional policy defining some aspects of the services and clarifying the broad criteria within which the various services would operate.

The artificial distinction between 'care' and 'education' with each the responsibility of a different department is perceived as a major stumbling block to integration of services. Also relevant, however, is the attitude of the different personnel to 'professionalism' which Watt considers an important factor affecting relationships between the various participants in preschool provision, one with potential for integration - and divisiveness. She refers to the dangers of certain services remaining on the periphery (such as childminders and private groups); equally important, however, the need for educational provision at the preschool stage not to become isolated from the mainstream education (further developed in Watt, 1983). She suggests that the initial modelling of the playgroup movement on nursery education, while understandable in the context in which it expanded so dramatically - a failure to develop state nursery education - may have done the movement a disservice. It may, she suggests, not only have blurred their distinctive functions but also have "encouraged an uneasy relationship of rivalry rather than a partnership of mutual trust" (Watt, 1977 p.83).

The advantages and dangers of preschool provision being organised within a single department are explored. To quote:

> "The dangers of integration within any one department are obvious - an unimaginative interpretation of community need based on the judgement of one department without wide consultation could be a very real step backward, could stifle initiative, could lead to bureaucratic proliferation of similar types of provision and could lead to a very much greater frustration than that engendered by the present system" (Watt, 1977 p.85).

CO-ORDINATION AND CO-OPERATION

The study by Watt had a detailed focus in a single area, involvement in discussions with a wide range of staffs within and beyond preschool provision, and of parents with children in and outside the provision. This helps to identify friction points and sources of misunderstanding as a base from which to explore possible developments.

The survey by Bradley identified areas, where at the time of his study there were successful initiatives. Taken together the studies seem to indicate the need for organisational planning at a high enough level for policy to be implemented in practice yet without centralized control inhibiting a variety of provision as required by circumstances and parental choice. They also indicate the need for procedures to facilitate co-operation between the various services at a more local level with optimum utilization of professionalism to support a variety of services to families. What is clear also is the extent to which different organisational features of departments involved in 'care' or 'education' services and budget priorities may inhibit developments.

According to Bradley major developments in co-ordination of services for under fives have taken place in England in the last ten years, with a variety of examples in different parts of the country (Bradley, 1987). In a review article setting such developments in their historical perspective, Bradley notes changes, particularly in people's attitudes to liaison with other workers, and the need to consider the local government setting for services. He stresses the importance of developing the necessary awareness and broad perspectives on work with young children in pre- and in-service training.

It seems appropriate to note at this point a recent initiative in the largest Region in Scotland in order to co-ordinate its services for children under five. Strathclyde Region in the West of Scotland, an area of multiple deprivation by any measure, set up a high level committee in 1981 to consider the needs for provision for under fives. This member/officer group after long consideration decided that the only way to achieve the goal of co-ordinated services for children under five was to make radical changes in the way the services are managed and funded (Strathclyde Regional Council, 1985). It was felt that the split responsibilities and resources left parents confused, resulted in poor planning of services, and a service which was very vulnerable to cuts each time budgets were under pressure. The recommendations therefore, to ensure that day care and education for under fives would achieve a higher priority and more comprehensive service were to establish a single 'pre-five' service, with its own budget. For a number of reasons it was decided to place this Pre-Five Unit in the Education Department. It is recognised that in the short-term, expansion will inevitably be limited: the long-term aim is to develop and expand Pre-Five services. The Region has about 155, 000 children under five and has within the Region a wide variety of services. Strathclyde is reported to be well provided with nursery schools and classes compared with other areas but to have fewer playgroups and far fewer registered childminders than England. The pattern in services varies greatly from one part of the Region to another (each of which was originally a separate local authority). Of greatest concern, however, was the feeling that the service often failed to reach those in most need. It is to be hoped that this and other initiatives will be monitored in such a way as to enable other areas to learn from their experiences.

CHAPTER 13 CONTINUITY IN EARLY EDUCATION

RESEARCH CONTEXT

'Continuity and Progression' was among nineteen items identified from the short-term studies on behalf of the Management Committee for the Nursery Research Programme. It should be noted that the following was the recommendation:

> "A descriptive study of children's experiences in schools between the ages of 3 and 7 or 8 years to show the extent and nature of continuity and progression in the curriculum. This might be followed by a development project to illustrate ways of achieving continuity and progression of experiences for children in the age range" (DES, 1975a p.72).

The features identified in the above quotation are as follows:

- to study 'continuity' and 'progression';
- to consider children in the age range 3 to 7 or 8 years;
- to describe experiences, and continuity and progression in the curriculum.

The urgency to obtain evidence to influence policy, and limitations in funding, may partly explain the fact that the studies which were funded within the Programme tended to consider transition rather than continuity; to focus on a very short time-scale and organisational aspects rather than curricular progression. The context for the Programme of research has been discussed here in the introduction, the constraints noted above are referred to by Kay (1975). The researches funded within the Programme will now be discussed and further evidence presented from more recent investigations.

The issues which have been addressed in the researches include the following:

- transition from home to preschool;
- transition from preschool to reception class;
- parents and continuity.

Clearly researches considered elsewhere in this report are also relevant to this issue. Those discussed in the present chapter are the investigations with continuity and transition as their main focus.

Continuity was one of the five priority areas for research identified by the DES Committee on the basis of their own studies and the report by Tizard to SSRC (DES, 1975a). A group of studies on continuity was funded within the 'Programme' to be undertaken by the National Foundation for Educational Research. These studies funded by DES, the Schools Council and NFER are listed in *Under Fives: A Programme of Research* (DES, 1981). The research on continuity which was funded by DES from 1977-81 has been published as a book entitled *And So To School* (Cleave, Jowett and Bate, 1982); the research funded by NFER was published as *The First Transition* (Blatchford, Battle and Mays, 1982). The action research funded by the Schools Council was concerned with the development of liaison groups whose development would then be monitored and evaluated. The aim was to produce materials to assist such groups. A paper by Bate (1983) summarized the findings.

Three researches undertaken since 1980 are also relevant to the issue of continuity. A study funded by DES, directed by the present author, under the title, 'Early Education of Children with Communication Problems : Particularly those from Ethnic Minorities', was undertaken between 1982-84. All children entering reception (first) class in five primary schools were studied and samples of language in preschool units were available for a selection of children from different ethnic backgrounds. The report submitted to DES is the main source for information on that study (Clark, Barr and Dewhirst, 1984). More recently a research project was commissioned by the Assistant Masters and Mistresses Association (AMMA) in 1985, 'An Evaluation of Responses of Reception Children to School'. This project directed by Gill Barrett of the University of East Anglia will also be discussed based on the report (Barrett, 1986). Aspects of longitudinal studies on 'Parents, Teachers and Infant School' at the Thomas Coram Research Unit are also relevant to continuity and the education of under fives. Reference will thus be made to some recently published articles on that study.

A research funded by the Scottish Education Department was undertaken by Joyce Watt and Marion Flett whose report to SED was submitted in 1985 under the title *Continuity in Early Education : The Role of the Parents* (Watt and Flett, 1985). That study addresses the issue of parents and continuity in early education and changes in roles and expectations by and of parents. Watt considers these further in a recent article (Watt, 1987).

THE FIRST TRANSITION : HOME TO PRESCHOOL

This study, one of the three NFER studies within the 'Programme', was concerned with children's transition from home to preschool (Blatchford, Battle and Mays, 1982) which as the authors indicate is indeed now the first transition for many children. It is stressed that there is a need not only to consider children's experiences after entry to preschool provision but also to study the situation prior to entry. The authors also stress the need to consider this not only in one direction but "in terms of a continual and changing interplay of effects between the child's experiences in the preschool and his home environment" (Blatchford *et al.*, 1982 p.3).

It is stated that the majority of children will at some point in the preschool years enter some form of preschool provision, though the type and age on entry may vary. The team decided, however, to study only one form of transition namely that from home into nursery class or school. Children were studied prior to entry, at the point of entry, and after entry, with a focus on similarities and differences in physical aspects and on social aspects. The research involved a survey and a more detailed observational study.

Survey on transition into preschool

Seven local authorities were involved in the questionnaires to staff and interviews were conducted in three areas more local to NFER (near London). Quantitative information from the two sources was combined. The response rate for nursery schools and classes was 88%. A sample of playgroups was also included for questionnaires in four of the seven local authorities already sampled with regard to nursery schools and classes. The response rate was however much lower at 68%, a point of significance in any comparisons between nursery schools and classes and playgroups.

The findings of the survey aspect of this study with regard to entrance into preschool units reported in Blatchford et al.(1982 Chapter 2), indicate a variety of patterns whereby newcomers were admitted to an existing group. Wide differences in approaches were clearly expressed ranging from those units where mothers were expected to stay initially to those where mothers were expected to leave as soon as possible. The extent of parental involvement reported varied as did attitudes expressed by staff to parental contact. Playgroups were more likely to encourage mothers to help as a matter of policy than nurseries (63% and 41% respectively) there were also some of each which it is reported discouraged help (13% and 21% respectively).

Staff when questioned on children's reactions on entry reported varied patterns from initial hesitancy to excited 'flitting' from one activity to another. They also noted attachment to a specific member of staff and that some children were finding it easier to relate to other children than to staff.

In some of the nursery sample surveyed a number of their children had previously attended playgroups. Yet few playgroups reported contacts with nurseries and indeed the majority of those who did not have contacts were reported not to want them (Blatchford et al. 1982, p.47). Within each type of provision there were stereotypes held by some of what was believed to happen in the other type.

Observational study of transition

The research involved an observational study of 51 children as newcomers into nursery classes in two local authorities. A schedule and additional notes were used to form case studies of a limited number of the children. Children were observed each day for their first three weeks then again on their ninth week. The children were assessed and questionnaires on their adjustment were completed by staff. Information on these children's experiences at home prior to entry were obtained from parental interviews (not by observation). A more comprehensive coverage of parental views was obtained by interviewing an additional group of parents whose children were not observed in school.

The interviews of parents prior to their children's entrance to school took place in only two nearby local authorities (both involved in the survey). In one area parents with a child born in 1976 were identified and approached by health visitors to seek agreement to be interviewed. Fifty parents were interviewed in 1979. In addition the head teachers of the two nursery schools to take part in the observational study provided lists of the new intake. Parents from this list completed the sample of 86 parents interviewed. This was not a 'random' sample although it did cover a range of backgrounds and views. The findings are reported in Chapter 3 of the study. The sample is weighted to those who did wish preschool provision for their children as nearly a third of those interviewed had a child about to enter a nursery class. Because the figures for different attitudes and characteristics are given only for the total group of parents, it is difficult to be sure to what extent these selection features are influencing the responses. Most children whose mothers were interviewed in this study lived in two-parent family units, in single child families or with one sibling, in adequate accommodation which usually had access to a play area. About 30% of the mothers worked but the majority of the children spent the major part of the day with their mother as the main adult companion. It is noted that the parents (usually mother) interviewed stressed the importance of social learning for children to mix with each other. Parents reported that they would have wanted to visit the preschool unit with their children before their entry, they would then have anticipated less adverse reaction from their child. They are stated to have reported helping their children with a variety of number games, nursery rhymes, colours, etc. The researchers comment, however, that:

> "parents tend to undervalue their own influence and potential as vital factors in their children's learning except over matters where they see themselves as competent" (Blatchford *et al.*, 1982 p.68).

Parents it is suggested did not appear to appreciate that many of the everyday activities they did with their children, such as reading stories and looking at books, were of significance towards learning to read.

The observational study was of 51 children during their first three weeks in two purpose-built nursery classes and during their ninth week there. The parents of only 33 had been interviewed prior to entry. Both nurseries 'staggered' children's entry. Details are given of the two units and the observational procedures. There was found to be little statistical difference between the findings in the two units, therefore the information was pooled. The average age of the children on entry was 41 months.

Some general information is given on the patterns of the group of children on entry indicating that at free-play they were inclined to spend time on solitary activities. Where there was contact it was more likely to be with other children and only about ten per cent of the children's time over the first four weeks was reported to involve adult/child contact; this is shown analysed by type of contact. Global measures for the group of children might have included, for example, some children who had a great deal of adult contact and others who had little or none, or for whom it was all 'disciplinary' in nature. What is more important is to consider children exhibiting different patterns of entry behaviour. This is reported within the same chapter.

The first group is referred to as 'distressed' and it is reported that:

"these children were generally poor in intellectual ability, in their attitude to teachers and pupils and in their concentration, use of equipment and behaviour in directed sessions" (Blatchford *et al.*, 1982 p.110-111).

The second group referred to as 'bright constructive-non-social' were reported to be busily involved in constructive (gross) activities.

A third group was identified as 'child relaters', children who were rarely involved in solitary activities, clearly interested in contacting other children.

A fourth group was identified whose preference appeared to be to relate to adults, this then influenced the type of activities at which they were observed.

The limited number of units involved and the naturalistic setting make it difficult to assess the generalisability of such groupings. They could have been influenced by any or all of the factors of size of unit, particular available playmates, the organisation of the unit in relation to available play activities, placement of staff either at specific activities or alternatively, in charge of groups of children. Experimental studies such as those reported in *The Ecology of Preschool Behaviour* (Smith and Connolly, 1980) have an important contribution to make in assessing the generalisability of grouping. These might be found not to withstand experimental manipulation of the physical setting, size of groups, numbers of activities available or specific children available as playmates.

There was an attempt to relate behaviour on entry to pre-entry experiences. This must, however, be treated with extreme caution and certainly no causal relationship could be established. It should be noted furthermore, that there was no observational study of the children pre-entry, also that information is based on parental interviews of only 33 of the 51 children observed. The mothers of 30 of the children were interviewed after their children had attended the nursery class for about a term.

Parents were generally reported to be 'satisfied', but this was based on little 'informed' knowledge, most was gained from their children. They also seemed confused as to what part they could play in helping their children. This it was felt was partly, at least, because staff had not communicated their aims effectively to parents.

The findings on transition

This study of transition thus concerns mainly the point of entry to the preschool unit. It is based on two aspects, a survey of views of staff undertaken in the late seventies in a number of preschool units on aspects related to entry, and a more detailed consideration of the views of parents based on interviews linked with observation of children in the preschool units. It is difficult to know to what extent arrangements for entry and a smooth transition for mother and child would differ now and whether observational studies on a greater number of units and over a longer timescale would have confirmed the findings in this small, short-term observation. In general the patterns found in the observational study were comparable to those found in other research in preschool units about the same period.

What one cannot tell is whether the groups identified at this early stage would have remained stable over time. Indeed, what is to be feared is that some of the negative early patterns may for some children have become more extreme, with some children remaining solitary, or 'drifting' or lacking in concentration. What is important is to identify the type of settings which support such children. Should the suggested link with behaviour before entry, based on the interviews, be confirmed by observational studies this would strengthen even further the claims of those who suggest the need for close and harmonious links between home and school in the education of the young child.

It should be noted that in any study of which parental interviews in the home are a part, the sample is inevitably biased to the more interested, less stressed mothers. Here the sample is also biased to parents who have committed themselves to a choice of nursery attendance for their child.

The above study relates only to a limited aspect of continuity because of the timescale over which it was studied, the nature of the sample of children and the fact that the observation was in only two units.

AND SO TO SCHOOL : PRESCHOOL TO PRIMARY

The project on 'Continuity of Children's Experiences in the years 3 to 8' undertaken by NFER, funded by DES between 1977 and 1980, is reported in a book entitled *And So To School* (Cleave, Jowett and Bate, 1982). That publication subtitled, 'a study of continuity from preschool to infant school', is the source for the following discussion. It is important to note the above limitation of the focus of the research decided upon by the research team. There are references in the text to older children within the observation sample. These were, however, only those in classes in which school entrants were in 'vertically' grouped classes (with six and seven-year-olds in the same class). The activities of the older children were not studied separately nor were observations undertaken of 'middle' or 'top' infant classes. This research is more appropriately regarded as a study of transition from preschool to infant school.

There is a further important limitation to note before discussing the detailed study of the group of 36 children. There was only one child who entered school direct from home, and she was a child whose mother had chosen to keep her at home. In spite of this, there are in the text a number of tables citing percentages of time on different aspects for sub-groups of the 36 target children preschool (for example on pp. 77, 79 and 84 of Cleave *et al.*, 1982 where the numbers in the sub-groups are not given). The generalisability of the data with regard to children entering reception class direct from home must be called into question not only because of the uniqueness of the child but also the background of that child, who forms one of three case studies to which a complete chapter is devoted (Chapter 13). Celia was the only preschool child in her family, with two older siblings who were in primary school and doing well at school. The mother had chosen not to send her daughter to the local playgroup only after visiting it and for reasons she could substantiate. She knew the school which Celia would enter well as she had worked there frequently as a helper. In spite of this, entry to school was a traumatic experience for what was clearly an advanced and socially conscious child whose older siblings were already at school. There are lessons to be learnt from detailed study of such a child. It is important to note that there are still children whose first experience of school is indeed the entry to reception class; furthermore, that for some of these children this has been a conscious decision by the parents in spite of the presence of preschool units. There were such examples also among the children in the study by the author of *Young Fluent Readers* (Clark, 1976). These are not typical of the type of child whose first experience of school, or even of a group setting outside the family, is the reception class. From other evidence such children are more likely to come from lower social classes, large families or single parent families.

The parameters of the NFER study have now been clarified as have the ways in which it differed from those anticipated in the short-term studies by DES where the priority area identified for study was 'Continuity and progression in the curriculum for children between the ages of 3 and 7 or 8 years of age'(DES, 1975a). The two aspects of the study will now be reported and their findings discussed.

A survey of entry to primary school

The survey aspect of the research was undertaken in seven local authorities, including London boroughs and four non-metropolitan counties. Six types of provision were studied namely nursery schools and classes, infant classes, playgroups, day nurseries and childminders. A sample was selected, balanced for the proportion of each type of provision available and representing education, social services and the voluntary sector, thereafter units were 'randomly' included. Sixty-three of these 181 provisions studied were infant classes catering for entrants, some 'vertically grouped' (that is including a wide age range in a single class), others were reception classes for children who had just entered school. This aspect involved interviews of staff concerning their aims, and visits during which the physical environment and materials could be studied. In addition a profile of how the children spent their time was investigated by a two-hour 'scan' type of observation, timetabled activities were also noted. Differences between types of provision in a variety of features, physical, organisational and in relation to activity are reported. This shows wide differences within as well as between types of provision. The researchers in this aspect were making general observations but were able to test their observations further from the more detailed, but less extensive study of 36 children before and after entry to infant school.

The observational study

It is perhaps appropriate to note here the characteristics of the small sample for the longitudinal study. It will then be possible to report the findings more precisely, showing the extent to which that extended and confirmed the survey. The 36 target children were in four different local authorities (three of which were in the survey) to provide a variety of types of area. Clusters of infant schools were selected and their related preschool provision. Children were then randomly selected from the transfer lists. For practical reasons children were required to have a good record of attendance. As noted earlier only one of the children entered infant class direct from home, the remaining children entered from a variety of provisions, two children were attending two types of provision. These children entered twelve different infant schools, 21 in September intake, the remainder in January. The ethnic origin of the children is not stated. Each child was observed during the last six weeks before entry to infant school, at the preschool unit or at home, and for the first six weeks in infant school. Children were observed for ten minutes in each hour, once a week, such that the observation covered the last two hours before lunch and first two after lunch. The observer noted systematically what the child was doing, with whom, with how much choice and adult involvement. Informal observations were made at other times of the children's behaviour and reactions to different types of routine. In addition there were parental interviews in the child's home before and after transition. The adult in charge of the preschool, the head of the infant school and class teacher were also interviewed.

The findings and their relevance to early education

Based mainly on the survey data of 181 units the researchers discuss differences between units in physical features, available resources and the scale with which children had to cope within both the immediate group and the extended unit or school. A profile of how the children spent their day is reported based on a two-hour observation in each unit and timetabled information (see Cleave et al., 1982 p.63 for a comparative table of types of activities).

With regard to the preschool units, sufficient similarities were found for nursery schools and classes to be treated together in the analysis. Their 'joint profile' is reported to be surprisingly similar to that of playgroups (Cleave *et al.*, 1982 p.60). This may of course mark wide differences within types of provision with regard to individual units. Such units would have relatively comparable age groups. It is difficult to assess the extent to which the age range of children present would have influenced the findings in day nurseries(or at childminders) where very much younger children might have been present during the observations. It is noted that in the nursery schools and classes and playgroups three types of activity predominated occupying more than half the child's time, namely:

> spatial, perceptual and fine motor activities; art and tactile activities; and imaginative and representational activities.

These same activities are reported in the day nursery but with less evidence of fine motor and imaginative and creative activities (see comment above).

A profile was also prepared of infant classes which was compared with the preschool settings. The sample of 63 such classes includes single age classes and 'vertically grouped' with older children as well as the new entrants. It is thus difficult to assess the extent to which the observed differences in the 'profiles' between these classes and the preschool units relate to the activities of the younger children - the focus of the study. The age range may have varied from a few months to several years. All such infant classes are settings with which a new entrant might be faced. It is thus important to note the points made by the researchers from the general survey and to assess the extent to which these were substantiated by the study in depth, with its focus on the experience of individual children.

The main types of activity frequently seen in the preschool units were no longer prominent in the infant classes. Gross motor activity was mainly confined to timetabled periods and playtime; there were fewer opportunities for art and tactile expression and imaginative expression became minimal. The children were frequently observed in what are referred to as 'verbal and symbolic tasks'. In view of the age range in many of the classes the predominance of '3Rs' activities would be no surprise. Observational studies of individual children over a much more extended period of time would be required to assess the appropriateness of the activities and the extent to which these supported and extended children's competence. Some evidence on this aspect will be reported later from a study by the author covering a longer period of children's school experiences in preschool and infant school (Clark, Barr and Dewhirst, 1984 and from the research by Barrett, 1986).

There are several important points made by the researchers in the NFER study about transition.

1) The first of these concerns the effects of organisational differences. These may be related partly to the presence in many infant classes of only one teacher, and indeed of only one adult for all or most of the day. The reception class is also part of a much larger unit to whose demands it must be tailored and some of whose facilities it must share. To quote:

"Perhaps the most striking difference between preschools and infant classes in general is in the amount of 'dead' or non-task time. Infants did at least three times as much waiting, queueing and lining-up as preschoolers" (Cleave *et al.*, 1982 p.64)

This may have been associated partly with organisational features and in particular the adult/child ratio and the size of the larger unit of which the child is now part. It may also have stemmed from very different attitudes and expectations of these young children by their teachers. From the in depth study the researchers note that some preschool units were indeed preparing their oldest children for the routines and expectations which they would meet upon transition. Likewise it was found that a number of infant classes 'made allowance' for the new entrants with regard to abiding by the rules of the classroom.

2) A second point of difference observed between the preschool and infant school settings relates to the proportion of time during which the child made 'choice' from the available activities. In the preschool units most of the time the children were free to make choices as to their activities; in the infant classes choice was seldom available. Since the children were observed to make such choices at the younger age one is perhaps led to consider whether more available opportunity for choice, could have avoided at least some of the 'dead-time' referred to earlier.

3) Likewise a third difference noted was a more explicit distinction between 'play' and 'work' between the preschool units and the infant classes. The role of play becomes very different and an activity confined to the playground or a reward for work completed.

4) Finally there were dramatic differences between preschool and infant class settings in the numbers of children with whom children are in direct and indirect contact.

These features may differentiate a child's experiences in the infant school and beyond from earlier experiences in preschool units and in the home in terms of choice, of play or work and of mobility. As issues in early education they have been discussed elsewhere by the present author in relation to the NFER study and others (see Clark, 1983). These were found to be useful distinctions in comparing and contrasting the preschool and infant settings and the perceptions of the infant teachers in my study of early education (Clark, Barr and Dewhirst, 1984). Before turning to that study there are, however, several further studies on transition and continuity whose findings are relevant to the issues raised by the NFER study on transition to school and between units. The next research to be discussed on 'Starting School' has only recently been completed.

STARTING SCHOOL

Following the publication of a survey concerning the behaviour of 'Children Starting School' by the Assistant Masters and Mistresses Association (AMMA) the association decided in 1985 to commission a study to improve understanding of the responses of young children to starting school and to make suggestions for practice. The research was undertaken by the Centre for Applied Research in Education in the University of East Anglia. The report on the research, entitled *Starting School* (Barrett, 1986) describes a 'naturalistic' research in which no attempt was made to control for differences between schools and children but rather to represent them in a case study of children starting school and by collaborative research involving teachers of reception class children. The report thus represents a variety of views and contains many and extensive quotations of the views of those interviewed, adults and children. Because of the nature of the research it is difficult to reflect its content by brief reference in this report.

The Study

The research was brief, from September 1985 until June 1986 and had two phases. The first phase involved teachers who studied their own reception classrooms, activities and organisation, and observed target children's responses for the first months of each term during that school year. Details of the background of the schools were also collected. The other phase was comparable to the NFER study reported above in that it involved observation of children in playgroup or nursery during the month prior to their entry to school and for the first month in school. Parents were also involved in making observations of the children at home and were interviewed. Following the case study the factors appearing to influence the children's responses were discussed within the wider group of teachers involved in the other aspect of the project.

Main conclusions and their practical implications

The main conclusions of the research as summarised in the report (Barrett, 1986, p.2-5) include the following five points:

1) There is a need for children to learn 'survival' skills including what they can do and how to cope with 'not knowing' and the feeling this may arouse.

2) The ideas teachers learnt in training did not appear to help them understand what children know on entry and how they respond to school.

3) Teachers need to be able to respond to children as individuals because of the wide differences in children's entry skills and survival skills.

4) The staff-pupil ratio in infant class was felt to be inadequate. Teachers felt that summer born children entering school in the summer term suffered particularly when they entered existing classes.

It is important to note, however, that most schools involved in the study had three intakes of 'rising fives' per year and that the children observed by the research all entered reception class in January. Thus there could be little research evidence of possible effects for the youngest children of entry to school in September, at the beginning of the school year when aged about four years of age, and possibly for the full day.

5) It was felt that ideas about 'work' and 'play' need to be clarified so that parents, teachers and children can communicate about activities in school.

6) A need was felt by teachers, parents and other professionals for more links between themselves and between home and school.

The reader is referred to the study itself for practical suggestions and for some idea of the types of responses.

Two aspects are of interest to a wider readership because of their potential for teacher training:

a) the use of photographs of young children in a variety of reception classroom settings to elicit views from young children. Most revealing were the children's interpretations of contexts which they related to their own;

b) the study of the physical layout and organisation of the classroom combined with guided observation of target children by the reception class teachers. This provided not only information for others, but also heightened the awareness of the teachers who participated to the wide individual differences in the children's needs and responses.

In assessing the generalisability of the points made by those involved in the research it is important to note briefly the nature of the sample. The teacher observation study is described In Appendix 2 of Barrett (1986). It covered 34 schools in two local authorities in different parts of England. It is clear just how varied were the possible contexts which children might experience on entry to school. Most of the schools taking part in the study were 'first' schools (with a possible age range of from 3 or 5 to 7 or 9). All schools had at least one mixed age class. Most schools in the study admitted three intakes per year of 'rising fives'. Only a few schools admitted all children in September and those born later tended to attend part-time for the first part of the year. Thus this aspect of the study has few classes admitting the younger four-year-olds which is becoming more frequent. A number of the teachers who were involved were within their first few years of teaching, although there were some with many years of experience; a few had not previously taught reception class children. The reader is referred to Barrett (1986) for further details on the reported organisation of classes and schools, most of which is provided in a narrative style.

A case study is reported of only one class of 23 children observed in a first school, children who were to start mornings only in January 1986 as 'rising fives'. The rest of the age group who had entered school in the previous September were in vertically grouped classes. Because of numbers the school had created a separate and differently organised class for this group, taught by a part-time teacher who had not previously taught reception class children. Thus the class was atypical in a number of ways with only a limited age range of children on entry. Furthermore 15 of the 23 children went to the same playgroup only a few minutes away from the school and had attended for about a year, while four other children went to different pre-schools.

For most children in this case study, as in the NFER research, reception class was not their first experience of a group setting. What they were facing was continuity, conflict or contrast at transition rather than transfer direct from home. As most of the children were starting school with companions from the preschool setting, it is difficult from the case study to analyse differential effects between different settings.

In spite of these features and limitations of the sample, there are in the case study many insights into the children's reactions and relationships which the observer was able to highlight. Many confirm the sorts of dichotomy between preschool and reception class noted earlier. One quotation is pertinent showing the effect of direction as compared with considered choices. These children, now somewhat older, had to rely on the teacher indicating exactly what to do, not only the parameter of permitted behaviour. To quote:

> "Having done it, or having been told they had 'done it' they were either redirected, chose for themselves or returned to the mat to engage in free activity. For a number of children there was an increase in inactivity when they were uninvolved and appeared uncertain what to do" (Barrett, 1986, p.51-52).

Her interviews with parents, after as well as before the children's entry to school, enabled the researcher to explore and to illustrate ways in which these children were still being provided with many learning experiences by their parents, exhibiting there on occasion skills at a much more advanced level than they were able to exhibit in the classroom setting.

> "The children started school apparently eager and keen to learn, and learn they did from activities and each other, what they had to do. However over the four weeks, as they learned what was expected of them, it was increasingly easy to perceive them as a class as they engaged in the same teacher directed activities as each other with less teacher involvement and guidance in free choice activities.
>
> The special interests and knowledge that the children had developed at home were barely evident at school" (Barrett, 1986 pp.60-61).

The function of the case study was to raise issues for further exploration. Throughout the report the match or mismatch between pupils' pre- and out-of-school experiences and those in a variety of classrooms is considered. Possible practical implications are also discussed (Barrett, 1986, p.130 onwards).

EARLY EDUCATION AND ETHNIC MINORITIES

In none of the studies referred to so far has there been any focus on continuity or transition in groups where the children are from ethnic minority backgrounds, or more specifically where for many of the children English, the language of instruction in the classroom, is not their mother tongue.

Background to the research

A study funded by DES on 'preschool education and children with special needs' undertaken by the present author in the West Midlands in 1979-81 included all nursery schools and classes, day nurseries and a sample of playgroups in Coventry. In Birmingham there was a similar sample for an area of the City covering 21% of the children in preschool education (Clark, Robson and Browning, 1982). All 94 preschool units were visited and interviews undertaken with the person in charge to discuss their setting and to identify children perceived as having special needs. It became clear that in addition to children identified as having a variety of handicapping conditions there were many children about whom the staff were concerned because of their limited competence in English. There were also problems of differential diagnosis regarding whether they might also have difficulties in their mother tongue.

In some preschool units in these areas most children attending were from ethnic minority backgrounds and although most of the children had been born in this country many entered school with little or no English, often speaking a language in which the staff were not competent. Although the focus of that study was on special needs it was possible to highlight some of the issues, not only in identifying special needs in children whose language was other than English, but also in identifying gifted children where their command of English on entry was limited. In one unit it was possible to identify several such children since there was a member of staff who spoke several Asian languages fluently.

None of the studies reported so far have considered any of the issues for staffs, parents or children, where some, many or most of the children speak a language other than that of the staff. At most there is reference to inclusion in the sample of multi-ethnic areas. Where target children have been selected in studies in preschool units, and of language development in the homes, often children whose mother tongue is not English have been excluded. Yet by 1981, in Birmingham for example, 25.1% of the live births were to parents either or both of whom were of Asian ethnic origin; Afro-Caribbean origin accounted for a further 9.1%. In most instances both parents rather than one parent were of Asian ethnic origin (See Clark, Barr and Dewhirst, 1984, pp.6-11 for further details). Some teachers concerned with the education of children under five may thus have in their schools and classes few children whose mother tongue is English, or who speak a language understood by the staff. Such teachers could feel justified in questioning how relevant to their major concerns is much of the research, reported in preschool units or indeed of language interaction in the homes. Two headteachers of nursery schools where most children are of Asian ethnic origin, one in Sandwell, the other in Birmingham, have addressed the issues of greatest concern to them in observational studies in their own schools using techniques developed in studies directed by the present author. 'The Play of Sikh Children in a Nursery Class and at Home', was the focus for Davenport (1983). Patterns of interaction within her nursery school were studied by Pearson who as a result of her observations was led to make organisational changes in the setting (Pearson, 1987).

The Study

Because of the lack of evidence on this important issue, the present author sought further funding from DES for a study which would focus upon children entering reception class from a variety of ethnic backgrounds. Information on the language of a number of these children was available prior to the commencement of the funded research from recordings in the preschool units. Further children who entered school straight from home were also studied and language competence was assessed both in their mother tongue and in English. Contexts for learning in the preschool units and in reception classes were compared and contrasted. A number of these children entered reception class between 4 and 5 years of age, whereas in other schools between 4 years 9 months and 5 years of age. That study is thus clearly relevant to the current discussion, particularly since parental interviews in their mother tongue, Punjabi, were also undertaken for a number of the children from ethnic minorities.

The basis for the following discussion will be the report to DES (Clark, Barr and Dewhirst, 1984). Other related publications are also available on the language aspects of the study and the importance of assessing the competence of children across a variety of contexts (See papers by Dewhirst, by Payne and Coates in Clark, 1985). A summary of the study is also available (in Clark, Barr and Dewhirst, 1985). The interviews of the Punjabi-speaking parents set in the context of other studies on that aspect are reported in greater detail elsewhere (Whittaker, 1985).

The Sample

The research on 'Early Education and Children from Ethnic Minority Backgrounds' was initially funded by DES as a one-year project of children entering reception class in five primary schools during 1982-83. Limited additional funding in the following year made it possible to interview the reception class teachers and a sample of parents and to reassess the competence in English of the children whose mother tongue was Punjabi. Five primary schools in Birmingham and Sandwell were selected which differed in the proportions of children from different ethnic minorities. Samples of language for some children in preschool units collected before the commencement of funded research were available. Three of these schools admitted children to reception class on three entry dates in the year (aged 4.9 to 5 years of age); the remaining two schools admitted all children at the beginning of the school year (4-5 years of age). There were large and small schools with different organisational patterns. Three schools had a nursery class attached: children entering the other schools might have attended a nearby nursery school. There were 247 children who entered reception class in these five schools in 1982-83, 34% of whom were of Asian ethnic origin and 24% of Afro-Caribbean ethnic origin. For the majority of children (189) this was indeed not 'starting school', but transfer of class in three of the schools, and of school for most children in the other two schools. A minority only of the children entered direct from home, a few from other preschool provision or from another school or country. Some of the children, depending on their precise date of birth, and that of their friends, were able to enter reception class together with close friends. For others the experience was very different.

It was possible to assess the language competence in English of 215 of the children on a test specifically prepared for children about that age and which assessed their competence in responding to questions of different levels of difficulty and perceptual distance such as they might meet in the classroom. Samples of the language of some children in a variety of contexts with adults and peers were also recorded.

The findings and their implications

Language

In each school there were children who had impressive language abilities and others who could respond adequately only to simple questions closely tied to perception. Likewise, there were children within each ethnic group who were competent in responding to complex questions and others with limited competence in English. The children assessed in Punjabi also showed wide differences in competence in their mother tongue. From the parental interviews it was established that for a number of these children Punjabi was the language of the home when adults addressed these young children. It must be questioned how much of the classroom discourse could be comprehended by some of these young children in their early months in the reception class. Some attended 'withdrawal' classes to improve their competence in English. It should be stressed that there were young children competent in two languages. Furthermore, the apparent competence of the children was very different in different contexts, some enabling them to show impressive skills, others not. For some children these skills were more evident in the preschool setting, others in peer-peer interaction in a stimulating setting planned within the research (See Clark *et al.*, 1984 Chapter 12 and Coates 1985).

Contrasts in preschool and reception classes

Observations in reception classrooms revealed basic similarities in the curriculum offered but there were differences in the extent to which teachers encouraged or permitted talk by and between children. In general the classrooms were similar to those reception classes described in *And So to School* (Cleave *et al.*, 1982), and contrasted with the pattern in the preschool units:

　　'Work' was favoured (rather than play);

children were generally dependent (rather than independent);

static much of the time (rather than mobile);

set work featured largely (as compared with choices).

Interviews with teachers subsequently confirmed their commitments to the patterns observed in their classrooms.

There was evidence of discontinuity for some children who had shown at the pre-school stage an independence and prolonged concentration which did not appear to be stimulated in the reception classroom. There were other children who made rapid progress in the basic skills in the 'work' ethos of the reception classroom.

Concern must be expressed for some aspects including the context for children who entered reception class direct from home, with mother tongue not English, and/or who thus knew few other children or the expectations of teachers.

There appeared to be a pattern of expectations for reception class among the teachers which tended to take little account of the precise age of the children in a particular reception class. Similarly there was a tendency, in schools with three entry dates, to refer to children who entered in the Summer Term as having only one term in reception class, which is indeed a result of organisational decisions. Both of the above are important in relation to continuity and the appropriateness or otherwise of early education for children of different ages, in different organisation patterns and from different backgrounds. Some children had several changes of class within a short time of entry to school, as a result of organisational problems in smaller schools.

The policy for entry has now been changed in Birmingham one of the areas in this study, from three entry dates to one, mainly of September entry to reception class for children aged 4 to 5 years. Thus many children become 'reception class' at a much earlier age, with as a result, a very different school day and very different expectations. The aspects of 'discontinuity' are ones to which attention must be addressed. They can only be considered where there is real dialogue between those who are knowledgeable on early education, the evidence and the issues. To focus on four-year-olds in reception class or any such specific cut off would be unfortunate and dangerous. This would fail to draw attention to the important issues of continuity in the early education of young children from one stage to another, one class to another and between home and school.

Aims of preschool education

It must be a matter of concern that even in schools with nursery classes there seemed to be little understanding among reception class teachers of the aims of preschool education. That language development might be an important aim in the preschool did not appear to be realised. The aim was seen mainly as one of socializing. There was limited appreciation of what activities and experiences might have been encountered or in the expectations set for children who had attended preschool units. Thus the possible gulf for children entering reception class straight from home, which might not be English-speaking, was unlikely to be appreciated. Some of the children from ethnic minorities might have learnt something of school and its expectations from older siblings; for others there were no older siblings and the parents had no experience themselves of education in this country. The lack of continuity was perhaps greatest for some children whose parents had themselves insufficient command of English even to express their concerns. All parents interviewed felt welcome at school but some who would have welcomed more contact were reluctant to initiate it.

The schools in this study were committed, caring settings for the education of young children. They were integrated multi-ethnic settings where the children's friends could be and were often from different ethnic backgrounds. There must nevertheless be concern at the organisational difficulties in establishing continuity between these two stages of children's learning even where for most children this had been within the educational setting. Even more concern must be felt for the children who are in such classes but are never the focus in observational studies, namely, those who enter late, have poor attendance and/or change school frequently.

This study further underlined the gulf between those involved at the preschool stage of education and those involved in teaching in the reception class and beyond. There seems also to be a lack of knowledge of the aims and activities in the preschools by colleagues in the later stages. This apparent discontinuity was confirmed in a study by Wallace (1985) who explored the aims of nursery school headteachers, and compared these with how teachers with responsibility for infant departments saw the aims and purposes in preschool education. The latter saw this in terms of socialisation and preparing the children for school, rather than as a stage of education in its own right. They also felt that entry of children to reception class at a younger age was valuable as it enabled real teaching to commence. They were thus inclined to accept uncritically the change in the authority to one entry date, and thus younger four-year-olds in reception class. Perhaps this is one unfortunate result of the term 'preschool', and even of the focus of a research microscope on that aspect in isolation. Financial cuts and threatening headlines in recent years questioning the value of preschool education have all added to this conflict.

Discontinuity in aims and perceptions of education from one stage to another are confusing to child and parent. There is also the danger that preschool education is seen mainly as a preparation for the next stage - whose rationale has indeed not been researched.

PARENTS, TEACHERS AND THE INFANT SCHOOL

A recent study funded by ESRC as part of its grant to the Thomas Coram Research Unit as a Designated Research Centre and directed by Barbara Tizard has a number of aspects which are of relevance to the issue of continuity between home and school, between reception classes in different schools and between stages in the infant department within a school. Different aspects of this longitudinal study have included larger or smaller samples of children and a variety of techniques. Much of it covers children aged over five years of age and is thus beyond the current remit.

The children were observed in their classroom in each of their first three years in infant school and their attainment was assessed in top infants and at the end of the first year in the junior school. Information on the curriculum coverage was also obtained from their teachers both for the class in general and for specific children. The teachers' views on influences on children's progress were also considered and these were compared with the views of the parents. Particular attention was given to achieving a sample of children of indigenous white and Afro-Caribbean ethnic origin. Pre-entry skills were assessed in the nursery class immediately prior to entry to reception class and the mothers of these children were interviewed during that summer.

One aim was to assess whether prior to entry to reception class there were already differences between boys and girls and between the two ethnic groups in pre-entry skills and in parental support and views. Girls were found to have higher pre-entry skills in literacy and numeracy than boys, but differences were not linked with ethnic origin at this stage in a sample where school attended was matched and social class was comparable (Blatchford, Burke *et al.*, 1985). It should be noted that all children in this aspect had attended nursery class. A wider sample within the same schools was utilized in some of the later aspects of the study in the infant classes.

Several papers have already appeared on parts of this study, others are in press, or preparation (Blatchford, Burke *et al.* (1985); Farquhar, Blatchford *et al.*(1985); Blatchford, Burke *et al.* (1987a); Blatchford, Burke *et al.* (1987b); Farquhar, Blatchford *et al.*(1987).

The Sample

It is important to note the nature of this sample, its strengths and limitations. The sample is described in Blatchford, Burke *et al.*, 1985. The study took place in six divisions of the Inner London Education Authority (ILEA). The sample consisted of all children entering the reception classes from nursery classes of 33 infant schools in September 1982. To be included a school was required to have at least two children who were white indigenous and two of Afro-Caribbean origin. All schools chosen had a nursery class and the initial assessment of the 277 children (171 'white', 106 'black') was carried out in the nursery class. It should be noted that this study does not cover children of Asian ethnic origin, that the majority of the schools were in working class areas and that on demographic measures the schools were below the mean for ILEA as a whole. The mean age of the children when assessed was four years nine months (S.D. two months). All children were attending nursery class and it could be argued that the parents interviewed might therefore have been more committed to their children's education than a random sample. The researchers note that:

> "the majority of three- and four-year-olds in the ILEA do attend some form of nursery education" (Blatchford, Burke *et al.*, 1985 p.53).

For the purposes of making inter-ethnic comparisons the care in matching was important; for more generalised points about the range of children's entry skills on admission to reception class the study is, however, more limited.

Furthermore little reference is made to the aims of the nursery classes or to possible influences of this on the knowledge of some or all of the children. The children's interactions in the nursery class are not a focus in the study. It is important to note the age of the children on entry to reception class. The mean age was 4 years 9 months when tested at the end of nursery class (details are not given of the range of ages and whether this differed from one school to another). Attention is also not directed to differential attainment of younger and older children in the articles available so far.

Some findings

The aspects of this study in which the views of parents and reception class teachers are compared is of importance (See Farquhar, Blatchford et al., 1985). No parent refused to be interviewed and the sample included 202 parents (114 'white' and 88 'black'). The teachers' sample was 31 reception teachers. There were striking differences in the views of parents and teachers. The teachers appeared to place clear restrictions on the nature of academic related activities in which they felt it was appropriate for parents to engage at home. The researchers suggest that the teachers may have been influenced by educational views of deprivation, the association of social class with poor academic achievement and by the preponderance of working class children in the sample. While the parents of both ethnic groups regarded the school as having a major role in determining academic achievement, many still stressed that they would help their children at home once they started school, as part of their role as parents. Clearly the willingness to be interviewed shown by these parents, as in so many studies where parents have been approached shows a potential resource. It is possible from this study to assess parents' expressed views, but not the extent to which they were reflected in practice. There does appear here, however, to be further evidence of lack of co-ordination and of possible discontinuities in children's early education similar to that noted by other researchers. Had children who entered reception class direct from home, or from other preschool settings than the attached nursery class been included, even wider differences in pre-entry skills and greater discontinuities might have been revealed.

CONTINUITY AND THE ROLE OF PARENTS

'Continuity' and 'the role of parents' were both identified in the mid-seventies as critical areas for research. The projects which were funded tended to focus on only one or other aspect. More recently a research was commissioned by the Scottish Education Department, as part of an interdepartmental study of provision for children under the age of six years, which had as its focus the relationship between 'continuity' and 'the role of parents'. This research undertaken by Joyce Watt and Marion Flett of the University of Aberdeen during1983-84 adopted a case study approach. Three primary schools and related preschool provision each in a different Region in Scotland were included. Because of possible implications for policy it was felt to be important to study more than one Region; those selected were Grampian, Tayside and Fife (the area in which Watt's earlier study of co-ordination was undertaken just prior to Regionalization). All these areas were accessible to Aberdeen yet provided variety of patterns. It was hoped that the findings would be relevant not only to education interests but to the social work departments responsible for day nurseries and for registration of preschool playgroups and childminders. Thus the variety of preschool provision available to children entering each primary school was included in the research, a pattern which differed for the three selected primary schools. Because of the limited staffing and timescale of the project, and in view of the case study approach which involved participant observation and interviews, it was decided to confine the study to a limited geographical area (100 mile area). Another limitation noted is that 'parent in this study, as in many others, refers to 'mother'.

The information cited here is taken from the report submitted to the SED, which has a brief valuable outline on relevant research in Chapter 2 (Watt and Flett, 1985). From their study of the available literature Watt and Flett suggest that three general points emerge:

a) "that parents are in the best position to provide long-term continuity for their children":

b) "schools and preschool groups provide their own forms of continuity for children" .... "they are normally concerned to ease the transition between one educational stage and the next" and to provide "an internal continuity, based on professional assumptions":

c) how best "to link the continuity provided by the parent with that provided by the professionals" since "then it seems there are problems" (Watt and Flett, 1985 p.22-23).

These indeed are the types of issues which only a detailed study planned as this can analyse. Survey type studies or questionnaire researches on attitudes of parents and professionals inevitably miss the subtleties of the issues, failing to identify personalities and practices in sufficient detail for their roles in promoting or preventing continuity for the child to be assessed.

The Study

The focus in this study as in most others within the topic of continuity, was on transition. The provisions selected are not claimed to be other than 'instances', that is to be either 'typical' or atypical, but are selected to contribute to an overall picture. Two criteria were adopted in selection, the first the willingness of those in charge to participate and the variety of preschool provision they could provide. All these primary schools catered for children for the first seven years of their 'compulsory' schooling, a common pattern in Scotland, unlike a number of areas in England, where school organisation may be of 'infant' school and 'junior' school. Transfer to secondary school would normally be one year earlier in England than in Scotland, or be 'first' and 'middle' school. The children entered school at the beginning of the school year in August aged between about 4 years 6 months and 5 years 6 months, the normal pattern in Scotland.

These two features made the study design more easily implemented within a one year research, and made it relevant well beyond the areas in Scotland in which it was undertaken because of the typicality of its pattern. This, however, does not make it less relevant in England. What must be remembered in considering the implications elsewhere is that any discontinuities found in these areas for parents and for the children from 3 to 12 years of age may be even greater elsewhere.

The first term of the one-year research was spent mainly in the three primary schools so that a picture could be built up of transition into compulsory schooling. The researchers interviewed 45 parents of children in the reception class, attended meetings held for parents, collected documentation on transfer. They also asked teachers to keep records of visits paid during the first term by parents. Talks with children in the reception class were supported by discussions with some children now in the third class who were asked to recall their first memories of school. Nine further parents were interviewed with parallel interviews of their children's teachers. Much of the second term was devoted to studies of and in the ten preschools which include two nursery schools, six playgroups, one children's centre and a day nursery. By March 1984 meetings were arranged in each area, to which parents and staff in the primary school and preschool groups were invited, at which the main issues identified were raised and discussed. In the final term of the project the team observed the preparation for transition by preschool units and the receiving primary schools.

The findings

The report contains detailed case studies of each primary school and its related preschool provision, which is interesting reading giving a clear and balanced picture of the strengths and weaknesses of the various practices and their relationship to local or chance factors in their development.

Three general points are important:

a) that although the importance of the home was always accepted: "attempts to relate the child's experience at home or in the community at large with what he did in the group or school were few and spasmodic" (and were through the presence or interest of the mother);

b) that although many children at the preschool stage attended two or even more preschool groups there were few links between the provisions, (these also came through the interest and presence of the mother);

c) transition from preschool to primary school involved organisational planning between groups to make transition happy and not stressful, gradual familiarization and similarities at the point of transfer:

> "The parents' role at this stage, however, seemed largely incidental, geared largely to helping the school make the child's organisational move as easy as possible" (Watt and Flett, 1985 pp 30-31).

The general findings and recommendations of the study are reported in Watt and Flett, 1985 Chapter 9, where the researchers stress the dangers of a number of discontinuities:

1) between home and school groups where parents were not involved and there were dangers of misunderstandings since in these circumstances the child became the main 'channel of communication' between them;

2) in the parents' minds between the purposes of preschool and school (also to be found in many professionals involved at the different stages from evidence from other researchers);

3) between preschool playgroups and nursery schools;

4) of parents excluded when transition becomes a matter handled by professionals;

5) for parents whose children move from one group to another and who find their role changes from 'needed' to 'not needed' to 'excluded';

6) there was felt to be an unfortunate discontinuity in use or non-use of records;

7) although the project team were not themselves able to look at continuity/discontinuity in the curriculum there was evidence of discontinuity at the primary school level in the parents' perception;

8) the important final point made was the difference with regard to 'continuity' and the 'role of the parents' between theory and what was feasible in practice. The two related aspects of training and resources were stressed with dissatisfaction noted by most professionals in the lack in their training of guidance on work with parents. Concern is expressed that this may still be true, and not confined to Scotland. The importance of this as an aspect of in-service training is stressed.

The recommendations based on the study are listed as specific points on pages 144-5 of the report (Watt and Flett, 1985). These points are developed further and their implications for early education explored in a recent article by Watt (Watt 1987).

'Continuity with extension' between preschool and primary education, Watt argues should be the aim, based on acceptance of the major importance of the preschool years.

There will then be -

'Compatibility' without 'sameness', and 'stimulation' without 'shock'.

She indicates the following major difficulties in providing this 'continuity with extension' in early education:

a) the inadequate provision of preschool education;

b) the fact that parents and even some primary teachers see it only in terms of social benefits and as a preparation for school;

c) the short period children spend in preschool education and the fact that children may move in and out of several types of provision;

d) the danger that pressures for co-ordination of preschool services may lead to a neglect of links between preschool and primary.

CHAPTER 14 EARLY EDUCATION AND CHILDREN WITH SPECIAL NEEDS

In the last fifteen years there have been many experimental and other studies concerning children with perceptual difficulties and the developmentally young. An evaluation of such research would be a major undertaking in its own right. Research specifically into children with severe handicapping conditions has not been studied as part of this investigation. The interpretation of the remit to include children with special needs was to ensure that research relevant to those responsible for the education of children under five, a number of whom may have special needs, was considered. The aim in this chapter is to identify issues which may still be of concern, on some of which further research may be needed. A knowledge of the evidence on developments in early education in general is important as a framework within which to assess the extent to which changes in legislation and in provision may have altered the situation for children under five who may have 'special educational needs', and for those responsible for their early education.

THE RESEARCH CONTEXT

The education of children with handicapping conditions, or as they are now referred to, those with special needs, was considered to be an area which required further research both by those interviewed by Tizard for her report to SSRC (Tizard, 1975), and by those who undertook the short term studies for DES (DES, 1975a). Research concerned with the education of severely subnormal children was one of the items listed by Tizard (Tizard, 1975 p.67) and indeed there has continued to be funding for a range of research on a variety of topics related to handicapped children, particularly based at the Hester Adrian Research Centre in Manchester University. There have been experimental studies, projects involving parents, and some with a focus on a particular handicap, such as Down's Syndrome. It is not possible within this current report to do justice to the range and variety of studies on young, or developmentally young, children with special needs. Many of the experimental studies may indeed legitimately be regarded as beyond its remit. Tizard refers also to the work of Margaret Manning in Edinburgh as being one of the few funded studies concerned with non-cognitive aspects of children's behaviour preschool, namely aggression and hostility. By 1975 she was reported to be extending this work, and undertaking a follow-up study to assess the predictability with regard to later

behaviour of characteristics and problems shown at an early age. Sadly this promising work has not been fully reported as a result of the untimely death of Margaret
Manning, one of several such deaths in recent years of pioneers in research on young
children.

The issue of integration at the preschool stage of children with special needs, the requirements for its success, and the problems in its implementation, are clearly of
relevance to this current study, and both were identified as issues requiring research
in the two reports referred to above. Indeed one of the five priority areas for research
identified by the DES Management Committee was 'The problems associated with
the integration of handicapped children into normal nursery classes'. A proposal by
Maurice Chazan and Alice Laing of University College of Swansea to undertake research into the early education of handicapped children was accepted as part of the
Nursery Research Programme. At the same time there were other initiatives underway which led to commissioning or funding of major research projects concerning
handicapped children and their education, not within the above Programme.

In 1974 a Committee of Enquiry, chaired by Mary Warnock, was established "to
review educational provision in England, Scotland and Wales for children and young
people handicapped by disabilities of body or mind". In view of the size and breadth
of the remit the committee decided to divide the work between four sub-commit-
tees, one of which was concerned with the needs of handicapped children under five
(HMSO, 1978 p.1). One research on under fives funded by DES to provide evidence
for the Committee was a study by the present author in Scotland on 'Preschool
Education and Handicapped and Exceptional Children'. A summary of this study in
Scotland forms Appendix 6 of the Warnock Report. A major section of the report,
Special Educational Needs is devoted to 'Children Under Five' listed as one of the
'Three Areas of First Priority' (HMSO, 1978). Post-Warnock the present author was
again funded by DES to undertake a further study of 'Preschool education and
children with special needs', on this occasion in the West Midlands, the term 'spe-
cial needs' now replacing the previously used terms relating to handicap.

The studies by Chazan and by Clark referred to above were in ordinary educational settings, although each has included some consideration of special preschool units
in the LEAs in question. A further study of integration in a more experimental setting, Anson House, was undertaken by the Hester Adrian Research Centre.
Observational studies undertaken there included an assessment of the extent of social interaction between the handicapped children attending the nursery class and
the non-handicapped. While this is a valuable research model, especially with the
observational and other facilities which were available, only a very limited number
of children were present at the same time. The group of ten children studied included
six handicapped and four non-handicapped children (six boys and four girls); four
of the handicapped children in the study were Down's Syndrome (Sebba, 1983).
Thus the evidence on social interaction between handicapped and non-handicapped
is limited in its generalisability.

Some of the recommendations made in the Warnock Report have been incorporated in subsequent legislation, others have not, including the proposal for the establishment of structures for the promotion and co-ordination of research in special education. Some of the recommendations with regard to children under five are dependent for their implementation as intended on developments in other aspects of education. It is recommended in the Warnock Report, for example, that wherever possible children with special needs should be educated in ordinary nursery schools or classes. Coupled with this is a recommendation that nursery education for all should be substantially increased. It is stressed that it is neither practicable nor desirable to have preferential admission for children with special needs, and that special nursery classes should be available for children with the most severe or complex difficulties. A number of conditions are set out for provision in ordinary classes to be satisfactory (see HMSO, 1978 pp.86-88). These include the following;

favourable attitudes of staff and parents of all children;

suitable accommodation and equipment;

generous staffing ratios;

that the implications for all children have been thought out;

that teachers have regular advice and information.

In order to meet the varying needs of children it is also recommended that a range of provisions be identified, including playgroups, opportunity groups and day nurseries, and that the staffs in these should also receive suitable training and support. Evidence of the presence of children with special needs in playgroups, especially in rural areas is cited, and the preference of some parents for such provision where they themselves can be involved with the children. The pre- and in- service training of teachers is crucial with regard to the presence of children with special needs in any ordinary school as stressed in the Warnock Report. In preschool provision, this would apply to all staff, not only to teachers.

A valuable review paper setting the developments in the United Kingdom in an international perspective is entitled 'Special education for children below compulsory school age' (Grubb, 1982). A recent paper by the present author entitled 'Early education and children with special needs' provides a brief analysis of the implications for policy and practice of her research pre- and post-Warnock on preschool education and children with special needs and the early education of children from ethnic minorities (Clark, 1987).

Three major research projects have been funded in recent years concerned with key aspects of meeting the special educational needs of children following the passage of the 1981 Education Act. The three projects involved:

- In-service training for special educational needs (Manchester University)

- Support for the Ordinary School (National Foundation for Educational Research)

- Policy and Provision for Special Educational Needs (London University's Institute of Education).

None of the above projects was specifically concerned with the education of children under five, although clearly such children would come within their remit. A project to disseminate the findings of research into the Education Act 1981 began in late 1986. It is based at the University of London Institute of Education and is jointly funded by DES and DHSS.

The three funded studies referred to earlier, that by Chazan, within the Nursery Research Programme, and those by Clark for the Warnock Committee and after, provided research evidence for policy and practice concerning integration and children with special needs.

SOME OF OUR CHILDREN

The two-year project directed by Chazan and Laing of University College Swansea from 1976-78, funded by the DES under the Nursery Research Programme, followed an investigation by the research team into 'Services for parents of handicapped children under five' sponsored by the Warnock Committee. The book entitled *Some of Our Children* gives an account of the aims, design, and methodology of the research and a summary of the main findings (Chazan, Laing, Shackleton-Bailey and Jones, 1980).

Aims of the study

The main aims of the study were to identify all handicapped children in the selected age group (3 years 9 months to 4 years 3 months, children born between July and December 1972) in two local authorities, and to survey the educational provision for all handicapped children under five in these areas. Two local authorities in England and Wales were chosen, with together a population of about one million. The target age-group of children, aged about four years of age was about 1.7% of such children born in Britain in these months in 1972. For a sample of 82 of the children identified, an intensive study was planned. In the case of those receiving some form of education, the suitability of this was assessed and any specific problems, also the views of the teachers and what support they were receiving. The views of the parents were also studied and the children were assessed on a variety of standardised tests. For a sample of 20 of the more severely handicapped children in ordinary schools or classes an observational study was undertaken, lasting about three hours, to assess the extent of their interactions with adults and children.

The areas

The two local authorities were selected partly for accessibility to the research team, but also to provide a range of socio- economic conditions and varied provision for handicapped children under five. Neither of the areas, referred to only as A and B in the report, had severe problems with social disadvantage. Area A, has coastal features, some towns, some predominantly rural areas and had some recent immigrants at the time of the study. Any children identified whose problems were only connected with a mother tongue other than English were not included in the later stages of the study (Chazan *et al.* 1980, p.27). Area B, with a population nearly twice that of Area A, has high density areas of population, but had few immigrants at the time of the study.

There were wide differences in the available provision for under fives in the two areas. In Area A about 45% of three- and four- year-olds were in nursery schools or classes (many other under fives were in reception classes) and 15% attended playgroups. In contrast, in Area B, about 18% were in nursery schools or classes and over 50% in playgroups. Furthermore a much higher percentage of children in nursery schools or classes in Area A were in attendance full-time than in Area B (See Chazan *et al.*, 1980 p.142). For the six month age-group studied, 70% were in school in Area A, and less than 20% in Area B. This information has been cited in detail because it illustrates the dangers of generalisations from one specific area, particularly if the research does not provide enough detail on crucial factors such as the above.

The studies

I. For the first stage of the project a short screening schedule was completed by health visitors, teachers and playgroup leaders for children within the specified age range, to determine whether they were seen to have a problem (definitely, possibly, or not) in any of a number of defined areas of handicap. Returns were received for a high proportion of those estimated to be in that age group. The importance of more than one source for the identification of handicapped children is stressed as some children were identified by one source, but not by another. A second schedule obtained more detailed information for those identified, and also from this the sample for Stage 2 was drawn. Discounting the children who appeared to have mild or temporary problems, a total of 1, 149 children remained, 15.6% of the original sample. Many of these children were identified as having real difficulties in more than one aspect of development. By far the highest proportion of problems were in the two categories of speech and language and of emotional, social and behavioural adjustment. Those handicaps with the highest prevalence rates were also those most difficult to identify. Some difficulties were indeed being identified early, others were not. The more detailed study of a smaller sample of the children made it possible to pinpoint a number of important aspects.

II. The more detailed study involved 82 children (40 from Area A and 42 from Area B, 54 boys and 28 girls). Only one of 17 with severe handicaps was not identified early, but there was no clear pattern for the remainder. There was little evidence of formal assessment by the teachers themselves. Many of these children had a combination of handicaps and most were retarded in speech and language. The assessments made within the research on the Griffiths and Reynell tests showed the language difficulties faced by staffs, and parents. The majority of these children were attending ordinary nursery schools or classes, or reception classes of infant schools. While it was found, as expected, that a number of the children who were seriously retarded were in special schools, the researchers comment on the relatively high scores of some of the children in such units in both areas, and the low scores of some of the children in ordinary schools in one area. There were also differences between the two areas in the proportions of these children in different types of ordinary provision, although the age group was similar. In Area A 13 of 30 children in school were already in reception class (with 3 in nurseryschool and 14 in nursery class). In Area B none of 21 children were yet in reception class. The children in the reception classes had access to fewer adults, as there were seldom nursery nurses full-time there, and the pressures on the single-handed teacher were greater in a variety of ways. In the two areas the ratio of full- to part-time attendance for these children was also very different (over 2:1 in Area A full-time, and only two of 21 in Area B). There is a detailed discussion of the differential problems these children presented to the staffs in the various placements and advantages in the various types of special unit.

III. Twenty of the 51 children attending ordinary schools were observed for a total of about three hours, over two sessions. Five minute intervals were recorded in notes, for subsequent analysis (See Chazan *et al.*, 1980 pp.189-197 for details). An important finding, and one confirmed in the observational studies by this author to be reported in the following section, was the extent to which variations in adult-child contact were affected by the child's behaviour. The more restless and aggressive children were the subject of much adult-initiated contact, while withdrawn children were not given sufficient help and encouragement as they appeared not to have the skills to elicit this. This is indeed an extension of much of the evidence on non- handicapped children reported in earlier chapters. The high proportion of time spent in child-directed activities made matters worse for children who were unsuccessful in initiating adult contact. Some of these children were more successful with peers, but most of these contacts were non-verbal. They were thus not necessarily getting the opportunity which might have been hoped for of sustained communication with either adults or children. There was evidence, however, that a number of the children with problems were modelling their behaviour on that of other children, an important positive consequence of integration if successfully monitored. To sum up this aspect of the study:

"It would seem true to say, therefore, that young children with problems are neither ignored nor given extra attention by teachers or peers if the children are considered as a group. Looked at individually, there are marked differences between them in this respect, with outgoing children making and receiving most contacts, whether these were favourable or adverse. While teachers sometimes complained that some of the outgoing children were demanding of their time and attention, they seldom sought to draw out the withdrawn children" (Chazan *et al.*, 1980 p.197).

IV. Information on the preschool provision for handicapped under fives was obtained from a questionnaire in the two authorities to the headteacher, or teacher in charge of all schools, classes and units catering for preschool children. This included special schools and playgroups. There was an over 90% return to the questionnaire and amenities index. In both areas it appeared that children with obvious or severe handicaps were likely to be placed in special schools at five years of age or earlier. Those with less severe handicaps entered infant school and would then be seen by an educational psychologist if presenting problems. Most headteachers were in favour in principle of integration; about half had not had experience of handicapped children in their school. Furthermore, the experience might well have been of only one particular type of handicap. Had class teachers also been asked, the proportion without personal experience might well have been higher. The conditions regarded as essential for successful integration were similar to those noted in the Warnock Report, and cited earlier. An area which appeared to give great concern was that of discussing the child's problems with parents, and it is felt that there is a need to give teachers help in counselling parents.

V. One chapter of the report is devoted specifically to playgroups and their contribution (Chapter 6). It should be noted, however, that of a total of 312 playgroups known to the social service departments, 67 made no reply to the preliminary requests, and of those left, 63 did not return the questionnaire sent to them, thus there was only a 58% return. More than half of the groups responding had had handicapped children attending at some time over the previous five years (usually only one or two in that time), and some such children had been refused or excluded. In some instances a child's problems had become apparent only after attendance had commenced. Of those with handicaps currently attending, the commonest problems mentioned were connected with speech or language. Some of the children in the group for special study had attended or were attending a playgroup. Settling in difficulties were reported by some of the mothers. Few of the mothers helped in the group. The playgroup leaders were most positive in their willingness to accept partial hearing children, those with physical handicap provided they could walk, and mild emotional handicap. In some instances by the very act of accepting a handicapped child a playgroup may be providing a service, as this may be seen as a first step for mother and child, and even if the mother does not stay, she may welcome a brief respite. For some children much more is required if they are to be integrated in any real sense. This issue will be considered further in the following section.

Six important points are made concerning the placement in ordinary schools of children with problems (See Chazan *et al.*, 1980 p.186).

    1. Mild handicaps, and children with physical handicaps, where there are not other problems, present less difficulty at least at this early stage.

2. Physical handicaps (unless there are other problems) are accepted by teachers and children.

3. Professional advice is essential to the teacher in the case of speech problems and aggressive and restless behaviour in particular.

4. Withdrawn children are found particularly difficult to help, and those whose expressive language is affected, with the other pressures that are faced.

5. Without additional help it was felt that it was impossible to cope adequately. The observational studies showed, however, that available help was not always used effectively. Concern is expressed at the placement of such young children in reception classes, since neither programme nor staffing may be suitable.

6. Large open-plan nursery schools are felt to present difficulties unless they have some provision for small group work.

Children with behavioural difficulties

During the course of their researches into children with special needs Chazan, Laing and their co-workers found that many of the staff in nursery schools and classes felt a need for help and guidance in the management of children showing behaviour problems. A two year project funded by the DES from 1980 enabled them to prepare a handbook on *The management of behaviour problems in young children*, and with a supplementary grant from the Welsh Office a Welsh version (Chazan, Laing, Jones *et al.*, 1983). The aim in preparing the handbook was to provide material that would be of practical use and encourage the staff to think positively about ways of helping such children. The authors stress that they hope the ideas will be of value not only with children presenting severe problems in their management, but also in handling any children needing special help. A preliminary version of the handbook was tried out experimentally in a number of nursery groups.

The handbook contains schedules and a record book, aimed at assisting the staff in assessing a particular child's behaviour difficulties and planning and implementing an individual programme. The children likely to require help are considered under the headings of:

shy/withdrawn/timid, immature/dependent, restless/overactive, aggressive/anti-social/destructive.

Illustrative case studies are provided, examples are given of possible activities and approaches and relevant background literature is listed.

PRESCHOOL EDUCATION AND HANDICAPPED CHILDREN: PRE-WARNOCK

The present author undertook a project in Scotland for the Warnock Committee in 1976-77, about the same time as the study in England and Wales reported in the previous section. In spite of differences in the areas and the designs of the two studies, there were a number of similarities in the findings of relevance to the integration of handicapped children. The report on this study submitted to the Warnock Committee, and cited there (Clark, Riach and Cheyne, 1977), was subsequently incorporated in a book of empirical studies on preschool education, (Clark and Cheyne , 1979).

The aims

The aims of the study were:

a) to ascertain by means of interviews the numbers of children identified by those in charge of preschool units as handicapped and the nature of the handicaps, also their views on the suitability of their provision for handicapped children in terms of staffing, accommodation and resources;

b) to undertake observational studies of 25 selected handicapped children in ordinary units who had been speciallly referred, compared with control children in the same units;

c) to interview the parents of the observed children to obtain their views on their children's education;

d) to interview primary school teachers receiving 20 children identified as specially referred to preschool units to obtain their views.

The areas

The research took place in two Regions in Scotland only a year after local government reorganisation had led to the incorporation in each area of several previously autonomous local authorities, with very different policies for preschool education and resources for handicapped children. Thus any percentage figures for either Region could mask wide variation in provision. There were also contrasts in provision between urban and extensive rural areas, which were to be found in both Central Region, where the first stage of the research was undertaken, and Grampian Region in the Highlands where the main study took place. The annual intake to reception class in Grampian Region was about 8, 000 children, about twice that of Central Region. Since regionalisation there was one entry date to primary school each year (for children aged 4-6 to 5-6) in both regions.

Little attention has been directed in research to the problems of providing education for young children in rural areas, whether or not they are handicapped children, although it was an issue highlighted in the short-term studies by DES. For this reason it seems worth emphasising some features of Grampian Region, which are indeed not exclusive either to that area, or to Scotland. In the five divisions which constituted the Region the possibility of children being in preschool education varied widely. Not only was there ample provision in the City, but distances between provisions were relatively small in contrast to the widely scattered provision in sparcely populated rural areas. In three of the five divisions in Grampian Region about one third of the schools had a roll of under fifty (for children aged 5-12 years of age). Thus there was clearly more than a simple problem of matching the provision in the less well-provided areas to that in the cities. For a variety of reasons there-fore, more children attended playgroups than nursery classes or schools in parts of the Region. The distance involved in travelling to specialist provision is a further important issue, particularly when considering provision for such young children. The nature of this area made it possible to consider this also. There were a number of special schools and classes in the Region, and an interdisciplinary assessment centre, mainly for children under six years of age. While children from other parts of the Region could attend, and be in residence for assessment, the day nursery and nursery school could realistically be utilised only by those living in relative proximity to the Centre. Thus very different possibilities for children in different areas.

The studies

I. The first phase of the study involved all 14 nursery schools and classes in Central Region (with 834 children). The main study in Grampian Region involved 98 preschool units, including all nursery schools and classes and day nurseries, together with a sample of playgroups (with 3, 423 children). The sample of 28 playgroups was selected from the Social Work Department's list of 184 such groups to give appropriate geographical spread across the divisions and balance of com-munity and private playgroups. This latter distinction is important not only for this research, but for others where playgroups are referred to as if they were similar in characteristics. The distinction here was that the community playgroups, of which there were 19 in the study (with 399 children) , were organised by a committee of parents, most met in halls used for other purposes, and while some had full-time staff who might have qualifications, all used parent help. While it would perhaps be incorrect to refer to the private playgroups of which there were nine in the study (for 218 children) as 'profit-making', they were run by private individuals, most had trained staff, some met in purpose-built accommodation, and only one used regular parent help. There were also two private nursery classes in the study.

From the information in the two above paragraphs it should be clear how dangerous it is to give overall figures for a wide area, or for certain types of provision. As in the study by Chazan, the commonest types of handicap to be identified were speech and language difficulties and social/emotional difficulties, some children exhibiting aggressive behaviour, others withdrawn. In this study also, a number of children were identified within more than one category. Clearly a child who suffers from more than one disability may be a particular problem to the staff. Although the study was undertaken for the Warnock Committee, whose remit did not include gifted children, it was decided in this study to request staff also to identify any talented or intellectually gifted children. There was a striking unwillingness on the part of staff to identify children as outstanding, and few such were noted, in contrast to the New

Zealand study on which this was based. It does seem more likely to be a matter of expectations and attitudes rather than quite such a striking difference between Scotland (or indeed the West Midlands where there was a similar finding in a subsequent study) and New Zealand!

Full details are given in the report of the severity and range of disabilities represented. It was clear that some units had children with severe or multiple handicaps, this included playgroups, and also day nurseries where already their children were normally selected from the most socially deprived. Two-thirds of those in charge of preschool units who were interviewed had at some time had at least one child specially referred, and there had been some such referrals to all types of unit. There was some evidence of information accompanying such referrals, but those who had accepted such were less happy about follow-up support. There was generally a willingness to accept a limited number of handicapped children (except by the two private nursery classes) although the willingness to do so and experience of what this might entail varied. A few of those in each type of unit had experience of working with handicaps, but there was little evidence of special expertise. When asked the extent to which their basic training had prepared them to cope with handicapped children, those interviewed were divided not only as to whether it did, but also as to whether it should. At the time of this study, and many of the others reported here, the keeping of written records at the preschool stage was an area of controversy, and few preschool units kept such records for more than a minority of children. There was furthermore little evidence that any records were sent from the preschool units to the receiving primary schools.

It had been hoped to explore differential attitudes to various handicaps, and related to that the extent to which those in charge were only willing to accept handicapped children, rather than to make any special provision, such as might have been required for certain handicaps. Although there were differences expressed, this was seldom on the basis of first-hand experience with a range of handicaps and what the presence of children with these might entail. The perceptions were based in many instances either on limited, or no, experience of the handicaps in question. There was a tendency to regard children with speech problems as more appropriately placed in an ordinary unit, and those with cerebral palsy, who were blind or suffered from severe hearing impairment, in a special unit. Speech defect, difference and difficulty tended not to be differentiated, and all to be felt to present little difficulty, and as justifying priority admission. All that may be hoped for by admission of a handicapped child to an 'ordinary ' unit may be that the child has some experience with normal children. For many children there may be much higher expectations from those making such a placement and assumptions that some aspects will be tailored to the child's special needs.

II. With parental permission 25 children who had either been specially referred to an ordinary preschool unit, or whose handicap was evident, were observed in parallel with a matched control child. These children were in 16 different units, 16 in nursery schools or classes and 9 in playgroups, all attended half day only. Together they covered most handicaps identified, except visual and auditory handicap of which two only had been specially referred. The children in each pair were.observed in parallel for about two hours using a schedule devised for a previous study (See Clark and Cheyne, 1979 Chapter 19). The design of this study made it possible to assess the extent to which patterns were general, specific to a unit or type of unit, or type of handicap.

There were as might have been expected wide individual differences. When the handicapped and non- handicapped within a pair were compared, however, a number of findings held over each type of comparison. The handicapped children communicated with adults for a similar amount of time, less with other children, had more one-way than two- way speech patterns. They were also more likely to play alone, and less likely to engage in imaginative play. They spent a similar amount of time in a group with adult and children, and were marginally more likely to be alone with an adult although this did not result in more speech-time with adults. A more detailed analysis on similar lines was possible in the subsequent study in the West Midlands in which speech of and to each child by means of a radiomicrophone was analysed.

III. The mother of each of the handicapped children who was observed was interviewed. For about half of the children the unit now attended was not the only one available, but had been selected either by the child's mother alone or in consultation, or by specialists who had seen the child. Most parents were satisfied with the provision made for their child, most of whom had been given priority admission, some were also currently receiving help elsewhere. Some parents would have accepted a place in a special unit had it been offered. This, however, tended to be with knowledge of the particular specialised unit referred to earlier.

IV. Interviews of primary teachers who had received 20 of the handicapped children who had been specially referred were conducted after the children had been in reception class for about two terms. Half of these children had attended the nursery class attached to the primary school they now attended, which clearly made communication much easier for those involved than if they had come from a day nursery or playgroup, as did some. The children were now in classes which varied in size from 24 to 31. Most of these teachers felt less able to cope with handicapped children in their classes than had those interviewed at the preschool stage. Where these particular children were concerned, the teachers felt they were given adequate information, and that should it prove necessary the children would be transferred to a special class. The views of these teachers were not negative or rejecting, and they felt that such children should initially at least be in an ordinary class. The more explicit educational goals in the primary school, the realisation that extra attention to the handicapped child might be at the expense of other children and the possibility that the handicapped child, if disruptive or distractable, might disturb the concentration of others, were all important considerations.

Children with special needs in ordinary schools

The details given here are valuable in their own right, and also to set the scene for the next study. It would appear that if the only aim in placing a handicapped child in an ordinary unit is that the child have experience of being in a setting with non-handicapped children, then some comfort can be taken from findings of a study controlled as was this. A number of these children had been specially referred to pre-school provision and the handicaps of the others were obvious; yet there was not evidence that they were, or could have been, differentially treated. Indeed the staffs in the units seldom claimed to be making special provision for these children.

Children much younger than those still in preschool units in this study might in some areas already have to face the pressures and constraints of the reception class (children in these areas were not admitted to reception class until aged 4-6 to 5-6 years). The effect on possible integration of handicapped children of admission to reception class at a younger age, possibly at age 4+, and with few adults available, is an important aspect. In each of the studies discussed here one of the commonest forms of handicap identified was problems in speech and language, another was social and emotional difficulties, each possibly in association with other problems. These would present real difficulties to the reception class teacher, possibly single-handed, expected to meet the expectations of her colleagues, and the varied demands of the children entering her class from different preschool settings, or direct from home. Some children on entry may be less demanding, quiet, submissive, or appear to be settled without much individual attention. The hard-pressed reception class teacher could be forgiven for concentrating on those whose needs are more obvious, and those whose responses are more readily elicited. Yet this may leave many whose needs are not being met, or where quiet acceptance masks very real problems in relating to adults or to other children as a result of language difficulties, or for other reasons.

PRESCHOOL EDUCATION AND CHILDREN WITH SPECIAL NEEDS: POST-WARNOCK

The further study by the present author was conducted in the West Midlands in 1979-81, also funded by DES. There were four important differences between this study and that reported earlier:

a) this study was post-Warnock, the other pre-Warnock;

b) this study took place in England, in urban areas, the other in Scotland and in predominantly rural areas;

c) the date of entry to reception class differed and age on entry, both between the two areas in this study, and those in the previous study: in one area there was one entry date only per year, and children entered aged between 4 and 5, in the other there were three entry dates and entry between 4-9 and 5 years (whereas in Scotland

K

it was between 4-6 and 5-6). The latter authority now also has one entry date and of the younger age group;

d) there were many children from ethnic minorities in Birmingham and Coventry, the two areas in this study, and for many of these English was not their mother tongue, whereas there were few children in the areas in Scotland who were from ethnic minorities or who spoke a different language.

The aims

The aims of this study were similar to the previous one, but additionally a comparison of the results of the two studies seemed of value, differing as they did in the ways noted above. Greater emphasis was also placed on the observational aspects. The availability during the study of lighter radiomicrophones made it possible to record the language of children with special needs and control children during free play, both in ordinary units, and in a special unit. Full details of this research are to be found in the report to DES (Clark, Robson and Browning, 1982, and further information on the language studies in Robson 1983a;1983b;1985).

The areas

In Coventry the nursery classes and a nursery school were included in the study, also the day nurseries, together with a sample of 13 of 98 playgroups across the city. Together these 49 units catered for 2633 children, many more part-time than full-time. In Birmingham, which is about three times the size of Coventry, it was not possible to include all preschool units. It was therefore decided to identify an area of the city, and there include all units. There were in the research area selected 2972 children in preschool units, of whom approximately equal numbers attended full- or part-time, and this accounted for nearly one-quarter of the children in ordinary preschool units in the city. As the survey in the ordinary preschool units revealed relatively few very severely handicapped children in attendance it was decided also to include special schools or classes with children under five years of age. A total of 18 such units were also visited, where there were at the time 123 children under five years of age (See Clark *et al.*, 1982 Chapter 7 for discussion of that aspect). As might have been expected the staff ratios were much more favourable in such units, as were the resources and access to outside professionals. There were, on the other hand, fewer children with whom the children with special needs could interact, and because they also had special needs communication would not always be easy or stimulating.

The studies

I. In the research area in Birmingham, and also to some extent in Coventry, large numbers of children in the nursery schools and classes, and some in the playgroups, were identified as having special needs related in some way to English as a second language. Indeed in some of the units for many of the other children, English was not their mother tongue. The fact that a child's mother tongue was not English did not ensure that the child had no other difficulty, either physical or sensory, or indeed that the child did not also have language difficulty in the mother tongue. It did, however, make such a differential diagnosis difficult, if not impossible for the staff. This also raises the issue as to whether and to what extent such a preschool unit can still be regarded as an appropriate ordinary unit in which to 'integrate' a child with communication problems if one hope is to help that child through communication with peers. There are dangers in the fact that the Warnock Committee did not include any such considerations within its remit, and therefore special needs and second language may be treated as two separate issues, and may even be considered by two separate departments (See Clark *et al.*, 1982 Chapter 5 for a discussion of the issues, and also Clark, Barr and Dewhirst 1985 which deals more specifically with early education and children from ethnic minorities).

In the 32 playgroups visited there were no children identified with severe handicaps which could adversely affect their performance in the group, in contrast to the finding in the rural areas in the previous study, where among other things the distances involved meant that such children attended the local provision, in some instances attendance had been a matter also of choice. In the day nurseries there were children with special needs in addition to the social conditions which had led to their admission. The staff in these units were concerned that they felt their training was not adequate for the range of duties which they now required to perform, which progressively involves counselling of parents. The interviews of staff revealed that not all those in charge of preschool units had trained to work with that age group, also that few had any training for, or experience of children with special needs. While referral of specific children to a variety of professionals was possible there was little evidence of support within the units. In all these studies communication difficulties were a major cause for concern, and staff would have welcomed support and assistance in the diagnosis of the severity of the children's problems, and either reassurance or some guidance. With regard to children whose mother tongue was not spoken, or understood by the staff, differential diagnosis was also important.

II. Observation of children with special needs and control children was undertaken for 17 children with special needs in the Birmingham area, each matched with a control child in the same unit. This study was undertaken in 15 preschool units and covered a variety of handicaps. Each child was observed on three occasions by means of a structured observation schedule devised for the study, and subsequently used in a number of other studies. While as a group the children with special needs were observed to engage in similar activities to the control children there were within pair differences related to the child's handicapping condition. Differences in the amount of adult interaction were found for some over- and under-reactive children. Children with special needs were here also found to spend more time looking, listening and waiting (See Clark *et al.*, 1982 Chapter 8 for details).

III. The study of language by means of radiomicrophones involved two ninety minute recordings of five children with communication difficulties in ordinary units with controls, and of two children in a special unit. The children's language was also assessed on the 'Preschool Language Assessment Instrument'. The transcripts provided valuable examples for in-service training, showing where communication was effective and where and for what reasons it appeared to breakdown (See Robson 1983a;1983b).

IV. It was possible to interview the mother of 13 of the 17 children with special needs who were observed. It seems important that parents should have full information in order to be adequately involved in decisions on placement. A number of parents while wishing special provision for their child would have preferred this to be associated with a neighbourhood ordinary unit. It was expected that all 17 children who were observed would proceed to reception class, where it was planned to interview their teacher. In the event, only five of the children went when expected; the others were retained in the preschool unit. As so few did proceed, and those who did were less severely handicapped, it would be inappropriate to make generalisations. The nature of each child's difficulties, the help being given and the prognosis is discussed in the research report. Not all even of these children were likely to complete their education in the ordinary class at least without considerable additional help.

CHILDREN WITH SPECIAL NEEDS AND PRESCHOOL EDUCATION

For children who are identified preschool as suffering from handicapping conditions, it is important to distinguish ways in which ordinary preschool education is expected to make a contribution to their development, and whether more is expected than that they be accepted by their peers and the adults in the unit. Priority admission to scarce resources might be all that is intended.

If more is indeed expected, particularly where a child is a special referral, then this should be explained to the staff, who are entitled to adequate information about the children and their problems.

Staff in all preschool units are also entitled to reviews of and changes in the arrangements should these prove difficult to meet, either because of the needs of the child in question, or the effect on other children, or the staff.

To place some children with special needs in an ordinary unit may indeed not be to integrate but to deny their needs.

Where problems are related to difficulties in communication, which were among the commonest special needs identified in the three studies reported, a child may be in, but not of the ordinary unit, and possibly more isolated than in any segrated provision. In a special unit such a child may in contrast have the full attention of skilful adults who interpret even rather unintelligable speech, and who have time to spend encouraging the child to respond. However, in such settings the child may have little opportunity to interact with peers who have sufficient skills in communication. There is a fine balance between the need for additional help and the benefits of 'integration'.

Early special treatment may enable some children to acquire skills through which they sustain integration later. Other children may by their very acceptance in an ordinary unit preschool be given the opportunity to show that they can indeed cope within mainstream education.

In these studies it was possible to observe only either 'total' integration, or children placed in special units. Clearly for some handicaps, and for some children, either integration part of the time, placement in a special unit attached to an ordinary preschool, with specialist staff available on site and gradual integration, or placement in an ordinary unit with specialist teachers in part-time or at least regular attendance might be the preferred arrangement. Whether or not such alternatives are available for a particular child will, however, be influenced by all the various factors identified in these three studies in addition to the range of provision in a particular authority. As with attendance of any child at preschool provision, distance is an important variable, even where, as with children with special needs, transport may be available.

The particular problems associated with placement in, or attendance at, day nurseries of children who have handicapping conditions has been highlighted by the evidence from day nurseries discussed elsewhere in this report. Many, or indeed most children attending such units are already 'at risk' in many ways, to such an extent that it must be questioned as to how 'ordinary' such provision indeed is. It certainly does not differ from other preschool units only in providing all day or year care.

The more recent study in the West Midlands in areas with a high proportion of children from ethnic minorities and for whom English is a second language has raised still other issues in relation to the education of preschool children with special needs. How ordinary is a preschool unit in which few children speak the language of the staff? How does one encourage identification of and treatment for such children who may have language difficulties in their own language? Finally, is it appropriate to place a child with communication difficulties in an ordinary unit but one where few children speak his or her language and to regard that as integration? Evidence elsewhere in this report has shown how important peer interaction is in stimulating the children and in providing rich and varied communication in the course of shared activities. A child with communication difficulties, if sufficiently persistent and acceptable to the other children, may manage to take part in activities and gradually also to communicate if the other children in the unit are themselves competent and speak the same language. The above are among the issues raised and still remaining even with the developments post-Warnock and after the implementation of the 1981 Education Act involving identification and review. The extent and range of preschool provision has been shown to vary so widely even within a particular local authority that the choices available to a given family may be very different. They may be wide or limited depending on the precise area, no matter how efficient any early diagnosis of difficulties is. Furthermore, where preschool provision, particularly within the education sector is limited, certain handicapping conditions, especially communication difficulties, are much less likely to be identified preschool. Observation of a child with other children, and outside the family setting may be a valuable aid in diagnosis. In the absence of such provision the difficulties of some of these children may become apparent only on entry to reception class.

A final important issue is age of entry to reception class and its effect on the ability of children with special needs to cope in ordinary school. This issue was raised in different ways in these three researches where a child in the age group studied by Chazan would be found to differ widely in the two areas. In one area the child might already be in reception class. In the areas studied in Scotland age on entry to reception class was later. In the West Midlands it differed in the two areas studied. In one of these areas a number of children of the same age as those studied who were in preschool education would now be in reception class, not preschool provision. It is important that decisions concerning children with special needs and appropriateness of provision for preschool and beyond are made with knowledge of research findings and trends in the variety of preschool provision such as are discussed in the other chapters of this report.

PORTAGE AND PARENTS

The importance of regarding parents wherever possible as the main educators of their handicapped children under five is stressed in the Warnock Report (HMSO, 1978), and in particular their need for support, and for encouragement to help widen the children's restricted experience. Reference is made to the Portage Project in the U.S.A., which involved the development of materials and procedures which enabled home visitors to teach parents in their own homes to set and attain educational objectives for their young handicapped children. Its introduction into Wessex is also noted, to train the parents of young handicapped children in their homes to work with their children.

'Portage' took its name from a small town in Wisconsin, USA, where a service was set up to provide for preschool handicapped children in rural areas of Wisconsin. The children were visited by 'home teachers', who modelled for parents how to work with their preschool handicapped child. A visit to the States in the mid seventies aroused interest in developing such services in the UK; workshops were provided by staff from the States, following which projects were set up in several areas. Their reported success led to its adoption in other areas. Recently a National

Portage Association has been established to help existing projects and to provide standards for new services. Recognition by the Department of Education and Science of Portage home teaching schemes for funding is likely in the last year or so to have increased still further the number of such projects. There is extensive literature on Portage in the U.S.A.; in the last few years books and articles have appeared in the UK also. An assessment of the range of services for handicapped children is beyond the current remit; several major studies have been funded by DES to investigate the implementation of the recent legislation concerning children with special needs. There was, however, such extensive referencing of Portage that it seemed appropriate to consult a number of the frequently cited articles which reported research into the implementation of Portage in the UK.

In 1982-83 the Wessex Health Care Evaluation Research Team conducted a National Portage Survey to assess the extent to which Portage had been replicated in the UK. The following information was collected on what are described as 'Portage-type' home teaching services, for which seven criteria were established:

1. Families were regularly visited in their homes
2. Assessment included the use of a developmental checklist
3. Written instructions for teaching and recording were given to parents
4. The suggested teaching procedure was modelled for the parent
5. The parent was observed carrying out the teaching and recording
6. Baseline and post-baseline data were recorded
7. Home visitors attended a regular staff meeting.

There were identified 221 services, of which 130 satisfied all seven criteria. Unlike the service in the States, the survey revealed an absence of services in rural sparsely populated areas. Most services catered for preschool children, all were involved with mentally handicapped, and few children with other special needs were included. More details were collected on 59 Portage-type services, almost half of which were provided jointly by health, social services and education. About half the services had five or fewer home teachers, 91% of the home visitors had other employment, and 76% visited three families or less. Home visitors were from a number of professions including health visitors, teachers and social workers. Over a third of the services reported that they had carried out no evaluation or done a pilot a study. The survey was confined to home teaching services, and no measures were taken during the survey to assess the quality of the services, nor to investigate any evaluations reported by services.

In a review of Research and Evaluation on Portage, Cameron (1986) distinguishes four aspects namely implementation, replication, dissemination and adaptation. Within these categories he identifies research in the United States and UK. Sturmey and Crisp (1986) in their review of research stress the need for a wider range of dependent variables to be considered in research to assess the effect of the programme on both the child and family. They claim that little is known about the reliability of the Portage checklist, and that a number of the texts are written in language that is too complex for those who are expected to use them. Comparison between the original materials and the other materials adapted from them they suggest would be valuable. They list a number of methodological and other shortcomings in available studies which make their evaluation difficult, including lack of sufficiently detailed information on the subjects of the researches.

Studies in the UK tend to be descriptions of local services reported by those involved, or 'evaluations' of services, or specific aspects of these after a few years in operation, rather than researches as interpreted elsewhere in this report. The researches are thus mainly small scale, with one or a few home visitors, and few children. The influence of the characteristics of the particular home visitors or children on the results is difficult to assess. Seldom have pre- or post-test measures, control groups, or an alternative approach to home visiting been used against which to assess any progress the children have made. Parental satisfaction with home visiting which has been of Portage type is reported, but it is not possible to assess the extent to which any 'satisfaction' expressed by the parents is because of interest and support for the home by professionals, or specific features of Portage. Workshops for staff in units are reported, in which staff satisfaction with the workshops is assessed, but is not compared to effects of alternative innovations; information may also not be available on any measured changes in staff practices or children's development. The characteristics of the parents who are involved and of those who sustain involvement may not be stated (for example the level of literacy the parents require to utilise the materials) or the extent to which the materials used have been modified. The precise ages of the children, and their intellectual level may also not be clear.

The authors of a number of the articles studied do themselves acknowledge the exploratory nature of their investigations, that it is a pilot study only, or that it has very severe methodological weaknesses. The citing in secondary sources does not always acknowledge such limitations. In view of the points made above it does not seem appropriate here to discuss individual researches. The reservations expressed by Sturmey and Crisp (1986) were felt by the present author also on the basis of the researches she consulted. Clearly there has been a rapid and successfully maintained establishment of home visiting projects on Portage lines in UK. What is less clear is that there is currently evidence of research in UK which is rigorous and on any large scale, or which is reported in sufficient detail for the study to be replicated elsewhere.

CHAPTER 15 CURRICULUM MATTERS

RESEARCH ISSUES

In this chapter research specifically concerned with the aims and roles of staff in preschool education will be discussed. Curriculum Development Projects in language, mathematics, and for socially handicapped children will be considered, together with the evidence from experimental studies on number, cognitive development and aspects of reading. Information on record keeping will also be considered.

AIMS OF PRESCHOOL EDUCATION

A national survey of nursery teachers

Shortly after the publication of the Plowden Report in 1967 with its recommendation that preschool education be expanded to make it available for all children of three years of age or older whose parents wished them to attend, the Schools Council decided to add an investigation into the aims of nursery education to an ongoing study of the aims of primary education. That project which started in 1969 is still perhaps the most frequently cited reference to the aims of teachers in preschool education (although the emphasis may have changed considerably since that time), and has formed the basis for more recent, but smaller scale studies (Taylor, Exon and Holley, 1972). Its findings may help to explain the limited influence on preschool education of the various curriculum projects undertaken in the early seventies. The child-centred view of early education into which they were introduced, coupled with retrenchment rather than the promised massive and speedy expansion in preschool education would scarcely put a profession under threat in a receptive mood to innovations.

On the basis of a questionnaire to all local authorities in England and Wales it was established that there were at that time at least 1413 nursery classes and 485 nursery schools. Local authorities were categorised into four groups and a random sample of 40% of nursery schools and 20% of nursery classes was then drawn from within each group. Questionnaires were returned by 578 teachers, 74% of the sample, varying from over 90% in some authorities to about 50% in others. Information obtained on the experience and background of the teachers showed that most had considerable teaching experience; more than 30% had taught children under five for over ten years; and over 50% for at least five years. About 25% of the teachers had been in their present school for ten or more years. Most of these teachers were members of an organisation concerned with nursery education. They were clearly a committed and experienced group of professionals who showed a desire for in-service training, particularly in relation to current trends and new ideas and for refresher courses on teaching methods.

The teachers were asked to rank five possible areas for importance in nursery education. The general order established was as follows: social, intellectual, home-school, aesthetic, physical. There were differences in the order in which teachers placed the aims (some giving first priority to an aim to which others gave a low priority): these differences did not appear to be related to time of training or the nature of catchment area in which the teachers worked. The teachers were also asked to rate a number of objectives, the grouping of which reinforced the earlier finding in that objectives related to the development of social skills were stressed, and while language and general reasoning skills were given some importance, 'formal' educational skills were rated low. Teachers were given an opportunity in an open-ended section to state the aims of nursery education as they saw them. The aims as stated there were wider and less specific, but still tended to confirm the same emphases.

When asked to consider the role of the teacher under a number of categories the teachers were likely to identify with a 'teacher-centred: child-directed approach, although a more teacher- directed role was likely to be favoured by the older members in the sample. A final aspect of the study was to ask these teachers which parts of the course of training for nursery education they regarded as of most importance. There was considerable emphasis on practice of nursery teaching and child psychology, suggesting the need for considerable time in the nursery to provide the practical basis and material for these studies. Little emphasis was given to curriculum studies; it is difficult, however, to be sure what precisely the teachers understood by the term, and whether they regarded it as involving only theoretical study. The teachers reacted unfavourably to 'formal' education for such young children and did not appear to regard it as a major function of preschool education to undertake the first stages in the teaching of the basic school subjects.

The stress on social/emotional development did not necessarily mean that the teachers were unconcerned for the children's future success or the children's ability to communicate with others. What they clearly emphasised was that preschool education was regarded as a stage in its own right. Preparation for school, narrowly interpreted, or formal education, did not tend to find favour. The aims could still have incorporated a desire to make the children more mature and able to interact effectively both with adults and children on entry to primary school. In this national sample of experienced preschool teachers in the early seventies there were many who held a view of preschool education which emphasised its importance for the child's social/emotional development and who favoured a child-directed, if teacher-centred approach. The project did not include any observational studies which could have identified whether the teachers who differed in aims also differed markedly in their practice.

Aims role and deployment of staff

One of the first projects to be commissioned within the Nursery Research Programme was a study by the National Foundation for Educational Research into the aims and role of staff in nursery schools and classes. The fieldwork for this study was completed by 1977, until which time Martin Woodhead was project director; the published report was by Clift, Cleave and Griffin (1980). This research which was an attempt to relate the aims of staff to what they do in the nursery involved a study of staff, and not the children's behaviour as in the studies in preschool units reported earlier. The research was conducted in local authorities in the south of England, with a mixture of urban, semi-urban and rural areas. Forty nurseries were selected, 9 nursery schools, 5 units (with more than one teacher) and 26 classes. Interviews, observation schedules, questionnaires and checklists were used in the collection of information. This enabled some assessment to be made of the extent to which the views expressed by staff were reflected in what they actually did when working with the children during the sessions. The behaviour of nursery teachers and nursery nurses was observed, compared with and related to their aims and training. Each of the forty nurseries in the study was visited for a total of six half days, but only during nursery sessions.

Thus the empirical data does not provide insights into how either the daily planning or more comprehensive planning was organised, by whom, the extent to which the decisions were a result of collective discussions or were presented by the more senior member of staff as plans to be implemented. The research was designed to make parallel observations of the two professions working together. It is not possible to assess the extent to which the activities, equipment and day as observed would have been different had there been no teacher on staff. That the planning of the programme of activities was the responsibility of the teachers was reported both by the teachers and by the assistants. Few nurseries were reported to hold regular formal staff meetings; in some nurseries meetings were held at the beginning or end of the day, or at lunch breaks. Observational information is also not available concerning the relative interactions of different members of staff with parents, or with outside agencies. These are important reservations in any general conclusions on the nature of the activities and responsibilities of the staffs in these units. It is thus dangerous to extend interpretations beyond the observations conducted. Even more dangerous would be any assumption, in the absence of empirical evidence, and in the face of the evidence from the questionnaires, that these nursery units would have been similar had there been only one profession on staff, whether teachers or nursery nurses. It seemed important to stress these limitations at the outset.

The sample of forty teachers included head teachers of nursery schools and teachers-in-charge of nursery units. The majority of the teachers in this study had undertaken a nursery/infant training, and some of the others had taken a 'conversion' course; most of the assistants were qualified NNEB nursery nurses. The nurseries ranged from 20 to 60 place, and most were 'open-plan'. Criticisms made of their training by the teachers emphasised insufficient training in classroom management, child care, health and social welfare, specialism in the three to five age group and working with other staff in a team situation. The assistants' most common suggestion for improvement in their training was for a larger component dealing with the cognitive development of the child.

The aims of the staffs in this study were investigated by means of open-ended interviews, the information volunteered was then categorised into four broad areas; namely social, educational, preparation for school and linguistic. Both groups of professionals overwhelmingly emphasised 'social' aims, as had the teachers in the study reported earlier by Taylor *et al.*(1972). The assistants tended within this to emphasize more welfare type aims (manners, dressing, behaving). These staff were similar to those in Taylor's study in their lesser emphasis on cognitive or intellectual development. Preparation for infant school, while mentioned, and language development, were not stressed to the extent of social development. Teachers volunteered more than twice as many statements of educational aims as the assistants and differed strongly in the terms which they used. The categorisation of the responses after the interviews, rather than providing categories of aims to which the staff were required to respond, has strengths, but also weaknesses in the possibility of interpretations of the statements by the researchers with which some of the staff might not have been in agreement.

A questionnaire on perceived responsibilities was given to the head teacher or teacher-in-charge of the unit, and a similar questionnaire on perceived responsibilities to the staffs. The teachers were allocated greater responsibilities for administration, planning, involvement and adult talk and nursery assistants for welfare and housework. There was close agreement between the responsibilities as ascribed and as perceived. In half of the nurseries in the study parents were sufficiently involved to be included in the division of responsibilities; as in other studies, here also there were widely different views on the involvement of parents in the nursery. In the majority of nurseries the staff/child ratio was at or better than 1:13; since most children attended half day only, the administrative work and contact with families was much greater than that would suggest.

Each member of staff was observed, and wore a radio microphone for two half day sessions, during which their activities and interactions were monitored and compared. Staff spent much of their time involved with the children in their activities, and during the observed time, which was while the children were present, little time on dealing with equipment, administration etc. The fragmentary nature of the staff contacts with the children is commented upon, noted also in other studies, and something which is likely to be detrimental to extended and meaningful dialogue with the children, and encouragement of children to complete activities once started. It is reported that what staff did was normally self-directed; however, this is a rather misleading expression, by which was meant that changes did not appear to be a direct result of a demand by a child or adult. The sample was not large enough for a study of similarities and differences between different types of unit, or within the two professions, which is unfortunate. Averages so clearly hide many differences, some of which may have been educationally significant, showing some practices to be emulated, others to be avoided. Two general points are made, one refers to the greater involvement with children, particularly individual children when the staff ratio was favourable. The second refers to comparison between morning and afternoon sessions, which were found to be relatively similar, except that more work with larger groups of children was undertaken in the morning; this could in some instances have been with children who attended all day.

Teachers spent more time than assistants with groups of children, especially the class as a whole. In general, however, the quantity of involvement of the two professions with the children was comparable. An attempt was made to assess whether there were differences in the quality of interaction. The use of the radiomicrophones made it possible to record adult/adult and adult/child talk. Only a small amount of time during the observations was concerned with talk between adults, during which it was found that teachers' talk related most to administration and to the development of the children's abilities.

Two fifteen minute tapes had been made of each member of staff in interaction with children in each session. These tapes were searched for an incident when the teacher and nursery nurse in a unit were engaged in a similar activity so that a comparison could be made of the adult/child interactions between the two professionals in a comparable setting. This analysis of speech was made for ten pairs, in different nurseries, none of which was known to have taken part in a language programme recently. It is stressed in the report that overgeneralisation from such a small study must be avoided (p.68). Three factors were identified; the use the adult made of the activity, the style of discourse, and the complexity of speech used. With regard to use of the activity an attempt was made to assess whether the activity appeared to be used as an end or as a means. According to that categorisation, more teachers than assistants were using the activity as a means. This was, however, the assessment of the researcher, and might or might not have been predetermined by the adult. As in other studies reported here comment is made on the preponderance of adult comments in these situations, and that the children's utterances were mainly confined to single statement or one word utterances. An analysis of staff language showed only slight differences between the teachers and assistants as a group, with teachers giving more information and responding statements, and the assistants more directing statements. There were wide differences in style between those recorded, and in this connection it is worthy of note that ten matched pairs of staff shared the same style, which it is suggested was influenced by the fact that they worked in the same unit. There is no evidence as to whether this had been influenced by conscious modelling, or policy of the person in charge.

The evidence from this study supports that of Taylor *et al.*(1972) in finding that social aims were regarded as of great importance by teachers and assistants working in nursery schools and classes, and that lower priority was given to cognitive aspects, or specific preparation for the next stage of education. All twenty nursery units observed during this study in the mid seventies were found to have certain similarities in that a variety of activities was available for the children, and that at most only a limited amount of the day was time-tabled. Staff interaction with children took most of their time during the sessions, but the episodes tended to be short in duration. Conversations between staff and children analysed appeared to be mainly adult dominated, and children's responses were brief. There were wide differences in style between staff, but not clearcut differences between the two professions in their deployment during the observations. In some units the deployment of staff at specific activities could have been preplanned, or varied, in others it could indeed have been self-directed by the members of staff as need arose. It would have been valuable to have had some analysis of the organisational patterns in specific units as planned by those in charge, since this could have influenced the layout of equipment and positioning of staff; as it certainly did in the three units studied intensively in research directed by the present author at about the same time (see Clark and Cheyne, 1979).

A study was undertaken in Avon between 1979-81 which replicated some aspects of the above research, extending the timescale of observations to cover the full nursery day including the time before the arrival of the children and at the end of the day; the major emphasis was on the relative training and needs as perceived by the two professions (summarised in Heaslip, 1985). The study in Avon differed in that the sample of staff whose views were surveyed was larger, and that it was a comprehensive coverage of such staff in nursery schools and classes in Avon at the time, including staff from all but one nursery school and two nursery classes. Avon included Bristol, which had a long and famous tradition for the provision of nursery education and long established nursery schools, and other areas with little provision. Lack of expansion in the years immediately prior to the study meant that few staff had been appointed recently. Most of the headteachers had been in their post for over ten years. Some staff had attended frequent in-service courses, others none; and there was evidence of a considerable difference in this between teachers and nursery nurses. In this area there were requests by teachers for courses in language, numeracy, parental involvement, curriculum planning, research and testing. In the two years previously the authority had run many in-service courses on play, parental involvement and language (using Joan Tough's materials). There was an 88% response to the first questionnaire and a similarly high response to a second more structured questionnaire, with responses by 15 nursery headteachers, 67 nursery teachers and

102 nursery nurses. Most of the nursery teachers had been in their present school for at least five years, and a number for over ten years; similarly with the head-teachers and the nursery nurses.

Observations were carried out in ten classes in five nursery schools and in five nursery classes. A similar schedule was used to that employed in the NFER study, but the periods of the day observed were extended. There were similarities in the findings to those of the other study during the period when the children were present. In this study there is information on the informal planning that took place prior to the children's arrival, and for the work of any students. Often at the end of the day reorganisation of the equipment for the following day took place, during which time discussion might involve planning. The inclusion of the period 8.30-9.00 increased the proportion of time devoted to adult talk and administration. Each of the periods observed during the day had a distinctive pattern; thus to obtain a comprehensive picture of the work of staff in a preschool unit it is necessary to sample, and to analyse separately, the various parts of the day.

In a number of aspects this study supported the findings of Clift *et al.*(1980) concerning the two professions working side by side in the nursery. Heaslip stresses, however, that there are more differences than are apparent at first sight, differences in training, in reasons for entering the profession, expectations about the children, purposes for nursery education and in levels of commitment to their own professional development, all of which he explored in the study. Important points are made in this report about the needs of the two professions in pre- and in-service training (see Heaslip 1985;1987).

CURRICULUM DEVELOPMENT PROJECTS

Three major curriculum projects on preschool education were undertaken in the early seventies at the time of the planned expansion in preschool education. Each led to the preparation of materials and was aimed at the pre-service or in-service training of teachers. Each project involved, during its development and beyond, the commitment of large numbers of teachers in nursery schools and classes in attendance at group discussions, in analysis of their own practice, and in try out and evaluation of materials. The extent of professional commitment this represents is impressive. Two things are particularly unfortunate, first that the expansion for which the materials were intended was aborted when it had scarcely begun to take effect, leaving this particular sector of the teaching profession vulnerable and under threat. Second, the focus of the projects on the preschool units, while understandable gave the appearance that this aspect of education, preschool education, was somehow in a separate compartment. Thus insights relevant to the primary school were less likely to be disseminated. Furthermore where children of comparable age, from comparable background, or who had not attended nursery schools or classes, were in primary school, their teachers were unlikely to have similar insights, to use or even be aware of the materials. It seems important that any further curriculum development projects are not developed in isolation from the related stages in education, especially, one which has such a shifting and variable population as preschool education.

Language development

The first project, funded by the Schools Council, was the Communication Skills Project directed by Joan Tough in Leeds. This initiative commenced in 1971 with funds from the Schools Council for a pilot study. The preschool language project in collaboration with local groups of nursery and infant teachers, explored ways of promoting curriculum development concerned with children's language, while an associated project, funded by DES for one year in 1976 examined the role of nursery nurses in fostering children's language development. Further extensions by the Schools Council have enabled the project to develop materials for work with children from seven to eleven, and for work with children with moderate learning difficulties. The main aims of the project were to help teachers to assess children's skills of using language while listening to them talking; and to help teachers to foster children's skills of using language and thinking through dialogue.

The early childhood project was not concerned to develop materials for the children to use, but rather to encourage teachers in the utilization of the opportunities which already exist. This project involved many teachers throughout the country in the development of the materials. In-service materials, including such publications as *Listening to Children Talking* (Tough, 1976) and *Talking and Learning* (Tough, 1977b) and pioneering video materials for demonstration purposes, which have subsequently been updated, have been used extensively in training courses. One major strength in the project is that it has not been confined to the 'preschool' stage in isolation, thus providing some continuity in development. This is particularly important since a number of teachers who are working in the preschool field may indeed not have received training for that age group. It is not possible to assess precisely how much effect the materials have had on the practice of those involved specifically with children under five in the absence of an evaluation. The necessity for teachers and other staff to be trained to engage in discussion with children which will both show the range of competence they possess, and help to extend this, has been apparent from the studies discussed in earlier chapters. This requires skill in organising the setting, and planning the activities in such ways that any 'dialogue' with adults does not become a series of questions and answers, that the situation is meaningful and has 'reality' for the child.

Early Mathematics

A second curriculum development project funded by the Schools Council was the Early Mathematical Experiences project, a three year project directed by Professor and Mrs. Matthews, which commenced in 1974, later extended to 1979 to provide for wider dissemination of the materials. The aim of this project was to identify relevant experiences leading to mathematical ideas for young children and to help their teachers with suggestions on how to encourage these. The materials consisted of guides for teachers, video tape and slides. The National Foundation for Educational Research was asked to undertake an evaluation of the project in anticipation of the programme of dissemination. By the time the evaluation was designed and approved, however, in 1977 the final drafts of the materials had already been sent to the publishers. Delays in appearance of the published version, which differed in layout, though not in content, meant that it could not be used for the evaluation, as the Schools Council required the report of the evaluation by 1978. These limitations had serious constraining effects on the independent evaluation by NFER (Holmes, Woodhead and Clift, 1978).

The EME project hoped to show that early mathematical experiences can be integrated into activities and conversation in the nursery school, and need not be confined to or consist of the type of 'formal' education which was so clearly rejected by the teachers in the study by Taylor *et al*. 1972. It is reported in Holmes *et al*. 1978, that Professor Matthews organiser of the Nuffield Mathematics Project, which started from age five, had felt that some children were entering primary school at a disadvantage because of lack of sufficiently varied experiences and conversation, the project was thus aimed to assist teachers to provide such experiences at the preschool stage, and not to produce a nursery curriculum.

Some evaluation, and revisions had taken place during the project; this had not included any systematic assessment of children's learning or teachers' success in implementing the ideas. The evaluation by NFER was intended to provide potential users with evidence on which to decide whether it was worth investing in the materials. This was carried out by observing the effect of the materials on teachers' ways of teaching, to assess the extent to which it was compatible with different teaching styles and for children from different backgrounds. Within the constraints indicated above it was clearly not possible to undertake an experimental study. The alternative adopted was to ask a number of teachers to use the prepublication draft and to report their experiences, and to monitor closely their progress over one and a half school terms. This was thus more in the nature of a pilot study in the use of the guidelines by teachers who were not in contact with those who had been involved in their design. Changes in teachers or children were not measured as part of the assessment. The development of the EME materials, which had involved an extensive network of working groups throughout the country, is described in Holmes *et al*.(1978).

The evaluation included an attempt to collect information on the development of the project from the liaison officers and groups of teachers who had been associated with it. The response to a questionnaire was very low, however. There was evidence, in spite of some criticisms, that the team had managed to recruit and retain the support and collaborative working of teacher groups in widely dispersed areas. Twenty teachers of varied experience working in nursery schools and classes, were involved in the evaluation, in areas in different parts of the country which had not been involved in the project. The evaluation team did not have control over the teachers selected to take part, and found that the authorities had tended to nominate more young and inexperienced teachers than would have been representative at that time. Seventeen of the teachers had some nursery component in their training. Visits were paid to the participating teachers at different stages in the project. Initial expectations of the teachers included apprehension, partly because of the word 'Mathematical' in the title, followed by relief, in some cases followed by disappointment at the familiarity of the contents and approach. One problem in the evaluation was that the teachers were not able to be as selective in their use of the guidelines as might have been the case under more natural circumstances.

With such a wide variety of teacher backgrounds it is understandable that the opinions varied widely from approval to rejection. The more directive teachers are reported to have found the guides valuable for planning. Those who had trained very recently were inclined to feel that their training had covered what the guides were offering. The guides were found to be helpful for those whose main experience had been with older children. The materials were felt to be more useful with the older children, the 'rising fives'. There were concerns expressed at the amount of sustained adult attention that they required. The guides were not felt to provide novel ideas for those who had trained for work with younger children, but could be of value to others working with young children, and give common ground for liaison between the nursery and infant stages.

One strength of developing curricular materials through a collaborative project with groups of teachers is that the materials developed are likely to be acceptable to practitioners, reflecting as they will some features of current practice. They are, however, not likely to be as innovative as the practice of some of those who have participated, nor to represent completely novel thinking and approaches. It is therefore understandable if projects such as these have something valuable to offer to only some of the teaching profession. What should not be overlooked, is the possibility that such materials may provide a valuable framework for the pre- and in-service training of staffs concerned with the education of preschool children. They could also form a basis for discussions to make possible 'continuity with extension' in the education of young children as the children move from one stage to the next.

A curriculum approach for socially handicapped children

Under the general heading 'topics relating to the education of socially disadvantaged children' were four of the eleven areas requiring further investigation listed by Tizard in her report to SSRC (see Appendix I and Tizard 1974). A project was set up by

NFER in 1975 on 'Social Handicap and Cognitive Functioning in Preschool Children' with two aims:

> to develop strategies and ideas that would benefit such children, and to evaluate these in a controlled experiment.

A handbook of ideas was published entitled *My World* (Curtis and Hill, 1978), followed by *Meeting the Needs of Socially Handicapped Children* (Curtis and Blatchford, 1981) which describes the background to the study and evaluation of its use. The results of a pilot study had shown social class differences in children's ability to use previous experience to solve new problems, and in their attention to 'school orientated' tasks. It was hoped by involving teachers in the development of the materials in this project that they would better meet the needs of the children and the teachers. Teacher groups were set up in six areas in England and Wales selected to represent major problems of social disadvantage, and links were established with a seventh area. The identification of children who might be termed socially disadvantaged, and ways of helping them were discussed. Teachers brought suggestions on more and less popular toys and materials with children aged three and four, and information from observations of children and their degree of involvement with different activities. In these groups of teachers, as in other studies at that time, some were unwilling to intervene in children's play. A decision was made to develop materials on a thematic approach, for small groups of four children aged four to five years of age, which should include other children who were not classified as socially disadvantaged. The involvement of teachers in this planning encouraged them to observe and make a critical appraisal of their own practices. While flexibility in the use of ideas in the handbook which was subsequently produced was encouraged, it was suggested that the activities be carried out at a regular time and place, and with children from a mix of backgrounds.

The evaluation of this project involved a comparison on a range of tests between an experimental group of children with whom the materials were used, a control group, and another group who received extra attention for similar lengths of time, but not with the handbook. In the main sample the tests were administered by the teachers, in a smaller sample by researchers who also undertook further tests and observations. Details on the children were collected by means of a questionnaire to teachers, whose own evaluation of the project was also sought. The evaluation involved schools in 12 areas in England and one in Wales, and 99 teachers in nursery schools or classes, 67 experimental and 32 control. There was a wide range of teaching experience among the teachers. A list of categories of social disadvantage was drawn up on the basis of previous research and discussions in the teacher groups. Children who fulfilled three or more of these were regarded as socially disadvantaged, and two or less as non-disadvantaged (Curtis and Blatchford, 1981 p.71). Each group of four was to contain a child of each sex in each category, within the age range 3-7 to 4-3. There were 684 in the groups initially, half classed as socially disadvantaged.

Some it was found did not meet the criteria, leaving a sample of 663, for all but 83 of whom data was available. An in-depth sample of 56 children was selected from these.

The main sample was assessed on two tests, the Boehm Test of Basic Concepts and Stott-Sharp Effectiveness Motivation Scale, and the smaller sample on a wide range of additional measures. Children who took part in the programme were found to have significantly higher scores on the concept test, the difference on the other test was not statistically significant. The scores from the groups who had special attention, but without involvement in the programme, showed that any effects were not explicable by that alone. At the start of the project, on pretest, the socially disadvantaged children had lower levels of performance; a gap was still apparent two terms later, although it is reported that the socially disadvantaged appeared to have gained more. From the small in-depth study in two local authorities the results were disappointing as there was not evidence of any additional significant effects for the experimental groups. Results from the main group were analysed in relation to a number of variables. One interesting finding was that the teachers who expected nursery attendance to have little effect on children's intellectual development had children with lower scores on the two main tests, both pre- and post-test. Since the teachers were themselves responsible for the testing, it is not possible to assess the extent to which their attitude deflated the scores of the children they tested: from other evidence that is a possibility.

An analysis of the attendance during the evaluation of the children from the different backgrounds revealed an important point, that those who had been classified as socially disadvantaged in both experimental and control groups had significantly lower attendance records. Furthermore, those with the lowest attendance records had the lowest post-test scores. This when related to the evidence on demand and uptake, and information on attendance from other studies, further confirms the difficulties in ensuring that children in most need of support do indeed receive it.

Religious education in the early years

A two-year curriculum development project to produce multi-faith materials for use in early education, with children aged 3 to 7 years, has just commenced. The project, directed by Dr. John Hull at the University of Birmingham, which has received funding from a number of official and charitable sources, will have extensive teacher involvement in developing and testing new methods and materials for the multi-cultural education of these children.

RECORD KEEPING IN PRESCHOOL EDUCATION

Assessment materials

One of the first projects to be funded by DES within the Nursery Research Programme was a study proposed by NFER to provide teachers in nursery schools and classes with a simple means of assessing and evaluating the development and performance of nursery children.

> "What appeared to be needed was a collection of resources and strategies for assessment which used normal nursery equipment and activities, but picked out crucial areas and placed them in some order or succession" (Bate and Smith 1978 p.6).

The aim was to improve teachers' observations of children, but without introducing artificiality, or producing a set curriculum to which staff were expected to teach. The team made a study of already available tests, now available in a revised edition (Bate, Smith and James, n.d.). Observational studies in nursery schools and classes reflecting 'good practice, in a variety of different areas in nine LEAS and ILEA were undertaken and an advisory group of lecturers, advisers, headteachers and teachers worked with the team. Two sets of field trials were undertaken with the tasks identified, and a reliability and validity study was undertaken (reported in the appendices to the manual, Bate and Smith, 1978). Five main areas were identified for assessment namely:

social skills and social thinking,

talking and listening,

thinking and doing,

manual and tool skills, and

physical skills.

Two methods of assessment are used, one is assessment from observation, the other uses activities the child is asked to perform. Short selections of items are available for a quick assessment. Similar materials and equipment can be substituted where appropriate. The aim is to provide flexible approaches to assessment, showing a child's strengths, and weaknesses which can be reassessed after help has been given.

Developing a record form

A rather different type of record keeping was investigated as part of a project funded by the Scottish Education Department and directed by the present author. In a two-year study a record form was devised by collaboration between a headteacher of a nursery school and the researcher who attempted to meet the specific requirements of that school. One aim was to ensure that the record had a high enough ceiling to record the development at age five of even the most able children, another to ensure that abilities possessed by the child, but not necessarily readily apparent by casual observation, were included. The record form was designed from the outset to be used by nursery nurses, and to assist in their in-service training, since at that time the headteacher was the only teacher in the school (Lomax 1977b;1979b). During two years the staff made periodic assessment of all 100 children in the nursery; results for children who remained over a two-year period were available for 37 children. The longitudinal nature of the project made it possible to study changes in children's interests over time, and differences between boys and girls in activities selected.

Reactions by the nursery nurses were generally favourable, although the form was felt to be too long and time-consuming if used to keep up-to-date records on every child. Its training function was justified, as it heightened staff's awareness of the extent to which some children could monopolize semistructured situations, also some children were found not to have grasped concepts which staff assumed they had. The forms also helped to give information on new children for whom a member of staff became responsible as different grouping took place.

Six headteachers in charge of other nursery schools were asked to comment on the form. Their reactions varied with the extent to which their priorities were in line with the emphasis on cognitive development of the headteacher for whose school the record form had been devised. Something similar, or parts of it, was thought to be valuable in teacher training, though some were unhappy at the involvement of nursery nurses in aspects of the assessment. Most of these headteachers would not, as a matter of course pass on written records to the primary school on all children, thus they would regard any form of record keeping as mainly for internal use and staff training.

Records and their use

The variety of purposes for which assessment of young children may be undertaken, whether by tests, in semistructured situations, by observations or using rating schedules, and the advantages and pitfalls in each are discussed by Lomax (in Clark and Cheyne, 1979 Ch. 8). Examples are given of children's responses based on data collected during the research project.

During the SSRC and DES funded studies on 'Play Exploration and Learning' at Keele University directed by John and Corinne Hutt a need was identified for some means of measuring changes not only in children's cognitive skills but in wider aspects of their development. As a result, the 'Keele Preschool Assessment Guide' was prepared which assessed language, cognition, socialisation and physical skills (Tyler, 1980). More recently Tyler has reviewed forms of assessment for use with young children including the above (Tyler, 1984). Observation schedules initially developed as part of research projects have been used by others, or in training of staff (for example those of Sylva et al., 1980 and Clark et al., 1982).

A survey of record keeping with under fives in Britain was undertaken between 1981 and 1983 involving 125 LEAs (Moore and Sylva, 1984). An open-ended query about record keeping in nursery and infant schools and a request for samples of current and previous systems was followed by a detailed questionnaire for the adviser with responsibility for education of under fives. Of the 125 LEAs in Britain, 94% responded, 66% sent sample records and 72% completed the detailed questionnaire.

It was found that most systems of records had developed over the previous five years, typically with advisers and teachers working together, although specialists such as educational psychologists speech therapists or college lecturers might be asked for suggestions. Most LEA advisers were reported to regard record keeping as either very, or quite important in both nursery and infant settings. Written guidelines and in-service training on record keeping was offered in many authorities, most frequently to infant teachers, next to nursery teachers, but much less frequently to nursery nurses. Records in infant and nursery schools were used to aid planning; most of those responding stated that records were often or always given to the next school. It was found that parents were seldom shown records relating to their under fives, and were unlikely to contribute to the record keeping process. In nurseries record keeping was for the purpose of team planning and planning for individual children; in contrast, in infant schools it was reported to be for transfer.

EXPERIMENTAL STUDIES ON THE UNDERSTANDING OF YOUNG CHILDREN

Mathematics

Grants awarded by SSRC to Peter Bryant at Oxford University and to Martin Hughes at Edinburgh University enabled each of them to undertake a series of experimental studies aimed at providing greater insight into young children's growing understanding of mathematical concepts. Bryant was concerned that so many statements made about children's ideas of number are negative, and yet it is clear that in certain situations children are quite capable of sharing, and that in asking for more, they show a sensitivity to things taken away from them. Hughes investigated the extent to which, in game-like situations, where the concepts had some practical significance, the children showed an understanding of number. He also wished to assess the extent to which the abstract aspects of mathematics were understood by, or could be taught, to the children.

The aim of Bryant's experiments was to investigate the extent of understanding of sharing, and of addition and subtraction in young children aged four and five years of age (Bryant 1978, Final Report to SSRC). He found that the children had a considerable measure of success with regard to sharing, but could be misled by perceptual clues. They also tended to be successful in appreciating that something added to a greater quantity, or subtracted from a lesser quantity, does not affect their relative status. An interesting additional point was noted that when the correct answer to a task was that they did not know (that is, a correct answer could not be deduced) the children still tended to give an answer. Bryant found that a training experiment encouraged the children to respond more appropriately in these circumstances, suggesting that their original difficulty was in admitting their ignorance.

In an article entitled 'Can preschool children add and subtract?', Hughes (1981) reports a series of experimental studies with children aged three, four and five years of age who were given simple addition and subtraction problems in a variety of task forms. Like Bryant, he found that the children had a considerable measure of success, but that performance was significantly affected by age, social class, size of number involved and form of task presentation. Most children were successful when the numbers were small and the problems were embedded in concrete or hypothetical tasks: a number were still successful with larger numbers. The difficulty arose when the tasks were set in the formal code of arithmetic, even when the numbers were small (for example what does two and three make).

In another series of studies Hughes(1983) introduced four-year-old children in two nursery schools to some basic arithmetic notation in a game situation. The children were seen individually for eight sessions. He found that most of the children were capable of understanding and using a simple form of arithmetical symbolism (in games where symbols were placed on boxes to enable the number of objects inside to be determined after addition or removal of some, for example). Hughes suggests that two important points were relevant to the children's success; that the task was embodied in a game which the children found interesting and that the symbols were introduced in a way which gave a clear rationale as to why they were used. It is interesting that Hughes found that in such settings the children had no greater difficulty with subtractions which resulted in zero. He found a considerable social class difference in children's ability to deal with these tasks, both in the younger and the older children, showing that there were already wide differences in children's understanding even before mathematics instruction had commenced. Differences in intelligence were not found to account for these; the kind of games and interactions which some of the children experienced at home might well have contributed (although this was not investigated in these studies), Hughes notes with concern these differences so early in the children's career. The studies by Hughes on preschool children, and others with children over five years of age in which their written representation of number was investigated, are now available in a book entitled *Children and Number,* with discussion on their implications for the early teaching of mathematics (Hughes 1986). Studies such as these by Bryant and Hughes show that before the introduction of mathematics teaching in school, children have already developed some knowledge of number in use, and that wide differences are present in their levels of understanding. They also suggest the need for a shift of emphasis in the early teaching of mathematics, with less emphasis on providing a range of concrete activities in isolation, coupled with a growing emphasis on use of arithmetical symbols in communicative situations which will help the children to appreciate their function. In recent years there has been an increasing acceptance that we need to consider mathematics as a language. In introducing number to young children it is thus important to help them to appreciate when mathematics is being spoken, its relevance, and to help them to move from the concrete to the abstract. Some children come into school already showing the beginnings of such linkage, receptive to and interested in the challenge; for the others situations and tasks must be planned to provide the basis, and the progression. Some examples are to be found in the activities used by Hughes in his experimental studies (Hughes, 1986). Hughes commented that the children found some aspects of the games he presented difficult, but far from discouraging them, this led children to state that it was difficult, or that they would have to think. The following is relevant not only for mathematics, but for other aspects of the curriculum.

> "It is worth noting that many preschool children appear to appreciate and enjoy intellectual problems which are pitched at the limits of their understanding" (Hughes, 1983 p.170).

Rhyme and Reason

During the period 1978-1983 Bradley and Bryant at Oxford University, with a grant from SSRC, investigated the importance for children who are beginning to read and to spell of the skill of detecting rhyme and alliteration. The research had two aspects; the first was a longitudinal study of children initially assessed at either four or five years of age on a task involving identification of 'the odd one out' in words which might differ in first, middle or final sound. The second aspect involved training children aged about six years of age who scored low on these tasks, and assessing whether or not this significantly affected their progress in reading and spelling. The two related studies were necessary in order to establish whether any link found was indeed causally related to progress in reading and spelling (Bradley and Bryant, 1983).

The first study involved 403 children (100 others assessed were rejected for further study because they were already beginning to read). Over the four years only 35 children were lost to the study, which necessitated following children into around forty schools. An important predictor of the children's progress in reading and in spelling was their intellectual level and score on vocabulary tests, a further significant predictor was the child's preschool skill at taking apart and categorising sounds in words.

Briefly, the training study involved 65 children aged about six years of age who were at the lower end of the distribution on the scores on the rhyming tasks. These were divided into four groups, two experimental, and two control. One experimental group received training, the second training and further practical experience: one control group received training in conceptual categorisation, the other no training. The experimental groups both performed better than the control groups, and the effect was greater in reading and spelling than in mathematics which was also assessed. Each child received forty training sessions individually, thus the experimental programme was considerable in intensity. In terms of both its individual nature and length it would not be possible in the normal school situation, even were it considered desirable. What that aspect provided, however, was the possibility to confirm whether a causal relationship was likely in relation to the findings on the first study. Bradley and Bryant have reported their studies in *Rhyme and Reason in Reading and Spelling* (Bradley and Bryant, 1985)

As was found in connection with mathematics, here also, even at an early stage, there were wide differences not fully accounted for by differences in intelligence in young children's ability to play with, to analyse and appreciate significant differences between words. Many young children in their interactions with adults at home have already had experience of playing with words and rhymes, enjoyed these experiences and learnt from them. Such experiences would appear to be of value within the context of school for many children, if introduced systematically in interesting and challenging situations.

There is some related evidence from a study by the present author of young children who could read before entry to school. All these young children could successfully undertake a task involving discrimination of differences between words, where the difference was in the initial sound, middle sound, or final sound; a test which gave problems to an unselected group of 197 children of the same age. It was argued, however, that the differences could not simply be explained in terms of lack of ability to discriminate sounds in words. Evidence to substantiate that was provided by giving the large group of school entrants a simplified task, but which still involved discriminating between similar sounds in different parts of a word. In the picture task the results were high, the errors few. This study is reported in a chapter of *Young Fluent Readers* entitled 'Auditory Discrimination and What else?' in which cautions are sounded at any assumption that what children require is a series of simple tasks to train them in auditory discrimination, even of word similarities and differences (Clark 1976). Depending on the form of presentation, they could succeed at such tasks. What the young fluent readers had developed were cognitive skills which enabled them to cope with the more complex task of distinguishing, for example, whether the words 'mouse' and 'mouth' were the same or different, rather than merely the ability to point to the correct picture, depending on which word was said. They enjoyed such tasks, and sustained concentration necessary to achieve success in it.

This study, those by Bradley and Bryant, and those in mathematics by Bryant and by Hughes all have important implications for assessing what young children can do in order to identify what they cannot, yet need to know. The challenge then is to provide stimulating and interesting activities within which they can extend their thinking. The experimental studies of the cognitive development of young children of Donaldson and her team, of whom Martin Hughes was one, have provided further insights into settings which enable young children to reveal the extent of their abilities, and possible explanations for their misunderstandings in other situations.

Children's minds

A Personal Research Grant from SSRC for one year gave Margaret Donaldson an opportunity to undertake a review of the findings of her own team's experimental studies of young children's cognitive development, some of which took place in an experimental nursery class at the University of Edinburgh, to relate them to the work of others, and to consider the implications of the findings. In *Children's Minds* Donaldson stresses the extent to which young children are actively attempting to make sense of their environment, and that an important feature influencing whether or not they solve a task is whether it makes 'human sense' (Donaldson 1978). Where the questions as posed do not make sense to the child they may be reinterpreted with the assistance of the perceptual setting to which the child then responds.

> "In the early stages, before the child has developed a full awareness of language, language is embedded for him in the flow of the events which accompany it. So long as this is the case, the child does not interpret words in isolation - he interprets situations. He is more concerned to make sense of what people do when they talk and act than to decide what words mean" (Donaldson, 1978 p.88).

At this stage the child, while framing hypotheses, is still limited in ability to cope with 'disembedded' thinking. With the assistance of the now famous 'naughty teddy' experiments and others Donaldson and her colleagues were able to show that children could solve tasks that had previously been thought beyond them, provided they made human sense. This leads Donaldson to reappraise the significance of the evidence from the Piagetian studies. The points made more specifically about mathematics by Hughes, discussed earlier, also developed this theme and its implications, for example, when he considered 'What's hard about two and two?' (Hughes, 1986 chapter 4).

The importance of studying young children in a variety of contexts before passing judgement on their competence, stressed throughout this report, is exemplified in these experimental studies. Furthermore the importance of providing children with educational experiences which will stimulate their thinking and help them to move from interpreting specific and concrete situations towards more abstract or disembedded thinking is discussed by Donaldson in her book, which is itself both challenging and full of insights for those involved in the education of young children. Donaldson suggests that young children from 'more privileged' backgrounds are more likely to pay attention to the precise nature of questions as posed, while children from 'less privileged' backgrounds are more likely to substitute a 'more natural' question. My concern would be with the way that the above expression might be interpreted, for example in terms of social class background, which would be misleading and not supported by the evidence now available. What is important is that it is recognised that some children enter school, even at the stage of nursery school or class, with home experiences of dialogue with adults which is already helping them to articulate not only what they know, but to ask for further information when in doubt, and to pay attention to the specifics of the language. This was certainly true of the children in my study of young fluent readers who came from a variety of social class backgrounds and who all experienced enjoyable and stimulating interaction with adults. One problem in early education is to continue to provide challenge for such children; at least as important, and much more difficult, is to ensure that the educational experiences of other children help them to develop such skills. It is all too easy for us in education to assume that the successes are a result of our instruction, but to regard the failures as a consequence of either lack of ability in the children, or of lack of competence or concern on the part of the parents. The evidence from experimental and other studies of young preschool children shows just how dangerous such assumptions are.

One important finding from a range of studies over the past fifteen or more years, is just how competent the young child can be, and how prepared to meet new and challenging situations, yet how possible it is for this not to be apparent in some children where the circumstances are either not stimulating or are even threatening.

"By the time they come to school, all normal children can show skill as thinkers and language-users to a degree which must compel our respect, so long as they are dealing with 'real-life' meaningful situations in which they have purposes and intentions and in which they can recognize and respond to similar purposes and intentions in others" (Donaldson, 1978 p.121).

Donaldson suggests that the printed word has an important contribution to make in helping children's development of disembedded thinking, as it is inevitably more distanced. Learning to read has in this way an importance for the child's further learning. To be successful in fulfilling this function, however, the context in which it is introduced, and the materials which are used would require both to make 'human sense', and to extend and enrich the children's experiences. There have been few experimental studies concerned with learning to read in which children under five years of age have been investigated, and in few observational studies in preschool units has any attempt been made to assess the extent of the children's involvement in books and stories, or the staff's involvement in or commitment to this aspect of the curriculum. Some of the issues and evidence on this will be considered in the final section of this chapter.

READING AND RELATED SKILLS

Young fluent readers; what can they teach us?

To further our understanding of how to help children to succeed in learning to read it is important that we look at successes, and not only at failures, including children who already read fluently, with understanding and enjoyment before school has instituted a teaching programme. What is important is not only the strengths of such children and their backgrounds, but also any weaknesses in spite of which they had succeeded. A detailed study of 32 such children who could already read before entry to school at five years of age included assessment of the children on a variety of tests, interviews with the parents and their teachers, and follow-up of these children in their first few years in school (Clark, 1976). These children were successful in a range of language-related tasks, and not only on specific reading materials. During the assessment they showed intense concentration and were clearly stimulated by the challenge. Some were highly intelligent, but not all; some came from professional homes, others from homes with few books (Clark, 1976).

Parental interviews, discussions with the children themselves, and their responses to a wide variety of tasks, all showed how important their interactions with the adults in their homes had been to their language development, of which their precocity in reading was only one feature. Already they were becoming sensitive to the written medium of English, could spell some words, make a recognisable attempt at others; they also knew what they did not know (Clark, 1984). A follow-up of these children a few years later showed how effectively their own written language was developing, showing clear evidence of the influence of their experience of the language of a wide variety of books. These children's strengths were in language related aspects, not necessarily in visual discrimination, or in motor co-ordination, and showed how important it is not to predict from failures in specific perceptual tasks, or from home background, that particular children will fail.

At the time this study was undertaken little interest had been shown in young pre-school children and reading: indeed there was a tendency to behave as if children entered primary school at most ready to read, and the process of learning to read commenced only with the instruction. Furthermore, there were views expressed that teaching reading to children before five years of age might be detrimental: indeed a number of the parents in the above study were either greeted with disbelief, or made to feel guilty that their children could read on entry to school. Coupled with this was a view among many teachers that preschools should not involve themselves in teaching reading. Reading of stories seemed to be regarded as part of a preparation for reading, and little more, or perhaps as providing a relaxing few minutes for staff and children. Certainly its importance as the first steps in developing awareness of print was not acknowledged at that time. Even the importance of story-reading to children as a valuable contributor to their oral language and cognitive development was not fully recognised. This may explain why so little attention was devoted to that aspect in research into the education of children under five. Now it is becoming increasing clear from a number of case studies just how different in their knowledge of concepts of print in relation to reading and writing and understanding of the language of reading instruction, children are on entry to school, even those who cannot yet read or write (see for example Payton 1984).

Stories in the development of young children

Evidence of the contribution of story reading and related activities in the homes of preschool children to the children's later reading attainment has been provided by Wells from his recordings of the language of children in their homes which was discussed in an earlier chapter (see for example Wells 1986). Reference is also made to story reading at home and at school by Tizard and Hughes, who cite some less successful experiences in both settings. Their recordings were limited, however, to the afternoons at home. In school they cite examples where the potential in such experiences was not utilized; in some instances because the story was read to a large number of children, or because of the teacher's 'hidden agenda' which prevented the follow up of points raised by the children (see Tizard and Hughes 1984 pp.59, 206, 237). Sutton assessed the competence of 20 children aged four years of age in her nursery school on activities related to reading, and found already a wide range of competence, before reading instruction had commenced. On a story-reading task in which the children were involved individually in attempting to recreate and predict the subsequent events in the story, she found a number of children were successful, and in that setting she found an impressive level of concentration in the children, all of whom appeared amused and interested throughout two readings of the story (summarised in Sutton, 1985). In an observational study in playgroups for disadvantaged children in Belfast, Turner (1977 p.59) found the most complex and extended language in story sessions, where the children employed phrases from the stories when discussing them, and with apparent understanding.

The extent to which reading-related activities have been a part of the day in preschool units, and of what these have consisted, or of when these have been particularly successful in stimulating and retaining the interest of the children, has been little studied. Indeed some of the observational studies have omitted the large group situations, and concentrated observations on free play only. In a study in a nursery school where the headteacher did regard introducing 'disadvantaged' children to books and stories as one of her priorities there was evidence that listening to stories and looking at books were among the more frequent activities to be observed, including requests for repeated readings of popular stories (Lomax, 1979a). The children were becoming sensitive to the patterns of story, and growing in awareness of the difference between relatively elaborate book language and everyday conversational language (see Clark and Cheyne, 1979 pp. 109-110). There was contrasting evidence in the observations made by teachers in preschool units involved in the project described earlier in this chapter on 'Socially handicapped children', in which the teachers were asked to study how long children stayed at a particular activity, and whether they were deeply involved. On page 27 of Curtis and Blatchford (1981) it is reported that the least popular activities with both sexes were jigsaws, books, dolls house and small table top toys. These are all possibly activities which may require concentration, and probably teacher support and intervention, otherwise the children who are not experiencing such activities at home may well avoid them, or dabble in them only briefly in school.

Until recently it was regarded as premature for teachers, and particularly for parents, to teach children to read, or actively encourage them, before the children's entry to primary school at five years of age in Britain. Now we have growing evidence on the importance of a developing awareness of print to children's later success in literacy related activities. It is ironic, however, now that so many more children of four years of age are entering school, some with little competence in the language of instruction, that there should be such urgency to start them on the more formal aspects of instruction. One explanation for that is likely to be the very limited nature of adult-child interaction possible where for all or much of the day there is only one adult in the classroom. Another reason may be pressure from parents who see only formal instruction as 'real' teaching. One aspect which has become clear from the researches is the limited understanding of important aspects of the education of young children of under five by some teachers and many parents, a discontinuity between home and school and between different stages in education. It is important that a greater understanding of the aims of early education is developed in other teachers and in parents, and that increased dialogue is achieved which stops pre-school education being considered in isolation from, or merely as a preparation for later instruction.

CHAPTER 16 LONG TERM EFFECTS OF PRESCHOOL EDUCATION: ISSUES AND EVIDENCE

ISSUES

One of the reasons for the planned expansion of preschool education in the early seventies was to prevent later educational failure. With hindsight it may now be apparent that it was naive to expect that future failure for those most at risk could be prevented by a brief inoculation at preschool, without any later co-ordinated follow-up, or consideration of the extent of compatibility of aims between preschool educators and those in primary schools and beyond. The task set preschool education was unrealistic, and any assessment of its effects, particularly long-term effects, is inevitably bedevilled by the possibility that any washout effect could have been, not indeed a result of lack in the preschool stages, but failure in the later stages to build upon the early foundations laid for such children. Any or all of the following are factors which might plausibly lead to a washout of effects shown earlier:

1 undue haste in moving to the more formal and abstract aspects of the curriculum before such children had been provided with sufficient experiences related to their immediate environment;

2 lack of sufficient staff or resources for continued individual or small group support;

3 discouragement of parents from taking an active part in their children's education or even the creation of a climate leading them to believe that they were unable to contribute to their children's progress;

4 premature judgements of the children's likely progress, or assessments based on evidence from limited contexts.

Surprisingly, in any discussion of long-term effects, the possibility of within school factors at later stages leading to a disappearance of effects, or to differential effects related to type of school attended and its aims, has been largely neglected. Yet, the more comparable, or at least compatible, the aims at different stages in the educational process the more likely there is to be continued progress, and continuity with extension. It seems unrealistic to expect effects to be maintained over a long period without any reinforcement or without at least some maintenance of an approach.

The focus on preschool education and provision for preschool children, in isolation from other aspects of education, in research funding in the seventies had unfortunate effects. Projects supported were expected to be able to provide evidence speedily to influence policy; for that reason and constraints in available funding long-term studies were not supported. Thus research, here and in the United States, in which long-term effects are assessed was not originally designed for that purpose. Furthermore studies from which valuable qualitative information might have been available may not be included in such evaluations because they lacked resources for longer term follow-up or because of missing information. It is important to appreciate the following points before considering specific studies of effects of preschool education.

The change in economic climate, before the funded studies had even been completed, led to a lack of interest in or dialogue about the findings, to some extent seen as no longer relevant, or scanned for evidence to support the changed policy to that of 'low-cost' provision. During the intervening years there was a shift in emphasis in much of the discussion on provision for preschool children to include, or to focus on the needs of the mother, as well as, or rather than the children. Care, rather than education, including all day care to meet the needs of working mothers, the need for and lack of such provision, became a centre for political debate, both here, and in the United States (see Hughes *et al.*, 1980, and for a review of these issues in USA, Scarr and Weinberg, 1986). Clearly, in discussing provision for young children it should not be in terms of a dichotomy of 'care' or 'education'. Furthermore, if the provision does not meet the requirements of the family, the children may either not enter, or may attend only irregularly. Demand for and uptake of the available provision, and differences in the populations in attendance at different types of provision are relevant to any assessment of effects of preschool education and have been considered elsewhere in this report. Issues concerned with whether or not mothers of preschool children should work and if so what form care provision should take, and by whom it should be provided, have not been considered.

From observational studies in preschool units it was clear that in those studied, freedom of choice, mobility and peer group interaction were all important features. In reception classrooms, these features were much less frequently apparent. The encouragement in preschool education of children to be independent, to make choices, to interact with their peers in a range of activities could on transfer to the next stage of education make some of these children less acceptable to some teachers. More passive, unquestioning children might be more acceptable to a teacher who adopts a didactic role; to a teacher/instructor, who frowns upon talk by the children except in response to specific questions, seldom provides choice, and expects peer interaction to be confined to the playground.

From the evidence of the aims of teachers in preschool education in the early seventies it is clear that fostering the children's social and emotional development was high in their priorities, and preparation for school in any precise sense was much lower in priority. Thus it would seem important that in any assessment of the effects of preschool education account is taken of the priorities of those involved. It may be that in more recent years there has been a move towards a greater emphasis on language and cognitive development in preschool education, or preparation for school; no large scale study has investigated this. Any long term evaluation of effects of preschool education either here or in the United States, has been of children who were of preschool age in the seventies, or earlier, before any changes in provision or in aims could have taken place. At that time many reception class teachers would for the first time be receiving children who had attended preschool units. In contrast, now in some areas most children will enter reception class as at least their second experience in a group setting outside the home. The expectations of the teachers are likely to change over time, such that any child entering direct from home may be at a disadvantage.

The population in, and aims in the establishment of different types of preschool provision are very different; both important points in any evaluation of their effects on children's later progress. To assess the effects of attendance at day nurseries, for example on children's later attainment in school seems to say the least rather unfair on the staff in that type of provision. The provision itself was not established as an educational provision; the children admitted in the seventies were frequently priority admissions for social reasons and, from available evidence, are even more likely to be so now. The circumstances which lead to children being admitted to day nurseries are, in addition unlikely to be transitory problems; from available evidence they are more likely to increase over time. Thus the likelihood of the children maintaining any gains which attendance could have achieved is greatly reduced. Within specific types of provision there may be very wide differences, in aims and in population. Terms such as 'playgroup', for example, have been used as if this meant a particular kind of provision, whereas there is evidence that the term may be used for many different types of provision. The one most generally assumed is a group of children meeting under the supervision or at least with the active involvement of the children's mothers. This is clearly true of some playgroups; others, however, are established by, and may be staffed by voluntary or other agencies, and may have no or little parental involvement. The term may also be used for a group which has the characteristics of a private school, run for profit by an individual in their own home or other premises specifically adapted for the purpose.

The amount and type of preschool provision varied, and still does, from area to area. The uptake of the available services by families differs, both generally and with regard to specific services, related among other things to awareness of available services, of their aims and benefits; to the demands that attendance would make on the families in terms of travel or parental involvement for example; to the extent to which the available provision meets the family's needs for all day care for example. Not only are there differences between types of provision in their aims, but also within types of provision which are identified by the same term in many published sources. The age of entry to primary school has varied over time, although the statutory age for starting school has not changed, and in different parts of Britain, may be preceded by, or possibly be in place of preschool education. All of the above variables may influence or interact with effects of preschool education.

Effects of preschool education may be assessed immediately after a particular programme, after the completion of preschool, or at any of a variety of points in later school life or beyond. The nature of the measures used to assess effects may vary, and be general cognitive tests, tests of more limited aspects, or of achievement in school subjects, motivation or even success in later life. A great deal of publicity has been directed in Britain to the results of studies in the United States of effects of intervention studies at the preschool stage. The initial evidence of effects, the later evidence of 'washout', and the more recent evidence of longer-term effects have all been reported. There have been some studies in Britain of short-term effects, but only one large scale study of long-term effects. Brief reference will be made to the studies in the United States, and a more detailed analysis given on the national survey in Britain.

EVIDENCE FROM THE STATES: CAN IT BE GENERALISED?

The two major sources of evidence from USA on long-term effects of preschool intervention which have contemporary relevance are those of Bronfenbrenner (1974), *Is early education effective?*, and the more recent evaluation, *As the twig is bent: lasting effects of preschool programmes* by the Consortium of Longitudinal Studies (1983).

Bronfenbrenner is tentative in his statements, warning of the need to replicate results and eliminate alternative interpretations, also the narrowness of the forms of assessment used such as IQ and related tests as measures of the total development of the child. For his review of research, Bronfenbrenner included only studies which

    a) included at least two years information after the end of the intervention

    b) provided information on a matched control group

    c) provided data which was comparable to results in other studies.

He reviewed studies in group settings and home-based intervention. He claimed that without family involvement intervention is unlikely to be successful, and that the few effects are unlikely to last. He argued in terms of long-term intervention up to age twelve and on a wide front for disadvantaged families.

The Consortium was founded in 1975 to assess whether early education programmes in USA could be shown to have long-term effects on the performance of children from low-income families. This group represented a collaboration of researchers who had developed and evaluated early education programmes in the sixties, and the children who had participated were by then between 8 and 18 years of age. All projects which had an original sample in excess of 100 were invited to join the consortium, and all but one of the 15 eligible studies accepted. The volume contains a chapter by those who had been involved in each of the studies, and a pooled analysis of follow-up data from the individual studies on which the conclusions are then based. This is not an evaluation of Head Start, as all programmes included were closely supervised and carefully documented experimental programmes; they were similar to Head Start in curricular goals and the populations at which they were aimed. These studies were of low income families; 94% of the children were black, and in some samples 100%; only 62% were two parent families; these were intensive interventions, with at least moderate parental involvement, and they took place in the United States in the sixties. The studies and findings must thus be viewed against the educational context which these children entered. Represented in the analysis were widely different curricular approaches and types of programme. It is claimed that individually and collectively these studies show that early intervention with low-income families can have measured effects throughout childhood and into adolescence. Measures included in addition to test scores, grade retention and referral to special school.

> "The low-income, mostly black children who participated in this diverse range of programmes and curricula were more likely to succeed in school than were similar children who did not have any of those experiences. They also felt better about themselves, had more realistic vocational expectations, and were prouder of their achievements than were non-participants" (Consortium, 1983 p. 462-463).

More recently an article has appeared from High/Scope one of the curricular groups represented (but for a different sample from that above), which it is claimed encourages and supports children in initiating their own activities. It is argued that in a long-term comparison of certain features, those who had participated in that programme were superior to others who had taken part in a more instruction-based approach. An important point is made that

> "We cannot continue to excuse an almost exclusive focus on the use of intellectual and academic measures for programme effectiveness because valid measures of social competence are difficult to develop" (Schweinhart, Weikart and Larner, 1986 p.43).

Woodhead (1985), in a valuable review article has considered the relevance of the evidence from the States, and possible implications for Britain. General conclusions based on these studies he argues should be influenced by the nature of the populations, severely disadvantaged, mainly black. Second, the projects were all carefully designed well-supported programmes with low ratios of adults to children and active parental involvement. Third, the effects of any programme may be influenced by the family and other context in which the intervention takes place, together with the subsequent school procedures which could either reduce or increase the relative progress of those who have and have not been involved in the preschool programme. He argues for a more complex transactional model, by which it may be possible for short-term cognitive and motivational gains to have long-term influences on educational achievement and motivation. Such a model he feels would better fit the results which showed long-term effects from a variety of intervention projects, and at different ages. Cheyne (1987) in reviewing the available evidence from research in the States on short- and long-term results, makes the valid point that any effects of preschool intervention which last even for three or four years still represent a major influence, and yet these tend to be discounted. Any kind of instructional programme needs maintenance if its effects are to survive, yet the projects take no account of what happens in school in the intervening years. This is an issue to which attention was drawn in the introduction to this chapter, in arguing for an analysis of the relationship between the aims of preschool and primary school.

There are many contrasts between the educational settings in the United States and in Britain, not only with regard to the measures of effect used in these studies undertaken in the sixties. Grade retention would clearly not be a relevant measure of effect in Britain, and referral to special schooling a dubious one. That the age of starting school, expectations and context are still very different, is brought home in a recent article by Zigler, one of those involved in the Consortium studies (Zigler, 1987). In the article entitled 'Formal schooling for four-year-olds? No', Zigler claims that in the States there has been a recent movement towards enrolling four-year-olds in academic programmes. He explains it as an inappropriate solution to the current crisis in child care for working parents. He argues that full day school is not appropriate for four, or even five-year-olds, and pleads for developmentally appropriate educational components in a programme which would be primarily concerned with socialisation and recreation.

> "Our four-year-olds do have a place in school, but it is not at a school desk" (Zigler, 1987 p.259).

EMPIRICAL STUDIES ON EFFECTS OF PRESCHOOL EDUCATION IN BRITAIN: SOME ISSUES

Brief reference will be made to four researches on the effects of preschool education to indicate problems in designing such studies and in the interpretation of the results. Some researches discussed elsewhere in the report included either a study of the effect of aspects of the curriculum, or an intervention in which a programme was introduced and its effects assessed. In these four studies the assessment was of the effects of attendance at ordinary units. The first two were in Scotland in nursery schools, the third in Northern Ireland was in playgroups for disadvantaged children, the fourth in England was a comparison of playgroups and nursery classes.

I Measuring the effects of a new nursery school

A valuable opportunity to measure effects of preschool education was provided by the opening of a new nursery school in an area of multiple deprivation, where there had previously been no preschool provision (Clark and Cheyne, 1979). All children in the area would subsequently attend one of two primary schools, one non-denominational, the other Roman Catholic. Over a period of three years it was possible shortly after entry to reception class, to assess the children individually on a range of psychological tests. In the first year group no children had attended nursery school; in the second group some children had attended for one year; in the following year, some had two years preschooling, some had one, some none. The nursery school was large enough to accommodate all the children and every attempt was made to encourage the parents to enrol their children. A number of factors influenced when or whether children attended, which a detailed knowledge of the area made it possible to study. About 200 children were involved in this study, approximately equal numbers in each of the three year groups, with numbers who had preschool education increasing, but different proportions of those entering the two primary schools. An important aim for the headteacher of the nursery school was to help develop children's intellectual powers, her second aim was to help them form stable relationships. On the wide range of psychometric tests there were differences in favour of each group of nursery children, and those who had two years attendance performed better than those who had attended for one year. The design made it possible to assess the differential effect of a range of factors. When allowance had been made for these, the differences found were small, however, and were only a minor factor in accounting for the variability in the children's scores. The nursery effects were greatest in the tests involving copying and drawing, and in tests given closest to entry to primary school.

One important consideration is whether these tests were effectively picking up what might be small but real differences in a relatively small sample within each category. Although larger samples could improve the sensitivity and reliability of such comparisons this also introduces other variables. For example the head of another nursery school might have very different aims; further primary schools would be involved which might have very different expectations and methods. Even in this study, one of the primary schools used 'ita' for teaching reading, the other did not. Any attempt to assess long-term effects when the assessment bridges two stages in education results not only in greater sample loss but also the need to allow for variations in expectations and methods in the receiving schools. The variables were complex even in this setting where circumstances were unusual in that there was only one preschool unit, and were only two primary schools in a relatively closeknit community.

II Effects of preschool

In an experimental study designed to assess the effects of a programme involving the parents of preschool children of three and four years of age it was possible also to assess over a limited time scale the effects of nursery school attendance with and without additional involvement of the parents (Donachy, 1979). There were 96 children in six groups in the study; nursery only and nursery with parent programme, aged four years of age; non-nursery with programme aged three and aged four; distant control group aged three and four. The groups matched for age, sex, social class and vocabulary level were assessed on individual intelligence and language tests before and after the four month parent programme in which three groups were involved. Observations in the nursery school did not form a part of this study. Further details of the study are given in the chapter of this report on parents and preschool education.

Significant differences were found on the Stanford Binet Intelligence Scale after the four month period for the children attending nursery school whose parents had not been involved in the programme. More differences were found where the parents were also involved.

III Playgroups and disadvantaged children

A series of studies involved some or all of 48 of the 52 playgroups for disadvantaged children in the Belfast area subsidised by grants and organised by local boards or charities (Turner, 1977). These studies included an assessment of the effects of attendance on the children's language and cognitive development supported by a wide range of information on the children and their families and the playgroups. Some aspects of the research, the less disruptive, involved 48 playgroups including test-retest of the measures used, other aspects were in sub-samples of the playgroups. The aims of playgroup leaders were studied, and in general found, as in other studies, to emphasise social-emotional development, followed by intellectual development (see Turner, 1977 chapter 2).

Observations were undertaken for a full morning session in 18 playgroups from which it was possible to assess the extent of similarity in the experiences offered to the children. The results are given both as means and range across playgroups. Approach to artistic development was also studied, in eight playgroups. The playgroups had many features in common, in aims and in practices observed, and in equipment, partly, it is suggested because of the selection of staff, the training and supervision they received from an organiser, also the fact that they were subsidised. They provided a setting with some activities in which all or most of the children were involved and free play in which the children selected their own activities.

The mothers' aims in sending their children to playgroup were studied in a sample of ten mothers from each of 18 playgroups, with equal numbers of boys and girls. For both boys and girls a high proportion of the responses related to aspects of social-emotional development, some to cognitive development and starting school, few to physical development and virtually none to aesthetic development. A significant sex difference was found indicating that the mothers tended to stress physical development more often for the girls, related to greater expectation of dexterity from the girls, and good relationships and co-operativeness for the boys as a reason for sending them. Generally the children were considered to have benefited in the areas mentioned by the mothers. Advantages of the child's attendance were also considered, both for the child and the mother. Short periods of separation were thought to be valuable for better relationship between mother and child, and more time available with siblings. It also gave mothers more time for housework etc. A few mentioned part-time work, for a few in a playgroup, at most once a week, for some very infrequently. Some mothers saw no benefits to themselves, and disadvantages were also mentioned by some, which might relate to size of family and the child's position in the family and to distance of the playgroup. The size of families and child's place in family are important variables, and in this study such information is provided. About half the children, boys and girls, were in families of more than two (and 14% in families of five or more); over 60% were first or second children.

The specific aspect of the research in which effects of attendance on language and cognitive development was assessed involved a sub-sample of 12 playgroups, from each of which ten children were selected aged between four and five. Sub-samples of non-attenders were matched with these from the same communities, and were children whose parents wished them to attend but for whom places were not available. Every care was taken in matching, and any limitations are fully discussed. In this research the effect of attendance at playgroups without any additional intervention, or programme is assessed. There were 120 children attending, and 120 non-attenders. Significant differences were found between attenders and non-attenders on measures of listening vocabulary and general reasoning ability and no significant differences between playgroups in relation to geographical area. Within this aspect inter-playgroup differences could not be analysed specifically. Further analyses were possible from the larger sample of 480 children from 48 playgroups tested and retested, in which significant differences were found over the period of six months. There were differences in the playgroups and some of these are considered in relation to children who made greater or less progress from first to second assessment. By the very nature of their support, staffing and population attending it is not surprising that these playgroups were relatively homogenous in approach, and that there were not larger differences between groups in effects on the tests. Even within such groups there were differences which are discussed and related to specific aspects of particular playgroups.

IV Playgroups and nursery classes, a comparison

A study of the effects on entry to reception class of attendance by 'working-class' children at either a playgroup or nursery class is reported in a recent article by Jowett and Sylva(1986). Behaviour on entry to reception class was assessed based on classroom observation, results from a test of basic concepts and a school adjustment scale. The sample was 90 children who started school in 1978, half of whom had attended each form of provision. Ten schools were selected, matched on a number of important variables, five of which had a nursery class and other five without a nursery class, whose intake normally attended a playgroup. Within the schools children were matched on sex, age, family structure; children from social group 1 or 2 were excluded. Children were observed in their first term in reception class, then again six months later. The observation schedule, which was adapted from that used by Sylva *et al.*(1980) in the Oxford research, was used to assess the cognitive complexity of the activities in which the children engaged, how they reacted to difficulties and their social interactions. Note was also taken of language initiated by or addressed to the target child.

The results reported include a significant effect of nursery class attendance on purposeful and creative play, an effect which although less still persisted six months later was still present. Differences were also apparent in the more school-related activities, which by the second analysis had increased more in the nursery class children. The children from the nursery class devoted more time to self-initiated writing. There was a tendency for the playgroup children to spend more time watching peers. Associated with the greater amount of 3Rs work by the nursery children, they spent more time waiting, sometimes for relatively long periods. Social participation was comparable between the two groups. The children who had attended nursery class were more likely to engage in purposeful or imaginative activity when alone or in a group parallel situation.

Differences in amount of language apparent on entry to school had disappeared by the second observations. There was evidence that the nursery children were more likely to engage in connected conversation. The initial difference found between the social competence shown by the children had narrowed by the second observation. In both phases, however, the playgroup children were more likely to make requests to the teacher, the nursery class children to make 'contribution' comments. There were also differences in the children's persistence under difficulties without asking for help in favour of the nursery class children. Differences were not found between the groups on the Boehm Test of Basic Concepts.

A number of differences between the groups of children who attended either playgroup or nursery class are reported in this study, some of which persisted six months after entry to school, in some the gap had closed somewhat. There are some aspects which are not reported in this article and which may be relevant to the findings. The nursery class and playgroup children selected entered different schools, an aspect of the design. It is, however, as a consequence, difficult to assess the extent to which teacher expectation of children in schools with a nursery class differed, or differed for children known to have attended a nursery class, possibly even in that school. There may have been differences in the pattern of available activities and speed at which 3Rs activities were introduced. It would be helpful to have details on the aims and objectives of the teachers in the two groups of schools in order to assess this, and whether there were differences between the reception classes in what the children in the class in general had available as activities, what they were expected to do, and how soon. Evidence from other studies in reception class would suggest that there is limited freedom of choice, and limited mobility in many reception classrooms. The behaviours shown by the children may or may not have been different from classmates who had not attended any preschool provision. It is not possible from this study to ascertain what proportion of the children in these reception classes had attended any preschool provision, and thus how similar the behaviour of the target children was to that of their classmates.

It would also be relevant to know the proportion of target children in each class who had attended the same preschool unit, and for how long, since in addition to those aspects considered in the article this could have been a powerful influence on complexity of play, length of conversations, etc. An analysis of how many children each child knew, say by name, or had met prior to entry to reception class could have been a valuable piece of evidence, as there could have been differences between those from playgroups and those from the nursery class, possibly that school's nursery class. It is crucial to know just how many of the children assessed who had attended a nursery class, had attended the nursery class in that school. For these children familiarity with that school, its routines, and even some of its staff, could have been important variables influencing their adjustment in the reception class. The narrowing gap between the two groups on some of the measures, and the lack of difference on the test of basic concepts suggests that such variables could be as important as those discussed in the article, and even if differences remain over a longer term than reported so far.

A NATIONAL SURVEY OF EFFECTS OF PRESCHOOL EDUCATION

Reference has been made in a number of places in this report to findings from the CHES (Child Health and Education Study) of a national sample of over 13, 000 children in Britain born between 5th and 11th April 1970, and to a national survey in 1975 of preschool institutions. The CHES study has provided a wealth of information on the social life of a national sample of children, based mainly on parental interviews and assessment of the children in the home by health visitors when the children were five years of age (Osborn, Butler and Morris, 1984). Among the many aspects of development and background on which information was sought from the mothers was whether or not their child had attended a preschool unit, if so what kind of unit, and whether the child had by five years of age already entered primary school. There were regional and social class differences both in whether a child had attended preschool provision, and in which particular type of provision had been attended. The aspect of the study which will be discussed here is that concerning the relationship between the children's preschool experiences and attainment as measured at five and ten years of age. Assessment based on results at five years of age is reported in Osborn *et al.*(1984). Subsequently the team received further funding, from DES, to follow-up the children at ten years of age and assess the relative performance on a number of measures of those who had and had not attended a preschool unit, also any differences between attainment related to the type of unit attended. This has now been reported in *The Effects of Early Education* (Osborn and Milbank, 1987). In addition to these two publications, the two volume final report to DES which provides more extensive detail than the more recent publication has been studied for this investigation (Osborn and Milbank, 1985).

The complexity of the issues involved in assessing effects of preschool education has been discussed earlier in this chapter both in general and in relation to several small-scale studies. The CHES sample was born in 1970, and the children had completed any preschool education by 1975; thus the information contained in chapters 2 and 3 of this report, and comments in Osborn and Milbank (1987) are relevant when considering the generalisability of the findings and their relevance to the eighties and beyond. There have been major differences in the numbers of children in preschool education, their ages, and the proportions attending different types of unit.

The study

This research is on a national sample of over 13, 000 children. The study was not originally planned to study preschool education and its effects and the information on preschool education, the type of unit attended and amount of parental involvement was all collected retrospectively when the children were five years of age. This presents two problems; first there is no measure as to whether there were differences before at the preschool stage either between those who did and did not subsequently receive preschool education, or those who attended different types of unit. Some attempt is made to allow for this in the analysis by means of a social index, and also to allow for the pressures on different types of unit because of the children attending, by means of a problem index. It is difficult to assess whether these measures have fully dealt with such differences. There may well be differences which are associated not only with differential attendance preschool, but also variations in quality and type of schooling between the ages of five and ten years of age, or home circumstances not accounted for which could reduce or increase any differences.

The second problem was that it was necessary to match from the mothers' descriptions the particular type of preschool provision attended. From other evidence it is likely that while the mothers might have accurately reported whether or not their child had attended a preschool unit, for how long, and whether full or part-time, they were less accurate in describing the type of unit. Attempts were made to match the mothers' statements to specific types of unit by use of information in the national survey in 1975 of preschool units. Unfortunately this led to a considerable sample loss where such matching could not be achieved. The sample in this study is large, over 13, 000 for whom test information was available at five, but the sample for whom matching of unit could not be achieved was over 3, 000, and as large as the sample with no preschool experience. There was, as in most longitudinal studies, particularly when an attempt is made to retest several years later without continued involvement, a further sample loss between age five and ten, reducing the sample included in the analysis from about 9, 000 to about 8, 400 between these ages. In spite of the size of the initial sample, the numbers of children who were assessed at ten years of age who had attended certain types of provision were still relatively small, and too small for a comparison of relative effects on attainment. Although the numbers in nursery schools and classes and in hall playgroups were relatively large, there were only 105 children who had attended local authority day nurseries, 145 from independent day nurseries, only 36 in what were categorised as independent nursery schools and 166 in 'home' playgroups in the sample at ten years of age.

The results

Among other measures reported on which effects of preschool education was assessed were the following;

at five years of age

copying designs and a listening vocabulary test

at ten years of age

some aspects of an intelligence test, a picture language test, reading and mathematics tests , and communication (as assessed by teachers).

At five years of age the tests were given by health visitors and at ten years of age by teachers.

Differences on these measures were found in scores uncorrected for other variables (see Osborn and Milbank 1987 p.101). In view of the known social and family differences between children attending different types of unit these results as they stood could not be taken as a consequence of differing preschool experiences. The results were therefore adjusted for social index, type of neighbourhood and number of children in the household and show that:

1. Children who had not attended a preschool unit had lower than average scores on most tests

2. Children who attended LEA nursery schools or hall playgroups had higher than average scores. A comparison of socially disadvantaged children showed only three significant differences; higher scores for children who had attended nursery schools on EPVT (language test) at five years of age, and on communication at ten, and higher mathematics scores for children who had attended hall playgroups (Osborn and Milbank, 1987 p.112)

3. Attendance at nursery class was associated with lower mean scores than 2. above. a finding which was surprising to the researchers, but which they had not empirical evidence to explain. This may be an artefact of the retrospective way in which the data was collected, for example, some of these children may have been in classes which were more similar to infant classes than to the other preschool provision. If there are real and educationally significant differences in favour of separate preschool provision (in terms of staff, approach or resources), or there are ways in which nursery classes should be modified to be more in line with these, that could be important in view of the tendency for increase in preschool education to be in nursery classes rather than in schools (See Chapter 3).

4. Children who attended local authority day nurseries had lower scores on most tests than those who attended other provision. This is not surprising, in view of the multiplicity of factors which distinguishes referral to and attendance at such provision, and the fact that their aims were to provide all day care for children from families with special needs rather than preparation for school (See Chapter 8).

5. Duration of attendance was a complex factor to assess, since age of admission, and of departure to reception class, varied as did length of day. Furthermore, the 'main' preschool provision used in these analyses was the most recent, and a number of children had attended more than one preschool placement. There was some evidence that the children who started preschool early had better scores on the tests than those who did not start until after four years of age. Pattern of attendance varied both between and within types of provision, and since full-time attendance may have been a consequence of priority admission, or special needs in some instances, this was an issue on which the survey could not provide any definitive answer.

6. In contrast to the evidence on attendance at preschool provision, there was not evidence that early entry to infant class had an effect on the various test measures.

7. The statement that the children with the best scores were those who had attended 'home' playgroups must be treated with caution, and the following points noted. The national survey of preschool provision in 1975, cited in Osborn and Milbank in 1987, separates home playgroups from hall playgroups, a decision made during the study. (It might have been valuable to distinguish 'private' from 'community' playgroups - found to be an important distinction by the present author (Clark and Cheyne, 1979). Home playgroups accounted for about 4% of the children in preschool provision at that time, about half those in nursery schools and more than the number attending LA day nurseries.

home playgroups were on average much smaller,

were more likely to have staff with teaching qualifications (about 20% of staff as compared with 9% in hall playgroups and about 36% in nursery schools);

over 25% had a child adult ratio of less than 1:5;

over 50% were in well-to-do neighbourhoods (as compared with hall playgroups 20% and nursery schools and classes about 7%);

most obtained no score on the problem index;

over 60% had no parental help, and few had 'at least one parent involved' either in the management or on a consultative committee (this evidence on little parental help is confirmed from the reports by the mothers of the children in the CHES, most of whom reported that they had not helped);

the pattern of type of school attended subsequently was relatively similar for children who had attended home playgroups, except that a slightly higher percentage attended direct grant or independent schools.

Although attendance at home playgroups was associated with high scores on the tests, "this superiority over the other types of institution was statistically non-significant", yet the authors go on to observe that "the consistency of the finding across all seven tests cannot be ignored". In view of the lack of statistical significance these are surprising comments. They then suggest that

"the small scale and homely atmosphere of the home playgroups may explain this relative success" (Osborn and Milbank, 1987 p.239)

There were no observations within the preschool units either when the children were in attendance, or from the national survey, and on the questionnaire returns there are wide differences in emphasis in such units (See Osborn and Milbank, 1987, p. 64). One must therefore have reservations about this aspect.

The evidence from the assessment at five and ten years of age on this large national sample gives support for the general statement by Osborn and Milbank

"This study is the first to provide conclusive evidence that preschool education provided by ordinary nursery schools and playgroups in Britain can have a positive effect upon the cognitive development of the children who attend them" (Osborn and Milbank, 1987 p.238).

As the authors themselves stress, it is important to appreciate the success of the nursery schools in view of the higher proportion of children from socially disadvantaged homes, children with special needs and with behaviour problems who attend such institutions. What is not possible is to assess from surveys such as this what are the features which characterise the units that are successful, and to what extent others can be trained and supported to achieve their success. Such evidence is more likely to be available in more detailed studies which included observations in a variety of units of different types, such as those reported elsewhere in this report. To what extent measures which can be used in a survey, particularly a large scale national study, can be sensitive enough to assess the range and quality of effects which have been achieved must remain open to question.

From the studies cited in this chapter it should be clear just how complex an issue is the extent of long-term effects of preschool education, and the many factors which can bedevil attempts to assess these. Small-scale intensive studies planned to evaluate the effects might have too small a sample for effects to be statistically significant. In a large scale study in which data is already available on a variety of other and related factors it should not be assumed that no problems will remain. It is difficult to assess the educational significance of results that are found, and dangerous to attribute them to specific types of provision in the absence of detailed knowledge of the provision. Averages could disguise in any type of institution outstandingly good and bad practice. It is important to assess the extent to which particular approaches are successful in stimulating children's development, what features are crucial both in establishing and maintaining any effects that can be achieved.

It is important that in any further research programme concerning the education of young children there is not an artificial division either according to type and stage of educational provision, or by age group. It is to be hoped that attention can be directed to the content and quality of the provision rather than, as has tended in the past, be focused mainly on co-ordination and organisational aspects, or on provision distinguished by its category name rather than its characteristics. Only then can features which are important to children's development be identified and the insights from research be fully reflected in the pre- and in-service training of teachers.

CHAPTER 17 SUMMARY

OVERVIEW

The remit for this report was a personal commission from the Secretary of State to undertake a critical evaluation of research of relevance to the education of under fives. The need for such a survey and evaluation became increasingly apparent during the investigation which commenced in 1985 and has uncovered a wide range of funded and other studies, only a limited number of which are frequently cited. Furthermore, in such references attention is not necessarily drawn to factors which might limit their generalisability or current relevance. Some researches are either not available in published versions, or in sufficient detail for evaluation. In addition it is often assumed that recently published research refers to information collected in preschools as they are now, which may not be the case, since much of the major funded work was commissioned and the empirical work undertaken in the seventies (See Chapter 2).

In the eighties there are many more children under five in educational provision, with wide differences between areas in the amount and types of provision (See Chapter 3). Younger children are now in reception class in some areas, who at the time of many of the researches would have been at home or in preschool. The current remit of 'children under five' made it possible to consider implications both for preschools and for reception classes. There are now in some areas many children from ethnic minorities, and for whom English is a second language (See Chapter 4).

For the reasons stated above it seemed essential to provide details, at least for the major studies within each topic, and not merely a personal evaluation of their relevance to policy and practice and an assessment of gaps in existing research. The preceding chapters have been presented in such a way that the information can be of continuing relevance to funding bodies and others. Researches may provide evidence on more than one topic, and the topics themselves are interrelated; thus individual chapters are not intended to be treated in isolation. In this section the main findings,their implications for policy and practice, and gaps in existing research will be identified.

The Nursery Research Programme instituted by DES in the mid seventies, and many researches funded by DHSS, Schools Council and other bodies, were planned towards informing policy during the proposed rapid expansion of preschool education, which was to be available by the early eighties, either full or part-time, for all three- and four-year-olds whose parents wished it for them. The urgency felt by those advising policy-makers to have speedy results to inform policy and practice can be seen in the precise topics selected for commissioned funding, none of which were long-term and most of which related to preschool education in isolation from the later stages of education (See Chapter 2 and Appendices).

Most researches commenced when expansion of preschool education had scarcely started, when it was still mainly in areas of high priority for which specific funding was available, or in authorities already committed to preschool provision. Some of the units in which studies were undertaken had only recently opened; many staff had only recently trained for that field, some were not yet specifically trained; few had been long in that post. They had not necessarily had time to revise their aims to take on board the new and wider roles, or to appreciate the enormity of the burden which they were to be expected to carry. As one reads the research and development projects, what is impressive is the amount of professional commitment shown by this relatively small group of teachers in preschool education, many of whom were members of working parties for, or were involved in, curriculum projects such as those funded by the Schools Council (discussed in Chapter 15). Many also showed a willingness to attend courses and to develop their practice in the light of new insights from research.

It is important not to draw conclusions about, and certainly not to condemn, current preschool practitioners on the basis of observational studies undertaken some ten or more years ago, as has often been the case. Not all studies provide details on the background of the staff observed; some of whom were teachers, others were nursery nurses or other adults in the unit; some of whom might not yet have been familiar with, or trained for the complexities of working with that young age-group, or in that setting. There are lessons with regard to organisation, range of activities, pre- and in-service training of staffs, and not least the need for continuity in the curriculum through the years of early education.

Economic constraints led almost immediately to a reversal of national policy from a commitment to expansion in this non-mandatory aspect of education to a focus on low-cost provision for the under fives. The climate had already changed from one of expansion to protection, or even contraction in some areas, in the early stages of the empirical work for a number of the researches, and before practice could have been expected to reflect the new priority of children's language and cognitive development, where previously the promotion of social and emotional development had for many been the most important aim (See Chapter 15 for example).

The presence of researchers in units which in some areas were already under real threat of closure, meant that observational studies might be used as ammunition for a change to lower cost provision. In that climate, some researchers even moved to different types of preschool provision (See Chapter 7 for example). Any disenchantment with preschool education which has been reported is scarcely surprising in view of the impossibility of the task it was set in the seventies as a non-mandatory provision vulnerable to cuts, yet expected, almost in isolation, to provide an injection against later educational failure, and for the most disadvantaged, those most at

M

risk (See Chapter 2 where the context is discussed). To be expected to do this under a research microscope, and when subjected to financial and other restrictions was an impossible task. Any failure to achieve substantial long-term effects from pre-school education could as plausibly result from a failure to capitalize on any gains made in theearly stages, or be compounded by limited expectations by teachers in the later stages of education (See Chapter 16). Alternative explanations might in-clude a lack of sufficiently individualised and creative curricula to meet the wide and varied needs of children entering school at or about five years of age, either as a consequence of scarce resources, or inadequacies in training. Yet any such pos-sibility has been under scrutiny only incidentally where children were followed from the preschool into reception class.

Where there is information on under fives which extends into the primary school this reveals that any implications of research are not confined to the preschool field, and that problems in utilizing the insights from research on young children's learn-ing are probably even greater in the reception class and beyond. Some children make choices, act responsibly, engage in valuable educational dialogue with their peers and with adults, and concentrate for long periods on challenging tasks in the pre-school unit or at home (See Chapters 5, 6 and 7). It is important not to overlook this finding when assessing the evidence that there are preschool settings which appear not to direct children sufficiently to the more creative activities, where the adults fail to stimulate sufficient extended dialogue or encourage the children to con-centrate to completion of activities once they have chosen them. In the more formalized settings in some reception classes the more creative aspects of learning in which children were observed to engage preschool may no longer be apparent, even in these same children (See Chapter 13). This may stem partly from anxiety by the schools to be seen to be teaching 'the basics', to meet the expectations of parents or others, or a lack of appreciation of the importance to children's later development even in the basics, of some of the broader aspects of the curriculum. There is research evidence which is of relevance to the training of staff involved in early education to ensure that the curriculum, the activities available, the organisa-tion of the staff, and the style of dialogue they adopt provides a stimulating environment for an even wider range of children (See Chapters 6 and 7 for example). Where the settings offered in school are limited, the responses of some children will still go beyond the task set and will show their wider understanding; those of others will not, and staff are then likely to underestimate the competence and potential which these children could demonstrate if the contexts were varied and challenging enough (See Chapter 5). The teachers' expectations may then begin to influence these children's view of themselves, and that of their parents.

A lack of communication with many parents on the aims of early education and the purposes behind many of the activities, means that many parents fail to understand the significance of the more extended aspects of the curriculum, which they may see merely as 'play', rather than 'work' (See Chapters 5 and 10)! There may also be a lack of adequate resources, and/or of staff with training and experience to provide the stimulation to learning of young children in the primary school. Some parents may not extend and support their young children's learning, either because they do not realise how valuable informal dialogue with their young children about everyday experiences can be, or because they have been conditioned to believe that teaching is the job of the schools, that anything they do will make littledifference, or might even be detrimental (See Chapters 10 and 11).

The importance of active involvement by young children in wide ranging tasks, which stimulate their understanding and which make 'human sense' to them, both to the assessment of their present competence and to their subsequent development, is becoming increasingly clear. This applies to literacy and the understanding of mathematics, as it does to oral language and cognitive development (some of the experimental evidence is discussed briefly in Chapter 15). Such foundations are already laid for some children in their homes before entry to school, and their homes continue to both support and extent what is provided in school (information is cited in Chapter 5). Other parents are not aware of the valuable contribution they could make, or indeed are making, and this limited view may be reinforced by teachers if they are not aware enough of the growing evidence of contributions of homes to their children's development, including many parents who, for a variety of reasons, do not visit the school.

Parental involvement, whether it should be encouraged, and if so what form it should take is a topic on which there are widely divergent views among those involved in early education (See Chapter 10). There may even be opposing views between those involved at consecutive stages in a child's education. The value of parental involvement, the nature of such involvement, and for whose benefits it is intended, are all important topics which should be included in the training of those who will work in early education, within a framework which includes a knowledge of the evidence on contributions of the home to the development of young children.

There are differences in the backgrounds of children attending the various forms of preschool provision (See Chapters 3 and 11). Nursery schools and classes may have been placed in specific areas of deprivation, may give priority admission to children from certain backgrounds, and may have special referrals of children with special needs (See Chapter 14). Many playgroups have been established by parents some of whom are actively involved in their management, and attend on a rota basis. Others may have been set up and staffed by voluntary or other bodies; still others are run by private individuals in their homes or elsewhere (See Chapter 16). They also may have children with special needs attending, particularly in rural areas.

Day nurseries, which normally provide all day care for children from a younger age than the other provision accept children who are 'at risk' for a number of reasons, mainly social; the population served is thus very different from the other forms of provision, and has changed towards an even greater emphasis on such admissions (See Chapter 8 where research specifically on day nurseries and combined centres is discussed). Children whose parents require to or wish to work may attend a childminder for all or part of the day, in some instances in combination with other provision. The extent of such provision is only known where the childminder has registered, and thus research has mainly studied this group (See Chapter 9).

There are still children entering reception class without experience in preschool education, even where facilities are available. For someparents this has been a conscious and positive choice for a variety of reasons. Failure to take up the opportunity when it is available, to send the child regularly, or withdrawal of the child shortly after admission, may result from a lack of awareness of the purposes of such attendance, or may be a feature of some families in most need of help (See Chapter 11). Language interaction studies and home visiting programmes are less likely to include such families, who may not agree to take part, or continue to co-operate. If their attendance continues to be irregular, or there are frequent changes of school, they are also unlikely to be within the sample for detailed study in preschool or beyond. Yet among such families are some of the most isolated, children who are at high risk of failure in the educational system, and whose likely failure is often predicted early and confirmed later.

There is now much more information, and positive and hopeful evidence, on the valuable interactions with their parents, and with siblings and peers, which many children have experienced prior to entry to school. There is also evidence of the capabilities of young children which can be stimulated in preschool settings, where staff are alert to the potential. Where parents have been involved in their young children's education in school there is also growing evidence of a better understanding by the parents of the purposes behind the activities provided, and their own contribution to their children's education. This does not mean that parents should, or even wish to be present in the school on any regular basis. Particularly in the early stages, a dialogue between home and school could avoid misunderstanding, enable the school to build on the child's experiences from home, and the home to appreciate the value of its own contribution as well as that of the school. The families in need of greatest help are, however, those most difficult to reach, those 'high alienation' families overwhelmed by circumstances, who may neither have the energy nor the time to take their children to an educational provision which is non-mandatory, nor to provide stimulation for their children in the home. These families need to be recognised and their problems considered in any policies directed at improving reciprocal understanding between home and school.

The importance of planning services to take account of the many and varied needs of the families with young children must be recognised, and the effects on other services of changes in policy acknowledged (Co-ordination is discussed in Chapter 12). Equally important is the need for continuity in the education of the young child between home and school, and between the different stages in the educational system (See Chapter 13).

Compatibility though an essential minimum is not sufficient; nor indeed is continuity. There must be dialogue between members of the professions responsible for successive stages, and between more recent and longer established members of staff. There is a pressing need to examine pre- and in-service training of those involved with the education of young children to ensure that it reflects the increasing demands and the growing insights from research on the competence of young children and the importance of stimulating and challenging experiences in their early education.

TRENDS IN PRESCHOOL PROVISION: WHAT IS THE EVIDENCE? (Chapters 3 and 4)

In Chapter 3 trends in preschool provision for the various parts of Britain are reported, based on statistical records for England, Scotland, Wales and Northern Ireland of numbers of children in preschool education. Information is also given, in available places, for playgroups, day nurseries and registered childminders. There are so many differences in the statistical tables, even in the precise age-groups for which they are collected, and changes in these over time, that it is impossible to give a brief summary; it would indeed be misleading, to give a generalised picture for Britain. What is clear is that there has been a trend over the last ten or more years for increasing numbers of children in Britain to be in educational provision before their fifth birthday. This includes an increase in attendance at preschool educational provision and in the numbers of children under five who are already in reception classes. Chapters 3 and 4 show just how misleading a short summary could be and that statistical data on this topic could easily be cited to make many and varied points, most of which could readily be disputed! There are wide differences between local authorities, or Regions, in the constituent parts of Britain in the numbers of children under five who are in preschool provision. The pattern of available provision, whether educational, if so, full- or part-time, in nursery schools or classes, or by early entry to reception class varies; the latter is not necessarily greater in authorities with lower provision in preschool education. Likewise there are wide differences between authorities in the available places in other forms of preschool provision, such as day nurseries, playgroups and registered childminders; these may or may not be high in areas with little other provision for children under five. In a service for such a young age-group the availability to particular families cannot be assessed by a study of the number of places in a local authority; distance is an important variable influencing the possibility of attendance for a particular family. Availability of special funds may mean that provision is mainly within clearly defined areas even in authorities with high levels of provision. Furthermore places in day nurseries, for example, are unlikely to be available other than to priority cases in specific categories, whether or not the family lives within easy reach of the facility.

Statistical records do not provide information on all the key issues, and in Chapter 4 further details are provided based on research, concerning age of entry to reception class and trends in this, from which it is clear that although recently there may have been an increase in younger four-year-olds in reception classes in parts of Britain, it is not a new phenomenon. Even in a study of children born within a single week in 1970, there were wide variations not only in whether or not they attended any preschool provision and which, but also in the age at which they entered reception class. The policy with regard to entry of children to reception class, varies not only from authority to authority, but also in some areas from school to school. There also appear to be widely different practices with regard to whether or not extra resources and staffing are provided for children entering school before the statutory entry date. This policy may well prove to be as vulnerable as has been preschool education to changes in available funds, in staffing, or in the birth rate! Admission of younger children, some immediately after their fourth birthday is in the main a consequence of decisions to have only one admission date per year to primary school. The effect of policy with regard to numbers of entry dates and age on entry to school differs markedly in its effect on specific children depending on their precise date of birth.

To summarise:

for many children entry to reception class is well before their fifth birthday;

for many children entry to reception class is a transfer from another educational setting, which may be a nursery class or school, and not as previously their first experience of 'school';

for many children entry to reception class, although their first experience of 'school', may not be their first experience of a group setting, as they may have attended a playgroup, or for a few a day nursery or other establishment;

some children prior to entry to reception class may already have attended more than one group setting outside the home, a few children may have attended two concurrently;

some reception classes will receive children most of whom have attended some form of preschool provision, few or many provisions may have been involved, and may or may not have been educational;

some teachers of reception classes are therefore introducing children for the first time to larger groups of children; may have children as young as four years of age; may have children for whom English is not their mother tongue who may or may not have had previous experience of school;

in most reception classes there will be some children for whom that is their first experience in a group setting beyond the family, among whom are some of those most potentially vulnerable, who may know few other children and little of the expectations of schools, in contrast to the majority;

in nursery schools and classes teachers and other staff may now have children attending full or part-time, may have children for one year or two years, may have mainly three-year-olds, mainly four-year-olds, or both age-groups;

nursery schools and classes may 'feed' several primary schools, which may have different entry policies, and expectations of the children on entry;

nursery schools and classes, and other preschool provision may in recent years have been required to accept a different pattern for transfer of their children to the next stage of education, not only when younger, but also at a single entry date;

teachers in early education, whether in nursery school or class, or in the reception class, if they transfer from one school or local authority to another, may become responsible for children of very different ages and previous experiences, including few or most of their class with limited competence in English for whom it is a second language.

It is questionable whether the pre-service training of teachers of young children could have prepared them for such tasks, particularly as many trained some time ago; furthermore, their training may not have included practical work with under fives or a specific focus on the issues now current. Teachers of preschool children may be working in a variety of contexts, with other professionals and with parents. Teachers may anticipate working with a specific age-group and may find themselves working with younger or older children. It is essential that they are aware of the aims and expectations of colleagues from whom they receive children, and to whom the children progress. These new demands coupled with a lack of research on the appropriateness of teacher training to meet these, highlight the need for a review of this aspect of teacher training, and the importance of in-service training for those currently involved in early education, teachers and nursery nurses.

LANGUAGE AND THE HOMES OF PRESCHOOL CHILDREN (Chapter 5)

The research on children's language in the homes, discussed in detail in Chapter 5 has shown how much more stimulating and challenging the experiences of some children are in their homes than was thought in the early seventies and the dangers of identifying language deficit with social class. The assumptions current in the seventies were often based on differences in children's performance in so-called 'standardised' tests, or limited settings outside the home, which might include the classroom, to which children may respond differentially (See Chapter 2). The crucial role adults play in stimulating more complex language in young children has been shown and the importance of the quality and quantity of conversation, in settings which are meaningful to the children and in which they make real contributions to the communication. The major social class differences reported previously in more limited settings were not apparent in the homes in which the observations took place. Subtle, qualitative differences were noted in the adult-child dialogue in some of the homes, which may be important, and siblings seemed to adopt some of these same features in their discussions.

In one of the studies the children were also observed in preschool, in another they were followed into infant school. In both settings there was evidence of some children not showing the quality of language which had been recorded in the home. The importance of 'enabling dialogue' is stressed; otherwise teachers will fail to appreciate the competence of many of the children, and to stimulate those most in need. During the observations in the homes, some of the most complex and extended language from children was in the setting of story reading and sharing of stories, and the extent of such experience was found to relate to later literacy development. Where only one setting was used preschool in which to record children's language, some social class differences were found in one study. When, however, the children were later assessed at five and seven years of age the precise task set influenced how relatively competent the children appeared. Both 'social classes' produced long complex sentences in some settings; when encouraged and prompted to continue responses, the differences also became less. Retelling a story in a meaningful context evoked some of the most complex language from those referred to as 'disadvantaged'. The importance of these potentially stimulating settings both for the development of oral language and literacy, is stressed. Elsewhere in the report (in Chapter 13), the potential of peer group discussions as a way of extending opportunities for communication in young children in the classroom is discussed.

There are implications in these studies for the assessment of young children, and suggestions of settings which could be 'enabling' of communication in classrooms. There have been, however, overgeneralisations made concerning the findings, not justified by the samples, and other aspects (See Chapter 5). These four researches all took place in the seventies when a major focus was on the extent of social class differences in children's language, each in a different part of England, with a different size of sample, and methodology. Observations in the home might include recording of the dialogue between adult and child or analysis based on the child's responses in specific settings, or subsequent analysis of observations in the home and outside, or comparison of the same child in different settings, in the home and preschool or infant school.

Teachers in preschool education and in the reception class are likely to have children with much more limited language than even the most limited referred to as 'disadvantaged' in the first study, since there were a number of criteria children had to meet before they were included even in the disadvantaged group, including, for example, clarity of articulation. In the second study most of the children whose language was recorded in the homes were also attending preschool provision of some kind, yet often the impression is given by those who quote it that the children's entry to infant school, where some were observed, was indeed their first experience of school. The third study, while it included girls who might have been classed as 'disadvantaged' by their teachers, was a sample from small families, where the mother was at home in the afternoons, and a choice had been made to send the girls to nursery school, and part-time. In the fourth study the settings in which the young children from both social classes lived were mainly houses or low flats with access to outside play areas; these were two parent families, many with relatives living nearby. It is important to have information on the home experiences of children from more and less advantaged backgrounds where the findings are not confounded by other variables such as very large or single parent families, those living in poverty or overcrowded circumstances; but equally important to realise that such children were excluded.

Although these researches included between them a large number of children studied in great detail, there are homes not included, either in such studies, or in the home visiting programmes, reported in Chapter 10. Some were excluded, as a conscious decision by the researchers, such as those from ethnic minorities, those for whom English was a second language, and others detailed in the relevant chapter. There are other children whose families will not participate in such studies, who may not even respond to initial requests. Among these are families burdened by a range of adverse circumstances, and unlikely to appreciate the contribution they themselves can make to their children's development. Yet some of the children from such families are those most at risk of failure early in the education system, and are those where the teacher's skills are most needed.

These studies have shown clearly the dangers of identifying disadvantage with social class, or of assuming deficiencies in homes which are different. What is also clear is the likelihood that in the more formal test situation or classroom, or on a limited range of tasks, some children will show proportionately less of their competence or creativity, while others from the more stimulating homes, of whichever social class, will go beyond the demands of the situation. The importance of stressing the limitations in these studies is that otherwise the way they are quoted by others may give the impression that most if not all children enter school at three or four years of age able to speak clearly and relate to an adult and to other children; that the children are all better at home with their parents until formal schooling in the basics commences, which it isassumed they will be ready to receive.

The challenge faced by teachers and others in early education is much greater, and the skills required much more complex, than would be appreciated by the reader who consults only these four studies. The reader who does not study such evidence and remains with the assumptions of the early seventies, may all too readily relate limitations in responses by the children in the classroom only to circumstances beyond the teacher's control!

STUDIES IN PRESCHOOL UNITS (Chapters 6 and 7)

Selective factors not under the control of the researchers, influence who goes to which schools, who lives in which neighbourhood, and where particular teachers work. Preschool education, as a non-mandatory aspect of education, is particularly subject to such variations, not only within types of provision, but between types. It is seldom possible in educational research of relevance to practice to adopt a 'pure' experimental design; studies which adopt as nearly as possible that approach are important, not least in ensuring that hypotheses identified in more natural settings are tested where circumstances, and children, are matched as nearly as possible.

The studies reported in Chapter 6 show for example the importance of not assuming that changes in children's behaviour after the introduction of a language programme were necessarily caused by the programme itself. They show the problems for a teacher in introducing and sustaining an intervention even to which she is herself committed, single-handed with a class of young children. Limited effects were found when trainers from a variety of settings were in turn expected to train staffs and to implement curriculum innovation, and not necessarily those hoped for. The relative effects on children's play of different sizes of preschool unit, space, numbers of activities, were assessed in an experimental playgroup, giving insights which might facilitate the optimum use of available resources by staff. Several studies in preschool units with a predominantly 'free play' atmosphere, where there was also an emphasis on planned placement of staff and activities, indicate that in such settings many children will engage in sustained, collaborative play, and valuable dialogue with adults. There are still, however, some children who may drift, fail to complete activities, or select activities at which there is less involvement with staff. The importance of monitoring the children's behaviour over time is clear if such settings are to maximise the opportunities for all the children.

Three further studies are reported in Chapter 7, each of which involved observations in a number of preschool units, all of which took place in the seventies, were planned during proposals for expansion, and were still underway during threats of contraction. All three took place in England, in Oxfordshire, in two contrasting areas around Stoke-on-Trent and parts and Cheshire, and in Outer London Boroughs respectively. One of the researches involved nursery schools and classes and playgroups in observational studies, and for a study of conversation, mainly playgroup workers. In a second research aseries of studies was undertaken some of which included day nurseries. The third research which was in nursery schools, with a focus on teachers' interactions, included a language intervention programme.

For many staff in preschool units at that time, social-emotional development was an important priority; yet the major focus in much reporting of the studies has been on limitations on extended dialogue in the free play settings, although from the evidence it is clear that many children were in these stimulated to make choices and play collaboratively with their peers, often for extended periods. Indeed, several of the studies on transition reported in Chapter 13, in which children were followed from preschool into reception class, reveal that for many children that setting was less stimulating, provided less responsibility, choice and peer interaction. Thus children who have not attended preschool may be deprived of such experience, unless resources, staffing, and attitudes to children's learning change in a number of these later settings. In view of the repeated emphasis in much reporting on limitations in the preschool setting it is important to emphasise these aspects, but also to stress the organisation and skill in relating to young children which such settings require if they are to be educational and promote the opportunity to learn in the children most in need. The observational studies reported in Chapter 7 and elsewhere do provide valuable pointers for teachers in selecting activities, in planning their arrangement and in their approach to young children; which should form an important aspect in those training to work with young children. Unfortunately most of the observational studies have reported in general terms, and have not provided detailed analyses of settings and staff approaches which were observed to be particularly successful in stimulating children to sustained attention, and complex and extended language. Further studies with such a focus would be valuable.

These studies, and any limitations in the samples and methodology are discussed in Chapter 7; here only some key points drawn from several studies will be highlighted. The observations showed a readiness for sustained attention, and intellectually demanding tasks by some children. The facilitatory role of certain activities can be seen from these researches, and also the disappointing use of some activities which have been assumed in themselves to produce either creative or more complex play; when observed closely and continuously some were found to produce only repetitive and rather low level play. In contrast, activities which had an end product which was understandable by the child were seen to lead to more extended play. Clearly with large numbers of young children, relatively few adults, and many demands, children could receive only limited adult attention. Staff were, however, often observed to spend relatively short periods of time engaged in particular activities with children before switching elsewhere; to change this staff would require to be aware of this tendency and its effects, and some restructuring of activities might also be necessary. The presence of an adult at an activity not only attracted children to that activity, but also led to more stimulating interactions. Monitoring by staff of their own patterns and that of selected children, using for example observation schedules was not common at that time, but has been one positive outcome of observational studies of the type described here, one which is valuable not only as part of the planning of activities to ensure each child does have a range of experiences and of adult attention, but also for staff training.

Much of children's time in preschool units is spent in interaction with peers. The importance of and learning potential in such interactions appears to have been overlooked by some researchers, who have considered only the language during the adult-child interactions and by many teachers in the following stages of education. Yet there is evidence that if such settings are carefully planned and there are real purposes in the interchanges complex language and a sharing of information can be stimulated. In free play settings children in small groups were found to be more likely to engage in complex play.

There was very little evidence of sustained adult child-dialogue without interruptions. Several studies showed the adverse effects of adults engaging in a series of questions to elicit responses from young children, particularly those to which the adult already knows the answer. This resulted in shorter and fewer responses from young children and highlights the dangers of a focus on language teaching in isolation from its communicative purposes. Not only do the pressures and needs of the other children place constraints on the amount of extended dialogue in which adults can engage with young children in school; the young child's stage of language development is itself a constraining factor, and the stresses that communication 'out of context' place on young children must be appreciated. The experimental studies discussed in Chapter 15 provide evidence of the ability of many young children to solve puzzles and to be stimulated by difficult tasks, provided they make 'human sense' to them. All these points have important implications for those involved in early education, and suggest practical ways in which young children's learning in school can be stimulated.

RESEARCH ON DAY CARE (Chapters 8 and 9)

Day nurseries provide all day, all year care, in many instances for children from an early age. Young children admitted to such preschool units, depending on the needs of their families, may spend long hours there over a period of years, and may enter reception class direct from the day nursery. Such units may be provided by the local authority, be run by a charity, or provided by an employer. Several researchers have studied selected day nurseries in depth, and a survey of the changes in provision between 1975 and 1983 has been conducted. In 1975 the survey reported that the day nurseries were a service under considerable pressure, offering provision to severely deprived families, and one parent families. The ethos of the nursery was a care or 'welfare' approach, and these facilities, staffed mainly by very young nursery nurses were remote from other agencies, including educational provision, yet many had children from families under severe stress, and a proportion of handicapped children. By 1983, the situation seemed even more stressed, with long waiting lists, and criteria for entry having changed for many to give a priority to children considered to be at risk, for example from 'non-accidental' injury. In England over the period from 1976-86, although there has been a slight increase in numbers of places in day nurseries, this varies widely between authorities, and there has been a dramatic increase in waiting lists, which are now at a level about equivalent to half the available places. There seems therefore, less chance now of working parents, even single parents, obtaining a place for their child in a day nursery (Chapter 3).

The studies of specific nurseries in the seventies confirmed the picture from the survey. Even in a nursery selected because the level of care was high, the staff were mainly very young and inexperienced, they worked long hours and the turnover of staff was high. Many of the children came from homes under considerable stress, had attended from a very early age and experienced little continuity of care either within the nursery or between that and the home. Problems in making changes in the setting were considerable, even with the encouragement and support of the research team. The placement of a teacher in a day nursery, to work with older children, or to support and encourage nursery nurses in a more educational emphasis, was observed in that nursery, and such developments are also discussed by others. This approach although it may have potential, is a situation open to many conflicts in status, in approach and in working hours, which are likely to be exacerbated where the teachers involved are not well-qualified and experienced in working with a range of preschool children and their families. An alternative approach of sending older children for part of the day to a nearby nursery school, is mentioned in one study, but the success of that model was not investigated.

In the early seventies a number of local authorities began to develop a new kind of nursery, namely a 'combined nursery centre', to provide preschool education and care in a single unit. A research project was funded shortly after their opening to study four of the seven combined centres, compared with nursery schools and day nurseries in the same areas. As might have been anticipated there were many problems in all four centres, including that of staffs forming working relationships, some more successfully overcome than others. While some problems may have been teething troubles in a new form of provision, many were inherent in the type of provision, and the differences in background training and staff, criteria for admission of children etc. Any conflicts in training, expectations and approach are inevitably highlighted in such situations, and clearly from the evidence, such centres provide no easy solution to the need of some preschool children for education and extended day care. The separateness of training of the two professions of teachers and nursery nurses was, it was suggested by the researchers, one cause of problems; there were many others.

A minimum requirement for teachers appointed to such settings is surely that they have had varied experience with, and are trained for work with preschool children and their families, and have some appreciation of the training background of those with whom they will work. Where pre-service training has not met all these requirements, then in-service provision must; otherwise friction is inevitable. There are no doubt many qualified and experienced teachers who would be highly successful in an educational setting in school, yet who for a variety of reasons, would be less successful in working with staff and with children either in a day nursery or combined nursery, or family centre.

The purpose in establishing day nurseries and other similar provision has been to provide extended day care, rather than education; thus it is unfortunate where lack of evidence of later educational success of children who have attended such provision is regarded as a failure of the staff or the unit. Furthermore the circumstances which led to these children's admission to such facilities are unlikely to change dramatically for the better after the child enters school. It must be apparent that children who have been in all-day care in these settings may enter school with severe problems in communication, as a result of the stresses in the homes, any limitations in the day care unit and the children with whom they are in contact (Chapter 16). The importance of ensuring that these children do have access to stimulating and varied experiences both preschool and in reception class cannot be overstated, otherwise their own characteristics and their home circumstances are likely to lead to very early failure in the educational system.

It seems crucial to explore which types of intervention are likely to achieve most success in helping these children's transition into school and enriching their preschool experience so that they are better able to cope with the stresses and challenges in school. It is unrealistic to expect this to be provided by the staff in the day nursery, who quite apart from their more limited training already have many and complex problems to deal with, both in relation to the children, often including babies in their charge, and in working with their parents.

Mothers who require to work, or wish to work, are clearly unlikely to obtain a place for their preschool child in a preschool unit either from an early age, or for sufficient hours for them to work full-time. Childminders, who are paid to care for children other than their own in their homes, are an alternative utilised by some families who do not have relatives able to look after the child. Childminders are required to register, and there has been a considerable increase in registered childminders; what is not known is precisely how large an increase in available provision this represents.

In Chapter 9 research on childminders is discussed, inevitably mainly registered childminders; thus little is known about the nature of the service offered by unregistered minders. In a research undertaken in the early seventies great concern was expressed about the quality of care offered by childminders, who were described as hard-pressed, often insensitive to the children's needs, and of sad passive children. As a result further researches were funded. One study in Oxfordshire showed that in many instances the mother already knew the minder, or another mother who used the minder; many minders started minding to help a friend, and for some it was 'a once off' situation. The child's life at the minders in this study tended to be at a physically high level, and most had gardens in which to play. The picture painted was very different in this area where the children's home circumstances and those of minders were relatively more affluent, although concern was still expressed at the quality of care.

In a more recent study in a different area, where mothers and minders are described as 'working-class', a more positive picture was painted, not only with regard to the physical circumstances at the minders', but also concerning interaction between minders and children. The minders were careful not to usurp the mother's role, and while the child's behaviour might be different at minder and at home it was seldom in a way that might give cause for concern. A number of practical problems between minders and mothers were identified on which advice might have been valuable to the minders. In this area many two and three-year-olds who attended minders also attended a playgroup, and most four-year-olds were attending a nursery school or class.

Further studies have looked at support available for minders. In one study reported in Chapter 11, where drop-in facilities were provided for minders, and care was taken to ensure that the arrangements were known to and convenient for them, there were those minders who for negative, rather than positive reasons, did not avail themselves of the opportunity, among whom were minders who would give cause for concern regarding the quality of care they provided for the children in their charge. Clearly many children whose mothers work either full or part-time spend some of their time in the care of another adult,possibly in the company of other pre-school children. The minder may indeed be the adult who seeks out preschool provision and accompanies such children there. It is important thus that minders are kept informed of the range of preschool facilities and are also supported to ensure that the care they provide is as stimulating as possible for the children in their care.

PARENTS AND PRESCHOOL: DEMAND AND UPTAKE (Chapters 10 and 11)

Demand for and uptake of preschool services is clearly likely to be influenced by the range and convenience of the services available, the parents' knowledge of their availability, and of possible benefits for themselves and their children should they attend. Parents may not be aware of the available preschool services, and/or be misinformed about differences between services. They may, it has been found, either be unaware of the precise aims of particular services, or have different aims in send-ing their children from those of the staffs (See Chapters 10 and 11). That there is need for greater communication between those providing preschool services and the parents is apparent. Some parents make a decision not to send their children to a pre-school unit for carefully considered reasons and wish them to start school only when attendance becomes mandatory. In spite of expansion in preschool education there are, among children who could most benefit, families which do not take advantage of the facilities. Some mothers under stress and isolated do not make use of provision, or send their children only briefly or irregularly, even if they acknow-ledge it might benefit the children. Among these families are some in which the children will be isolated and may receive only limited stimulation in the home.

Some professionals would regard non-attendance when provision is available as mainly the consequence of parental attitudes; others feel that more could be done to support and cater for such children and their parents in preschool settings (See also Chapter 12). Some home visiting schemes have excluded such families, who may be isolated as well as under stress, or failed to recruit them. One way of identifying families with preschool children is through the primary school in whose catchment area they live. One project which used such an approach, and the support of health visitors, found that although the first parents to be recruited in the project were the more outgoing, they were still lacking in confidence with regard to any contribution they could make to their child's progress. Involvement with their child within the scheme might both lead them subsequently to enrol their children in preschool education, and through them attract other families in even greater need of help into the project (See Chapter 10). Parent volunteers might also in some circumstances be supportive of others, but to fulfil such a role they would themselves require guidance and support, and might well be rejected by some parents.

One research into playgroups for disadvantaged families, which included those provided by social services, voluntary groups and some independent groups considered among other issues whether such groupswere catering for high need children or were only in high need areas. It was found that there were children who had been special referrals, but beyond that there was neither the expertise nor resources to seek out other families in the area who might have special needs. These groups were clearly dependent on the skills and resources of committed leaders, who in many instances were paid very little for the stressful and taxing job they were undertaking. There appeared to be little contact with outside agencies, or even with a number of agencies who had specially referred children. The importance of continuing support from referring agencies is underlined by the fact that among those who left, or attended irregularly were a number of those who had been specially referred. There was little evidence of parental involvement in these playgroups, and where there was, it tended to include only a small number of the mothers.

Another study, in which self-help 'working-class' playgroups were studied over a period of years, showed the stresses and conflicts in the groups, only one of which survived, one which had the continued active support of one of the originators with access to a range of information and resources. Differences between these groups and a more 'middle-class' group in the area are considered. The greater difficulty in gaining access to outside resources in the less advantaged groups, conflicts between those parents who worked with the children and the parents whose children were attending, and concerning aims, were only some of the problems encountered. The mothers who are working as leaders in some playgroups, including a number of those in research discussed in earlier chapters, although they may be volunteers and mothers of children currently attending, may also have professional qualifications relevant to working with young children which may add to their credibility both inside the group and with outside agencies. This is not to suggest that such qualities are the prerogative of only certain sections of the population or are an essential attribute; the difficulties faced by young mothers in organising and maintaining a low cost provision should, however, not be underestimated. Such groups are also as susceptible to accepting and rejecting children and their parents as any other, and in the absence of professional skills there may be greater dangers of confrontation.

Wide differences have been found not only between types of provision, but within types, in whether and how many parents are involved, and in what capacity; parental wishes and staff attitudes both play a part in influencing this (See Chapter 10).

No single philosophy has been found even within types of unit with regard to the nature and extent of parental involvement, and equally important, even where there was active parental involvement there was a network of those who were active, and those who were not, and not always in the latter case from choice. Even where few mothers work full-time such differences were apparent. The purposes behind direct involvement by parents within preschool provision need to be considered and the extent to which it is for the benefit of mother or child, also the impossibility for some mothers because of other commitments of meeting such a requirement. The importance of communication with all parents to ensure that they appreciate the purposes behind the activities and approach, and their own possible contribution is clear, as are the difficulties; without this serious misconceptions remain. Yet like most of the points made in this section, extending such involvement either requires additional resources, or cuts in other importance aspects of the staff's work.

Some of the points made in connection with demand and uptake, and with parental involvement, concern the philosophy of early education and the extent to which its aim is mainly to facilitate the development of the child, as would be most people's perception of education in the later stages. Involvement of parents and communication with parents has then clearly set goals. Furthermore the extent to which increasing parental involvement, possibly without additional resources, is feasible without adverse effects on the service to the child becomes the major issue. In much of the dialogue about preschool provision it is not clear whether that issue has been resolved, or if the preschool services, including those in education, are expected over and above their provision for the children to meet a variety of family needs, and in particular needs of some of the families most at risk. The resources required, the nature of these and their distribution depends on the extent to which the aims are educational for the child, however broadly interpreted, or go beyond that to those of the families of preschool children.

EARLY EDUCATION AND CHILDREN WITH SPECIAL NEEDS (Chapter 14)

A knowledge of the evidence on developments in early education is an important framework within which to consider the availability of preschool education for children with special needs, possibilities of and advantages in partial or full integration in 'ordinary' preschool units. Even priority admission, possibly with special transport, and support from professionals, would not it must be clear make it possible even if desirable, for all children with special needs to gain access to preschool education. With the wide variations in the extent and nature of provision available in a particular area the choice available for a particular family may be limited. Policy recommendations for the integration where possible of children with special needs were made not only on the assumption that there would be support for the children and their families from a range of professionals, but also that there would be a substantial increase in preschool education, rather than that they would be priority admissions to existing relatively scarce provision.

For children identified preschool as suffering from handicapping conditions it is important to distinguish ways in which early education in 'ordinary' preschools is expected to contribute to their development. Priority admission to scarce provision might be all that is intended. If more is expected, then unless the requirements are made specific, and additional resources are provided, such admissions may be at the expense of the other children. Some children with special needs, particularly those with behaviour difficulties, and those who are outgoing or have certain forms of physical handicap may by their characteristics, or the nature of their handicap secure the additional attention they require. Other children who are more withdrawn or suffer from certain kinds of communication difficulties will not be integrated merely by their presence in an ordinary unit, but instead could be more isolated than elsewhere.

Communication difficulties, either alone or in association with other handicapping conditions, are common in young children with special needs. Such children may present particular difficulties for the staffs in ordinary units, if they are expected both to help such children, and do so without detriment to the other children in the unit, particularly if there is not extra support provided. There are preschool units in which for most children their mother tongue is other than English; the appropriateness of such a unit for the 'integration' of a child with communication problems must be open to question. The initial identification of communication difficulties isoften made by the staff in settings outside the home, such as a preschool unit. Diagnosis of communication delay or difficulty in young children whose mother tongue is different from that of the staff, and following that help in developing language competence, must present additional difficulties in preschool units.

Some children by the severity of their handicapping conditions may not be able to attend available ordinary provision, but may be able to enter a unit attached to such provision with professional support towards some limited integration. For other children with severe handicapping conditions, and for young children with severe developmental delays the most promising developments may be support for their parents in the homes. Experimental research into children with severe difficulties and sensory handicaps, and the developmentally young, which is now extensive, was beyond the remit of this investigation.

Research into the type of provision attended by children with different handicapping conditions showed just how much this might vary depending on the educational provision and policy in a particular authority. The reduction in age of entry to reception class in many areas raises particular issues in connection with children with special needs. Children of comparable age with those studied in the researches discussed in Chapter 14 might now be expected to be in reception class, and with a single teacher, and possibly only one adult responsible for the whole class. For some children additional resources might be made available. This change in policy will present potential difficulties not only for such children, but for those who teach them. Where children with special needs attending preschool units were followed-up at the age of entry to primary school at about five years of age, it was found that a number were retained in preschool units for a further year; others who did enter reception class, had or presented difficulties within the more formal academic setting with the additional demands for conformity and progress in the basic skills.

FOUR 'Cs' IN THE EDUCATION OF UNDER FIVES
(Chapter 12, 13, 15 and 16)

The three 'Cs' of co-ordination, co-operation and continuity are difficult to treat in isolation. It is perhaps helpful to consider co-ordination as that aspect which relates to the administrative structures which may facilitate or frustrate co-operation; co-operation as relating to the personnel involved whether professional, parent or volunteer; continuity as focusing on the children and their early experiences in education, at home and in school. It is also difficult to consider continuity in the absence of an analysis of the aims of education and the curriculum in early education and beyond. Any assessment of the effects of preschool education must inevitably be bound up with the relationship between the early and later stages of education and the appropriateness of any measures used to assess effects. The detailed evidence from research on each of these issues has been treated in separate chapters. In this final section it seemed more appropriate to consider them in relation to each other.

As a consequence of the non-mandatory nature of provision for children under five in Britain, co-ordination of services is of crucial importance, but difficult to achieve either nationally or locally. There is a wide range of services involved, some established to meet the needs of the families with young children, and even specific families with particular needs; others to achieve the most effective early education for young children; still others attempting to meet a range of needs within a single setting. Co-ordination is essential if there is to be a sufficiently wide range of services and these are to meet the needs of all families. It is crucial in an aspect as vulnerable to economic pressures as provision for children under five which is even more 'fragile' if it is dependent on initiatives by specific personnel and not within a management structure. Changes in priorities nationally and locally, boundary changes, non-replacement of committed personnel, are only some of the features which have adversely affected services for young children (See Chapter 12) To be successful co-ordination must involve a structure which encourages dialogue between, and represents the interests of, all those involved with preschool children; and ensures involvement by those at the level of policy decisions within a management structure which provides access to funds.

Co-operation between services, which is clearly a necessary requirement for effective and integrated provision, is not easily achieved in services which may have conflicting aims and be in competition for available resources, and between and within which there are professionals with very different training and experience. Even where provision is extensive difficulties may arise some of which hinder co-operation between services, and which are detrimental to the range of services available to families and the quality within these.

Much of the research on continuity in the education of young children has involved a study of transition from preschool to primary school, and mainly of children most of whom have had access to preschool units, either nursery schools or classes, or playgroups. The importance of establishing, or where they exist, strengthening links between preschools and primary schools, is clear if the foundations laid at the preschool stage are to be built upon in the succeeding stages. The differences between age at transfer over time and between areas, or even schools make this even more essential. Evidence at the point of transition shows that children may after transition be offered a narrower range of the curriculum and fewer opportunities to engage in stimulating activities or valuable learning experiences involving dialogue with adults and their peers. For some changes to be effected more resources of staffing and materials are clearly essential. Attitude changes are also important, in many professionals, in parents and in policy-makers. These include a greater appreciation of the educational significance to children's progress, including the development of literacy and numeracy, of a wide and varied range of experiences, and of dialogue with adults and with peers. Some of the relevant evidence is in Chapters 13, further evidence from experimental and other studies is reported in Chapter 15, supplemented by information from the homes of young children in Chapter 5 and from preschool units in Chapter 6 and 7. Record keeping is an important aspect of professional competence, which must be sensitive enough to the range of activities in which children are involved and their development over time to provide information for others and to facilitate the further development of the professionals involved. Communication of information between home and school and the different stages of education is essential for continuity in children's early learning experiences.

Lack of resources, or pressures to achieve measurable effects at an early stage, will inevitably result in a curtailment of the experiences available to children in early education. Few children who had not attended preschool provision, and particularly those whose preschool experiences at home may have been limited for a variety of circumstances, have been studied at transition. Yet for these children the stress at transition may be greatest, and the effects of the limitations most severe. It is important that such children are the focus of study, but must be recognised that there are major difficulties in ensuring their continued inclusion in any research in depth, since among them are the children with poor and irregular attendance and frequent changes of school.

There is little specific evidence on the home experiences preschool, preschool education or transition into school of children from ethnic minority backgrounds, and in particular those whose mother tongue is other than the language of instruction. Where such children do not have an opportunity for preschool education, and where links between home and school are not able to be established, for whatever reason, these children are likely to be under severe pressures. There is little evidence to indicate whether and to what extent the families of these children are supportive of, or even understand the aims of a number of the activities in education. Furthermore, there is little evidence as to whether the type of adult-child interactions and peer interactions reported in Chapter 5 are reflected also in the preschool experiences in their homes of children from different cultures. Such evidence is important to teachers who may otherwise not appreciate the problems faced by some of the children for whom they are responsible, for whom there may be both language barriers to communication and possible cultural differences in their expectations of relationships with adults.

Evidence and issues in assessing long-term effects of preschool education are considered in Chapter 16, where it is stressed that studies have not been funded initially to considered this issue in depth. Evidence is available from a number of studies of gains over more limited periods, and some studies have also shown longer-term gains. The difficulty in matching the aims of those who were involved in preschool education with the measures used to assess effects must be recognised, as must the real possibility that any lack of massive permanent effects might be a consequence of lack of continuity in achieving what had been started preschool, or even conflicting aims in the different stages of education.

The appointment at local level of professionals with sufficient seniority to gain access to decision-making committees is crucial for early education; professionals with responsibilities as co-ordinators and facilitators of development who have a wide knowledge of early education, the variety of services for preschool children and their families, and with a remit which gives them access also to the early stages in the primary school. Only with such support will those in early education be encouraged and enabled to develop their insights further, and the appointment of well-qualified staff be ensured. Only with such key professionals in post will educators, and policy-makers be made sensitive to possible implications of policy decisions, such as, for example, age and date of entry to school, and the necessary staffing and resources required if such policies are not to be detrimental to children's education. Yet in many areas where such personnel were previously available there is now no such post, or person with these skills. The inclusion of early education as a priority within in-service training nationally and locally seems essential in view of the new and competing demands. An essential requirement for this to become effective is a professional senior and articulate enough to express the need for such support in the face of other competing demands, and capable of planning courses of appropriate breadth to cater for the requirements of the variety of professionals.

CHAPTER 18   IMPLICATIONS OF RESEARCH FOR POLICY AND PRACTICE

PROVISION FOR UNDER FIVES

In Britain many children now attend some form of educational provision before their fifth birthday, either they are in nursery class or school and/or they have already been admitted to reception class. Statistics on available places for children under five in Britain in educational and other units show increased provision in general, but with massive inequalities in available provision and resources between areas. Whether or not a particular child attends, and which provision; whether there is any choice, whether attendance is full or part-time, depends on the exact area in which the child lives, the child's precise date of birth and the parents' knowledge of available provision. Availability of other forms of preschool provision such as playgroups, and day nurseries also differs widely. There are long waiting lists for day nurseries which provide all day/all year care. Those children who do attend, many of whom with very severe problems, may have frequent changes of carers and little access to a range of educational activities. Likewise, the staffing and other resources made available to those children who have been admitted to primary school before the statutory age for entry also differ widely. It is dangerous to assume that early entry to primary school gives children a good start, unless the appropriate resources and skilled staff are available.

Thus access to education has already become unequal for young children by the time they reach the statutory age for starting school. The effects could be further exacerbated unless the staffing in the early stages of the primary school is sufficiently generous and well-qualified to make effective communication with young children possible. The staff must also be free from constraints which might prevent them from offering the young children sufficient breadth and depth of experiences. It is possible from research evidence in homes and in preschool units to pinpoint contexts which are most likely to stimulate learning in young children and to lay an effective foundation for literacy and numeracy. What is also clear is that already by five years of age there are very wide differences in the readiness of children for more formal aspects of education and their grasp of the underlying concepts on which to build numeracy and literacy.

Inequality of provision, difference and changes in age on entry to primary school have important implications both for the preschool services, and for teachers of reception classes, some of whom may have children as young as four years of age, others children aged over five. For some children entry to reception class in primary school is a transfer from one, or more than one, preschool setting in which a foundation has already been laid; for others it is their first experience away from home. Added to this, in some reception classes and preschool units, English may be a second language for some or most of the children, and may not be the language used in the home, or one within which they are as yet competent. Furthermore, in some classes, there may be many different languages in use by the children, making dialogue between adults and children and between peers more difficult to sustain. In the light of such evidence the appropriate pace and range of experiences in both preschool education and reception class must vary to meet the children's stage of development and previous experiences.

THE CURRICULUM AND EARLY EDUCATION

Studies have shown that a very different curriculum may be offered to children, even of the same age, depending on whether they happen to attend a preschool or a reception class. Studies of transition also show that for some children the primary school may provide a less stimulating and challenging experience than these same children had previously, and to which they were responding making meaningful choices, concentrating for long periods, engaging in dialogue with adults, and sustained cooperation with peers.

Observational studies have shown that a free-play setting has potential for stimulating learning in young children. If it is to be an effective learning environment, particularly for the children in most need of support, it must be carefully structured with the adults playing a crucial role in its organisation and by selective intervention with the children in their 'play'. There is evidence of the language and cognitive tasks of which young children are capable, given appropriate contexts, and the need for greater challenge to some of the children. Communication with adults which is meaningful, activities which make sense to the children, and shared challenging activities with peers are valuable in laying a foundation for children's development of effective oral language, literacy and numeracy. Some children come to school already well on the way to literacy and numeracy and able to communicate effectively with adults and peers. The teachers who have such children in their class have a very different task from some of their colleagues.

Where the potential and present competence of young children is assessed by brief and formal contacts; in, for example, question and answer sessions, their present level of functioning and potential may be seriously underestimated and teacher expectation may colour their subsequent progress. Furthermore, the less experience with adults the child has had, the greater the danger of underestimation. Even greater skill and sensitivity is required of the teachers and support staff when assessing and helping young children who have communication difficulties, either because of special educational needs, or because they speak a language other than that of the staff. On transition to primary school, lack of continuity for children who have attended preschool appears to stem from a number of features including a lack of appreciation by many teachers in primary schools of the educational potential of the activities available in preschool units, seen merely as 'play' in contrast to 'work'; lack of resources, particulary of adults, to enable the necessary adult-child dialogue to take place; pressures from parents or administrators to be 'seen' to be teaching the basics interpreted very narrowly; lack of appropriate training either pre-service or in-service of some of the teachers working in reception classes, and now possibly with even younger children.

Attempts to achieve higher standards in the academic subjects for those training as teachers, and those nursery nurses intending to work in the educational scene, must not be achieved at the expense of breadth and of practical experience for those intending to work in early education. The courses must have a theoretical underpinning, provide practical experience with young children in a variety of settings, provide knowledge of implications for practice of recent research and be taught by staff who are themselves knowledgeable and so experienced. The current shortage of qualified staff, and other constraints, means that teachers of young children may indeed not have adequate qualifications for such work. Thus in-service training is essential if there is to be any effect in the short-term. With present funding arrangements this is unlikely to take place on any large scale because of competing demands, unless it is given the status of a nationally identified priority. It also requires a sufficiently knowledgeable and senior professional at local level to organise effective courses which should bring together staff teaching children aged three to about seven or eight years and from a variety of settings. Only then will the present discontinuities in children's learning become clear and be changed to 'continuity with extension', whether between different stages in schooling or from home to school.

Teachers of young children may find themselves under pressure to be 'seen' to be teaching to specific but limited targets. To go 'Back' to the Basics would be disastrous if this ignores recent insights and results in children being deprived, in their early education, of a broad range of experiences. There is an urgent public relations exercise to be undertaken, by those concerned with early education, to ensure that research evidence on the contribution of broadly based experiences at home and at school to children's early education, and as foundation for literacy and numeracy, is appreciated. Some administrators, fellow teachers and particularly parents, perceive 'good' early education in terms of 'work' (as opposed to 'play') and a narrowly interpreted programme of introduction to the basic skills at as early an age as possible. The ability to communicate effectively and creatively orally and in writing, to develop numeracy applicable in meaningful contexts, to solve problems of increasing complexity individually and collaboratively are important foundations for young children's learning. It would be unfortunate if these were sacrificed in attempts to achieve short term testable evidence of attainment.

CO-ORDINATION OF SERVICES

The need not only for greater resources and further training of staff but also for co-ordination of services for under fives is clear from the evidence. Different types of provision are the responsibility of different departments which, without co-ordination, may lead to waste of resources, and facilities failing to reach those most in need. Changes in policy in one aspect often have important implications for other services. Co-operation between services is not easily achieved in services which may have conflicting aims, professionals with different training and be in competition for available resources.

Any comparisons between the available services for under fives in different areas must, if they are not to be misleading, include all children under statutory school starting age, and not only those in so-called 'preschool' provision, the age-group for which differs so much. Furthermore some children attend more than one form of provision, some consecutively, a few concurrently. Unfortunately much of the research which was funded was specifically on preschool provision in isolation, which may refer to a different age-group depending on the area and time-scale of the study. It is important that a different error is not now introduced whereby four-year-olds in reception classes come to be studied in isolation from early education, as if they were a separate group in some special way. There may be an increasing number of such children, but the phenomenon is not a new one.

RESEARCH PRIORITIES

It is important that the following research topics are considered in association with policy recommendations in the earlier section of this chapter and related to the detailed discussion of the various research topics in the preceding chapters. Chapter 2, 'Preschool education: the setting for the research', has an important role also as a base from which to plan further research initiatives. To inform policy and practice future research should build on current evidence, make good its deficiencies, fill gaps in existing knowledge and open up new lines of enquiry. The following priorities are thus listed as a framework within which to consider such issues, not to be treated in isolation.

a) Studies of continuity of children's experiences between three and seven or eight years of age would be valuable, with a remit which has a focus on the curriculum and links between home and school. The aim would be to identify examples of 'good practice' which provide children with a breadth of experience, stimulate their creativity, and within that framework encourage oral language development and set the foundations of numeracy and literacy. It is important that good practice in early

N

education in Britain is studied, and the necessary conditions for its extension. The urgency to obtain speedy results to 'inform policy' in the seventies for a planned speedy expansion of preschool education meant that transition rather than continuity became the focus of study. Within such studies consideration of records which are helpful in monitoring children's progress and facilitate communication between professionals and between school and home would be valuable. This might identify how to make assessment serve the curriculum rather than have the curriculum dictated by the tests.

b) Further research would be valuable on the development of literacy and numeracy in young children, and contexts in which their cognitive development and creativity appear to be expressed and stimulated. There have been promising beginnings. Fundamental experimental research must not be neglected for short-term, but possibly transitory, information. Such research requires an 'act of faith' in its funding and may not, at least initially, appear to be highly relevant to education.

c) Research is urgently needed into the particular problems of children for whom English is a second language in order to assess the quality and appropriateness of their experiences in early education. Linked to this should be studies into the expectations of early education of parents from different cultural backgrounds, the extent to which they are similar to or different from those of the teachers and parents who have been studied in their homes.

d) One aspect on which research was recommended from the short-term studies commissioned by DES but to which little attention has been paid is the needs of children in rural areas. In a country like Britain, with such very different problems in the inner cities and remote villages, it is important that the needs of the latter are not neglected as a consequence of the high profile of the inner cities.

e) Surveys of pre-service and in-service courses available nationally for teachers and other staff working with young children are important. Any change in practice and attitude is dependent to a large extent on regular in-service training which includes more than a small band of enthusiasts.

f) An evaluation of the extent and quality of educational and other provision for children under five would be timely in order to assess the extent to which this is meeting current needs, which in some areas may have changed greatly in recent years. Any such appraisals must include children under mandatory school age who are in reception class in primary school, otherwise comparisons between areas and over time will be misleading..

There have been lessons from this investigation for funding bodies which go beyond the specific remit of children under five. The value of coordination of research information to ensure that knowledge of completed and on-going research is readily available is clear. The absence of such records caused particular problems in studying children under five. Only a very limited amount of research was known to many people, even those involved in funding, or conducting research. Some basic information will be made available to other researchers as an offshoot from this study.

The timescale and funding of any research should make possible, and require researchers to provide a full report. Such reports should be explicit and detailed enough for evaluation and replication to be possible. Furthermore, it is essential in educational research that summaries are readily available which provide information on the precise area in which the study took place and any significant characteristics; children, staff and parents included and excluded and on what grounds; dates of the empirical work; methodology as well as results.

There must be concern at the timelag in availability of research findings, and also that some are ultimately available only in popularised versions from which any assessment of the legitimacy of the findings is not possible. Clarity and absence of jargon is to be commended, but not if it results in the findings being overstated, and limitations and timescale omitted.

Researchers are no more protected from misrepresentation by others than are politicians, of that I am only too aware as I complete this report!

APPENDIX I

ISSUES FOR RESEARCH IN PRESCHOOL EDUCATION IDENTIFIED IN 1975

A. Some Topics Requiring Research or Development Projects as identified following short-term studies undertaken on behalf of the Management Committee of the Department of Education and Science Nursery Research Programme. (See *Preschool Education and Care*. DES, 1975a).

1. Demand and uptake,

   a) parental demand for places for 3 and 4 year olds and for full and part-time attendance

   b) local authority policies

   c) children catered for in relation to social and ethnic composition of area

2. Co-ordination of services,

3. Day long care and education,

4. Length and duration of attendance,

5. Rural areas,

6. Parental participation - effects on the children, the school, the parents,

7. Home visiting to discover differences in children's development, whether gains are maintained, whether there is greater understanding of the nursery by parents, whether a continuation of home visiting is required and by whom,

8. Programme and curriculum - for children from different social and ethnic backgrounds and of different abilities,

   a) adult intervention

   b) development of empirical thinking

   c) fostering imaginative play

9. Assessment techniques to assist teachers,

10. Continuity and progress - a descriptive study of children's experiences in schools between the ages of 3 and 7 or 8 years, to show the extent and nature of continuity and progression in the curriculum,

11. Group size examining:

   a) effects on children's play concentration, etc.

   b) number of adults with whom they interact and effect on quality of interaction

c) use children make of resources and equipment

d) staff deployment

12. Roles and deployment of staff examining how staff with different qualifications and experience perceive:

a) children's needs

b) their own goals

c) their role - how these affect the children in different types of institution and proportion of different staff, adult- child ratios

13. Teacher training - project to evaluate courses of initial training attention to preparing teachers:

a) to work in nursery class or school

b) to guide nursery assistants

c) establish relationships with parents

d) extend children's language development, also development of materials

14. Minority groups, cultural problems,

15. Minority groups, language problems - to evaluate alternative strategies,

16. Minority groups, parental involvement,

17. A longitudinal study of handicapped children in a number of different social and educational preschool environments to assess the effects on:

a) educational progress

b) support for families who can be incorporated and under what conditions

18. Educational programmes for handicapped children (work like that of Dorothy Jeffree) extended to other handicaps from Down's syndrome,

19. Playgroups - to assess the effects of direct and indirect help in relation to the quality of experiences when professional staff lead, parents lead, there is a mixture of the two - also type and amount of parental involvement.

See Appendix II for details of the short-term studies from which these issues were identified.

The Management Committee considered the above list and the report by Tizard to SSRC. In the light of this evidence they determined the following five areas of priority for further research:

1) What parents want and why in the realm of preschool provision,

2) Co-ordination of services for the under-fives,

3) Parental involvement in nursery education,

4) Continuity and progression in the educational experience of children between 3 and 8 years of age,

5) Problems associated with the integration of handicapped children into normal nursery classes.

See Appendix III for a summary of a discussion by Kay, Secretary to the DES
Management Committee, on the researches which were funded and the reasons for
their choice (Kay, 1975).

B. Important areas for future investigation as listed in *Early Childhood Education:
a review of research in Britain* B. Tizard (Tizard, 1974; Tizard, 1975).
Topics related to the education of socially disadvantaged children:

1. Research concerned with assisting young disadvantaged children to acquire
skills,

    a) Remediation by nursery school attendance

    b) Remediation through work with parents: via parental involvement in school
    c) Remediation through work with parents: via home visitors

    d) work with parents: via television

    e) Work with parents: via classes for adolescents

    f) Remediation through development of specific educational strategies

    g) Assessment of remediation programmes in the schools

2. Characteristics of the socially disadvantaged child,

3. The transmission of educational and intellectual disadvantage,

4. Adapting the school to the socially disadvantaged child.

Topics not directly related to the education of socially disadvantaged children:

5. Problems of school organization and staff attitudes,

6. Transition to primary school,

7. Staff training,

8. Research concerned with the education of severely sub-normal children,

9. Problems in early school socialization,

10. Problems in early cognitive development which relate to education,

11. The general provision of services for the under-fives

    a) The contribution of health services

    b) The safety of children

    c) Group care of under-fives outside their home

    d) The need for services for young handicapped children

    e) Pre-school services for the children of immigrants

APPENDIX II

SHORT-TERM STUDIES ON PRESCHOOL EDUCATION AND CARE (DES, 1975a)

The sample

The Management Committee set up by DES in 1974 to commission and monitor research in connection with the expansion of nursery education undertook short-term studies. The following is an outline of these as reported in DES(1975a), followed by some observations by the present author. Six areas were chosen differing in

"their character, social and ethnic composition and the problems they present to planners of preschool provision" (DES, 1975a p.1)

1. a rural area served almost entirely by playgroups;

2. a stable working class community - all primary schools admit four year olds - little preschool provision;

3. a new town with young families attracted to a new neighbourhood - because of restrictions on expansion of nursery education during the town's growth has most provision through support of voluntary playgroups;

4. an inner city area with a large Asian community concentrated into a small district, with a relatively large number of nursery classes;

5. another urban area with "high density housing", much of it in multistorey blocks, large West Indian Community - has nursery school, classes, playgroups, play bus, day nurseries and child minding;

6. an inner-city area undergoing major redevelopment - many high-rise flats - declining population has resulted in admission of children to reception classes of primary schools full-time from four years of age - younger children in nursery schools and classes and many children of three years of age attend full-time - a few playgroups - also a special nursery school for socially handicapped, also a nursery centre.

The studies

Each area was visited for ten working days during which time approximately 30 establishments were visited by one or more members of the team (which included two members of the inspectorate on secondment). Information was gathered by use of three forms:

(a) with questions to head of establishments;

(b) an observation checklist used by members of the team;

(c) an aide-memoire for leading discussion between team members and staff.

Supplementary information on provision was provided by education and social services departments

- on overall provision and policy
- also on in-service training,
- on teaching English to immigrants
- and from officers of local PPA
- also background statistical information.

In the publication the study is described as "an exploratory investigation" (involving visiting 167 establishments) and the data is described as indicating "apparent trends only, and the conclusions are tentative" - substantiated where possible by "research findings and information from other sources" (DES, 1975a p.4).

Findings

Striking differences were found

(1) between inner-city and rural areas - illustrated diagrammatically for two areas

(2) whether attendance was full or part-time.

Although it was intended that the expansion in preschool provision would be part-time note is made of the need for extended care for some children.

Evidence was gathered that some needy children were not being catered for - listed are the following

(1) children of single parents and working mothers;

(2) children whose parents are apathetic;

(3) in rural areas (where parents could not afford transport costs to playgroups, for example);

(4) where nursery education was too far away;

(5) children of inadequate mothers who could not bear to part with them;

(6) disadvantaged children where nursery schools were full and aiming to retain a balanced group.

One major area considered by the team was the problems for rural areas(with some alternatives suggested on p.20).

Some parents did not know about the availability of nursery provision, differences between types, or that it is free.

Issues identified for research

Nineteen research projects were suggested on the basis of the short-term studies (see Appendix I). Five aspects were given priority for research on the basis of these and the report by Tizard to SSRC (see Appendix I).

A number of issues identified on the basis of the short-term studies as urgently requiring research do not seem to have been funded for research projects. Others were the subject of research but perhaps not in a way which has provided the information sought by those involved in the short-term studies. number of these issues are of current concern including the following:

(1) *rural areas:*

"to monitor selected LEA schemes for providing nursery education in sparsely populated rural areas and to evaluate their effectiveness in meeting the children's educational needs" (p.21)

(Reference is made again to rural areas on p.27 with regard to educational home visiting (The home visiting study funded was not in rural areas.)

(2) *continuity* (as set in context there):

"a descriptive study of children's experiences in schools between the ages of 3 and 7 or 8 years to determine the extent and nature of continuity in the curriculum, and the factors which encourage or impede it" - followed by "a development project to explore ways of achieving continuity of experiences for children in this age range" (p.37)

(3) *teacher training:*

"a project to develop and monitor courses of initial training for teachers of young children, with particular reference to the needs of nursery teachers" (p.45)

(a second project on developing materials is probably reflected in the continuation of J.Tough's work with DES funding).

(4) *ethnic minorities:*

Issues are discussed in detail (p.47-54) where a number of issues are listed a number of projects are suggested, and notes are made that other projects should take account of these, e.g. demand and uptake. Three specific areas are noted:

(a) educational needs in assimilating two cultures;

(b) extent of the language problem and an evaluation of alternative strategies;

(c) how to help ethnic minority parents to understand nursery schools and classes.

Possible reasons for lack of research

There are a number of reasons why some of what were seen as crucial areas by those conducting the short-term studies were either not funded, or not in the way they were conceived. One reason clearly was cost; another was that some would inevitably have been long-term studies and urgency is clearly evident in the paper by Kay(1975). A further reason it would appear is the way those commissioned to undertake the researches were selected, and subsequently selected their samples (some excluded part of the area or population with certain characteristics). This, while inevitable, has on occasion resulted not only in studies which are now dated (which is true of some) but studies which, while they may address the topic as listed in DES (1975a) fail to set it in the educational context(s) so clearly identified and described in the short-term studies.

These studies could have provided a valuable context for research planning which seems to have been overlooked, except to identify areas of priority in general terms. See Appendix III for points from an article by Kay, Secretary to the Nursery Education Research Management Committee, in which he set out the plans for research and the constraints (Kay, 1975).

APPENDIX III

BACKGROUND TO THE NURSERY RESEARCH PROGRAMME

The following notes are based on an article by J.L. Kay, HMI, Secretary to the Nursery Education Research Management Committee in which he sets out the intentions, progress over the first eighteen months, and constraints under which it operated (Kay, 1975). By then it had established five research projects (set out below) and had developed a strategy for the deployment of the remaining resources. There had also been, he reports, a subtle change in emphasis from the quantitative to the qualitative. An appreciation of that setting in the mid-seventies helps clarify why certain approaches were selected, particular researchers funded - and other approaches or projects rejected or not considered. Kay states that the pressure for provision of nursery education in 1972 was as much socially as educationally motivated, and that:

> "the urban aid programme was already directing the only new resources available for nursery education into areas of social disadvantage" (Kay, 1975 p.22-23).

Kay refers to possible values of large-scale longitudinal studies

> "which might indicate some possible correlations between later benefits and earlier practices" (p.23)

He rules such possible studies out as (a) expensive (b) too late with results to affect policy decisions. Kay notes thus that any research proposals must lead to

> "useful results relatively quickly" (p.23).

He suggests that,

> "the advent of the computer has made it possible, however, to amass information in advance of any hypothesis", and " to formulate hypotheses after the correlations have been established" (p.24).

He states that even before the short-term studies team had reported back it was clear that certain areas of research would need to be included in the Programme -

(1) the evaluation of the combined nursery centres (then jointly commissioned by DES and DHSS from NCB.

(2) the aims of practitioners of nursery education (such a study was proposed by NFER).

(3) NFER also proposed a project to develop materials for teachers to use to assess progress. If nursery education is compensatory he suggested there might be a

need for 'norm referenced' tests (which might be questioned now). He states

> "the norm must be set by the normal home" (p.25) (a term we might be less willing to use so easily now).

Thus a proposal from Prof. Hutt of Keele University to study the home in the pre-school years was also approved.

A further proposal from Prof. Hutt to study the way children learn through play was also approved.

Kay states that the short-term studies team and SSRC Research Review confirmed the importance of the two above NFER proposals which were then supported. The five areas agreed for priority were therefore over and above these. This paper indicates how the 19 issues identified by the team would be incorporated under these broad areas:

(a) *parental demand*: could possibly include a large-scale sample
> "if the right questions could be asked without an unacceptable escalation of the costs" (Kay, 1975 p.26)

A more intensive study was thought to be better, if a number of representative areas were chosen - so that regional variations, social class, availability of local work, and special needs for rural areas could be considered;

(b) *co-ordination* was seen to need two related projects, with both educational researchers and a department of social administration involved;

(c) *parental involvement in nursery education:* should consider effects of different patterns and teachers' attitude, which could have implications for their training.
> "This rigorous research might hopefully take the form of a series of case studies" (p.27-8).

(d) *continuity and progression* in the educational experience of the child in, and through, nursery and infant education was, he stresses, a region where there was "urgent need" for research
> "So that each child can be helped to progress as continuously and as smoothly as possible during the years from three to eight" (p.28).

(e) problems surrounding the admission of children with varying degrees of *handicap* to normal nursery classes.

REFERENCES

Ahmad, K. (1986). *The Language of Young Punjabi Speaking Children on Starting School.* (unpublished M.Ed. dissertation). Faculty of Education, Birmingham University, Birmingham

Bain, A. and Barnett, L. (1980) *The Design of a Day Care System in a Nursery Setting for Children Under Five.* Final Report to DHSS of an action research project 1975-79. London: Tavistock Institute of Human Relations.

Barrett, G. (1986). *Starting School: an Evaluation of the Experience.* Final Report to AMMA.

Bate, M. (1983). Liaison groups in early education. *Educational Research,* 25(2), 105-109.

Bate, M. and Smith, M. (1978) *Assessment in Nursery Education.* Windsor: NFER.

Bate, M., Smith, M. and James, J. (n.d.) *Review of tests and assessment in early education (3-5 years).* Windsor:NFER.

Bayliss, S. (1985). Infant behaviour sparks study of reception classes. *Times Educational Supplement,* (28.6.85).

Bernstein, B. (1970) A sociolinguistic approach to socialisation: with some reference to educability. In Williams, F. (Ed) *Language and Poverty - Perspectives on a theme.* Chicago: Markham Pub.Co.

Blackstone, T. (1973) The structure of nursery education: some reflections on its developments in the past and future. In Chazan, M. (Ed.) *Education in the Early Years.* Swansea : University of Swansea.

Blatchford, P., Battle, S. and Mays, J. (1982) *The First Transition: Home to Preschool.* A report on the "Transition from Home to Preschool" project. Windsor: NFER-Nelson.

Blatchford, P., Burke, J., Farquhar, C., Plewis, I. and Tizard, B. (1985). Educational achievement in the infant school: The influence of ethnic origin, gender and home on entry skills. *Educational Research,* 27(1), 52-60.

Blatchford, P., Burke, J., Farquhar, C., Plewis, I. and Tizard, B. (1987a). A Systematic Observation Study of Children's Behaviour at Infant School. *Research Papers in Education,* 2(1), 47-62.

Blatchford, P., Burke, J., Farquhar, C., Plewis, I. and Tizard, B. (1987b). Associations between preschool reading related skills and later reading achievement. *British Educational Research Journal,* 13(1), 15-23.

Bone, M. (1977) *Preschool Children and the Need for Day Care.* OPCS Social Survey, London. London: HMSO.

Bradley, L. and Bryant, P. (1983). *Reading skills in young children and the recognition of auditory similarities* Final Report to SSRC (C/00/23/0047/1). SSRC, London

Bradley, L. and Bryant, P. (1985) *Rhyme and Reason in Reading and Spelling.* Ann Arbor : University of Michigan

Bradley, M. (1982) *The Co-ordination of Services for Children under Five.* Windsor: NFER-Nelson.

Bradley, M. (1987) The co-ordination of services for children under five, with particular reference to practices in England. In Clark, M.M. (Ed) *Roles, Responsibilities and Relationships in the Education of the Young Child. Educational Review* Occasional Pub. No.13. Ch.3. Faculty of Education, University of Birmingham.

Bronfenbrenner, U. (1974) *Is Early Intervention Effective?* Teachers College Report, 76(2), 279-303.

Bruner, J. (1980) *Under Five in Britain.* Oxford Preschool Research Project. London: Grant McIntyre.

Bryant, P. (1978). *The Preschool child's understanding of some basic concepts of number.* Final Report to SSRC. Grant No. HR 3305/2

Bryant, B., Harris, M. and Newton, D. (1980) *Children and Minders.* Oxford Preschool Research Project. London: Grant McIntyre.

Cameron, R.J. (1986). Research and Evaluation: How effective is Portage? In Cameron, R.J. (Ed.) *Portage: Preschoolers, Parents and Professionals. Ten years of achievement in the UK.* Ch.6. Windsor: NFER-Nelson.

Campaign for the Advancement of State Education (CASE) (Dec. 1985). *Survey of Local Education Authorities.* (Unpublished).

Cashdan, A. and Meadows, S. (1983). *Teaching Styles in Nursery Education.* Final Report of Grant No. HR 3456. London: SSRC.

Cazden, C.B. (1970) The neglected situation in child language research and education. In Williams.F. (Ed) *Language and Poverty - Perspectives on a theme.* Chicago: Markham Pub. Co.

Chazan, M., Laing, A.F., Jones, J. *et al.* (1983). *Helping Young Children with Behaviour Difficulties.* London: Croom Helm.

Chazan, M., Laing, A.F., Shackleton-Bailey, M. and Jones, G. (1980) *Some of Our Children: The early education of children with special needs.* London: Open Books.

Cheyne, W.M. (1979) Problems of design and analysis in the investigation of preschool education. In Clark M.M. and Cheyne, W.M. (Ed) *Studies in Preschool Education.* London: Hodder and Stoughton (for SCRE).

Cheyne, W.M. (1987). *Long-term Effects of Preschool Programs - A Review* of American Studies. Department of Psychology, University of Strathclyde, Glasgow. (unpublished).

Clark, M.M. (1976) *Young Fluent Readers. What can they teach us?* London: Heinemann Educational Books.

Clark, M.M. (1979) Developments in preschool education and the role of research. In Clark, M.M. and Cheyne, W.M. (Ed) *Studies in Preschool Education.* London: Hodder and Stoughton (for SCRE).

Clark, M.M. (1982). Review of reports of the Oxford Preschool Research Project, Under Five in Britain. *Educational Review,* 1, 79-81.

Clark, M.M. (Ed) (1983a). *Special educational needs and children under five.* Educational Review Occasional Publications No. 9. Faculty of Education, University of Birmingham.

Clark, M.M. (1983b). Early education: issues and evidence. *Educational Review,* 35(2), 113-120.

Clark, M.M. (1984). Literacy at home and at school: Insights from a study of young fluent readers. In Goelman, H., Oberg, A. and Smith, F. (Eds.) *Awakening to Literacy.* Ch. 9. London: Heinemann Educational Books.

Clark, M.M. (Ed) (1985). *Helping Communication in Early Education.* Educational Review Occasional Publications, No.11, Faculty of Education, University of Birmingham.

Clark, M.M. (1987). Early education and children with special needs. *Journal of Child*

Psychology and Psychiatry, 28(3), 417-425.

Clark, M.M., Barr, J.E. and Dewhirst, W. (1984). *Early Education of Children with Communication Problems: particularly those from ethnic minorities.* Report of a Research funded by the DES. Educational Review Offset Publication No. 3, University of Birmingham, Birmingham.

Clark, M.M., Barr, J.E. and Dewhirst, W. (1985). Early education in multi-cultural schools. *Concern,* No.57, 3-6. National Children's Bureau.

Clark, M.M. and Cheyne, W.M. (Eds.) (1979) *Studies in Preschool Education.* London: Hodder and Stoughton (for SCRE)

Clark, M.M., Riach, J. and Cheyne, W.M. (1977). *Handicapped Children and Preschool Education.* Report of a research for the Warnock Committee funded by the DES. University of Strathclyde, Glasgow.

Clark, M.M., Robson.B. and Browning, M. (1982). *Preschool Education and Children with Special Needs.* Report of a Research funded by DES 1979-81. Educational Review, University of Birmingham, Birmingham.

Cleave, S. (1985). NFER evidence to the Select Committee on Education, Science and Arts for its inquiry into achievement in primary schools. *Educational Research,* 27(2), 117-126.

Cleave, S., Barker Lunn, J. and Sharp, C. (1985). LEA Policy on admission to infant/first school. *Educational Research,* 27(1), 40-43.

Cleave, S., Jowett, S. and Bate, M. (1982) *And so to School: A study of continuity from preschool to infant school.* Report of the "Continuity of Children's Experience in the years 3 to 8". Windsor: NFER-Nelson.

Clift, P., Cleave, S. and Griffin, M. (1980) *The aims, role and deployment of staff in the nursery.* A Report of the National Foundation for Educational Research in England and Wales. Windsor: NFER.

Coates, E.A. (1985) An examination of the nature of young children's discussions, both in peer groups and with an adult, and the implications of these for the development of linguistic skills in the infant classroom. In Clark, M.M. (Ed.) *Helping Communication in Early Education.* Educational Review Occasional Publications No 11. Faculty of Education, University of Birmingham, Birmingham.

Consortium for Longitudinal Studies (1983) *As the twig is bent: lasting effects of preschool programmes.* New Jersey: Lawrence Erlbaum Associates.

Cooper, M.G. (1979) Verbal Interaction in Nursery Schools. *British Journal of Educational Psychology,* 49, 214-225

Curtis, A. and Hill, S. (1978) *My World.* Windsor: NFER-Nelson.

Curtis, A. and Blatchford, P. (1981) *Meeting the Needs of Socially Handicapped Children - the background to my world.* Windsor: NFER-Nelson.

Davenport, E. (1983). The play of Sikh children in a nursery class and at home. *Educational Review,* 35(2), 127-140.

Davie, C. (1986). *An Investigation into Childminding Practice in North Staffordshire.* Final Report to DHSS.

Davie, C.E., Hutt, S.J., Vincent, E. and Mason, M. (1984) *The Young Child at Home.* Windsor: NFER-Nelson.

Davies, A. (Ed.) (1977) *Language and Learning in Early Childhood.* London: Heinemann Educational Books Ltd.

Department of Education. (Northern Ireland) (1986). *Pupils and teachers in Grant-Aided*

Schools. January 1986. Statistical Bulletin 3/1986

Department of Education and Science (1967) *Children and their Primary Schools.* Plowden Report. Central Advisory Council for Education (England). Vol.1 Report and Vol.2 Research and Survey. London: HMSO.

Department of Education and Science (1975a) *Preschool Education and Care: some topics requiring research or development projects.* London: DES.

Department of Education and Science (1975b) *A Language for Life.* Bullock Report. London: HMSO.

Department of Education and Science (1981) *Under Fives: A Programme of Research.* A Handbook published by the Under Fives Research Dissemination Group. London: DES.

Department of Education and Science (1982). *Pupils under five years in each local authority in England - January 1981.* Statistical Bulletin 4/82.

Department of Education and Science (1986). *Pupils under five years in each Local Authority in England - January 1985.* Statistical Bulletin 10/86.

Department of Health and Social Security (1986). *Children's day care facilities at 31st. March 1986 in England 86/6.*

Department of Health and Social Security and Department of Education and Science (1976). *Low Cost Day Provision for the Under-fives.* Report of the Sunningdale Conference.

Donachy, W. (1976). Parent Participation in Preschool Education. *British Journal of Educational Psychology,* 46, 31-39.

Donachy, W. (1979) Parental Participation in Preschool Education. In Clark, M.M. and Cheyne, W.M. (Ed) *Studies in Preschool Education.* London: Hodder and Stoughton (for SCRE).

Donachy, W. (1987). Parental Participation in a Language Programme. In Clark, M.M. (Ed) *Roles, Responsibilities and Relationships in the Education of the Young Child* Educational Review Occasional Publication No.13. Ch. 4. Faculty of Education, University of Birmingham.

Donaldson, M. (1978) *Children's Minds.* Glasgow: Fontana/Collins.

Farquhar, C., Blatchford, P., Burke, J., Plewis, I. and Tizard, B. (1985). A Comparison of the Views of Parents and Reception Teachers. *Education 3-13,* 13(2), 17-22.

Farquhar, C., Blatchford, P., Burke, J., Plewis, I. and Tizard, B. (1987). Curriculum Diversity in London Infant Schools. *British Journal of Educational Psychology.* 57(2), 151-165.

Ferri, E., Birchall, D., Gingell, V. and Gipps, C. (1981) *Combined Nursery Centres: A New Approach to Education and Day Care.* London: Macmillan (National Children's Bureau Series).

Ferri, E. and Niblett, R. (1977) *Disadvantaged Families and Playgroups.* A National Children's Bureau Report. Slough: NFER. Finch, J. (1981). *Working Class Women and Preschool Playgroups.* Final Report of SSRC supported project. University of Lancaster.

Finch, J. (1983). Can Skills be shared? Preschool playgroups in 'disadvantaged' areas. *Community Development Journal,* 18(3), 251-256.

Finch, J. (1984). The Deceit of Self-Help: Preschool Playgroups and Working Class Mothers. *Journal of Social Policy,* 13(1), 1-20.

Flynn, R. and Oates, J. (1981). *Preschool Observational Research: A register of British Research with preschool children from 1970 to 1979.* Open University Early Education Research Group.

Gahagan, D.M. and Gahagan, G.A. (1970) *Talk Reform.* London: Routledge & Kegan Paul.

Garland, C. and White, S. (1980) *Children and Day Nurseries, Management and Practice in Nine London Day Nurseries.* Oxford Preschool Research Project. London: Grant McIntyre.

Grubb, J. (1982). Special education for children below compulsory school age. *Early Child Development and Care,* 9, 283-315.

Haystead, J., Howarth, V. and Strachan, A. (1980) *Preschool Education and Care.* Sevenoaks: Hodder and Stoughton (for SCRE).

Heaslip, P. (1985). The Training and Roles of Nursery Staff. *Tutors of Advanced Courses for Teachers of Young Children Journal,* 5, (No.2).

Heaslip, P. (1987). Does the Glass Slipper Fit Cinderella? Nursery teachers and their training. In Clark, M.M. (Ed) *Roles, Responsibilities and Relationships in the Education of the Young Child.* Educational Review Occasional Publication No.13. Ch.5. Birmingham:Faculty of Education, University of Birmingham

Hevey, D. (1984). *Linking Research and Practice - The Experience of a Research Liaison Officer.* Economic and Social Research Council, London.

HMSO (1978) *Special Educational Needs.* Warnock Report London: HMSO.

Hohmann, M., Banet, B. and Weikart, D.P. (1979). *Young Children in Action. A Manual for Preschool Educators.* Ypsilanti: High Scope Press.

Holmes, J.E., Woodhead, M. and Clift, P.S. (1978). *Early Mathematical Experiences: An Evaluation Study.* Evaluation Report for Schools Council.

Hughes, M. (1981). Can preschool children add and subtract?. *Educational Psychology,* 1(3), 207-219. Hughes, M. (1983). Teaching arithmetic to preschool children. *Educational Review,* 35(2), 163-173.

Hughes, M. (1986) *Children and Number - difficulties in learning mathematics.* Oxford:Blackwell.

Hughes, M., Mayall, B., Moss, P., et al. (1980) *Nurseries Now: A Fair Deal for Parents and Children.* Harmondsworth: Penguin.

Hunt, J.McV. (1961) *Intelligence and Experience.* New York: Ronald Press.

Hunt, J.McV. (1969). The psychological basis for using preschool enrichment as an antidote for cultural deprivation. In Hunt, J.McV. (Ed.) *The Challenge of Incompetence and Poverty.* Urbana: University of Illinois Press.

Hutt, S.J., Tyler, S., Hutt, C. and Foy, H. (1984). *A Natural History of the Preschool.* Final report to DES - prepared at University of Keele (unpublished).

Ingham, E. (1982) Britsh and West-Indian children in day nurseries: a comparative study. *New Community,* 9(3), 423-230

Joseph, K. (27.2.85.). A written reply. *Hansard,* 180.

Jowett, S. and Sylva, K. (1986). Does kind of preschool matter?. *Educational Review,* 28(1), 21-31.

Kay, J.L. (1975). The direction of the nursery education research programme. *Trends in Education,* 3, 22-28.

Kysel, F. (1982a). Preschool Provision in a area of Lewisham. ILEA Research and Statistics Report. RS 816/82. ILEA, London

Kysel, F. (1982b). The ILEA Preschool Survey. *ILEA Research and Statistics Report.* RS 817/82. ILEA, London.

Labov.W. (1970) The Logic of Nonstandard English. In Williams, F. (Ed) *Language and Poverty - Perspectives on a theme.* Chicago: Markham Pub. Co.

Lomax, C.M. (1977a). Interest in Books and Stories. *Educational Research,* 19, 100-112.

Lomax, C.M. (1977b). Record Keeping in Nursery School: A two-year study. *Educational*

Research, 19(3), 192-198.

Lomax, C.M. (1979a) Interest in Books and Stories. In Clark, M.M. & Cheyne, W.M. (Ed) *Studies in Preschool Education.* London: Hodder and Stoughton (for SCRE).

Lomax, C.M. (1979b) Record keeping in nursery school: A two-year study. In Clark, M.M. and Cheyne, W.M. (Ed) *Studies in Preschool Education.* London: Hodder and Stoughton (for SCRE).

Lomax, C.M. (1979c) The assessment of young children. In Clark, M.M. & Cheyne, W.M. (Ed) *Studies in Preschool Education* London: Hodder and Stoughton (for SCRE).

MacFayden (1980). The Background to, and the operation of, the Lothian Region Educational Home Visiting Scheme. In Raven, J. (Ed.). *Parents, Teachers and Children. A study of an educational Home Visiting Scheme.* Ch.2. London: Hodder and Stoughton (for SCRE).

Mayall, B. and Petrie, P. (1977) *Minder, Mother and Child.* London: University of London, Institute of Education.

Mayall, B. and Petrie, P. (1983) *Childminding and Day Nurseries: What kind of care?* London: Heinemann Educational Books.

McCail, G. (1981) *Mother Start. An account of an educational home-visiting scheme for preschool children.* Edinburgh: SCRE.

Meadows, S. and Cashdan, A. (1982). *Children's Free Play in Nursery School. Paper presented to the British Psychological Society* Developmental Section, Durham. (unpublished).

Moore, E. and Sylva, K. (1984). A survey of under-fives record-keeping in Great Britain. *Educational Research,* 26(2), 115-120.

Moxon, L. (1979). *Language Stimulation in a Day Nursery.* 2 parts Barnardo Social Work Papers, No.6. Barnardo's, Hertford.

Murphy, H.F. (1980). Staff Behaviour in Nursery School-An Observational Study. *Scottish Educational Review,* 12(2), 99-107.

Murphy, H.F. and Wilkinson, J.E. (1982). Cognitive socialisation of 4-year-old children in nursery school. *Child: Care, Health and Development,* 8(4), 203-217.

National Children's Bureau (1982a). Why Provide for the Under Fives? A Review of Research (E.Grey). *Highlight,* No.52.

National Children's Bureau (1982b). Preschool Provision in Schools, Nurseries and Playgroups: A Review of Research (E.Grey). *Highlight,* No.53.

National Children's Bureau (1982c). Home Based Services for the Under Fives: A Review of Research (D.Birchall). *Highlight,* No.54.

National Children's Bureau (1982d). Preschool Activity and the Curriculum: A Review of Research (D Birchall). *Highlight,* No.55.

Neill, S.R.StJ. (1982). Preschool design and child behaviour. *Journal of Child Psychology and Psychiatry,* 23(3), 309-318.

Neill, S.R.StJ., Denham, E., Markus, T.A. and Schaffer, H.R. (1977). *Psychological influences of spatial design factors in nurseries.* University of Strathclyde, Glasgow.

Nisbet J and Watt, J. (1984). *Educational Disadvantage: Ten Years on.* Scottish Education Dept. Occasional Papers. Edinburgh: HMSO.

Osborn, A.F. (1981). Under-fives in school in England and Wales 1971-9. *Educational Research,* 23(2), 96-103.

Osborn, A.F., Butler, N.R. and Morris, A.C. (1984) *The Social Life of Britain's Five-year-olds.* A Report of the Child Health and Education Study. London: Routledge and Kegan Paul.

Osborn, A.F. and Milbank, J.E. (1985) *The Association of Preschool Educational Experience with Subsequent Ability, Attainment and Behaviour*. Report to the DES of the CHES study. Vol.1.- report, Vol.2.- tables. Bristol: Department of Child Health, University of Bristol.

Osborn, A.F. and Milbank, J.E. (1987) *The Effect of Early Education: A Report from the Child Health and Education Study*. Oxford: Oxford University Press.

Payton, S. (1984). *Developing awareness of print: A young child's first steps towards literacy*. Educational Review Offset Publication No.2, University of Birmimgham, Birmingham.

Pearson, S.A. (1987). *Language interaction between child/child and adult/child among Moslem children who are about to transfer from Nursery School to Infant School*. (unpublished B. Phil.(Ed.) dissertation) Faculty of Education, University of Birmingham, Birmingham.

Plowden, Lady, (1982). We didn't know then what we know now. *Times Educational Supplement*, (2.4.82.), p.21

Pugh, G. and De'Ath, E. (1984) *The Needs of Parents: Practice and Policy in Education*. London: Macmillan.

Pugh, G., Aplin, G., De'Ath, E. and Moxon, M. (1987). *Partnership in Action working with parents in preschool centres*. Vol. 1 and 2. London: National Children's Bureau.

Raven, J. (1980) *Parents, Teachers and Children. A Study of an Educational Home Visiting Scheme*. Sevenoaks: SCRE/Hodder and Stoughton.

Robinson, W.P. (1980) Language Management, Socioeconomic Status and Educational Progress. In Hersov, L.A. and Berger, M. (Ed.) *Language and Language Disorders in Childhood*. New York: Pergamon Press.

Robson, B. (1983a). Encouraging dialogue in preschool units: the role of the pink pamfer. *Educational Review*, 35(2), 141-148.

Robson, B. (1983b) Encouraging Interaction between Staff and Children with Communication Problems in Preschool Units. In Clark, M.M. (Ed.) *Special Educational Needs and Children Under Five*. Ch.2. Educational Review Occasional Publications No.9. Faculty of Education, University of Birmingham.

Robson, B. (1985). *Young Children with special educational needs; integration and segregation*. Ph.D. Thesis, University of Birmingham (unpublished).

Scarr, S. and Weinberg, R.A.. (1986) The early childhood enterprise: care and education of the young. *American Psychologist*, 41, (10), 1140-1146.

Schweinhart, L.J., Weikart, D.P. and Larner, M.B. (1986). Consequences of three preschool curriculum models through age 15. *Early Childhood Research Quarterly*, 1 (1), 15-45.

Scottish Education Department (1984). *Provision for Preschool Children* (published jointly with the Social Work Services Group.) 8/A2/1984.

Scottish Education Department (1986a). *Provision for preschool children* (published jointly with Social Work Services Group.) 6/A2/1986.

Scottish Education Department (1986b). *Placing Requests in Education Authority Schools*. Statistical Bulletin 5/B6/1986.

Sebba, J. (1983). Social Interactions among Preschool Handicapped and Non-Handicapped Children. *Journal of Mental Deficiency Research*, 27, 115-124.

Sharp, C. (1987). Local Education Authority Admission Policies and Practices. Presented at joint NFER/SCDC Seminar. In *Four-Year-Olds in School: Policy and Practice*. NFER/SCDC 1-9.

Shinman, S.M. (1981) *A Chance for Every Child: access and response to preschool provision.* London: Tavistock.

Smith, J (1986) The development of Portage in the United Kingdom. In Cameron, R.J. (Ed.) *Portage: Preschoolers, Parents an Professionals. Ten years of achievement in the UK.* Ch.3. Windsor: NFER-Nelson.

Smith, P.K., Dalgleish, M. and Herzmark, G. (1981). A comparison of the effects of fantasy play tutoring and skills tutoring in nursery classes. *International Journal of Behavioural Development,* 4, 421-441.

Smith, P.K. and Connolly, K.J. (1980) *The Ecology of Preschool Behaviour.* Cambridge: Cambridge University Press.

Smith, P.K. and Connolly, K.J. (1986). Experimental studies of the preschool environment: the Sheffield Project. *Advances in Early Education and Day Care,* 4, 27-66.

Smith, T. (1980) *Parents and Preschool.* Oxford Preschool Research Project London: Grant McIntyre.

Strathclyde Regional Council (1985) *Under Fives Final Report of the Member/Officer Group.* Glasgow: Strathclyde Regional Council.

Sturmey, P. and Crisp, A.G. (1986). Portage Guide to Early Education: a review of research. *Educational Psychology,* 6(2), 134-157.

Sutton, W. (1985). Some factors in preschool children of relevance to learning to read. In Clark, M.M. (Ed.) *New Directions in the Study of Reading.* London; Falmer Press.

Sylva, K., Smith, T. and Moore, E. (1986) *Monitoring the High/Scope Training Programme.* London : VOLCUF

Sylva, K., Roy, C. and Painter, M. (1980) *Childwatching at Playgroup and Nursery School.* Oxford Preschool Research Project. London: Grant McIntyre.

Taylor, P.H., Exon, G. and Holley, B. (1972). *A Study of Nursery Education.* School Councils Working Paper 41. London: Evans/Methuen Educational

Tizard, B. (1974) *Preschool Research in Great Britain : A Research Review.* London: SSRC.

Tizard, B. (1975) *Early Childhood Education : a review and discussion of research in Britain.* Slough: NFER/SSRC.

Tizard, B., Carmichael, H., Hughes, M. and Pinkerton, G. (1980) Four year olds talking to mothers and teachers. In Hersov, L.A. and Berger, M. (Ed) *Language and Language Disorders in Childhood.* Oxford: Pergamon Press.

Tizard, B. and Hughes, M. (1984) *Young Children Learning: Talking and Thinking at Home and at School.* London: Fontana.

Tizard, B., Hughes, M., Carmichael, H. and Pinkerton, G. (1983a). Children's questions and adults' answers. *Journal of Child Psychology and Psychiatry,* 24(2), 269-281.

Tizard, B., Hughes, M., Carmichael, H. and Pinkerton, G. (1983b). Language and social class: is verbal deprivation a myth?. *Journal of Child Psychology and Psychiatry,* 24(4), 533-542.

Tizard, B., Hughes, M., Pinkerton, G. and Carmichael, H. (1982). Adults' cognitive demands at home and at nursery school. *Journal of Child Psychology and Psychiatry,* 23(2), 105-116.

Tizard, B., Mortimore, J. and Burchell, B. (1981) *Involving Parents in Nursery and Infant Schools: a source book for teachers.* London: Grant McIntyre.

Tizard, B., Philps, J. and Plewis, I. (1976). Staff behaviour in preschool centres. *Journal of Child Psychology and Psychiatry,* 17, 21-33.

Tough, J. (1973). The Language of Young Children: the implications for the education of the young disadvantaged child. In Chazan, M. (Ed.) *Education in the Early Years.* Swansea: University of Swansea.

Tough, J. (1976) *Listening to Children Talking: a guide to the appraisal of children's use of language.* London:Ward Lock Educational (for Schools Council).

Tough, J. (1977a) *The Development of Meaning. A study of children's use of language.* London: Allen and Unwin.

Tough, J. (1977b) *Talking and Learning: a guide to fostering communication skills in nursery and infant school.* London: Ward Lock Educational (for Schools Council).

Turner, I.F. (1977). *Preschool Playgroups Research and Evaluation Project.* Final Report submitted to Government of Northern Ireland Department of Health and Social Services. Dept. of Psychology, The Queen's University of Belfast, Belfast.

Turner, I.F. and Whyte, J. (1979). *The Language Dimension: an action programme in the reception class.* No.17. The Northern Ireland Council for Educational Research.

Tyler, S. (1980) *Keele Preschool Assessment Guide (Experimental Edition).* Windsor:NFER-Nelson.

Tyler, S. (1984) Carrying out assessment with young children. In Fontana, D. (Ed) *The Education of the Young Child.* Ch.9 Oxford: Blackwell

Van der Eyken, W. (1982) *Home-Start: A Four-Year Evaluation.* Leicester: Home Start Consultancy.

Van der Eyken, W. (1984). *Day Nurseries in Action: a national study of local authority day nurseries in England, 1975-1983.* Final Report to the Department of Health and Social Security (marked as 'draft' by DHSS). University of Bristol, Department of Child Health, Bristol.

Van der Eyken, W., Osborn, A. and Butler, N. (1984). Preschooling in Britain: A national study of institutional provision for under-fives in England, Scotland and Wales. *Early Child Development and Care,* 17, 79-122.

Wallace, F. (1985). *The aims of nursery education as perceived by headteachers of nursery schools and teachers with posts of responsibility for reception children in large primary schools.* (unpublished M.Ed.(Ed. Psych.) dissertation) University of Birmingham, Birmingham.

Watt, J.S. (1977) *Co-operation in Preschool Education.* London: SSRC.

Watt, J. (1983). In-service education: an opportunity for growth? *Educational Review,* 35(2), 195-202.

Watt, J. (1987) Continuity in early education. In Clark, M.M. (Ed) *Roles, Responsibilities and Relationships in the Education of the Young Child.* Educational Review Occasional Publications No.13. Ch.2. Faculty of Education, University of Birmingham. Birmingham.

Watt, J. and Flett, M. (1985) *Continuity in Early Education, the Role of Parents.* Dept. of Education, Aberdeen University, Aberdeen.

Wells, G. (1977). *Language use and Educational success: a response to Joan Tough's 'The Development of Meaning'* (1977). Paper presented at the Child Language Seminar,Nottingham.

Wells, G. (Ed.) (1981) *Learning through Interaction: the study of language development.* Cambridge: Cambridge University Press.

Wells, G. (1985a) *Language Development in the Preschool Years.* Cambridge: Cambridge University Press.

Wells, G. (1985b). *Language, Learning and Education*. Selected papers from the Bristol study: 'Language at Home and at School'. Windsor: NFER-Nelson

Wells, G. (1986) *The Meaning Makers - Children Learning Language and Using Language to Learn*. New Hampshire: Heinemann Educational.

Wells, G., Barnes, S. and Wells, J. (1984). *Linguistic influences on educational attainment*. Final Report to DES. University of Bristol/Ontario Institute for Studies in Education, Toronto.

Wells, I. and Burke, S. (1986a). *Nursery Questions and Teachers' Answers* - Report 8. Research and Consultancy Service, Northern Ireland Council for Educational Research.

Wells, I. and Burke, S. (1986b). *Nursery Education: Provision and Need* - Report 9. Research and Consultancy Service, Northern Ireland Council for Educational Research.

Welsh Office (1986). *Statistics of Education in Wales*. No.10, 1985

Whittaker, H.M. (1985). *The assessment of language competence in young Punjabi-English speaking children*. (unpublished M.Ed. dissertation). Faculty of Education, University of Birmingham, Birmingham.

Wilkinson, J.E. and Murphy, H.F. (1983). "Flitting" in nursery school children. *Child: Care, Health and Development*, 9(1), 19-28.

Williams, F. (Ed.) (1970) *Language and Poverty - Perspectives on a theme*. Chicago: Markham Pub. Co.

Wood, D., McMahon, L. and Cranstoun, Y. (1980) *Working with Under Fives*. Oxford Preschool Research Project. London: Grant McIntyre.

Wood, D., Wood, H., Griffith, A. and Howarth, I. (1986) *Teaching and Talking with Deaf Children*. Chichester: Wiley.

Wood, H. and Wood, D. (1983). Questioning the Preschool child. *Educational Review*, 35, No.2, 149-162.

Woodhead, M. (1985). Preschool education has long-term effects: but can they be generalised?. *Oxford Review of Education*, 11(2), 133-155.

Zigler, E.F. (1987). Formal schooling for four-year-olds? No. *American Psychologist*, 42(3), 254-260.

OUTLINE OF CHAPTER CONTENTS

Most chapters commence with a brief outline of the studies considered there in detail, their dates and other relevant information. Some chapters have detailed discussion on a limited number of researches with mention of other relevant studies, including some reported elsewhere in the book; for other topics a number of studies are reported briefly. The notes below do not give information on all researches mentioned, for that the reference list should be consulted.

Chapter 1: The remit and scope of the investigation, the approach and the sources of information consulted

Chapter 2: Types of preschool units in Britain, previous research initiatives, their context and dissemination

Chapter 3: Trends in educational provision for children under five in Britain since 1975, based mainly on statistical documents for England, Wales, Northern Ireland and Scotland

Chapter 4: Changes in children in preschool education in Britain, including age of entry to primary school, regional contrasts and effects by date of birth, with briefly reported research evidence

Chapter 5; Detailed discussion of four researches on the language of young children by Tough; Wells; Tizard and Hughes; Davie, S. J. Hutt, Vincent and Mason

Chapter 6: Brief discussion of a number of experimental and interventional studies in preschool units including Tizard, Philps and Plewis; Moxon; Turner and Whyte; Murphy and Wilkinson; Lomax; Neill, Denham, Markus and Schaffer; Smith and Connolly; Sylva, Smith and Moore

Chapter 7: Three funded studies in preschool units are discussed in detail those by Sylva, Roy and Painter; Wood, McMahon and Cranstoun from 'The Oxford Preschool Research' directed by Bruner; by S. J. Hutt, Tyler, Foy and C. Hutt; by Cashdan and Meadows

Chapter 8: Detailed discussion of the studies of day nurseries by Garland and White; by Bain and Barnett and of combined centres by Ferri, Birchall, Gingell and Gipps; brief comparative reference is made to other studies including those by Van der Eyken

Chapter 9: Brief reference to the study of childminders by Mayall and Petrie and several others studies and detailed discussion of two studies, those by Bryant, Harris and Newton; Davie

Chapter 10: A number of issues on parental involvement are considered with evidence from Osborn and Milbank (CHES); Tizard, Mortimore and Burchell; T. Smith (from the Oxford Preschool Research); by McCail and Raven (The Lothian Project); Donachy

Chapter 11: Further information on parents with a focus on research into demand and uptake, in particular research by Haystead, Howarth and Strachan; Shinman; Ferri and Niblett: Finch

Chapter 12: Research on co-ordination by Bradley and on co-operation by Watt are the focus for discussion of the issues

Chapter 13: Transition studies by Blatchford, Battle and Mays; by Cleave, Jowett and Bate; by Barrett; on early education of children from ethnic minorities by Clark, Barr and Dewhirst; on continuity and the role of parents by Watt and Flett are all considered in some detail

Chapter 14: This report does not claim to provide a comprehensive review of research on children with special needs, which would have been a project in its own right, evidence from Chazan, Laing, Shackleton-Bailey and Jones; and two contrasting studies directed by Clark provide a framework for discussion of the issues; research in Britain on Portage is also considered briefly

Chapter 15: Curricular issues are considered with evidence from a number of studies including that on aims and deployment by Clift, Cleave and Griffin; an evaluation of a mathematics project by Holmes, Woodhead and Clift; on socially handicapped by Curtis and Blatchford; on record keeping, by Bate and Smith and by Moore and Sylva; the implications of experimental studies on mathematics, on reading and on cognitive development including those by Bryant and Bradley; Clark; Hughes; Donaldson

Chapter 16: Evidence on effects of preschool education, including the relevance to Britain of the Consortium Studies in the United States; research by Donachy; Turner; Jowett and Sylva; Osborn and Milbank from the Child Health and Education Study

Chapter 17: An overview and brief resume chapter by chapter

Chapter 18: Implications of research for policy and practice to be considered in association with the research evidence, gaps in current knowledge and promising further developments identified and related to current needs in the earlier chapters.